Photography Now

An Hachette UK Company
www.hachette.co.uk

First published in the UK in 2021 by
ILEX, an imprint of Octopus Publishing Group Ltd
Octopus Publishing Group
Carmelite House
50 Victoria Embankment
London, EC4Y 0DZ
www.octopusbooks.co.uk
www.octopusbooksusa.com

Distributed in the US by Hachette Book Group
1290 Avenue of the Americas, 4th & 5th Floors
New York, NY 10104

Distributed in Canada by Canadian Manda Group
664 Annette St, Toronto, Ontario, Canda M6S2C8

Publisher: Alison Starling
Commissioning Editor: Ellie Corbett
Managing Editor: Rachel Silverlight
Editorial Assistant: Ellen Sandford O'Neill
Art Director: Ben Gardiner
Design: Leonardo Design Studio
Picture Research: Giulia Hetherington
Senior Production Manager: Peter Hunt

ISBN 978-1-78157-620-5

A CIP catalogue record for this book
is available from the British Library

Printed and bound in China

10 9 8 7 6 5 4 3 2 1

Charlotte Jansen

Photography Now

Fifty Pioneers Defining Photography for the Twenty-First Century

ilex

Contents

Introduction

If a photograph does its job, it speaks to us without words. It presents both fiction and fact, obscuring reality from us while at the same time forcing us to see with greater clarity. More than a simple act of benign representation, photography now is made up of many such paradoxes. There is nothing photographs cannot show us, from the insides of our bodies to the outer edges of the cosmos, but they do not actually tell us anything. Diane Arbus once said, 'A photograph is a secret about a secret. The more it tells you the less you know.' And yet photographs can convince us, even when we are aware that what we're seeing isn't real. They allow us to be intimate while remaining far away, conveying a sense of familiarity with things we have never encountered. The result of motion, they are static.

Today, people's addiction to photography is so overpowering that it has become almost a reflex, an impulse so strong that it often replaces the desire to exist in the moment. Photography is integrated into contemporary experience to such an extent that we consume the world through it and, as the curator Bonaventure Soh Bejeng Ndikung has suggested, we now think photographically.

Does photography still have a role as an artistic medium? An artist picking up their camera (whatever form it takes) might feel the act is futile; it might even be a more audacious statement to resist the impulse and not take photographs at all. Yet this book proves, through the images and ideas of fifty living artists, there is always more to say. In revealing the complexities of our photographic psyche, these artists have significantly shifted the discourse on photography not only as an art form but also, through its purpose and place in the world, as a form of activism that can hold a mirror to the contemporary condition. I have always been fascinated by the idea that a photograph allows us to see the world as another sees it. The artists I have chosen continue to define photography for the twenty-first century, ranging from masters to pioneers in different genres who are pushing at the boundaries of what we think of as a photograph. Sometimes their approaches, concerns and techniques converge; at other times they contradict one another. Together, they prove that the possibilities of photography are still vast. Regardless of when they first came to prominence, all fifty artists have played a significant role in shaping a unique time in the history of photography, during which it has become a singularly popular and indispensable visual medium.

Before thinking about what photography is now, we need to address its past and acknowledge the way the camera has been and continues to be used as a means of control. Photography is often called the 'democratic medium', but how democratic is it really? What does it mean to witness or to look away? We have moved on from the postmodernists, who dismissed photography as a sham, and now embrace the performative aspect of the medium. We also know it's a fallacy to say that everything has already been photographed; rather, we are now in the process of discovering what has been concealed from view. Who is behind the camera is of as much interest as what passes in front of it – in other words, photography should be seen as a subjective art form, just like any other.

The purpose of this book is to close the gap between the photographer, the photographed and the viewer by exposing the fact that not all photographers are equal and not all photographs are treated equally. Photography might be the global language of today, bold and borderless, yet its universality is called into question by the photographers in this book, who remind us that photographs are subject to the machinations of capitalism, distorted and debased by biased systems that favour the dominant. The writer and photography critic Teju Cole wrote perceptively in the *New York Times* in 2019 that 'photography's future will be much like its past. It will largely continue to illustrate, without condemning, how the powerful dominate the less powerful.' How can we disrupt this?

The photographers featured here work in different contexts and in overlapping, often indefinable genres, moving the conversation about what photography is to what photography does. The creative instinct is an affirmative act, a way of expressing our existence. But a photograph leaves its own trace in that it has to face outwards, towards something beyond us. For me, this explains the inexorable pull of photography: the desire to frame what it means to be human; to see ourselves more clearly by looking elsewhere. In the wake of the Covid-19 pandemic followed by the explosion of the Black Lives Matter movement at the start of this decade, photography has the power to become the mouthpiece of humanity, tethering us to reality as events spiral out of control. It is the clarion cry in a world adrift.

Laia Abril

Photographs are often assumed to be passive – they are static, inanimate, fixed. Laia Abril has looked for ways to make photography an active medium, by disrupting the chronology of the archive, bringing images from the past vividly into the present. Her ongoing project is visualizing the history of violence and discrimination against women, in order to look forward, not back.

Born in Barcelona in 1986, Abril trained as a journalist before going on to study photography in New York and then worked as a researcher and photo editor at *Colors* magazine (which ceased publication in 2014). Abril's background has evidently affected her approach to her work, which often begins with a news story that has left a deep impression. Although she has emphasized that her work is not only documentary any more, her process involves intensive research, assembling archival materials and mapping out real-life stories in order to coherently visualize global problems. Usually starting with a book or publication of some sort, Abril's multimedia projects also take the form of exhibitions, films and conferences. Her recurrent subject is women's bodies and the violence inflicted on them as a result of the society we inhabit. However, Abril does not present these as issues related only to women, but contextualizes them as global, societal problems that affect everyone, everywhere, now as much as in the past.

Abril's work to date can be divided into three major projects, each subdivided into what the artist refers to as 'chapters' and each using varied lens-based media, including filmed footage, found imagery, archival images, reconstructions, documentations, portraits and texts. This innovative way of combining photography to tell engaging, complex and multilayered stories won Abril the Paris Photo/Aperture Foundation PhotoBook of the Year Award in 2018 and saw her shortlisted for the 2019 Deutsche Börse Photography Foundation Prize.

On Sexuality, Abril's first project, began with *Femme Love* (2009), exploring the ordinariness of lesbian lives – a deliberate reversal of the way the private, domestic day-to-day lives of same-sex couples are usually portrayed in the heteronormative eyes of mass media. Conversely, the second part, *Last Cabaret* (2011) investigated couples who perform online peep shows for profit, and the role of boredom in contemporary sexuality. The final part of the project, *Lobismuller* (2016), was based on a mid-nineteenth-century account of a Spanish serial killer who claimed he was a werewolf. Some evidence suggests that the murderer was born intersex and originally raised as a woman.

Scales **from the series** ***The Epilogue*****, 2014**
In 2014 Laia Abril worked closely with the Robinson family, who had lost their daughter Mary Cameron Robinson – known as Cammy – to bulimia. Retracing Cammy's debilitating battle with the disease through family photographs, letters, medical records, testimonies, interviews and Abril's own snapshots, we are presented with a picture of Cammy from multiple perspectives, charged with the emotional intensity of the heartbreak of the family she left behind as they attempt to understand what has happened. This simple, minimal image of white bathroom scales is symbolically shot through with pain as an apparently innocuous object becomes a form of daily torture for the sufferer.

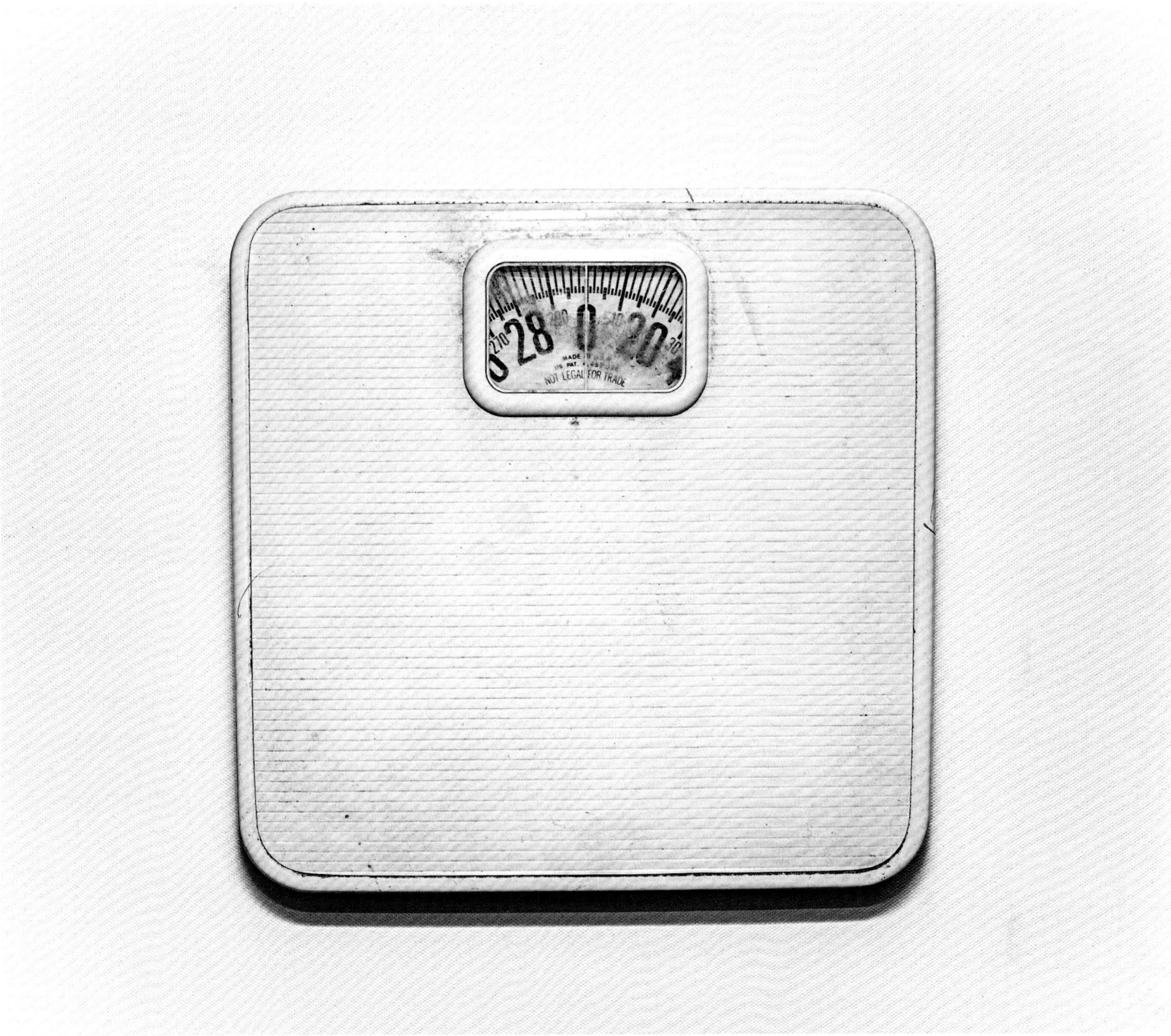

On Eating Disorders, Abril's next project, included three episodic parts: a short film, *A Bad Day* (2009), about a twenty-one-year-old bulimia sufferer, Jo; a fanzine titled *Thinspiration* (2012) reproducing screen-captures of self-portraits posted online by pro-Ana bloggers; and a book, *The Epilogue* (2014), telling the story of a family grieving the loss of their twenty-six-year-old daughter to bulimia. *On Eating Disorders* is a harrowing look at the excruciating pain of these women and their loved ones. Understanding the way visual media works so well, Abril arranges different kinds of images and texts to shock and unsettle, but she does so without sensationalizing the problem; each chapter moves slowly and sensitively through the subject.

A challenge for Abril has been to engage audiences with issues that are highly stigmatized and taboo – to make us see when our instinct is to look away. This is essential in her groundbreaking, long-term project, *A History of Misogyny* (2016), a visualization of the 'invisible war on women', in the words of critic Sean O'Hagan.[1] With access to safe and legal abortion and reproductive care increasingly under political threat around the world, *Chapter One: On Abortion and the Repercussions of Lack of Access* could not have come at a more relevant moment. First exhibited in 2016 at Les Rencontres d'Arles, the project was published as a book in 2018 and it has been exhibited in twelve countries to date, most recently, the USA. *On Abortion* is an extensive, unprecedented research project into a subject that has been neglected in history and in contemporary art. Confronting the viewer with the voices of women from all over the world, with statistics, medical information and case studies, *On Abortion* is evidence of the myths and misconceptions that have covered up a global problem – and the hundreds of thousands of deaths that have resulted from lack of access to safe and legal abortion. As Abril says, 'It's about human rights – and human rights are always going to be jeopardized by the political situation.'[2]

***Marta, 29, Poland*, from the series *On Abortion*, 2016**
On Abortion assembles different kinds of photography to convey information in the most effective way possible. Comprising interviews with women who have performed or experienced abortion in the last century, as well as documentation of women whose lives have been lost and detailed accounts of illegal abortion practices, it is a platform for the voices of women who have been silenced for centuries. For this reason, the portraits in *On Abortion* are particularly important – giving faces to the women who share their stories, without which this project, Abril acknowledges, would not exist. This portrait is of Marta and includes the extended caption below.

'*On January 2, 2015, I traveled to Slovakia to have an abortion. [In Poland, abortion is illegal except in cases of sexual assault, serious fetal deformation, or threat to the mother's life.] I was too scared to take DIY abortion pills alone. What if something went wrong? So I decided to get a surgical abortion in a clinic abroad. I felt upset about borrowing money for the procedure, and lonely and frustrated because I couldn't tell anyone what was happening. The hardest part was facing my boyfriend, who opposes abortion. All the same, I felt stronger and more mature afterwards.*' —Marta

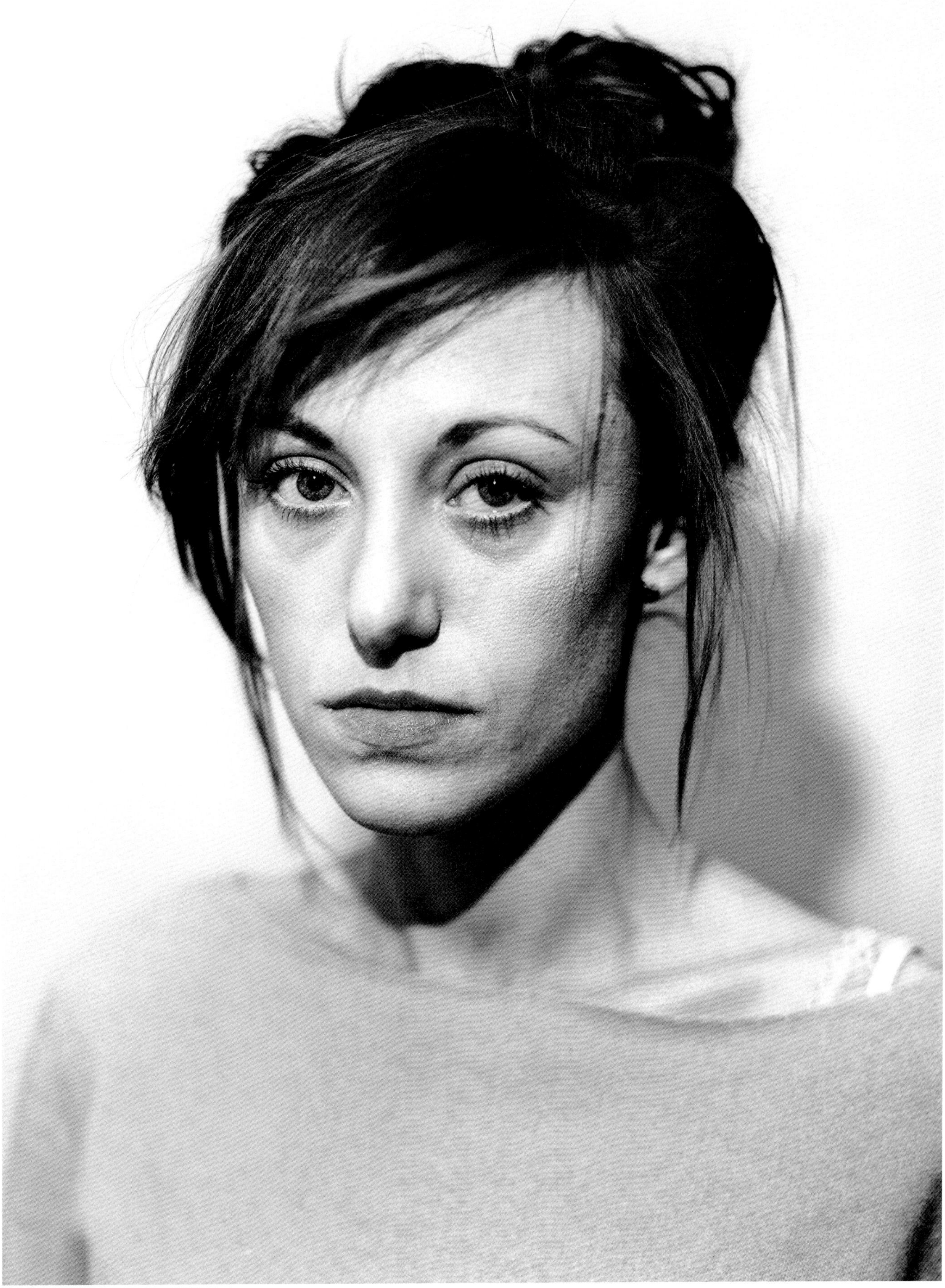

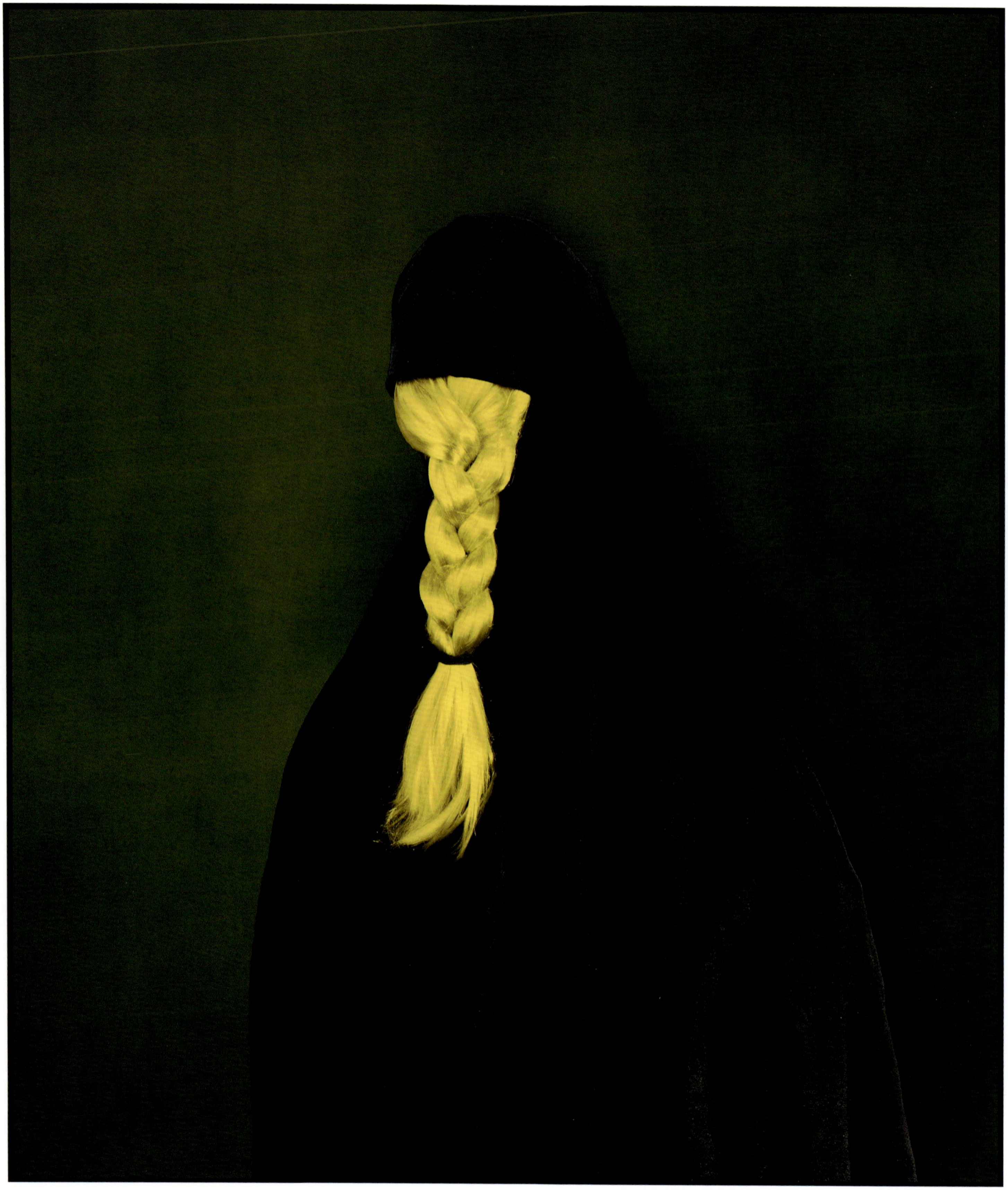

Hoda Afshar

'I believe in the power of images to change the world by changing the way that we see it,' Hoda Afshar has stated,[1] and this conviction informs all of her work to date. Born in Iran in 1983, from an early age Afshar knew that she wanted to become a photographer. She was enthralled by what she has called the 'magic of photography',[2] watching negatives develop in the darkroom. After completing a Fine Art Photography degree at the University of Tehran, she originally planned to become a war photographer. Instead, she worked for a news agency, until it was closed by the government. Meanwhile she had been taking her camera into Tehran's underground party scene, giving a glimpse of a side of life in the city usually hidden from view. The pictures evolved into her first long-term project, *Scene* (2004–5), which was the beginning of an ongoing investigation into the unseen and the invisible.

In 2007 Afshar emigrated to Australia. Arriving in a Western culture as a young Muslim woman, she suddenly found herself being seen as 'Other'. The narrow stereotypes of Middle Eastern women she was confronted with angered her, especially the assumptions that all veiled women are subjugated, suppressed and lacking autonomy. This did not match her own experience, or those of the women she knew and had grown up with in Iran. In 2013–14 she created a series of satirical self-portraits in response to these misconceptions, targeted at a Western audience and entitled *Under Western Eyes*. Born out of her initial indignation, Afshar nonetheless felt that 'this not belonging became some kind of a positive thing for me.'[3]

Afshar's main motivation as a photographer and teacher has been to find a new language in documentary photography, one that addresses the 'intrusive nature of the camera'[4] but can also translate stories into images that are staged, performed and charged with emotion and narrative nuance – a blurring of the real and the symbolic. Though critical of traditional documentary representations used by the mass media, Afshar has not given up on the power of the photograph. Her work relates to what the literary critic Edward Said asks us to do in his collection of essays *Culture and Imperialism* (1993): 'to think concretely and sympathetically, contrapuntally, about others [rather] than only about "us".'

This was Afshar's approach when, in 2018, she travelled to the idyllic setting of Manus Island in Papua New Guinea to work with male asylum seekers who had been imprisoned in the infamous Australian detention

***The Westoxicated #1* from the series *Under Western Eyes*, 2013. Archival pigment print. Edition of 5**
When Afshar moved to Australia she was faced with an image of herself she did not recognize. Her response was to retaliate with images that ham up the absurdity of Islamic female stereotypes as they are displayed in the art world. Using the seductive global language of pop art and the codes of exoticism, she expresses an idea inspired by the Australian indigenous artist Richard Bell in his 2002 paper *Aboriginal Art – It's a White Thing!* – a comment on mass-produced 'Otherness' as a commodity manufactured for the art market. 'With this image in the series, I was trying to express the same concern, that "Veil Art" is a white thing too,' Afshar reflects.[5]

centre there until it closed the year before. Her subjects remained in a kind of purgatory of pain inflicted on them over the years they were imprisoned. In a two-channel video work and a series of portraits, Afshar reinstated the men's individual identities that had been erased and denied by the Australian government. Afshar went to Manus Island on a tourist visa after making contact with Behrouz Boochani, a Kurdish-Iranian writer and journalist who spent six years detained there after fleeing Iran in 2013. Afshar and Boochani talked for months via WhatsApp, planning the video and portrait project *Remain* (2018), which became a close collaboration with the prisoners. 'The most important goal was to make people feel empathetic,'[6] Afshar said. Although the portraits touch on universal themes – fear, the loss of hope, death – they each convey a sense of the individual's suffering.

***Untitled #4* from the series *Behold*, 2016. Archival pigment print. Edition of 5**
While visiting Iran in 2015, Afshar was approached by a group of young homosexual men who invited her to the men-only bathhouse that was their safe public meeting place. The series of images is a rare rumination on male intimacy and male bodies. Showing the men shrouded in steam, with drops of sweat just visible on their bare flesh as they hold each other, this image is undeniably sensual, but the homoerotic charge is a subtext, not the centre of the work. There is little information to locate these men and their bodies, and the bathhouse no longer exists. Only the tenderness of the moment and the comfort of the embrace remain.

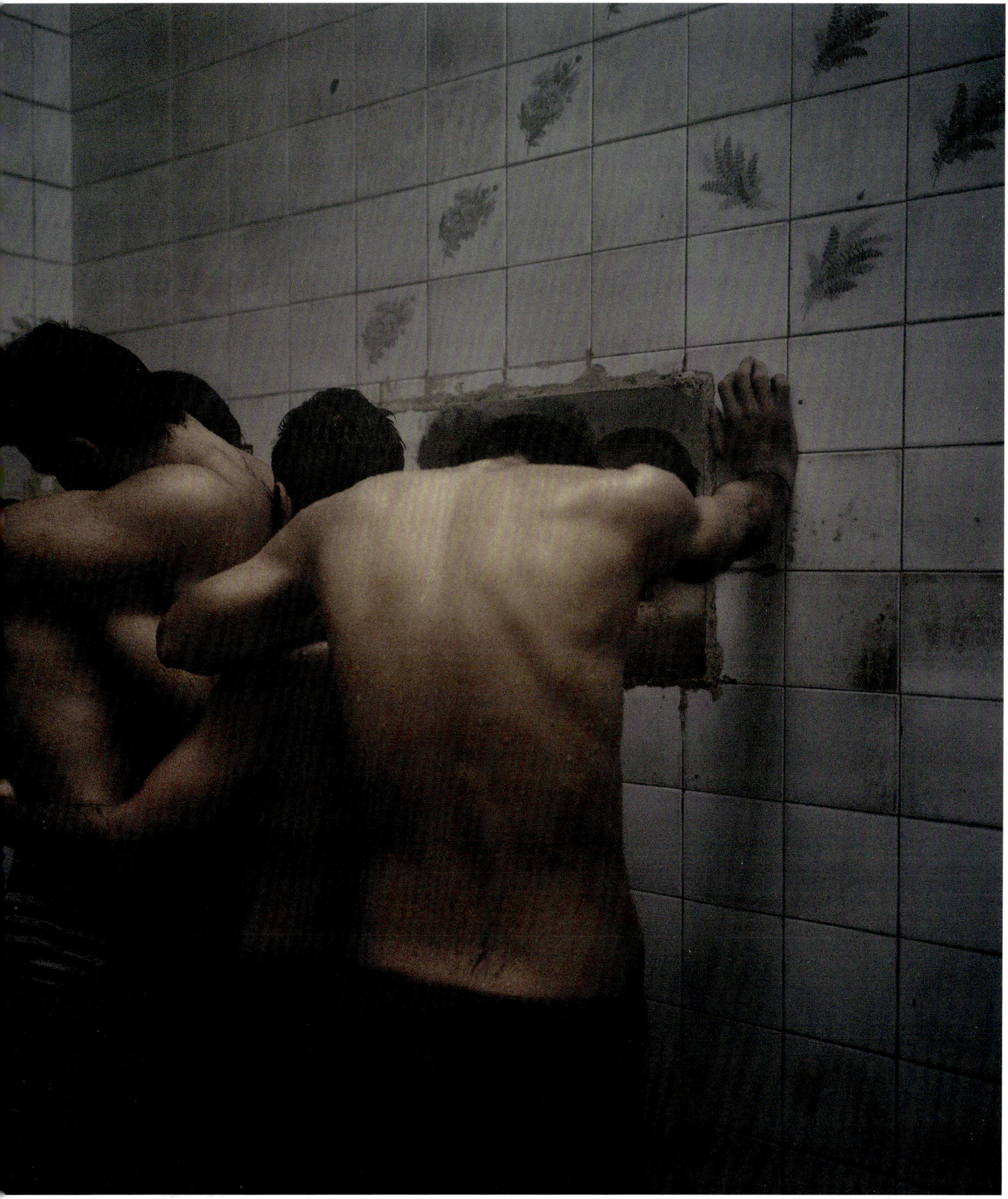

Antoine d'Agata

'I just use photography in the most coherent way, while experimenting with the world in the most intense way,' Antoine d'Agata explains.[1] Plumbing the depths of the subconscious, defying morality as we know it, he uses every possible means to lose control in order to exist in the purest state. This is how he produces his pictures, treating photography as 'some kind of martial art'.[2]

Once you've seen a photograph by d'Agata, you're unlikely to forget it. His divisive methods and subject matter touch on every possible taboo – the trafficking of bodies and narcotics, drug abuse, sex, violence – depicting real-life situations in which he himself is often involved. His willingness to participate in contentious acts, to 'become an image' himself,[3] is the only way, he believes, to wrest his work from the documentary. D'Agata is not a spectator or even a voyeur – there are no boundaries between himself and his subjects; he wants to be inside their bodies, to be with them in the most physical and emotional sense. His images are therefore a reflection of events not only as he sees them but also as he lives them: 'I don't want to look at the pain, but feel the pain.'[4]

His methods might be controversial, but d'Agata is not interested in shock value. His photography represents his way of experiencing the world and his attempts to bring himself to the brink – to be 'as close as possible to death'.[5] Seeing settling down 'as some kind of failure',[6] he has led a nomadic lifestyle since leaving his hometown, Marseille, aged eighteen, getting lost and losing himself in people and places all over the world ever since. D'Agata has stated that he is willing to take any risk, whether through drugs (he is open about his own addiction), sex or crime, and he is drawn instinctively to places where he is not welcome but where he believes life is to be found at its most honest and raw. He has addressed criticisms about the deeply problematic nature of what he does, maintaining that his motive is not to exploit but to learn to know himself. He has lived with disenfranchised communities everywhere: refugees in Bangladesh, prisoners in Libya, drug addicts in Cambodia, sex workers in the Canary Islands. D'Agata does not try to expose anything about these places, but his photographs reveal the profound fractures caused by politics and economics.

By putting himself in these situations, d'Agata is making a radical statement: we are part of all of this. Sometimes this plays out in the images themselves: blurred bodies merge with each other; furniture blends into flesh; prison cells in Tripoli look like rooms in a brothel in Phnom Penh. The critic Teju Cole has written that photographs of brutality and suffering should be

***Playa del Ingles, Canary Island, 2004* from the series *Stigma*, 2004**
This image appears to depict a man masturbating alone in a room that is bathed in an ethereal pink light. The soft focus of the photograph conceals details, but the man is d'Agata, who is nude and hunched over in an animalistic pose. This self-portrait belongs to his photobook *Stigma*, a collection of sexually explicit photographs depicting couples and individuals engaged in different sex acts. Sex is a recurrent theme in d'Agata's work, particularly sex in brothels. The artist has said, however, that he isn't interested in sex as a perversion or pleasure, but as an 'existential attempt', a moment when ego and control are lost, bringing us closer to 'what being means'. He sees sex, therefore, as a 'pathetic and tragic state of being'. By photographing himself in this way, d'Agata shows his willingness to involve himself in his work and become vulnerable. As he puts it, 'I ended up being an image.'[12]

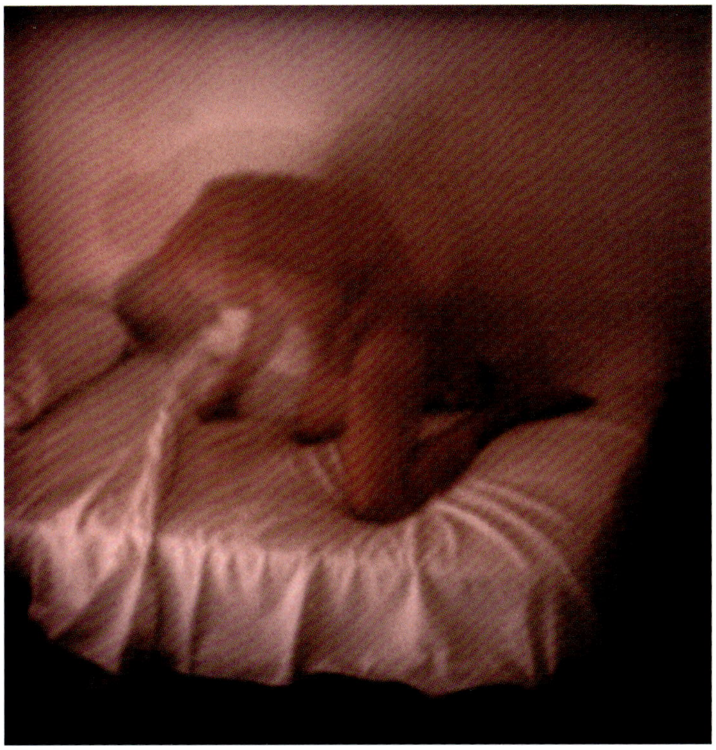

'mirrors, not windows. We look into them, and what they reflect back to us is something monstrous and hard to reconcile with our notion of ourselves.'[7] This is the effect d'Agata's works have: we cannot consume them without accepting our own complicity. The most unsettling aspect of his approach is that d'Agata gets to choose to exist in these ways and is then able to leave. Yet the viewer too can choose to look away; to turn the page and forget – as Cole suggests, 'perennially missing the point'.

Born in 1961, d'Agata came to photography in his late twenties, describing the process as painful: 'a desperate attempt to stay alive'.[8] It was the moment he began to try to communicate his perspective on life. Having left France in 1983, in the early 1990s d'Agata studied at the International Center of Photography in New York, where he met Nan Goldin and Larry Clark, who would become friends and influences. He published his first photobooks, *Mala Noche* and *De Mala Muerte*, in 1998, and in 2004 joined Magnum Photos as a full member. While still a student at the ICP, d'Agata visited Boy's Town – a district in Nuevo Laredo, Mexico, known for its bars and brothels – which became the subject of his first two works. They established the tone for his future work: shot almost exclusively at night, in intimate and insalubrious spaces, a desultory set-up with long exposures that embrace accidental blurring and chances of the light. The paintings of Francis Bacon, LSD trips and the nightmares d'Agata suffered as a teenager all inform the resulting atmosphere of anxiety tinged with desire. It conforms to d'Agata's view that photography is 'the art of perspective and not the art of description'.[9] When he presents his photographs, they are often organized as grids of repeated similar images, made up of tens of frames, similar but with slight differences. This relates to d'Agata's attraction to excess but also reflects a more authentic expression of the moment. 'The single image is much more of a lie,' he believes.[10]

D'Agata doesn't look for resolutions; he doesn't try to understand the world intellectually. He has come close to abandoning photography altogether and often goes for long periods without shooting at all. It is a complex relationship, one he is constantly negotiating, acknowledging the role his camera has played in allowing him to push the boundaries of his own existence. It may be divisive and difficult, but his work is uncompromising in its pursuit of the essence of life. As he has said, 'Photographers have to accept they can only convey fragments of illusory realities and relate their own intimate experience of the world.'[11]

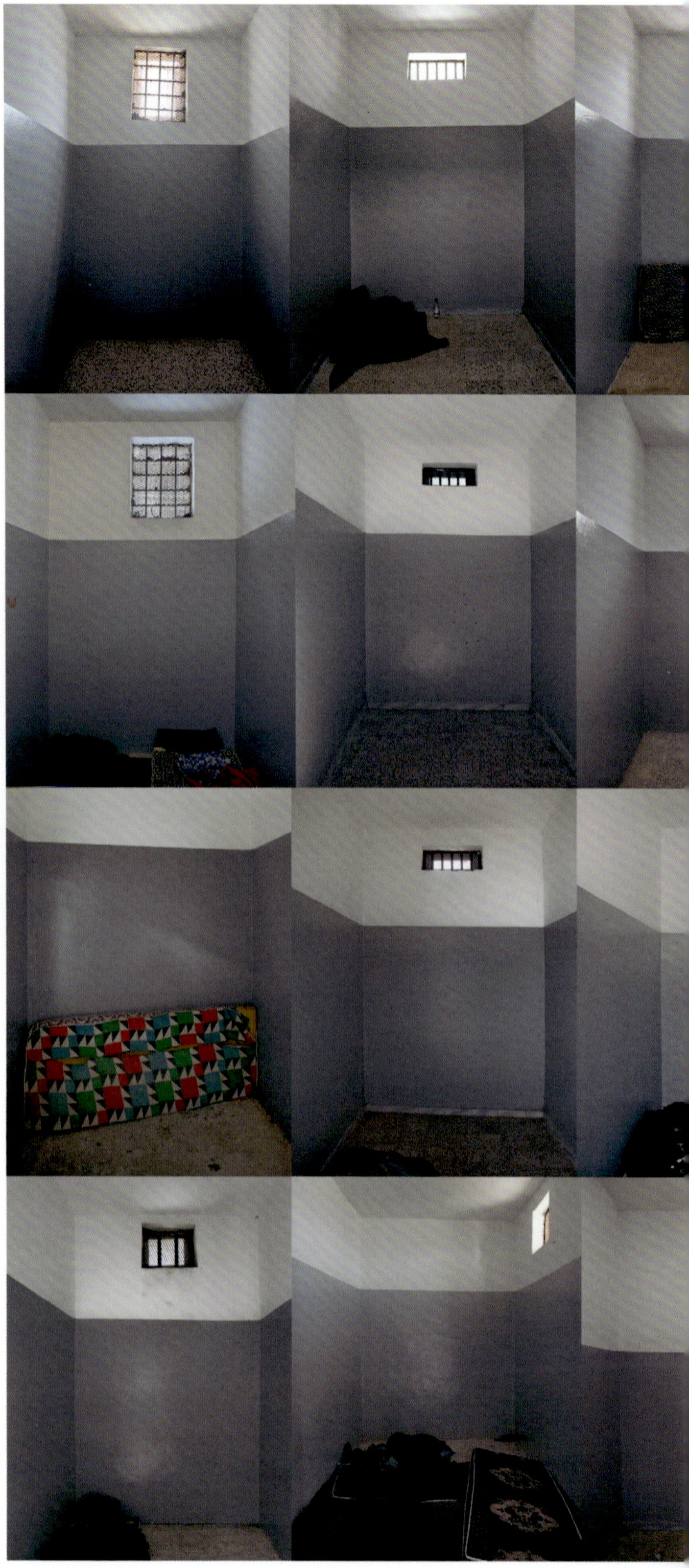

***Abu Salim Prison, Tripoli, Sept 7 2011*, 2011**
Abu Salim was a notorious maximum-security jail in Tripoli, where political prisoners were held under Gaddafi's rule. In 1996 a massacre took place there in which more than 1,270 inmates were said to have been killed. During the Libyan Civil War in 2011, the jail was captured by rebels and the remaining prisoners were set free. D'Agata arrived the day after and didn't have long to shoot because the conditions – the country was still at war – were too dangerous. This image juxtaposes photographs of the recently vacated cells and traces of the men who had inhabited them. It is only these items that give any hint of the inmates' stories and of the kinds of conditions in which they were held. Perhaps even more haunting and disquieting are those cells that are completely empty. D'Agata does not present us with the view of a war-torn country we might have anticipated; instead the horror and violence are embedded in the architecture of the cells – the lack of light and absence of any washing or toilet facilities, for example. As d'Agata has said, 'A picture only shows a given situation under a very specific perspective, consciously or not, openly or not, relevantly or not.'[13]

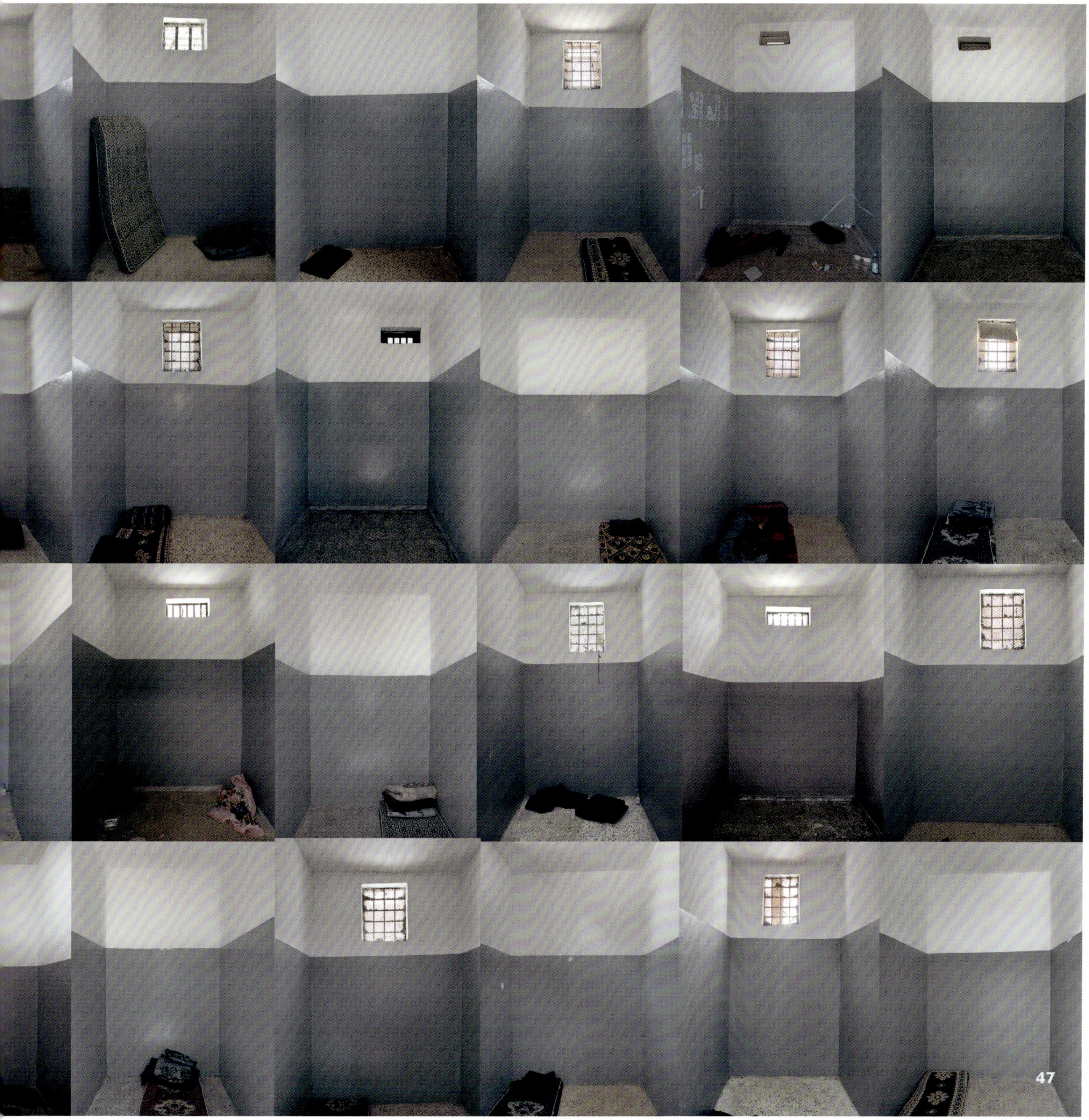
47

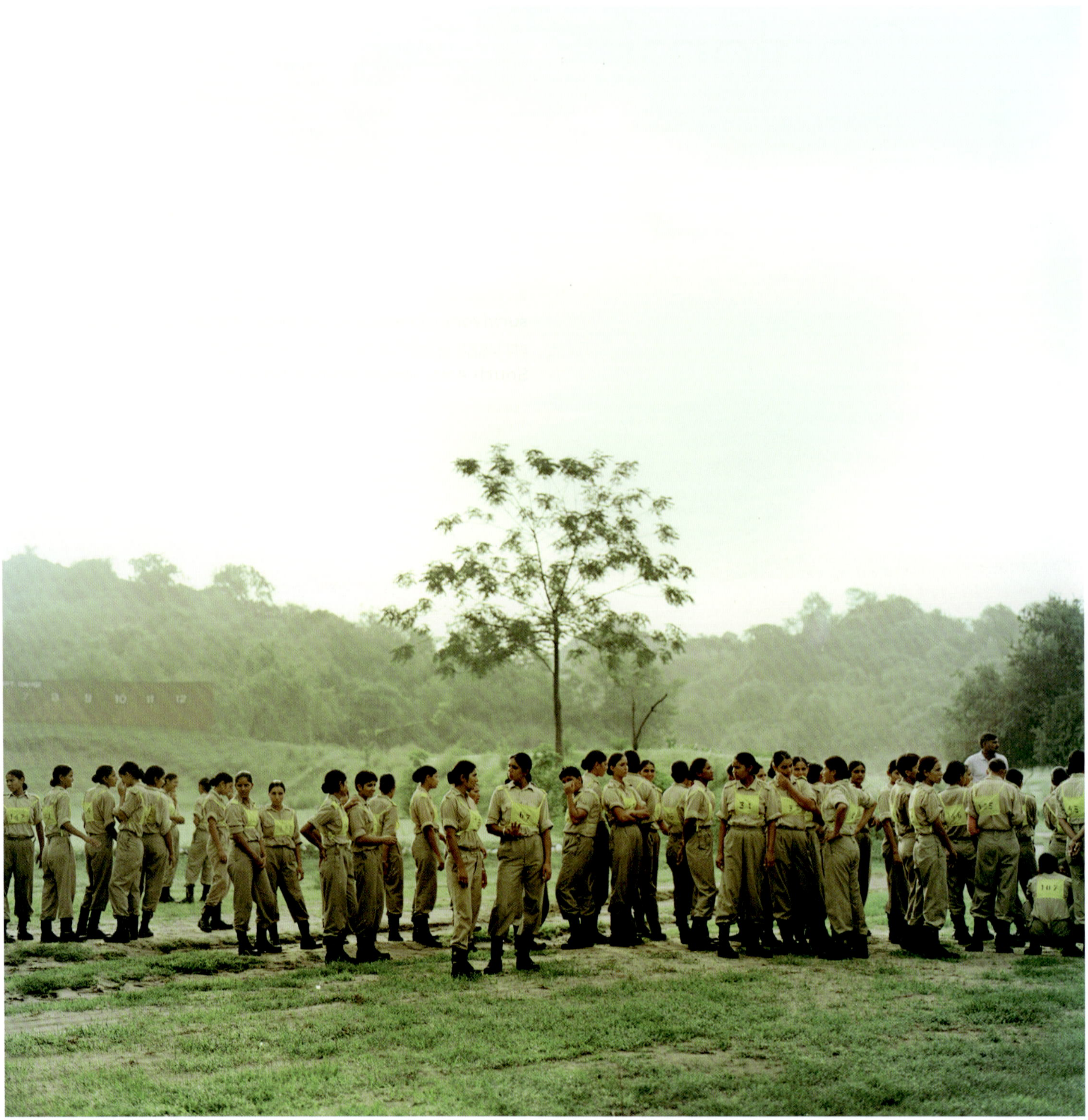

Poulomi Basu

'We are not looking "at" but spending time "with" – this is an important distinction for me,' Poulomi Basu has said of her work.[1] The artist and human rights activist, who was born in Calcutta in 1983, does not stop at observing but instead plunges right into the space her subjects occupy – space that is often contested, polemical, fragile.

Basu's most frequent subjects are 'ordinary women in extraordinary situations'[2]: female soldiers, survivors of rape and violence, mothers and daughters struggling with the particular patriarchal structures of South Asia, where women often face inequality on multiple fronts. Beautiful but also apocalyptic, her photographs and films pulsate with psychotropic light. As an activist, Basu knows that the impact her images have on viewers is of paramount importance, and indeed in some cases her work has been so effective that changes in government policy have followed.

Basu's groundbreaking transmedia project *Blood Speaks: A Ritual of Exile* (2013–) is a revelatory study of the practice in Hindu communities across western Nepal known as *chaupadi*, which forces women out of their homes to remote huts while they are menstruating. Isolated, exposed and vulnerable, the exiled women are often subjected to abuse and rape, and even killed. The work includes LED-lit photographs and a sound installation, but centres around three VR experiences of young women. One documents a sixteen-year-old named Saraswati, who was forced to live in a hut with no access to sanitation immediately after giving birth and while suffering postpartum bleeding. Basu left the camera set up in the hut, taking viewers right in there and giving them a 360-degree portrait of Saraswati, who sits, despondent and alone, clutching her newborn baby. Time seems to move at a glacial pace. It is an alarming, claustrophobic and frightening situation – one in which Basu makes us not only a witness, but also an accomplice.

Social conditioning through religious and cultural attitudes around menstrual blood has ensured that it is viewed as shameful and unacceptable all over the world. Basu, who was raised in a Hindu household in Bengal, sees this as an 'endemic, deep-rooted and subtle form of patriarchal control' that is not limited to the Nepalese context, but, as she says, 'Through the prism of one culture we may see another more clearly.'[3] *Blood Speaks* created an international furore and ultimately resulted in a change in the law, criminalizing *chaupadi* in 2018.

Basu's work is unlimited in its scope, but each of her projects begins with everyday individual acts of

From the series *To Conquer Her Land*, 2009–12
'The border between India and Pakistan is its own world. Since Partition, it has seen war, smuggling – of people, arms and drugs – shooting, jingoistic parades, killing, suicide bombings, fireworks, lonely tears and little moments of glory. In September 2009, India's first women soldiers were deployed on the India–Pakistan border from Punjab to near the first line of control in Kashmir. Comprising women from different parts of the country, these female battalions are a microcosm of the Indian state, cutting across intricate and complex issues of poverty, case, youth and gender,' Basu explains when talking about this image. Between 2009 and 2012, the artist-activist followed a group of women from their last days at home to their first days on active duty. 'Patrolling these barren lands, they try to come to terms with their new responsibilities, undergoing an intense transformation in the process. It is impossible to recreate or restore what they've left behind.'[4]

resilience and resistance – often silent and overlooked – against oppressive systems, connecting contemporary problems in the East with their origins in the West, where they are rarely reported. One such story is unravelled by Basu in *Centralia* (2019), a photographic publication that focuses on the female Maoist guerrillas of the red corridor in central east India, where the land is rich in resources and has consequently been torn apart by violence and injustice. Basu sees this conflict between the state and indigenous people as 'crucial to understanding my country, and yet it is almost completely unknown or at least completely misunderstood,' she told the *British Journal of Photography* in 2019.[5]

Inspired artistically by the 'lyricism' and 'fire' of Arundhati Roy,[6] the dark ambivalence of David Lynch and the perplexing novels of J. G. Ballard, Basu comes hurtling towards us, blistering with urgency, soaring with compassion. Yet it's the artist's own story that connects her most profoundly with the women she meets and whose rights she advocates for in her work. Basu fled her family home at a young age to escape being married off and a life of domestic abuse. Sharing her story is a fundamental part of the process of making her work: 'Photography is an exchange – you have to make yourself vulnerable, because you're asking for a lot in return.'[7]

From the series *Fireflies*, 2009–
'*Fireflies* was a combination of ideas and accumulated experiences that made me feel compelled to turn the camera upon myself – to tell my story of resistance and stand in solidarity with the women who have opened their lives to me,' Basu says of this image. It is part of an ongoing work made in response to her own trauma, which she explores through her relationship with her mother. 'When I was seventeen, my mother told me to leave home so that I would be able to live a life of freedom and choice that had been denied to her, and my grandmother, who were both child brides and then young widows. Rooted in my experience of domestic violence, this work navigates the bloodlines of our collective trauma, mapping an elemental journey of survival. From the claustrophobia of the home, through to dreams of escape and transcendence, this is a kinetic and spiritual work, lingering on the fragility of time and our earthly insignificance when contrasted with the celestial wonder of the natural world.'[8] In *Fireflies*, Basu continues to examine the preoccupying themes of her work – gender, power and violence – extending them beyond the documentary and into the 'hinterland between fact and fiction',[9] within the atmosphere of a dystopian, female-centric place, familiar yet fantastical.

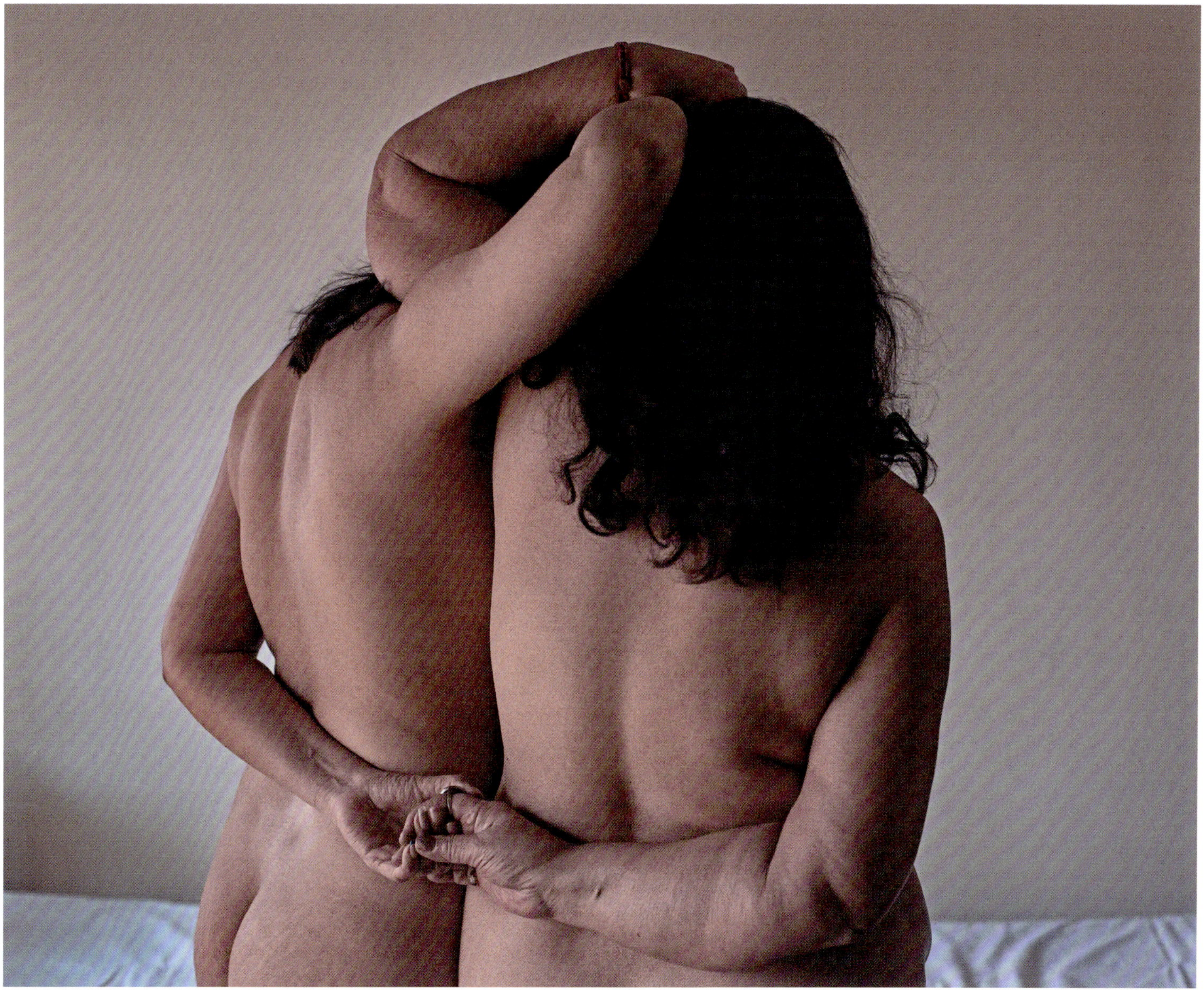

Mohamed Bourouissa

Born in 1978 in Algeria, Mohamed Bourouissa moved to France at the age of five and grew up in the Parisian suburb of Courbevoie, one of the most heavily populated municipalities in Europe. The particular geography and social dynamics of the Parisian *banlieue*, and similar places on the periphery of the urban metropolis, are the starting point for much of Bourouissa's work as an artist, which involves moving images, photography, drawing and photo-based sculptures.

Throughout his career, a central concern for Bourouissa has been the place of the individual in society. He has investigated this through the relationship of bodies to the structures – architectural, political, economic, sexual, social – that constrict them. These structures also include photography, since the artist's hand and intention are inescapable; a fact that Bourouissa reveals in his work. His interventions have sometimes been literal: his lauded early video work *Temps Mort* (2009) – a collaboration with a friend in prison – was shot on a smuggled camera. His friend followed directions from Bourouissa about how and what to photograph and film, and the artist compiled their exchanges into an 18-minute, low-resolution video work comprising grainy and pixelated texts, photos and MMS messages to give a first-hand insight into prison life that's far from the sensationalized impressions we're used to seeing on television.

Nonetheless, the fact that the directions came from the artist on the outside reminds us how much of what we see is structured by invisible forces. The way images are constructed (or deconstructed) is as important as what is in the picture. Bourouissa constantly reminds us to look beyond what we think we are seeing. Communities that are highly politicized are often considered to be geographically, physically or socially 'outside', but this is only because the person making the assumption – the observer – is 'inside'. This tension is apparent in one of Bourouissa's best-known series, *Périphérique* (2005–9), about young men living in the Parisian *banlieue*. The pictures replicate the language of social documentary but are in fact staged re-enactments, some based on classical paintings by the likes of Delacroix, using the gaze, gestures and framing to carefully elicit emotional responses. Who is 'inside' and who is 'outside' are matters of where you stand. At

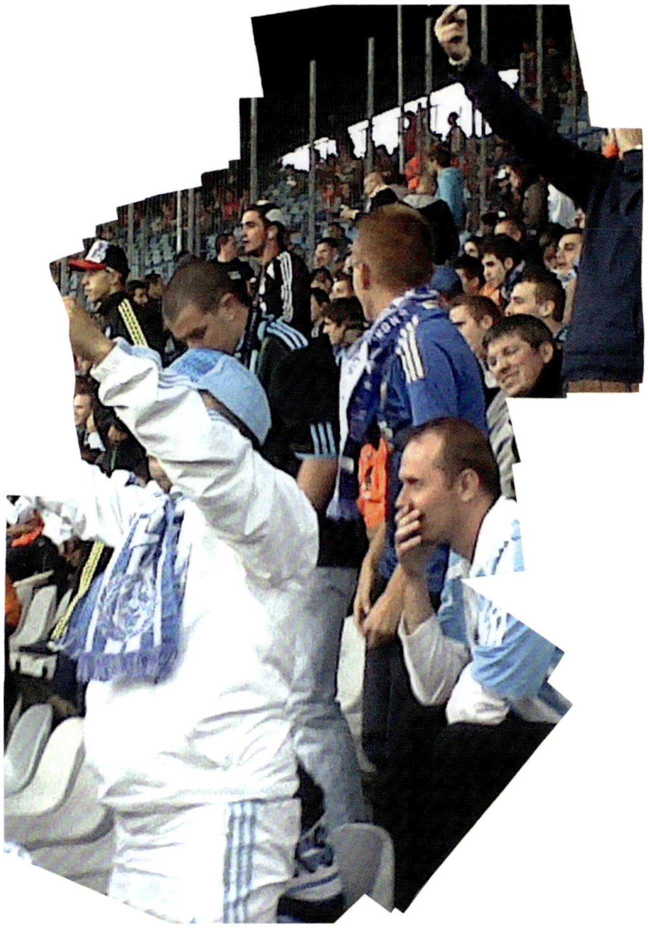

***Sans Titre* from the series *RIP*, 2011. Fine art paper print, 29.5 x 20cm (11 ⅝ x 7 ⅞ in)**
Written across a banner being waved at a football match in Marseille once were the letters RIP, commemorating two fans who had passed away. The letters could, of course, without any context, also be read as the word 'rip'. This ambivalence articulated for Bourouissa the way gestures and chants – including the torn pieces of paper fans often throw – make their way round football stadiums. It inspired him to create a series of works that question the material aspects of the photograph, including images pasted onto Plexiglas and a video work in which photographs of fans before and after a match are printed out and land in the tray of an inkjet printer. Bourouissa asks if the dissemination of images, their physical presence (or absence) and the way they circulate now are just as important as what is depicted in the image itself.

Bourouissa's exhibitions – which include solo shows at notable institutions such as the Musée d'Art Moderne de la Ville de Paris, the Centre Pompidou, Paris, and the Stedelijk Museum, Amsterdam – the photographs and videos are fragmented, pixelated, split across screens, torn, worn or crumpled (and even printed onto flattened car parts). We have to work hard to 'see' the photograph, and in itself it does not fully reveal what it means. For Bourouissa, photojournalism has become a deeply problematic way of representing people, and he responds to it with trenchant criticism in the way he creates and displays his work. He believes images should be complex, difficult to read, to remind viewers that what we see is not always what we think we see.

In Bourouissa's work, the artist's presence is always felt, and he moves between the positions of insider and observer. Full immersion in the community he is working with, intuitively getting to know its contours, is fundamental to his artistic practice. In 2013 Bourouissa spent several months with the Fletcher Street Urban Riding Club in North Philadelphia. The club is a non-profit organization that maintains a century-long tradition of African-American cowboys and horsemanship and teaches local young people to ride and care for horses. Wanting to address the specificities of the Fletcher Street community in his own way, Bourouissa decided to organize a pageant event with them, which became the subject of a short film, *Horse Day* (2014–15).

The beating heart of Bourouissa's practice is to puncture our assumptions about photography and its uses in different contexts. As John Berger writes in *Understanding a Photograph* (2013), 'A photograph is not necessarily a lie, but it isn't the truth either. It's more like a fleeting, subjective impression.'[1] Bourouissa's work constitutes a radical interrogation of the subjective role of the photographer today, leading us to question the purpose of the 'photograph' itself.

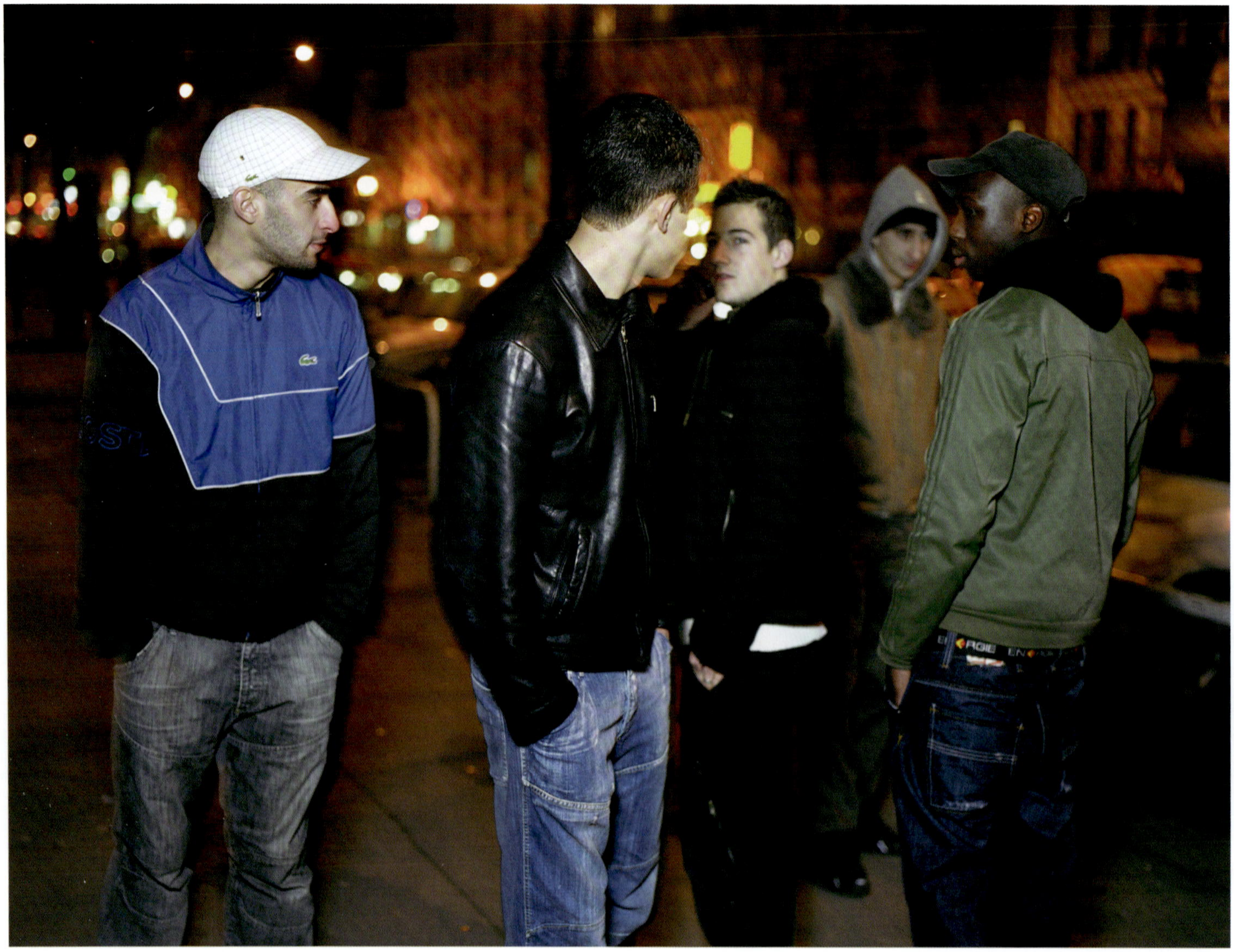

Le rencontre from the series _Périphérique_, 2005. C-print, 90 x 120cm (35 ½ x 47 ¼ in). Edition of 10.

In the series *Périphérique* we encounter familiar images of disenfranchised male youths, loitering and posturing, as in *Le rencontre*, above. However, these scenes that appear to be documentary images are in fact carefully staged and often reference classical paintings. Our reading of the images is flipped on its head when we realize that what we are looking at has been 'faked' – a sharp reminder that no photograph ever represents the complete truth. Bourouissa created these images in the immediate aftermath of the 2005 riots in the Parisian *banlieues*, stating that he wanted to elevate the ubiquitous and politicized mass-media representations of these people and the suburbs they live in to the realm of poetry.

The Twins from the series _Nous sommes halles_, 2002. Lambda print, 30 x 21.2cm (11 ½ x 8 ¼ in)

Périphérique followed on from Bourouissa's first project, *Nous somme halles*, creating in collaboration with his friend and fellow photographer Anoush Kashoot while Bourouissa was studying painting at the Sorbonne. The portraits play on works from the history of art: here, the inspiration comes from Jan van Eyck's *The Arnolfini Portrait*, and group photographs of men by August Sander and Jamel Shabazz. His preoccupations with what stories are told and how people are represented are already on display in this series, for which he photographed the marginalized youths of the Parisian neighbourhood of Châtelet-les-Halles.

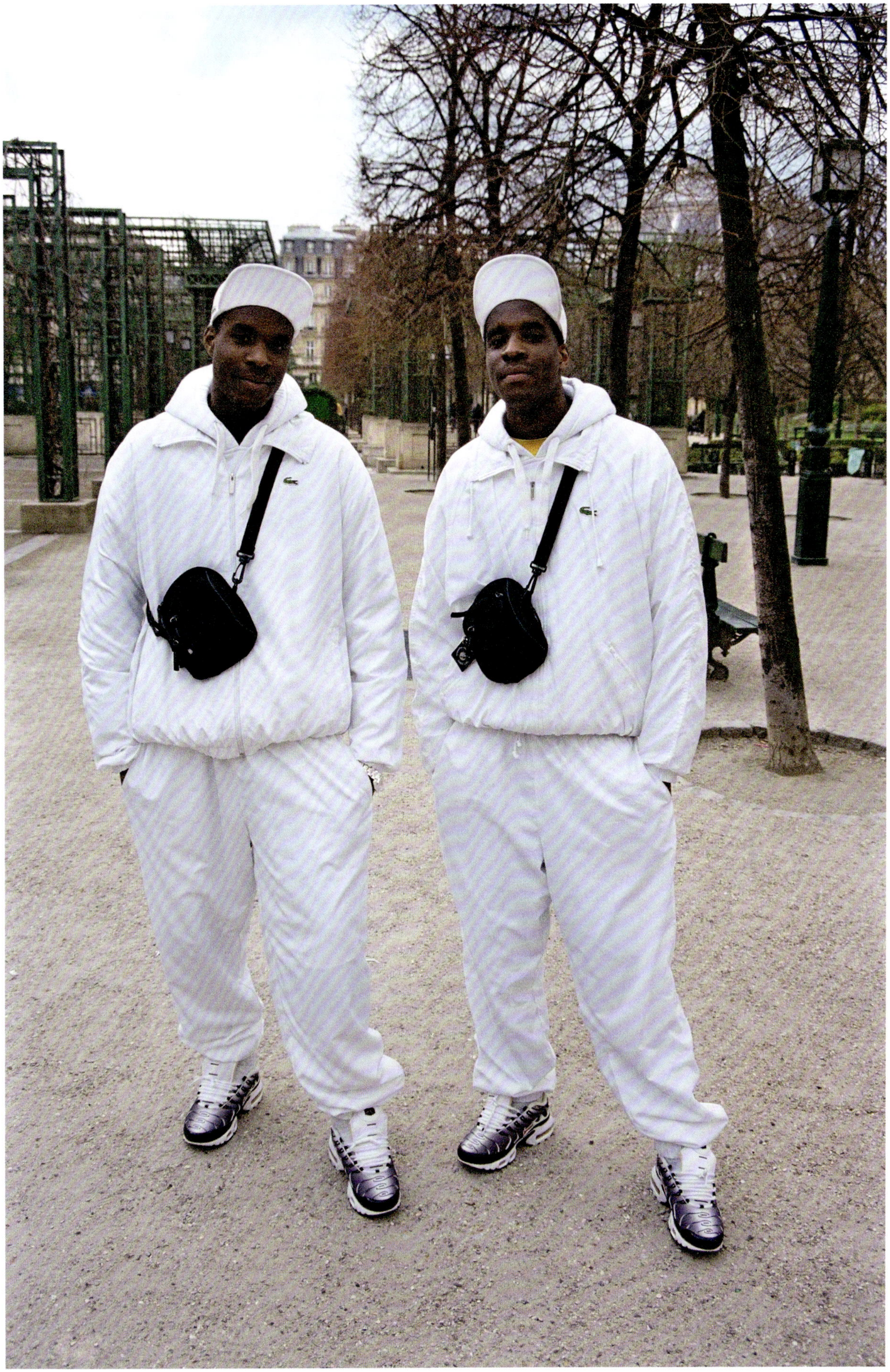

Sheila Pree Bright

Sheila Pree Bright's photographs aren't well known outside the USA, but she has become a key chronicler of the Black Lives Matter movement over the last decade, bearing witness to the seemingly endless struggle for social and racial justice in the USA. Born in Georgia, the heartland of the American civil rights movement, in 1967 – a year before the assassination of Martin Luther King Jr – she spent her early childhood in Germany and then moving around the USA, as her father was in the army. She eventually returned to the South, where she now lives, and the region has become, as she says, 'a foundation for my research'.[1]

In the 1990s Bright worked as a commercial photographer, taking promotional portraits of hip-hop musicians for independent record labels. By portraying rappers with guns or posing impassively among staged dead bodies wrapped in white sheets, she was inadvertently contributing to a stereotype of young black men that became entrenched in the mainstream. When Bright went back to college to do an MFA in Photography, she experienced something of an epiphany once she realized the effect photographs had on the public conscience. She turned away from her early work – she no longer exhibits it in public – and began to focus on subverting those same stereotypes, encouraging people 'to think critically, beyond what they see on the news, and to inspire dialogues between people of different races, genders and generations'.[2]

Bright's first acclaimed series was *Plastic Bodies* (2003), in which she spliced Barbie Doll figures with photographs of real women using Photoshop. The work, which was completed as her MFA thesis, directly contrasts the plastic, manufactured version of femininity with human skin. The conceit was a straightforward but effective way to show how all women are judged against racialized beauty ideals, which are turned into norms by products. As toy manufacturers have begun to adopt new body types and skin tones, Bright has observed how black body types have been appropriated and made acceptable through a Eurocentric, white model. She cites Sara 'Saartjie' Baartman, one of several African women who were exhibited at freak shows in the nineteenth century across Europe for the size of their buttocks, and the recent trend for 'butt-pumping', popularized by Kim Kardashian, as an example of the way black female bodies

***Untitled 12* from the series *Suburbia*, 2005. C-print, 61 x 76.2cm (24 ⅛ x 30in)**

It is surprising how subversive this photograph is. Part of the series *Suburbia*, documenting middle-class African American lives, it depicts an ordinary domestic scene in a family home in the suburbs of Atlanta. A woman reclines, reading *Business Week*; the furniture, the magazine and her clothing all suggest a comfortable existence. The reactions the series provoked have become part of the work, with some commenting that the images 'didn't have enough signifiers in them to show they were black homes', as Bright recounts.[4] What certain viewers expect to see – and what they don't – is profoundly revealing. The signifiers of race, Bright has said, are in fact there, if you look closely enough, but they exist in a way that American mass media and mainstream culture deny. The images in *Suburbia* prove how deeply rooted stereotypes are by giving us a truthful – if less sensational – image of African American homes.

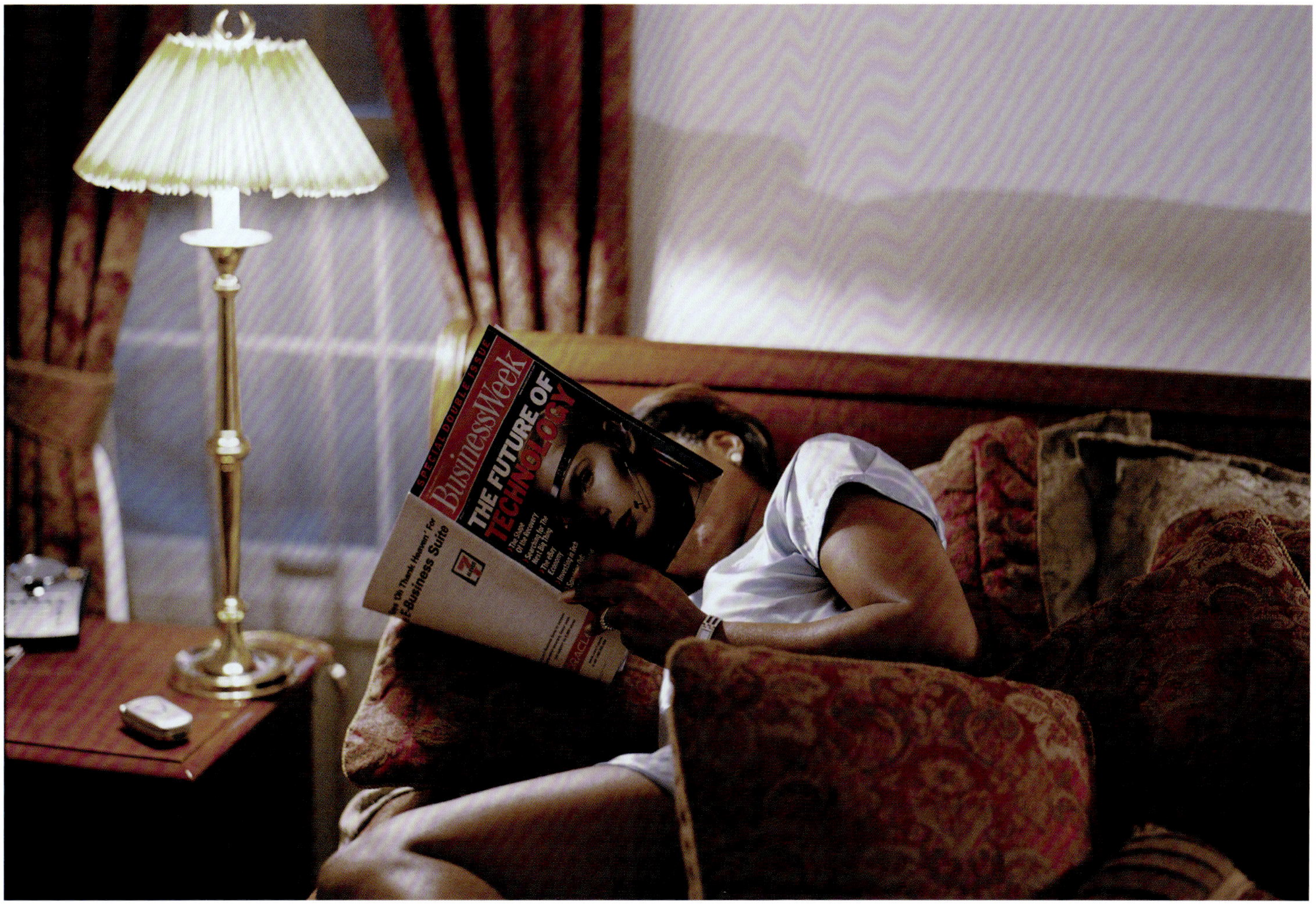

have been objectified and commodified without recognition of the past discrimination and degradation black women suffered. *Plastic Bodies*, Bright says, addresses the 'loss of personal identity many women experience, specifically women of color',[3] when confronted with these fabricated representations of female bodies.

Providing a counter-narrative to the photography disseminated by mass and mainstream media continued to be a concern for Bright throughout the 2000s. Her series *Suburbia* (2006), for example, focused on middle-class homes in the suburbs of Atlanta, while in *Young Americans* (2008) she collaborated with Generation Y subjects, asking each to use the American flag to express what being an American signified for them. The *Young Americans* portraits give a surprising and concise picture of the complexities of a nation that is both fractured and proud: one subject uses the flag to bind his hands like a prisoner; another wears it patriotically as a robe. In 2012, Bright pasted eleven works from the series on the streets of Miami during Art Basel. She felt then – and continues to feel – that taking her work beyond galleries and museums, into the streets or onto social media, is a crucial part of her practice if she is to fulfil her purpose of giving an alternative perspective on life in contemporary America.

It is possible that Bright's most important work is yet to be done. In 2013, as the Black Lives Matter movement galvanized action across the USA following the death of Trayvon Martin in Florida the previous year, Bright started to take portraits of little-known but important figures from the civil rights movement in the 1960s. With the emergence of BLM, she began to connect the struggles of previous generations under Jim Crow laws with those of the young activists now leading the new movement in the South. In the wake of widely publicized police brutality and murders in Atlanta, Ferguson, Baltimore, Washington, DC, and Baton Rouge, Bright took to the streets with her camera, documenting marches and protests, pain and power, capturing moments of vulnerability, anger and anguish that are not typically shown in news coverage. Her photographs have given the movement against racism in the USA a poignant new identity, with the sombre weight of history behind the current voices. The photographs evolved into an expansive public art project, *#1960Now* (2016). The series also conveys a profound feeling of frustration and urgency. Bright shot all the images in black and white to give a sense of continuity between then and now, so that past and present merge, posing the question: has anything changed in all these years?

Black Lives Matter, Atlanta Chapter Rally for Tamir Rice, Atlanta GA, 2016 **from the series** ***#1960Now*****, 2016. Archival inkjet print, 76.2 x 76.2cm (30 x 30in)**
'My work is about controlling the narrative,' Bright has said.[5] Her major series *#1960Now* shows not only the rage and anger of people fighting for social and racial justice, but moments of pain and tenderness, particularly as experienced by young black men, who are frequently maligned in the press and misrepresented in photography. In this image, photographs of Tamir Rice, the twelve-year-old who was shot and killed by a police officer in Cleveland in 2014, are held up on a placard by protesters in Atlanta at a Black Lives Matter march. It is raw with emotion – the pain, loss and grief that followed Rice's murder cut into the faces of the protesters. The photograph within the photograph reminds us of the importance of images. The image of Rice here – clearly only a boy – is a powerful counter-narrative to the image the police officer who fatally shot him had of a threatening black youth. Would he have died if the smiling, innocent image was the one that people saw?

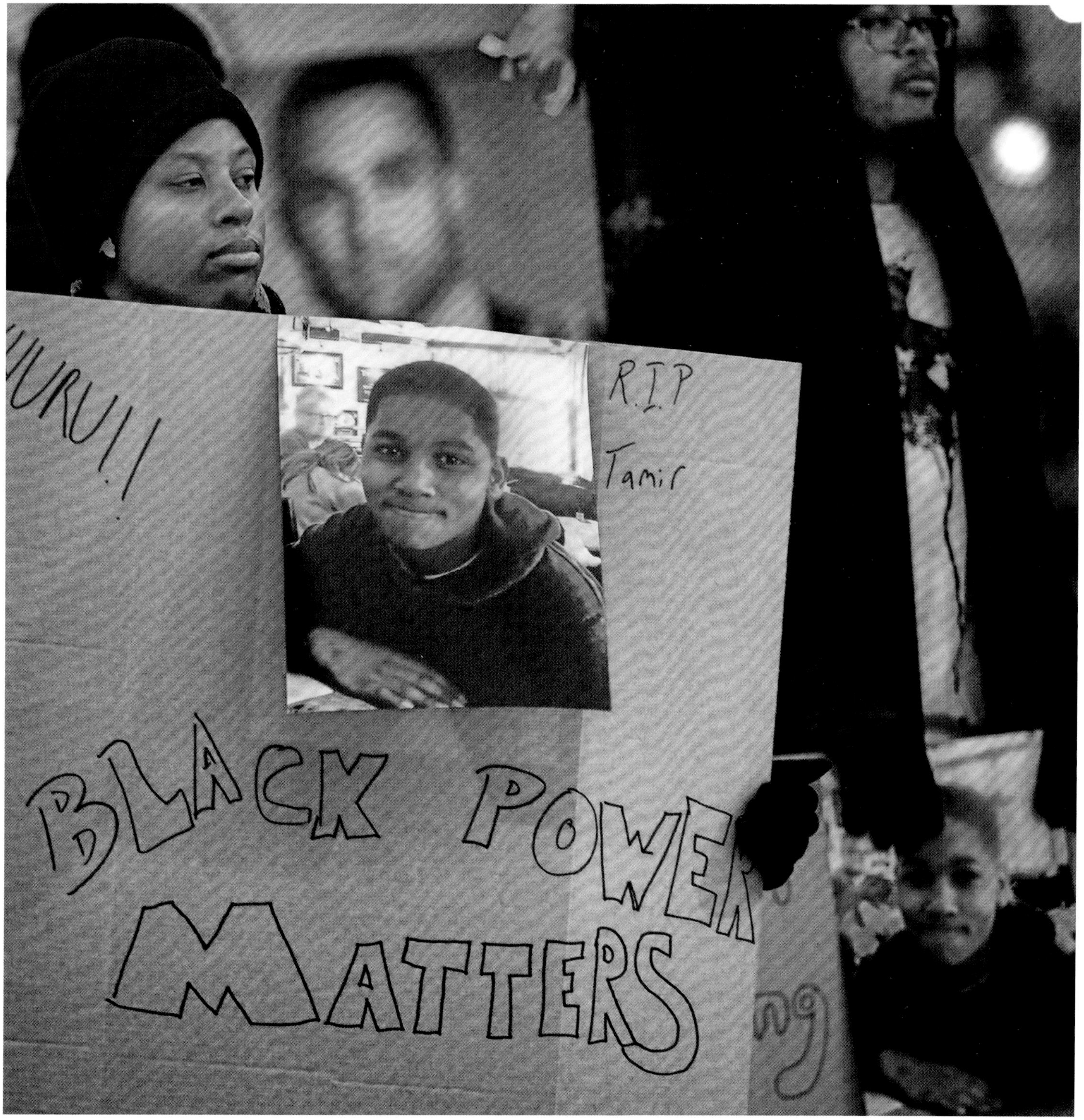
R.I.P
Tamir
BLACK POWER
MATTERS

Jo Ann Callis

Born in Ohio in 1940, Jo Ann Callis's work has remained largely overlooked beyond the USA for most of her career. She started to take photographs in her thirties as a student at UCLA, having first experimented with drawing and painting but finding that photography offered a more immediate pleasure. Her first photographic encounters with works by Hans Bellmer, Pierre Molinier and Duane Michals exposed her to the erotic potential of the camera and the possibilities of theatrical staging.

A faculty member of the Photography and Media department at CalArts, where she began teaching in 1976, Callis has been an influence on more than one new generation of photographers. As is the case with most avant-garde artists, it was only after many years that Callis's wider importance and originality became clear, largely thanks to a 2009 retrospective at the J. Paul Getty Museum in Los Angeles. In the late 1970s Callis was among the early pioneers of 'fabricated photography', using staged sets created solely for the purpose of photographing images that were meant to look constructed. At a time when conceptual photography was becoming popular, Callis's work by contrast was loaded with personal melodrama and emotion. As the artist has revealed, 'I've always wanted to please myself.'[1]

Callis's early works are charged with psychological tension – the artist had divorced her husband, moved to Los Angeles and was bringing up two children on her own. She admitted that she felt the strain of surviving financially as an artist. Having spent a lot of time in domestic spaces, looking inwards, she often featured interiors, furnishings, tables and domestic objects in her photographs, and trained her lens on animals, babies and food. These sound like unsexy subjects, but Callis totally transforms the way we see them, making the prosaic appear camp, comic, mysterious and playful. An ordinary scene of salt and pepper shakers and a cup of coffee is split asunder by a burning dinner plate; a scoop of ice cream unsettles a pile of spaghetti. These private psychodramas build on the legacy of surrealism. Callis often arranges ordinary, everyday objects into grids in order to find free associations between forms and similarities between apparently disparate things: a cake, a hat and a pillow; a glove, a balloon and a shoehorn. There is humour in these juxtapositions, but Callis is also interested in the tactile beauty of the objects.

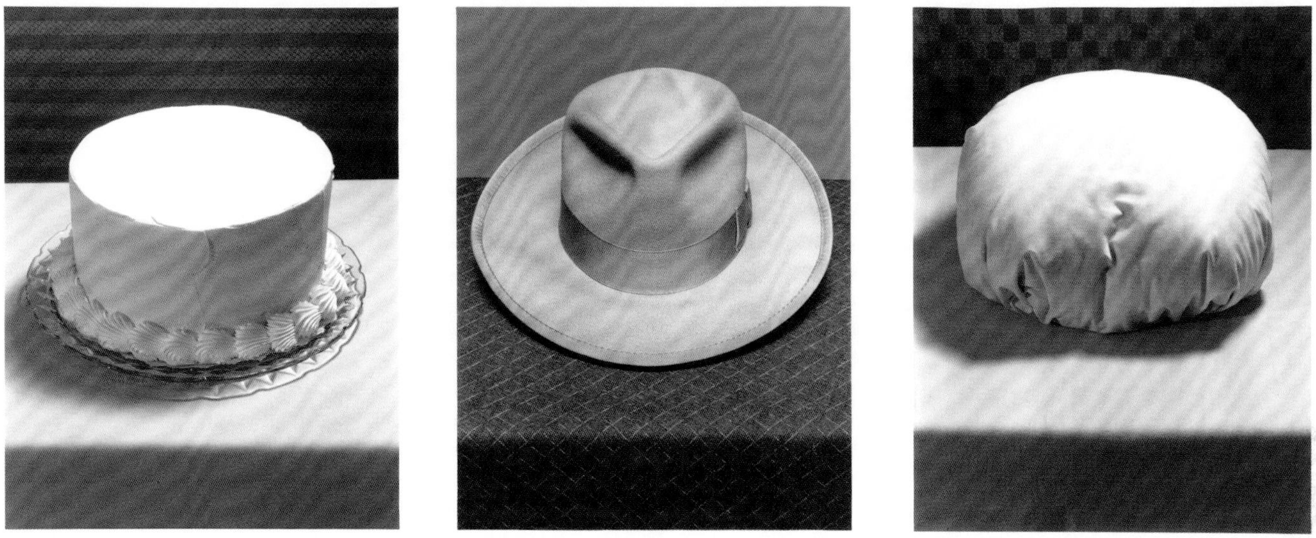

Cake, Hat, Pillow **from the series *Grids*, 1982. Gelatin silver print, 20.8 x 54.7cm (8 ¼ x 21 ⅝ in)**
'What does it mean?' is not the right question to ask when viewing a work like this. It is not a puzzle and there is no one right answer. In the early 1980s Callis was considering the presentation of the still life photograph. Typically, a still life is arranged hierarchically, with the most important item in the foreground of the image. Callis wanted to reverse this conventional order and present all the objects in the image as equal, drawing the eye to the connections between their formal and material qualities. All the individual images were printed onto a single sheet of paper, so they could not be moved or changed. There is not, Callis has emphasized, any political intention to her works. She has always worked from her curiosity about the world and translated this into her photographs, hoping to communicate something about the parts of us we can't explain. The work is about the sheer delight of looking.

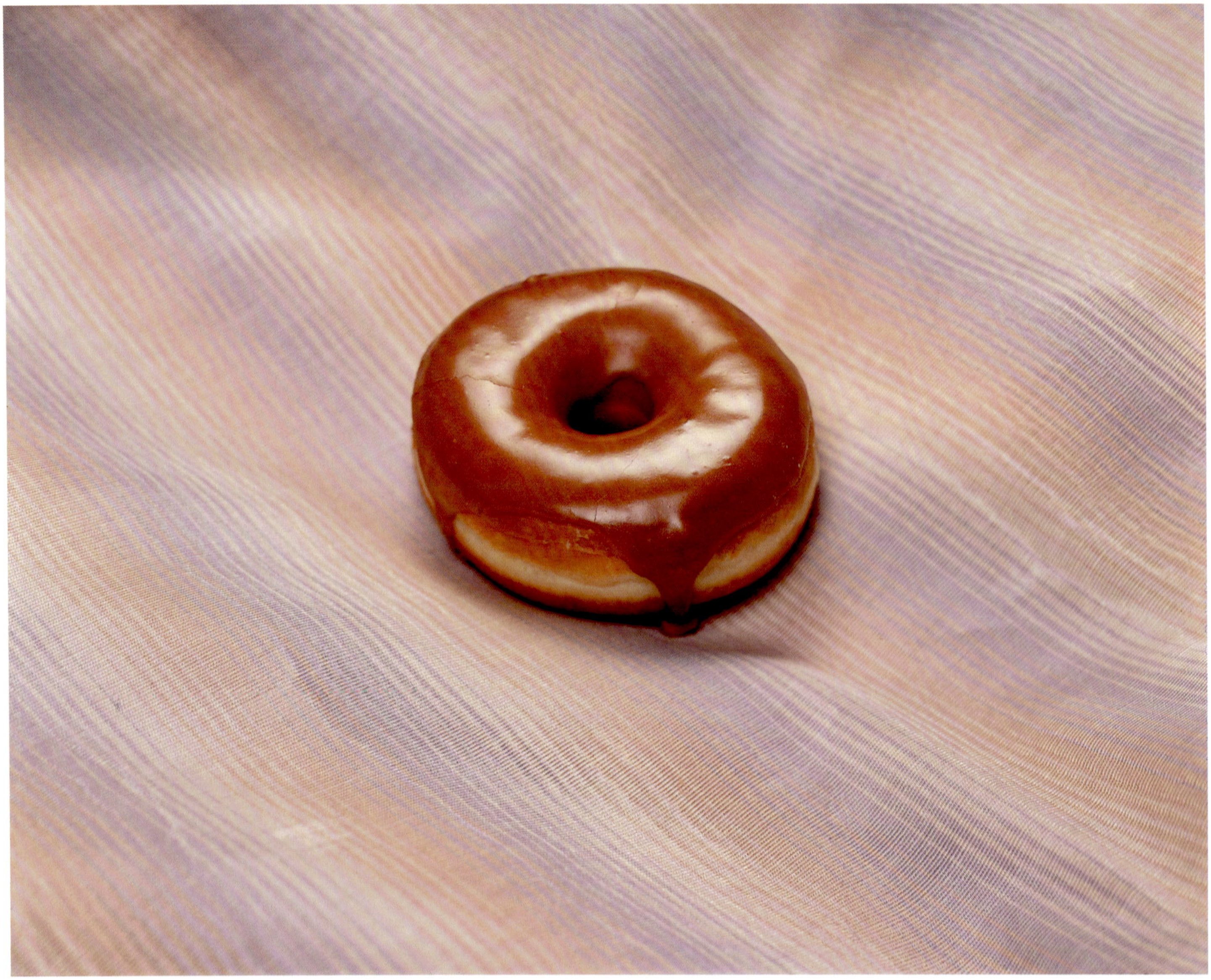

***Untitled #12* (above left) and *Untitled #8* (above right) from the series *Cheap Thrills and Forbidden Pleasures*, 1993. Silver-dye bleach prints, both 27.9 x 35.6cm (11 x 14 1/8 in)**
'I love desserts,' Callis confesses.[3] That is obvious in this series of glorious, sensual jollifications of a variety of cakes, tarts, eclairs, doughnuts and pies. The artist travelled all over Los Angeles buying desserts – an exercise in the cheap thrill of indulgence. Cherries, glossy with glaze, wobble atop titillating piles of whipped cream, each sweet treat nestled in a lusty frisson of fabric. The suggestiveness here is deliberate and typical of Callis, who is a kind of voyeur of confections, likening the guilty pleasure of eating to sex. *Cheap Thrills and Forbidden Pleasures* connects to a wider interest in food explored throughout her work.

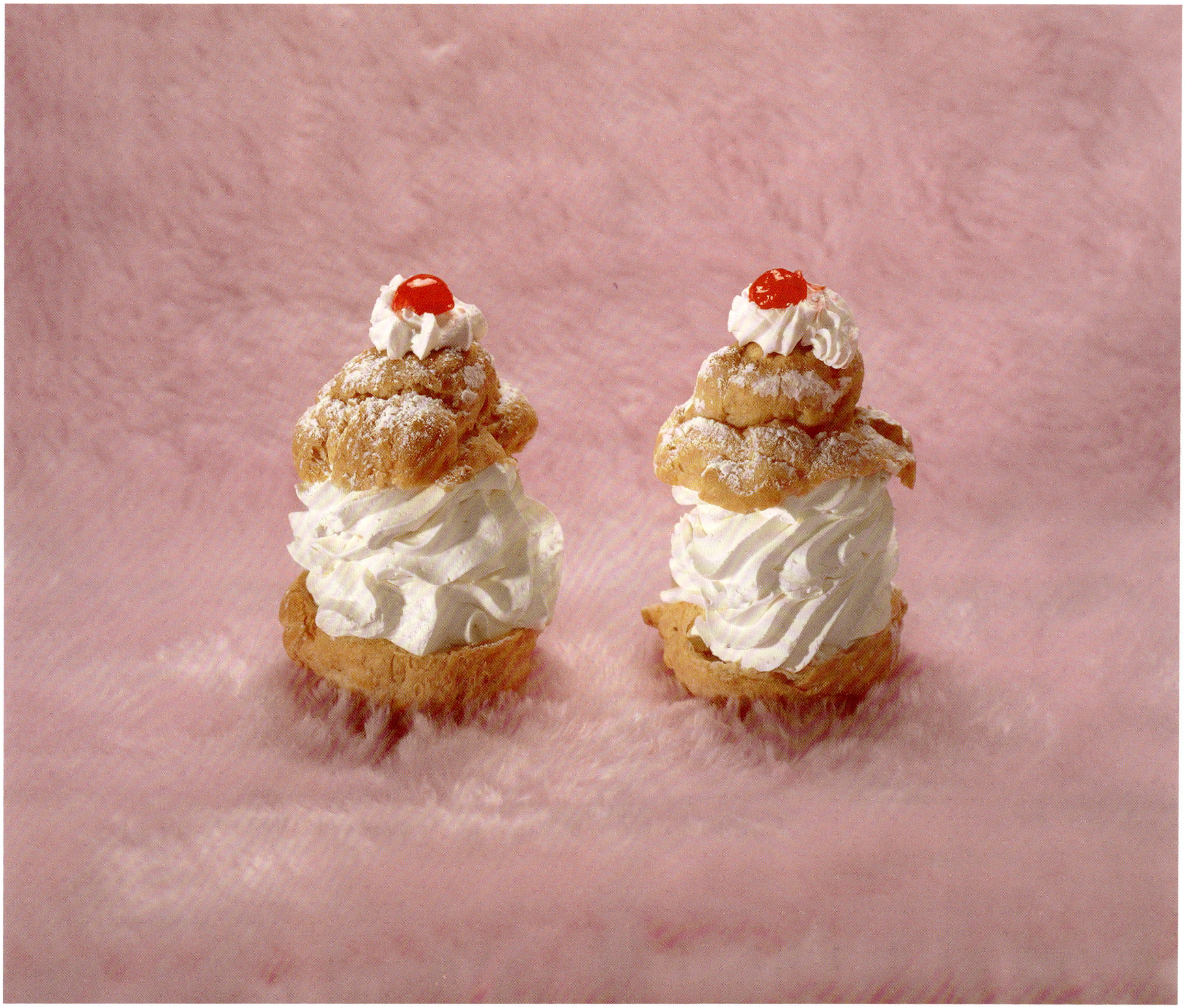

Photography allows Callis to 'make my own world and occupy it in the way I want to'.[2] In her early pictures, created in the first two decades of her photography practice, anxiety emanates through constant tensions, stillness is erupted by action. Unafraid to be overtly feminine, Callis embraced the female objectifying gaze well ahead of its becoming a widespread phenomenon in photography. This is equally the case with her sexually charged *Early Black and White Portfolio* and *Early Color Portfolio*, both shot in the 1970s, which were explorations of innuendo, moving between the eye and imagination. She looks at bodies with the strange regard of a surrealist and the sexual intrigue of a voyeur. Even now, they're wild reinventions of fetish and erotic photography.

Juno Calypso

Juno Calypso started dressing up for the camera because, like many of us, she wanted to have some nice photographs of herself. Taking the pictures gave her control. This early impulse lay the foundation for what soon became a more serious endeavour. While Calypso was a student at the London College of Communication, she devised her first series, *Joyce* (2011), in which she portrayed a semi-fictional protagonist/alter ego who is desperate and deadpan, lonely and exhausted by self-care routines, a suburbanite female stereotype who is doused in baby oil, pink drapery and fluffy dressing gowns. It makes the consumerist dream look dystopian.

Born in London in 1989, Calypso works differently from the typical photographer in the age of social media. She prefers to operate entirely alone (even in deserted mansions and seedy hotels). She then rigorously pares her photographs down to only a few images, releasing one body of work at a time and usually only once a year. In an age where so many images float in the ether without context, Calypso also contradicts the millennial paradigm by speaking extensively about her work, considering this discussion a valuable way to bring her practice full circle.

Joyce won Calypso the Catlin Art Prize in 2013, but it was her next work, the *Honeymoon* series, first released in 2015, that was Calypso's major breakthrough – winning her the BJP International Photography Award and the Foam Talent Award in 2016. The series takes the spectator on the solo voyage of a female fantasy played out in a love hotel meant for couples. Visually perfect and highly choreographed, *Honeymoon* is an exploration of self-love and the auto-erotic, and the psychology of how we construct our own image. Calypso's interest in the products of the self-care industry is mostly aesthetic, but it's more than skin-deep: 'I got fed up of seeing my own face very quickly. I didn't decide to use myself as a model because I wanted to confront myself. It was just a convenient body. So now I make it more convenient by covering my face.'[1]

The themes present in Calypso's early works – enquiring into the female experience through the lens of consumerism; disappointment; our obsession with ageing and preservation, and our avoidance of death – have continued to evolve over a decade and still preoccupy the artist. She grew up with parents who are doctors, which has perhaps influenced her fascination with

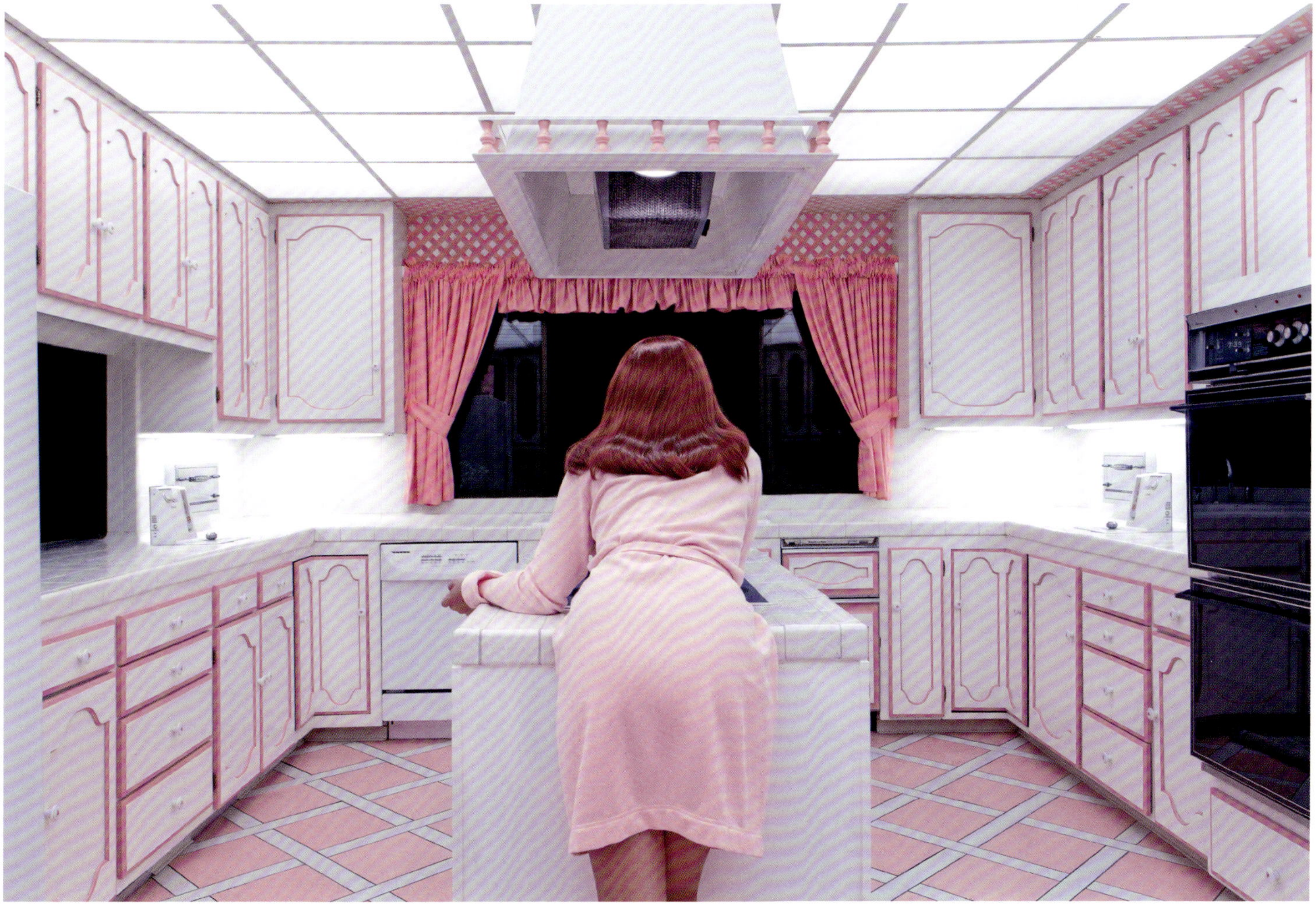

Subterranean Kitchen **from the series** ***What To Do With A Million Years*****, 2018**
This image belongs to Calypso's ambitious project *What To Do With A Million Years*, which was shot in the vast underground home of Avon Products director Girard 'Jerry' Henderson. Henderson had the place built as an extravagant bunker to escape from nuclear war – and remains perfectly preserved as a 1970s time capsule. The highly unusual house now belongs to the Society for the Preservation of Near Extinct Species. This image is full of suggestion and tension – possibly in part due to the fact Calypso really was alone in the sprawling, ominous estate, some 26 feet underground.

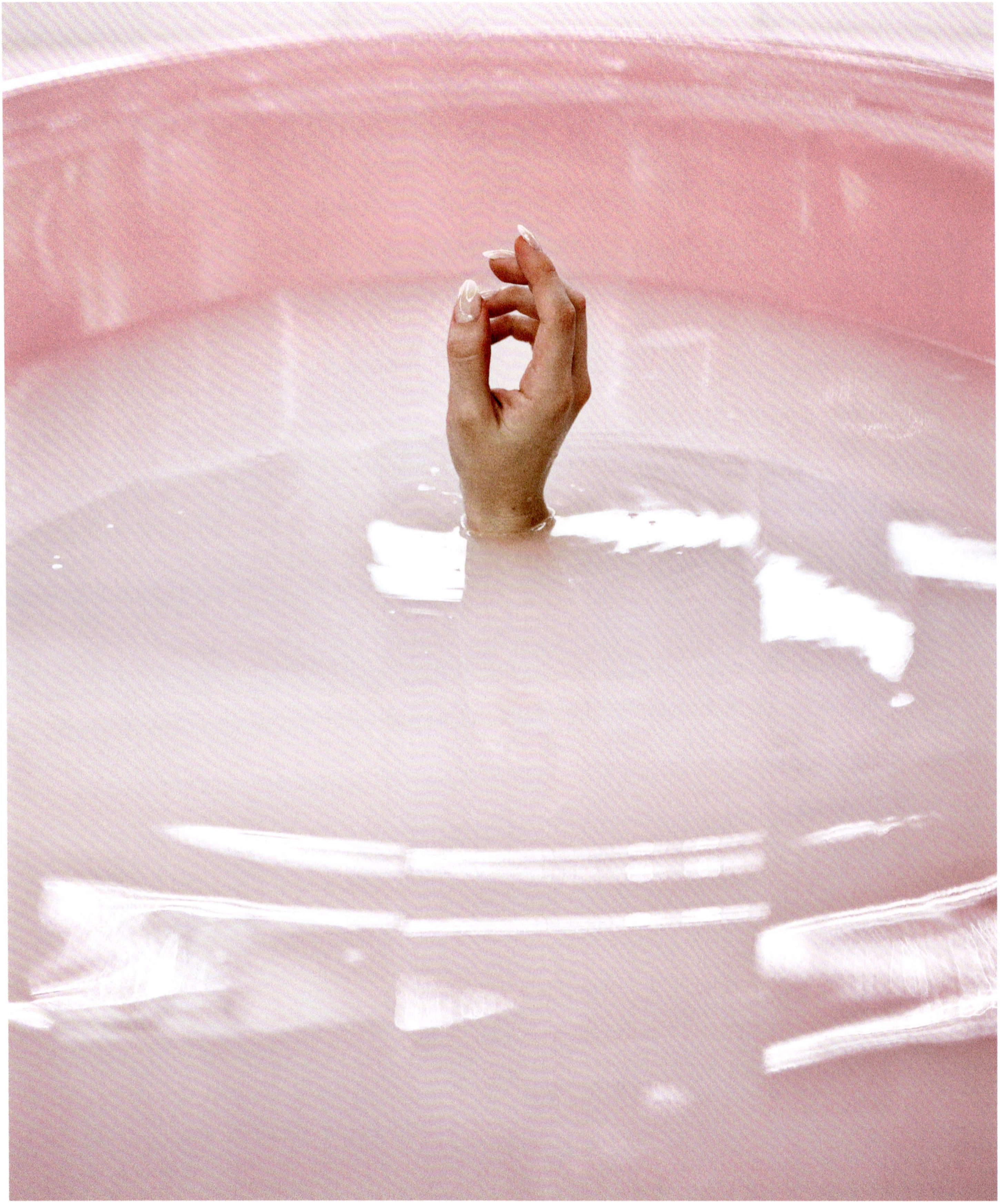

apparatus and the clinical aspects of beauty, as well as the exaggerated, sterile perfection of her constructed scenes. She has also tackled medical procedures, such as egg-freezing (a commission for TOPIC in 2017), and in 2018 she invited the public into a salon in central London where gown-clad mannequins, including a cast of the artist herself, were the clients, surreally basking in throbbing red lights.

The tones of haunting, psychological horror in Calypso's work are always expressed with a dry sense of humour – complicity between the viewer and the creator, or what Calypso has referred to as the 'looped gaze',[2] is an essential part of the power of her images. We are meant to find these scenes terrifying and unnatural, but they are also laughable in their absurdity. This laughter is liberating. As author Naomi Wolf writes in *The Beauty Myth* (1990) – a book Calypso has noted as an influence – 'You do not win by struggling to the top of a caste system, you win by refusing to be trapped within one at all.'[3]

If You Can't Live Without Me, Why Aren't You Dead Yet **(left), 2015, and *A Dream in Green* (overleaf), 2016, from the series *The Honeymoon Suite*. Archival pigment prints**
Many can identify with the feeling of going into the bathroom like a monster that needs to be tamed, and then emerging, after hours of grooming, resplendent. This feeling is represented in *A Dream in Green*, a reinvention of the Botticelli *Venus* for our times showing a woman play-acting a fantasy in front of the mirror. *If You Can't Live without Me, Why Aren't You Dead Yet?*, meanwhile, is typical of Calypso's provocative irony. A flawlessly manicured hand emerges from the surface of opaque pink-hued bathwater, leaving the viewer to wonder if what is in there is dead or alive.

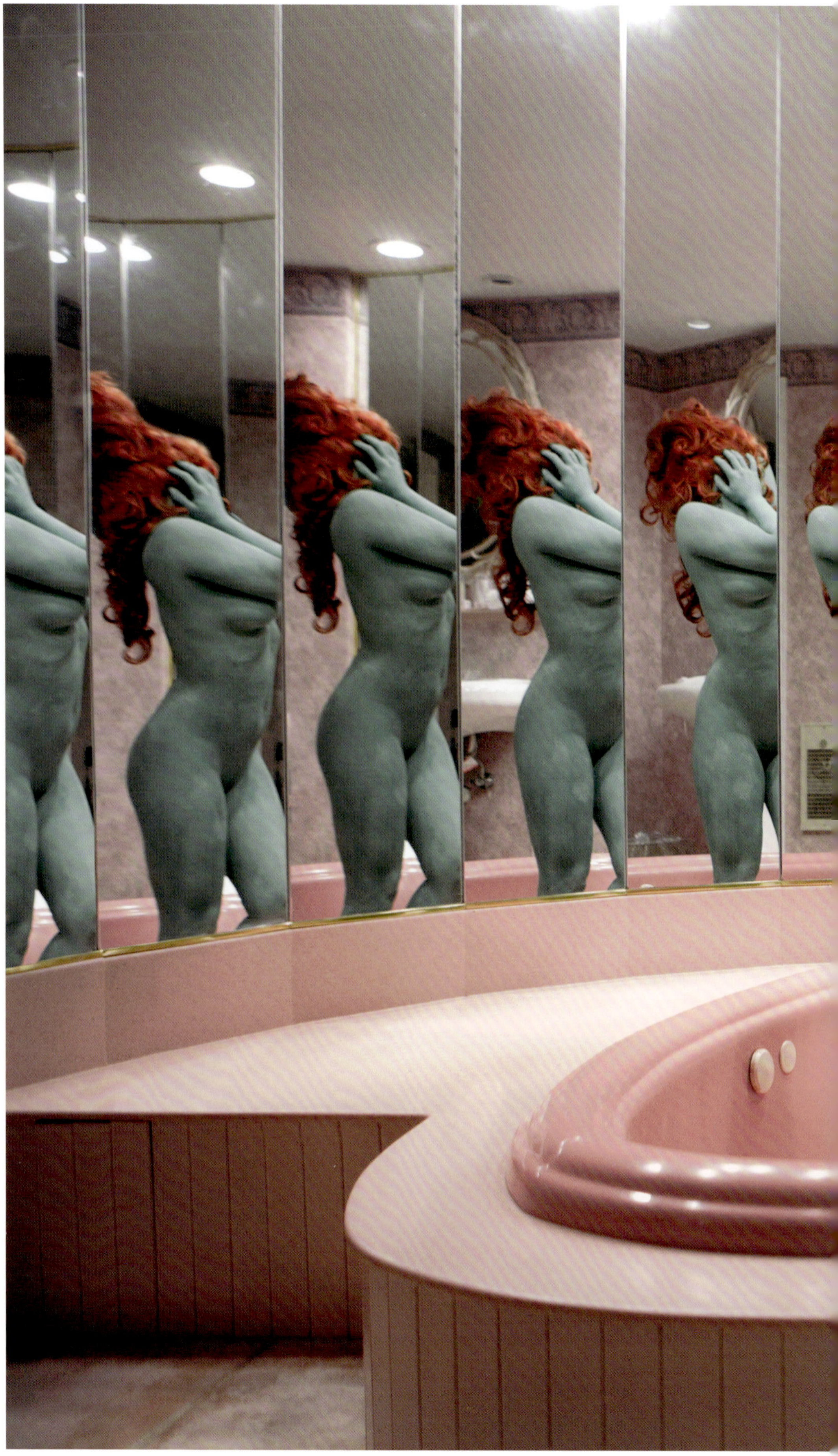

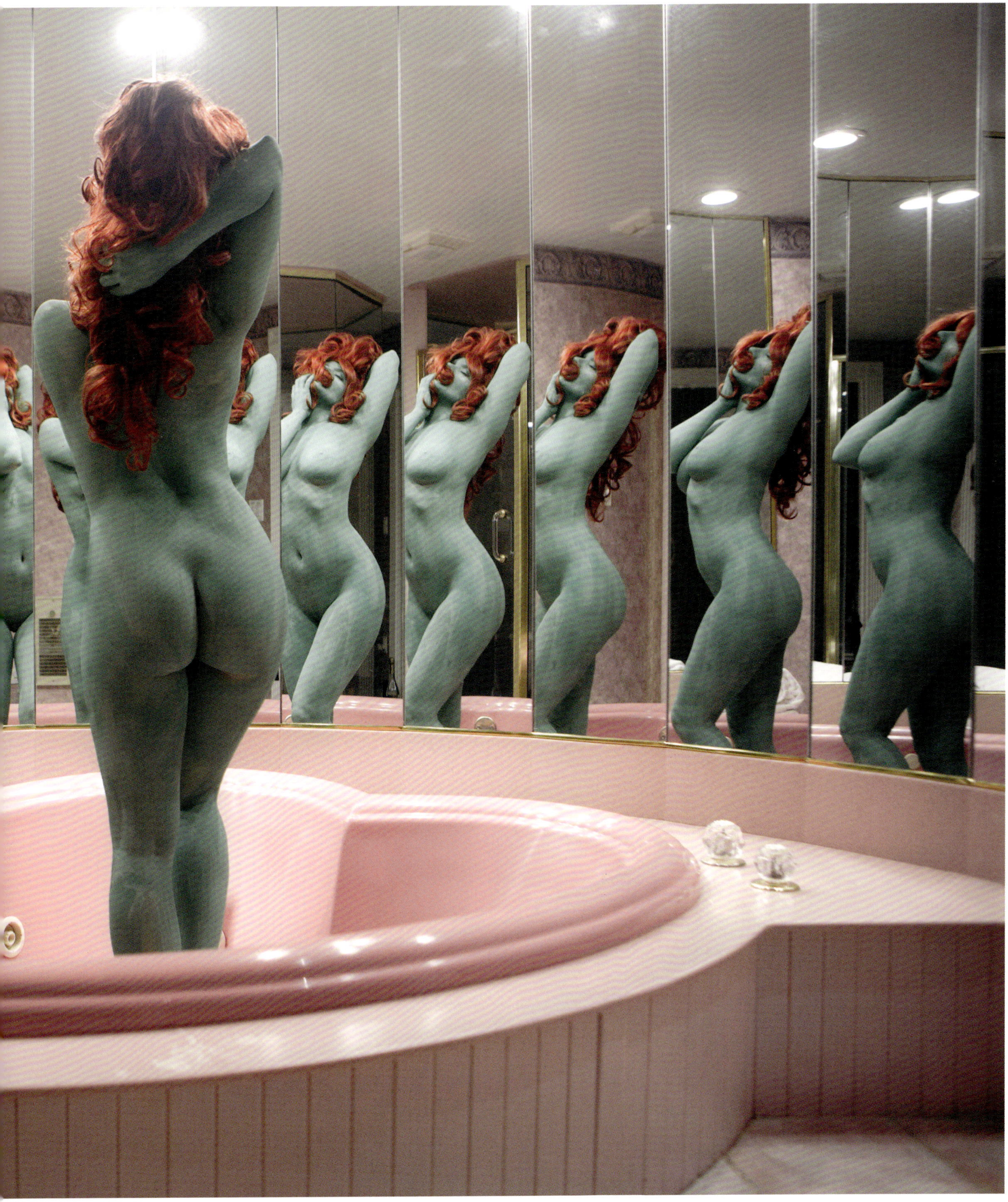

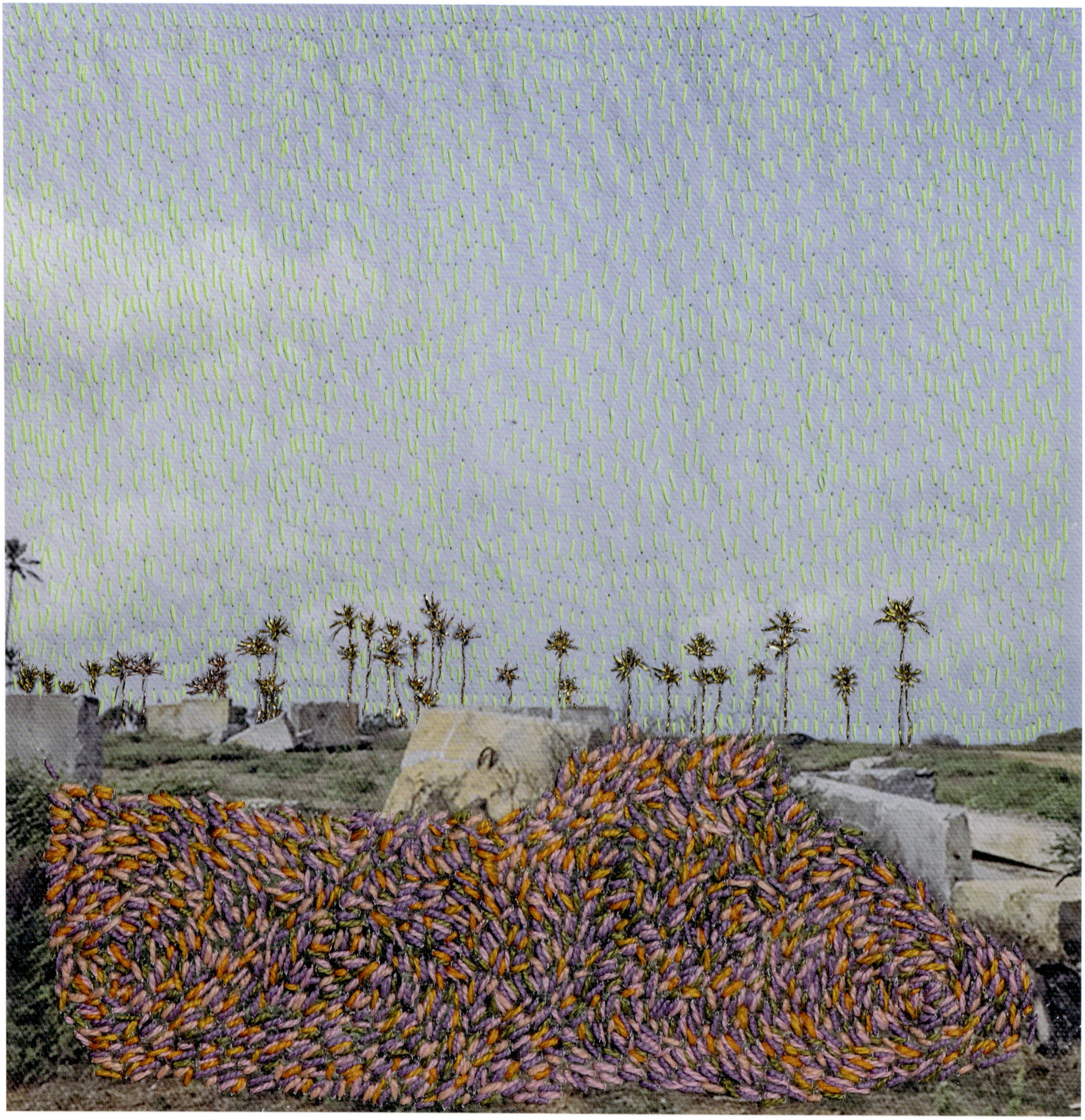

Joana Choumali

The small, sleepy town of Grand-Bassam, Ivory Coast, an hour's drive from the city of Abidjan, has special resonance for the artist Joana Choumali, who spent Sunday afternoons on the beach there with her family throughout her childhood. In March 2016 three gunmen opened fire on the very beach Choumali regularly visited, killing nineteen people. The attack left an indelible mark of trauma, and two weeks later she visited Grand-Bassam to try to make sense of what had happened. She took photographs on her iPhone – less intrusive than her usual DSLR camera – of a community picking up the pieces in the aftermath. She printed the pictures onto cotton canvas and began to work over them by hand, embroidering them with cotton, Lurex and wool. This meditative act was a way of stitching a place back together. Choumali entitled the series *ça va aller* – meaning 'It will be OK' – to give hope, but also to point to the way Ivorians tend to use the expression to avoid dealing with psychological issues. They had experienced a post-election war as recently as 2011, so the Grand-Bassam attacks sent shockwaves across the whole nation.

ça va aller (2016–19) was awarded the 2019 Prix Pictet, making Choumali the first African artist to receive the global photography prize. A breakthrough work for her, it has been recognized not only for bringing hope to many through the healing power of art, but also for expanding the perspectives and possibilities of photography. Choumali describes her embroidery technique as a search to 'overcome the limits of the photographic medium'.[1]

Born in 1974, Choumali trained in graphic arts in Casablanca before returning to her native Abidjan in 1998, where she worked for a time as an art director in an advertising agency. Her early practice as a photographer was photojournalistic in approach but showed her interest in documenting life in the Ivory Coast. Her award-winning series *Hââbré/The Last Generation* (2013–14), for example, consists of studio portraits of people with scarification – the making of superficial, decorative incisions into the skin. The practice is disappearing with shifting social and cultural attitudes, as well as the introduction of clothing into the tribes where it originated, and the older generation she photographed for the series may indeed be the last to wear these marks.

***Sans Titre* from the series *ça va aller*, 2019, iPhone photograph printed on cotton canvas, hand-embroidered with cotton, Lurex and wool thread. 24 x 24cm (9 ½ x 9 ½ in)**
Two weeks after the terror attacks at Grand-Bassam beach, Choumali visited the town as a way to deal with her own pain and reflect on what had happened there. With images that are empty of people, or with solitary figures lingering against the backdrop of the tree-lined beach, the mood is contemplative and melancholy, reflecting the loneliness and sense of loss in the immediate aftermath of the attack. In the image shown here, the vegetation is richly embroidered – the distant coconut palms with golden thread – and the sky is adorned with fluorescent yellow dots that scintillate. Choumali fills empty spaces – the desolation in the wake of the collective trauma – with these abstract representations of an inner world of hopes, dreams and desires we cannot see.

It was while shooting a documentary portrait project that Choumali noticed the transformative effect of fabric on women dressing in traditional textiles; this would later inspire her to introduce thread directly into her photography. Moving away from the documentary style, while still subverting ideas about contemporary life in African cities, Choumali turned her attention to the urban environment. The quiet, dreamlike atmosphere of her compositions owes a lot to the particular light in her photographs, which are taken during habitual early morning walks between 5 a.m. and 7 a.m. Silhouettes of figures remain small against vast backdrops, giving an unusual feeling of space and serenity that inverts stereotypical views of overcrowding and chaos in a city. Introducing hand-sewn thread into her photographs imbues Choumali's work with a tactile quality that contrasts with the momentary engagement of a digital camera, suffusing the digital image with the intimate, painstaking effort of the hand.

Above all, what motivates Choumali is a deep affection for her home city: 'We often say that the city of Abidjan is "the City of Joy". Whatever happens, the Ivorian will always find a way to create concepts through neologisms, music and humour. Ivorian culture is a pulsating source of inspiration for me.'[2]

***Trapped Soul* from the series *Alba'hian*, 2019. Mixed media, embroidery and manual collage on digital photo printing on cotton canvas embroidery on chiffon and tulle, 50 x 50cm (19 ¾ x 19 in). Unique piece**

Alba'hian is an ongoing series in which Choumali photographed neighbourhoods in Johannesburg, Accra, Dakar, Casablanca, Sal Island and her home city, Abidjan, at sunrise, responding to the snapshots later with embroidery at her studio. The resulting pictures constitute a deeply personal 'quiet diary'.[3] The soft, celestial hues of the city as it begins the day create an alternative narrative of life in a swelling urban centre, distinct from the dominant impression of African cities as vibrant, bustling and bright. In this image, a young man leans against the Radio Nostalgie building in the business district of central Abidjan known as the Plateau. As he looks down into the phone that is swallowing his face, Choumali conveys the isolation of individuals in an urban context and the increasing disconnect between individuals in real life that cannot be compensated for by social networks online.

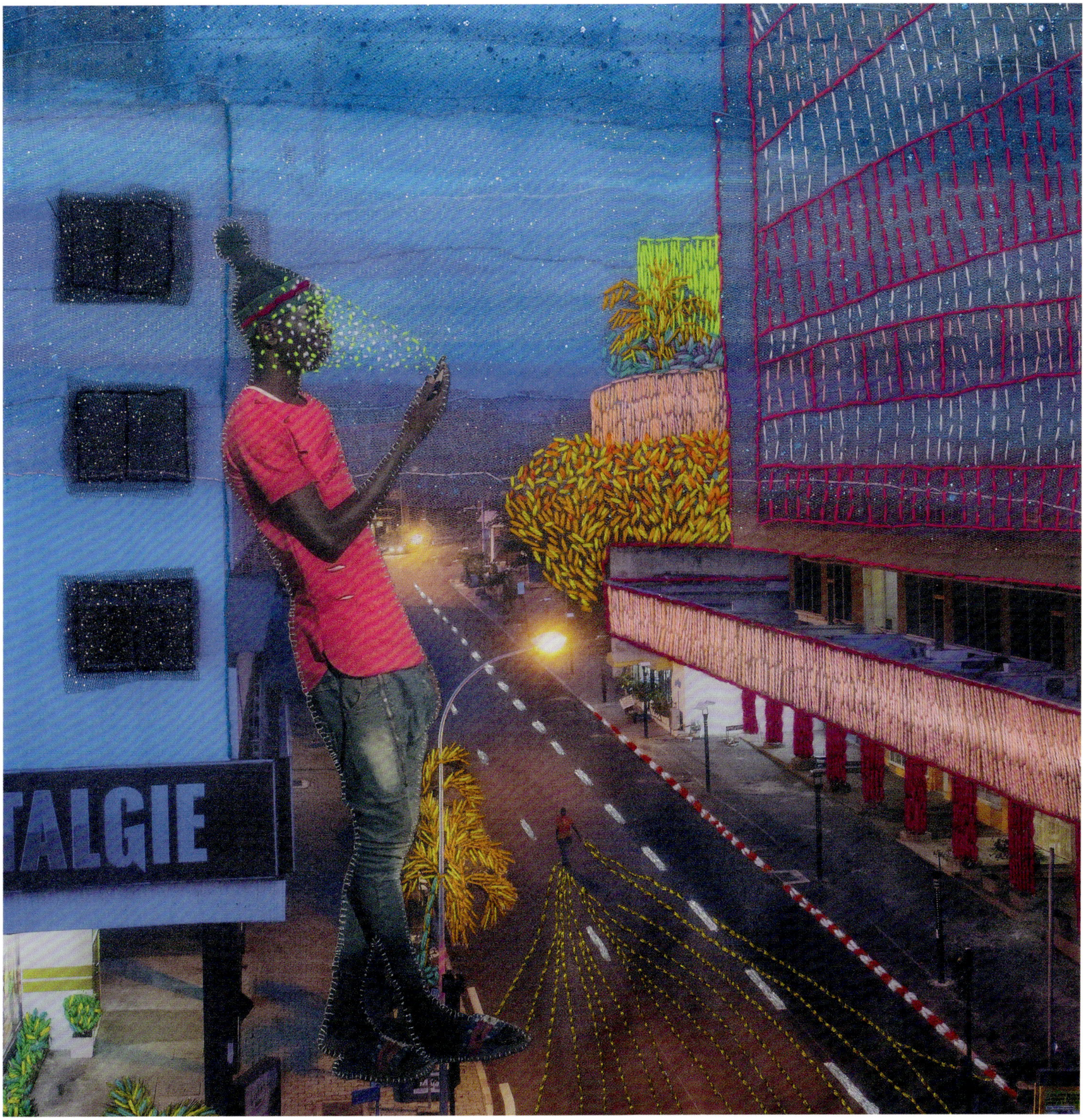
TALGIE

Gregory Crewdson

In Edgar Allan Poe's poem 'A Dream within a Dream', 'All that we see or seem is but a dream within a dream.' Seeing and seeming, dream and reality, and the elusiveness of existence are at the heart of Gregory Crewdson's photographs, which are cinematic tableaux that transform the most ordinary suburban scenes into disturbing settings for the unspeakable.

Crewdson is a Poe for our times: a master of the uncanny, his photographs capture the emotions of the modern age of anxiety – loneliness, alienation, longing and fear. Active since the 1990s, and a professor at Yale since 1993 (where he is now the director of graduate studies in photography), Crewdson has become known for his sinister aesthetic: solitary, hazy-eyed characters (it's sometimes hard to tell if they are human) stare vacantly or wander aimlessly through deserted streets; snow, fog or mist enshroud these empty settings in a heavy atmosphere edged with terror.

Born in Brooklyn in 1962, Crewdson now resides in a church near Becket, Massachusetts, a place he used to visit as a child. The small rural town has provided the backdrop for several of his works over the years, including *Fireflies* (1996) and *Cathedral of the Pines* (2013–14). Crewdson's settings speak of ordinary America – suburban every-places, familiar landscapes and nondescript streets, innocuous domestic interiors – but there is an eerie undertone to the seeming normality. His interest in the uncanny as a psychological phenomenon is explored through this process of identification with an image. By placing the viewer-spectator explicitly inside the frame, looking out of a window (a device borrowed from the likes of Alfred Hitchcock, who has been a significant influence), Crewdson keeps us suspended between the pleasure of looking at something we know and an uncomfortable, creeping sense of foreboding.

Crewdson is known for working like a film-maker: each image requires equipment, budget and crew akin to an independent cinema production, and can take years to realize. He begins with a detailed description of the image and then works with a crew of up to fifty people. Crewdson's close relationship with cinema is reflected in more than his way of working; he has said that 'movies probably shaped my sensibility more than photography has.'[1] In 2012 he was the subject of a film himself,

***Sisters* from the series *Cathedral of the Pines*, 2014. Archival pigment print, 114.3 x 146.2cm (45 x 57 ⅝ in) (framed). Edition of 3, plus 2 artist proofs**

Crewdson pared back his usual production to create *Cathedral of the Pines*. Working with a smaller crew and depending on the ambience of the natural and particular light of the forest environment where it was shot, the series took two years to complete. Each of the images constitutes its own complex and ambiguous narrative. Here, we observe twin sisters in their bedroom, lugubrious and vulnerable; naked, despite the icy winter that frames them outside, they convey a sense of longing and loss. This is all, however, read between the lines, in gesture, because although we look into a private room, there are few details to give us a clue about the sisters' identity, and the bedroom is as barren as the snowy landscape outside. All the people who appear in this particular series – including the two unnamed sisters – are known to Crewdson, a decision he took because he 'wanted the pictures to have a greater degree of intimacy, even though they will never be seen as cosy'.[3]

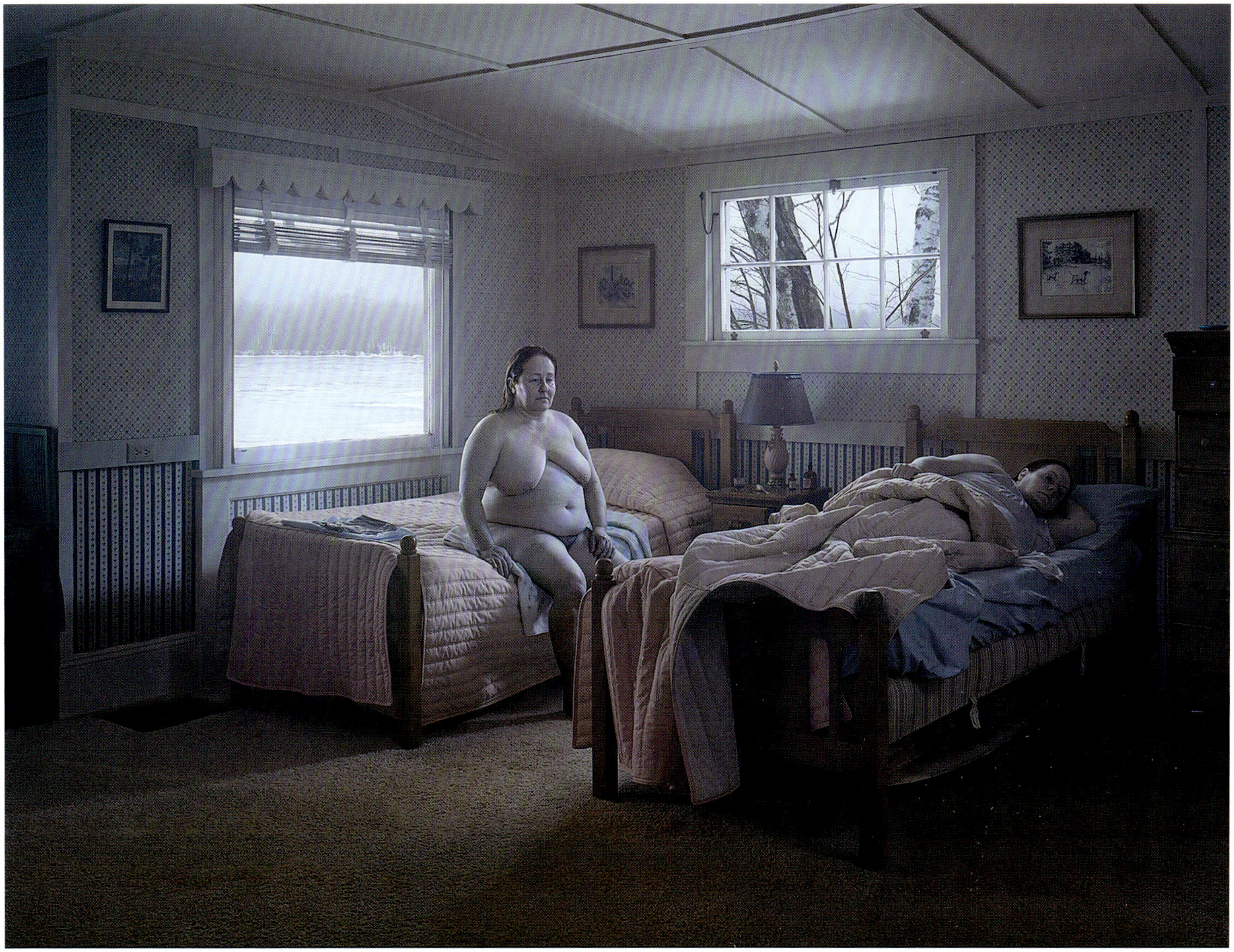

Gregory Crewdson: Brief Encounters, and he is in the process of writing his directorial debut, *Reflective Light*. Crewdson has explained that the medium of photography allows him total control, which is not possible in film-making. A single photograph – or a 'frozen moment', as he refers to it – allows the story to unfold purely visually, without the constraints of dialogue, plot and narrative.

Over thirty years, Crewdson has continued to tell the same stories in his images, about the pervasive melancholy of the contemporary condition, while also locating wonder in the mysterious. As he has said, his photographs 'suggest some possibility of hope, through the aesthetic act. If my pictures were just completely bleak they'd be less interesting as photographs. To me what's interesting is their aesthetic, their ambition to try to be beautiful and mysterious objects – that, I think, in the end, is what makes them what they are.'[2]

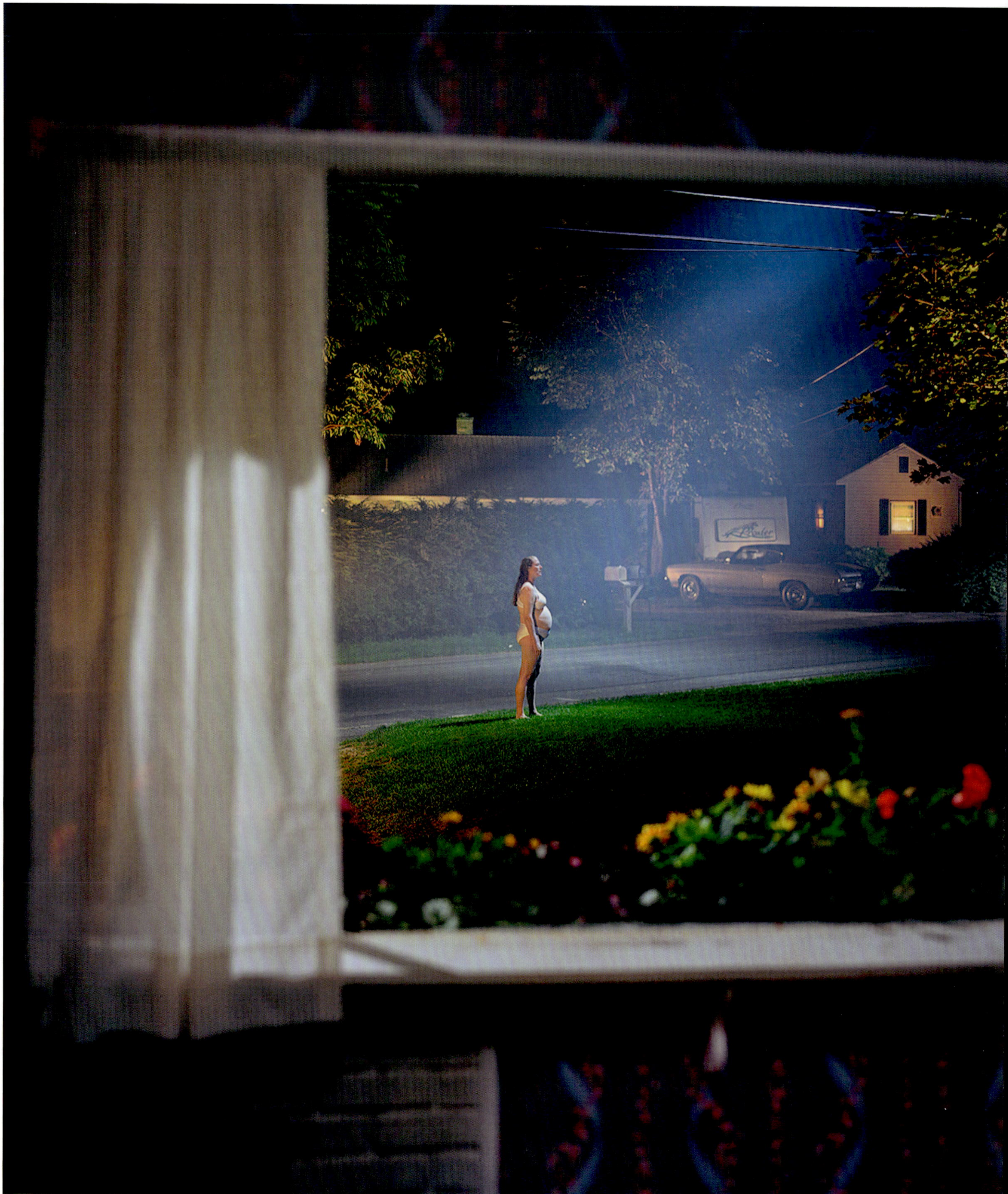

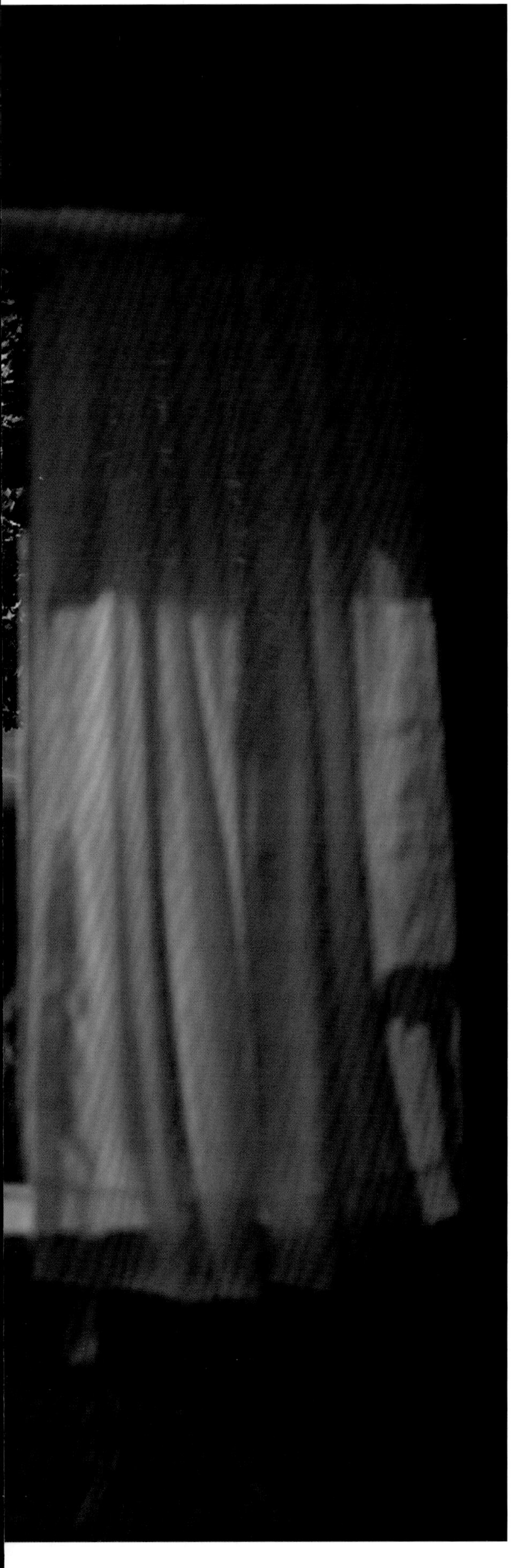

Untitled (Sleepwalking Woman) from the series _Twilight_, 1998–2002. Digital C-print, 135.25 x 166cm (53 ¼ x 65 ⅜ in) (framed). Edition of 10, plus 3 artist proofs

Twilight remains one of Crewdson's central works, an exploration of his fascination with the 'poetic condition'[4] of the light at dusk and its transformative effects. The images in the series were all shot at twilight, but this was the first time Crewdson worked with cinematic lighting to ramp up the drama artificially, so that the light appears to come down in a diaphanous beam from the sky, casting a spooky glow over the solitary, pregnant female figure who stands outside, inexplicably, naked. There is a spine-chilling stillness in the image – another quality of twilight that Crewdson says he 'lives for'.[5] In this image, Crewdson places us, the viewer, directly inside the image, explicitly in the position of a voyeur who peeks out from their window at the strange and disturbing scene that is unfolding on the street outside. But as we know from Hitchcock, the person who looks out in silence is often the one we should be most afraid of.

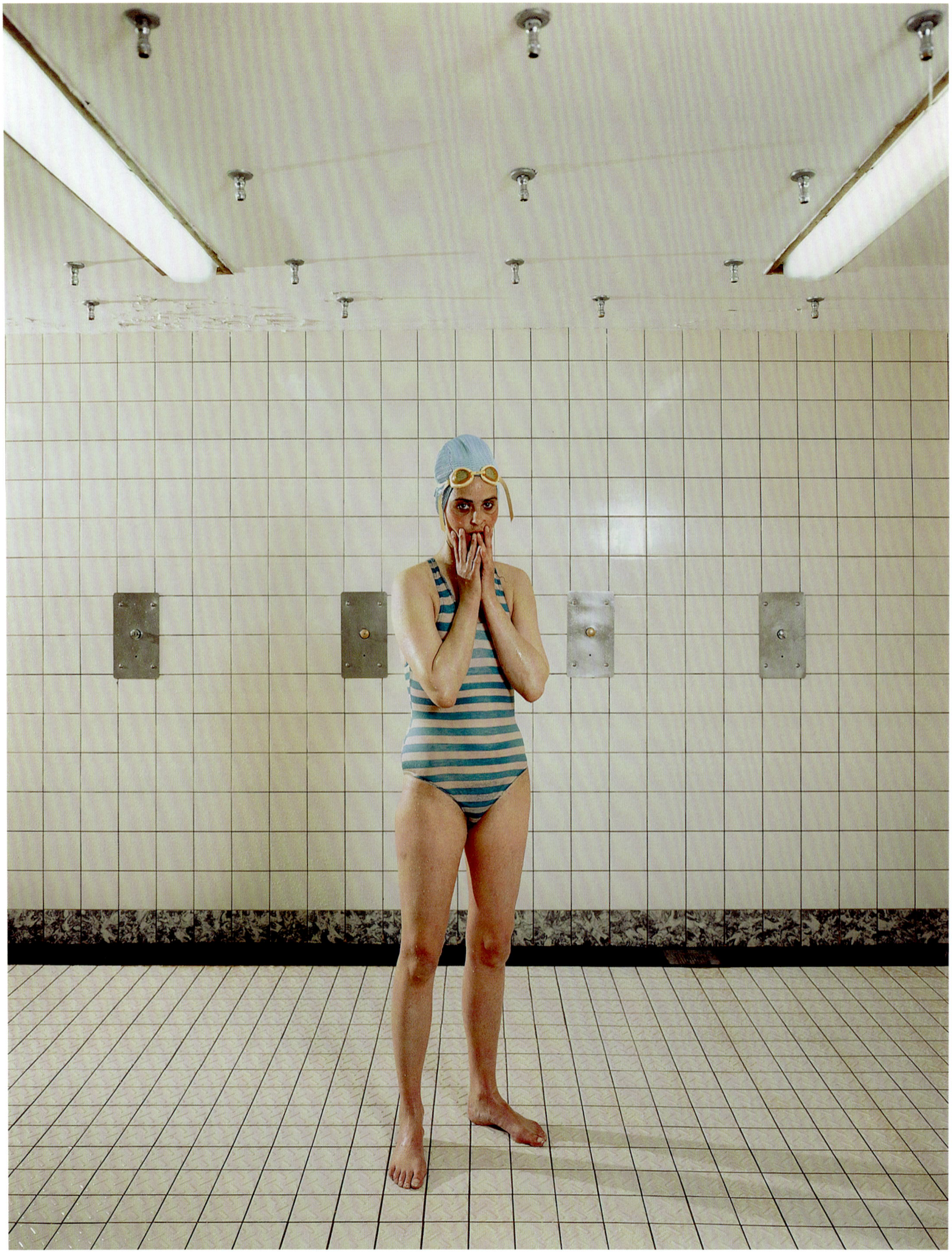

Rineke Dijkstra

***Self Portrait, Marnixbad, Netherlands, June 19, 1991*, 1991**
This photograph was taken after Dijkstra had pushed her body to its limits by swimming thirty laps of a pool. At the time, swimming was rehabilitation from a serious bike accident, adding to the physical intensity that permeates this picture. A significant photograph in Dijkstra's work, this self-portrait prefigured several major series, including *Beach Portraits*, in both style and concept. It was also one of the first photographs she shot on her then new 4x5-inch plate camera – the same camera she still shoots with today.

In 1983, when she was twenty-four years old and at the very beginning of her career, the Dutch photographer Rineke Dijkstra said in an interview, 'There is something mysterious to me about people, so many things you don't know. That determined the way I make my portraits. It's by deciding what to show and what to leave out that I try to tell my own story. I like the fact that the pictures can then be interpreted differently by others. That, to me, is the value of photography.'[1]

From her first breakthrough series, *Beach Portraits* (1992–98), which comprises photographs of teenagers on beaches in Europe and the USA, children and adolescents have been a dominant presence in Dijkstra's portraits. She finds young people interesting because she relates to their state of flux at a time when everything is still possible, nothing yet determined, and she to capture the physical and emotional complexity of her subjects in such moments of transition between childhood and adulthood. By isolating them from their daily context and framing them only with the sand, the sea and the sky, the focus shifts more towards postures, gazes and small details. The result is a contrasting play of monumentality and intimacy.

Dijkstra has taken photographs of the same people many times over the years. She first photographed six-year-old Almerisa, a refugee from Bosnia, in 1994, and continued portraying her every two years, now as a young woman with three children of her own. Then there's Shany, an Israeli soldier photographed between 1999 and 2003, and Oliver, who served in the French Foreign Legion and was Dijkstra's subject for three years. Presented together, these photographs chart considerable physical and psychological shifts, giving a sense of how much an individual can alter in even a short period. In addition to the superficial changes to hair, clothes and make-up, there are also notable differences in poise and gaze, conveying the many ways experience etches itself into a person's expressions.

Another aspect of Dijkstra's portraiture is her quest for authenticity while maintaining a certain kind of distance – even opacity – towards the person she is photographing. This allows the mystery inherent in trying to understand someone to play out purely by looking at them. 'I think of a portrait as an encounter,' she explains.[2] In these encounters, by capturing a subtle gesture or expression, Dijkstra hopes to find a moment in which her subjects reveal something of themselves.

The intensity of these moments is often the result of a lengthy, arduous process. For almost four decades,

Dijkstra has used the exact same set-up: a 4x5-inch plate camera with a standard lens and flash. This portable studio lends a stylistic consistency to her photographs, but it also demands concentration and commitment. Though she leaves room for improvisation during the session, the camera does not allow her to move fast. Her portraits are the result of setting certain parameters and taking deliberate decisions – arranging the lighting, colour and composition, then waiting for these elements to come together at the right moment. This moment can take hours to manifest itself, making the artist's practice more like that of a painter than of a contemporary photographer. The sharpness of her camera and the quality of her life-size prints reveal details you would never notice in reality.

A large number of Dijkstra's portraits are of siblings, and these, together with video installations such as *I See a Woman Crying* (2009) and *Night Watching* (2019), allow her to explore group dynamics and social hierarchies in families and among friends, peers and colleagues, and how they might inform the way we see and interpret the world. As Dijkstra explains, 'I am interested in the paradox between identity and uniformity, in the power and vulnerability of each individual and each group. It is this paradox that I try to visualize by concentrating on poses, attitudes, gestures and gazes.'[3] A classical portraitist for a contemporary age, she has created a body of work that conveys the enigma of being and the mystifying nature of looking at one another.

***Saskia, Harderwijk, Netherlands, March 16, 1994* from the series *New Mothers*, 1994**

In this image a woman called Saskia is photographed with her baby one week after giving birth. The wound from a Caesarean section is visibly still healing and her cheeks are flushed. She holds the baby proudly and awkwardly, poised yet vulnerable. Childbirth is one of the most universal of experiences, yet it is rarely represented in art. Taken in 1994 and exhibited in Amsterdam that year, the three portraits that make up *New Mothers* were created after Dijkstra attended the birth of a friend's child. Considered very radical in its treatment of the subject at the time, the series provoked strong reactions from some viewers, who suggested that women should not be shown in such a raw way. Yet for Dijkstra, the series was not about motherhood or birth, but about the enormity of the moment when primal emotions surge and renewal seems possible. Dijkstra was still at a relatively early point in her career, but the series nevertheless anticipated some of the qualities that would mark her later work; superfluous information is minimal, so that attention is focused on the subject and her newborn. In a similar way to her earlier self-portrait after swimming, in *New Mothers*, extremes of physical pain and exhaustion lead to a state in which the true self can emerge, revealing itself to the portraitist.

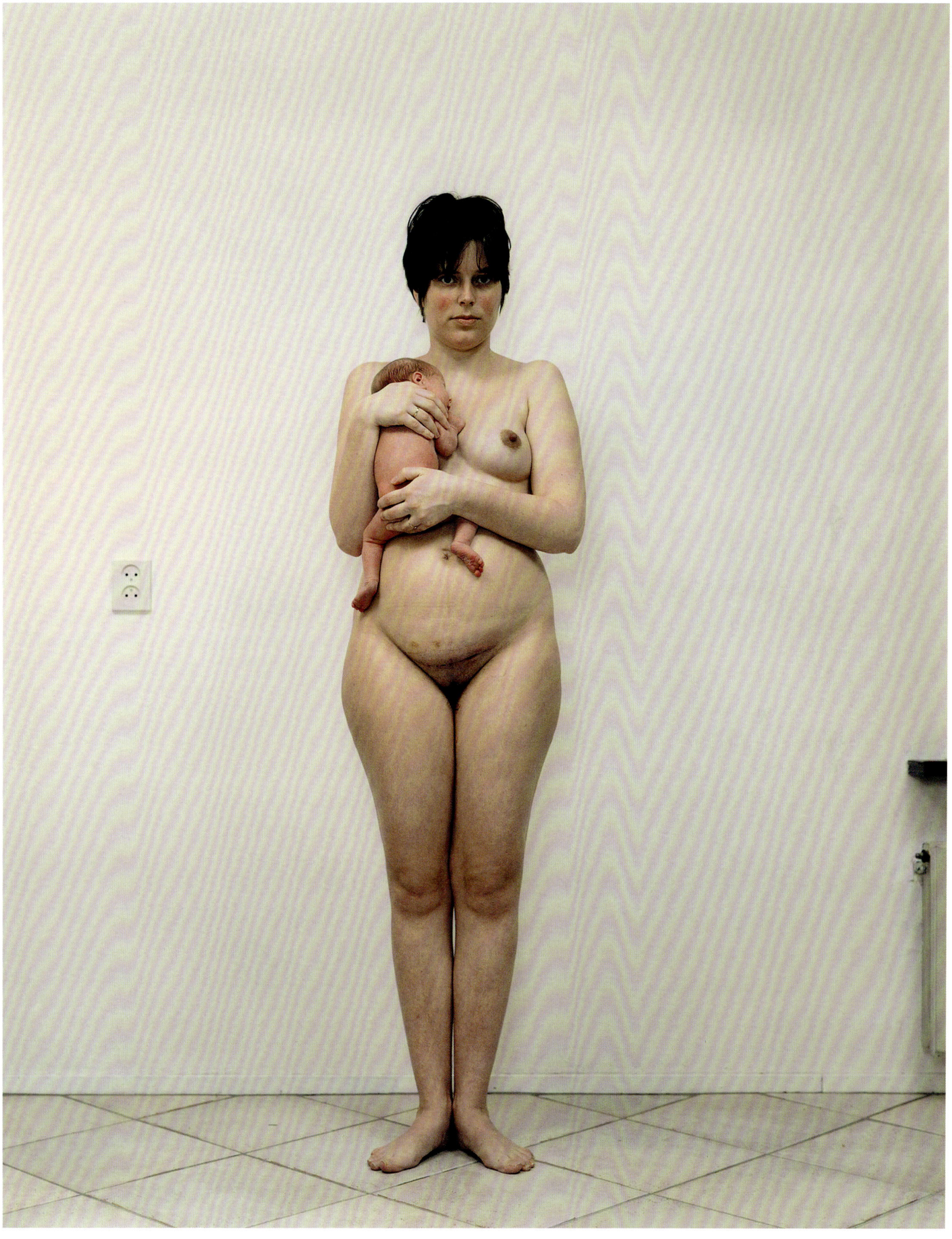

***Villa Franca de Xira, Portugal, May 8 1994*, 1994**
This image comes from a series of portraits of Portuguese *forcados*, or amateur bullfighters, who perform the final event in a Portuguese bullfight, challenging the bull as a group. Dijkstra captured the men – like the new mothers – immediately after they had been engaged in a gruelling and potentially fatal fight with their bare hands in the ring. She does not show the spectacle or consider its ethics; she is interested only in the human condition. The portrait is stripped of its setting and context, positioning her sitter against a blank background. She moves in close, so that only the head and shoulders are seen. The face and suit are stained with blood and the young man's direct look seems to exude a mixture of relief and pride.

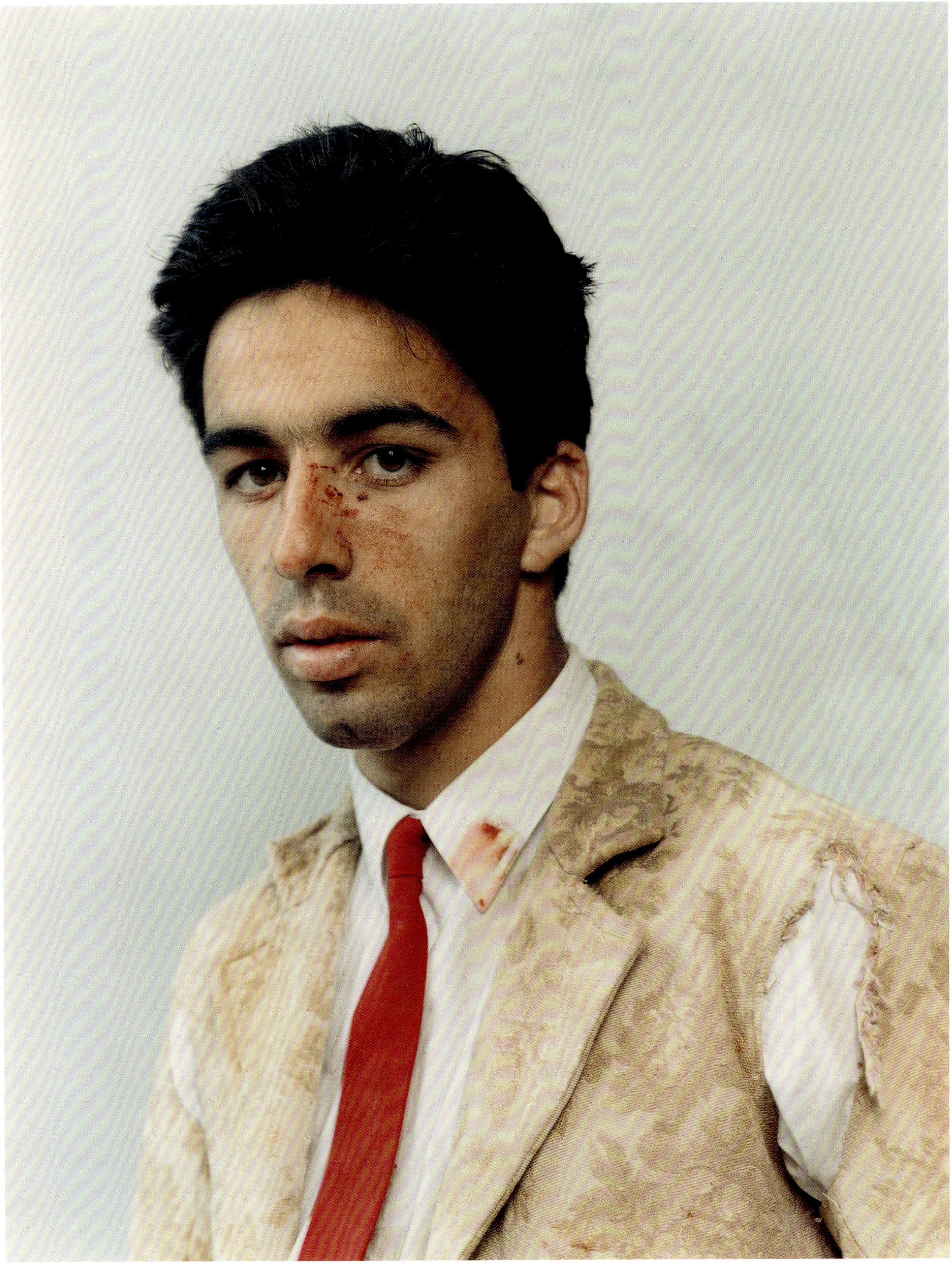

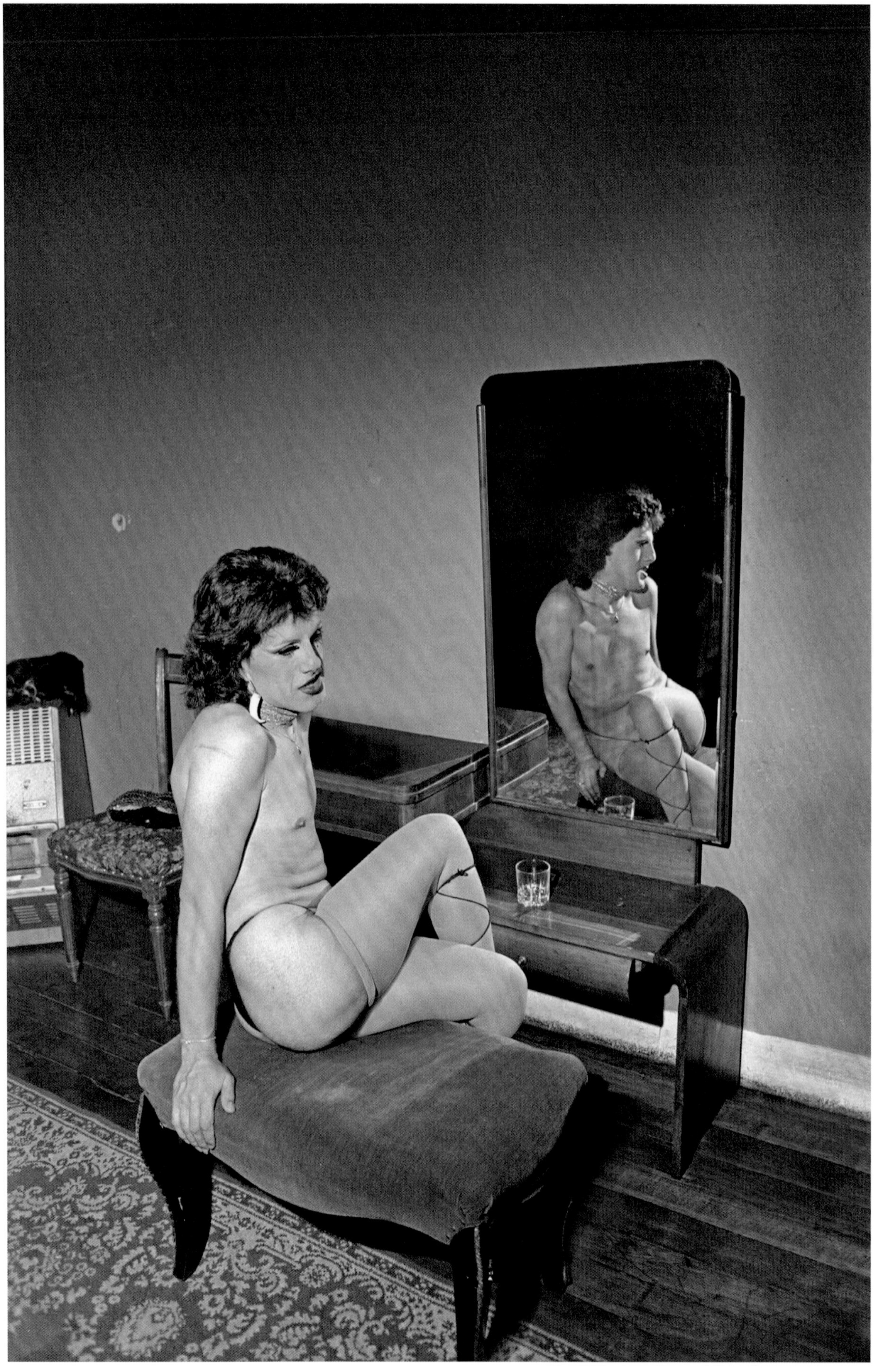

Paz Errázuriz

La Manzana de Adán **('Adam's Apple'), 1983. Gelatin silver print on paper, 46 x 29.6cm (18 ⅛ x 11 ¾ in)**
Errázuriz identifies *La Manzana de Adán* ('Adam's Apple') as one of her most important and meaningful photo essays. Together with the journalist Claudia Donoso, she spent more than four years living with a community of transvestite prostitutes in Santiago, centring on the lives of Pilar and Evelyn, and their mother, Mercedes, who became one of the most important figures in the artist's life: 'I dedicate all this work to her,' Errázuriz said.[3] This image was taken in the 1980s, under Pinochet's military regime, which was an extremely difficult and dangerous environment for gender-non-conforming people, who were persecuted by the police and often had to move on. Reminiscent of an early twentieth-century boudoir photograph, it shows Pilar, wearing make-up and lingerie, seated in front of the mirror, posing playfully – Errázuriz has said her subjects loved the camera. Pilar does not look back at her own reflection; instead her eyes are directed towards something we cannot see out of the frame – a subtle suggestion of the world beyond the safe, intimate setting of the bedroom. 'Pilar was more easy-going than Evelyn. She had a big sense of humour and was a very generous person. She liked being photographed,' Errázuriz remembers.[4]

Paz Errázuriz was born in 1944 in Chile. In 1973, when Augusto Pinochet seized control of the country in a coup, she was forced to leave her teaching job in a primary school. By this time, Errázuriz had already begun to photograph children and felt comfortable with the camera. With two young children to support, she was a freelance family photographer for many years, but she was also working covertly on her own investigations into the disenfranchised. She was one of the few women photojournalists on the streets of Santiago during the dictatorship, when strict curfews and censorship laws curtailed what, who and when she could photograph. Self-taught, Errázuriz's images have an instinctive impulse, guided by intuition, empathy and urgency. As she has said, for her, 'the need to photograph was constant'.[1]

Because of the circumstances, Errázuriz's early works, which take the form of visual essays, used metaphor to speak of Chile's sociopolitical issues. In 1979 her first exhibition presented *Los Dormidos* ('People Asleep'). In the photographs, Errázuriz documents the homeless in Santiago while they sleep. Ostensibly a vivid depiction of an endemic social problem in the city, the series was intended as a metaphor for the inertia prevalent in Chilean society under Pinochet's regime – a form of critique that might get past the censors but would be felt and understood.

Since the 1970s Errázuriz's enduring interest has been identity. As a woman in a patriarchal society, she has said she always felt an affinity with those who transgressed tradition and defied the norm. Growing up with conservative Catholic family values, in addition to the oppression under Pinochet, Errázuriz found that the camera was a way to affirm the existence of those who were ostracized or powerless. She has been explicit in not referring to the people she has photographed as 'marginalized': 'I'm not trying to make judgements about anything. Pinochet's regime like any other dictatorship makes you very aware of power, and the danger of power. On the other hand, you develop a lot of solidarity.'[2]

Though she did not intend to shock or provoke with her pictures, the two series Errázuriz shot about life incarcerated in Chilean psychiatric institutions still elicit strong reactions. In *Antesala de un Desnudo* ('Anteroom of a Nude') (1992), she photographed elderly female patients as they took a communal bath: the scenes expose the austere, squalid conditions they endured and the mistreatment of the women, herded like cattle and deprived of dignity. In *El Infarto del Alma* ('Heart Attack of the Soul') (1992), we get another perspective on life in the institution: patients who had found love against the odds within the confines of the asylum's walls but were not permitted, as many of them wished, to marry. These two series resonate with Diane Arbus's images of the mentally ill in their emotional gravitas and empathy. The subjects' bodies are disfigured by medication, illness and neglect, but it is not the patients who are meant to disturb the viewer; they go about their lives in an ordinary way – washing, dressing, falling in love. It is their environment that is abnormal. Errázuriz, like Arbus, uses the camera to represent the people society refuses to see.

Errázuriz's work has defined a specific period in Chile's history, making her one of the most important photographers both within Latin America and beyond; in 1986 she was the first Latin American photographer to be awarded a Guggenheim Fellowship. The democratic Chile she lives in today is very different from the place in her most acclaimed pictures, but she always understood when taking her photographs that they would serve the future, affirming the existence of those who would otherwise have been erased from history. Her photographs are a testament and a proof. In later works such as *Cuerpos* ('Bodies') (2002) and *Memento Mori* (2004)n in which she focuses on ageing and death, she reflects further on this purpose of photography and the way it represents us after life. At the heart of Errázuriz's work is the impulse to learn something about the world she lives in and her place in it: 'Photography is still teaching me about humanity… it's like a school for your soul.'[5]

From the series *Tango*, 1988
Ageing and the elderly are enduring interests for Errázuriz. She spent a lot of time visiting various homes for the elderly, to observe the way people there lived and interacted with each other, in particular as couples. After observing one dance class attended by the elderly, she began to visit tango clubs, 'where you could not find any young people. I became fascinated with these couples who go to practice this erotic dance of the tango every week.'[6] She struck up friendships with many of the amateur dancers, who would go to the clubs every Saturday. The resulting series, *Tango*, from which this image is taken, is an exploration of passion, desire and the body through dance, but frozen in Errázuriz's pictures without music or movement, so that we experience these aspects of tango in an entirely different way.

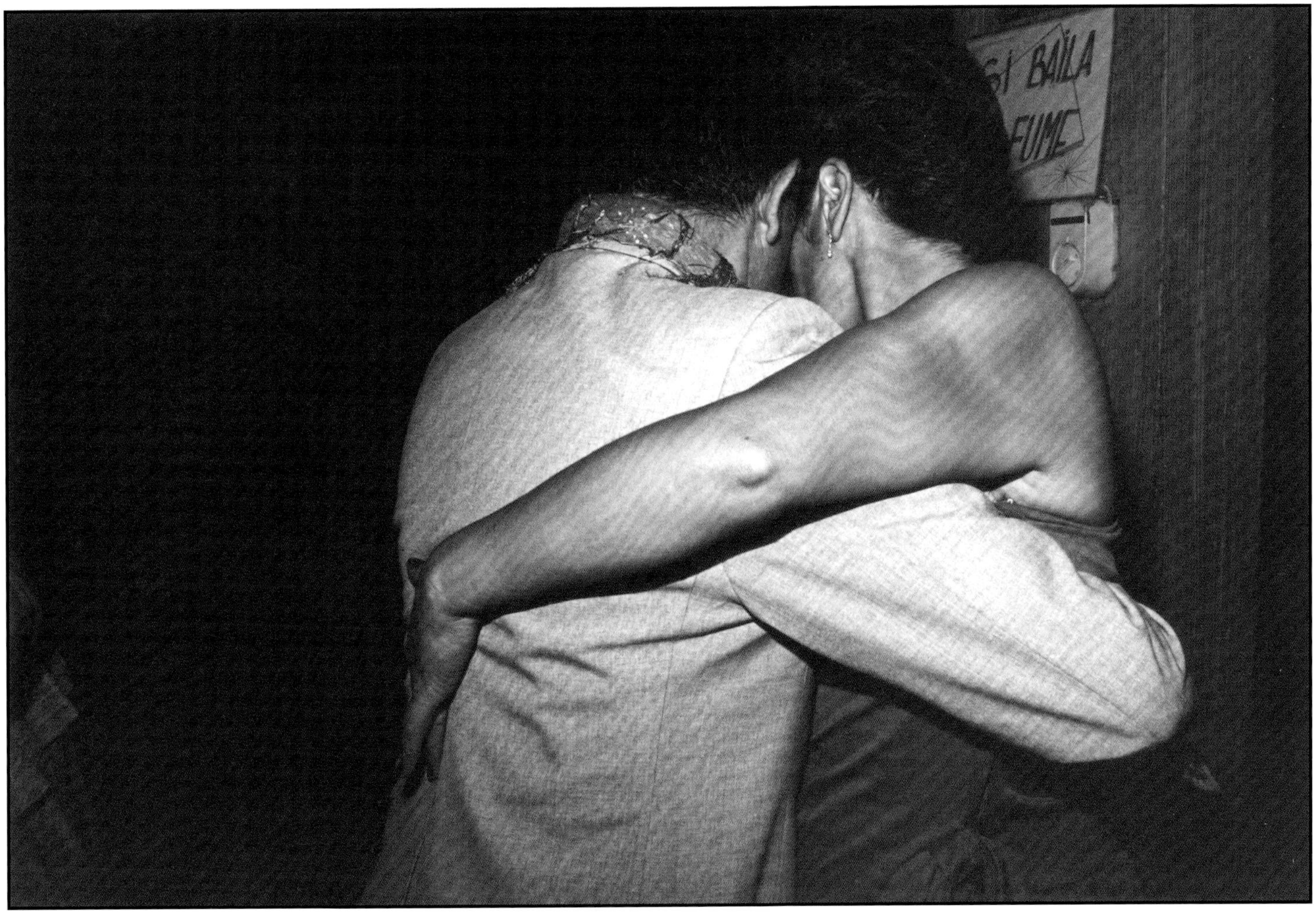
SI BAILA
FUME

Samuel Fosso

***Autoportrait* [SM20] from the series *70s Lifestyle*, 1975–8**
From the ages of thirteen to sixteen, Fosso created his first self-portraits at the commercial studio he ran in Bangui. When the clients had left, he would dress up, emulating the people he had seen in magazines and on album covers, and turn the camera on himself, initially as a way to use up the ends of his rolls of film. He has said that he felt handsome and flawless, and wanted to capture this moment to show his children in the future. There is a sense of the confidence of youth in the images he made at this time, before he had any intention of displaying them in public. Yet Fosso was already taking a conceptual approach to his self-portraits; these were not random acts of vanity. In this picture, for example, he wears a suit he had custom-made in the style African ministers were obliged to adopt under French colonial rule. Clothing in Fosso's photographs always has a political purpose and these early self-portraits, taken under Bokassa's dictatorship in the Central African Republic, were politically charged.

There are many versions of the story of Samuel Fosso, a mythology in part disseminated by the man himself. According to one established version, Fosso was born in 1962 in Cameroon to Nigerian parents and was a sickly child who was paralysed until the age of three when he was cured, according to some accounts, by his grandfather, a respected healer. He spent his early years in Nigeria, but in 1972, following the Biafran War (1967–70), Fosso eventually fled to Bangui, Central African Republic, where an uncle lived. In Bangui, Fosso was apprenticed to a local photographer and by 1975, at the age of thirteen, he had opened his own commercial photography studio: his services including family portraits, passport pictures and wedding photography. His studio's strapline was: 'You will be beautiful, elegant, delicate and easy to recognize.'

Fosso took the same approach when he began to take self-portraits after work, making use of any leftover rolls of film. In these portraits Fosso was certainly beautiful and elegant, but, deliberately assuming different personas, he was not easy to recognize. With his Hasselblad on auto-timer, he would dress up in a range of outfits – sometimes bell-bottom trousers, tight-fitting, patterned shirts and high-heeled platform boots; sometimes in little more than underwear and gloves. He would have his clothes made by a local tailor, who copied styles Fosso had seen in American magazines or on album covers. These fashions were politically dangerous in the conservative society of the day, under Emperor Bokassa I, where certain attire was banned. Even in the privacy of his studio, 'I couldn't just do whatever I wanted,' Fosso reflects.[1]

Using the camera in lieu of an audience, Fosso set the stage for his own cast of characters. Inhabiting these costumes, poses and props, he gave powerful performances of personal freedom, claiming authorship of his own identity. Yet, at first, Fosso intended nothing more than to send the pictures back to his grandmother in Nigeria. 'I didn't know I was making artistic photographs,' he recalls.[2]

It was only in 1994, when he met the French photographer Bernard Descamps who invited him to exhibit his black and white self-portraits from the 1970s at the Rencontres de Bamako, that Fosso realized the scope of what he had been doing. Descamps, a co-founder of the Rencontres, was in Bangui scouting for participants for the biennial's first edition. In Bamako, Fosso met the masters of West African studio photography, Seydou Keïta and Malick Sidibé, and saw

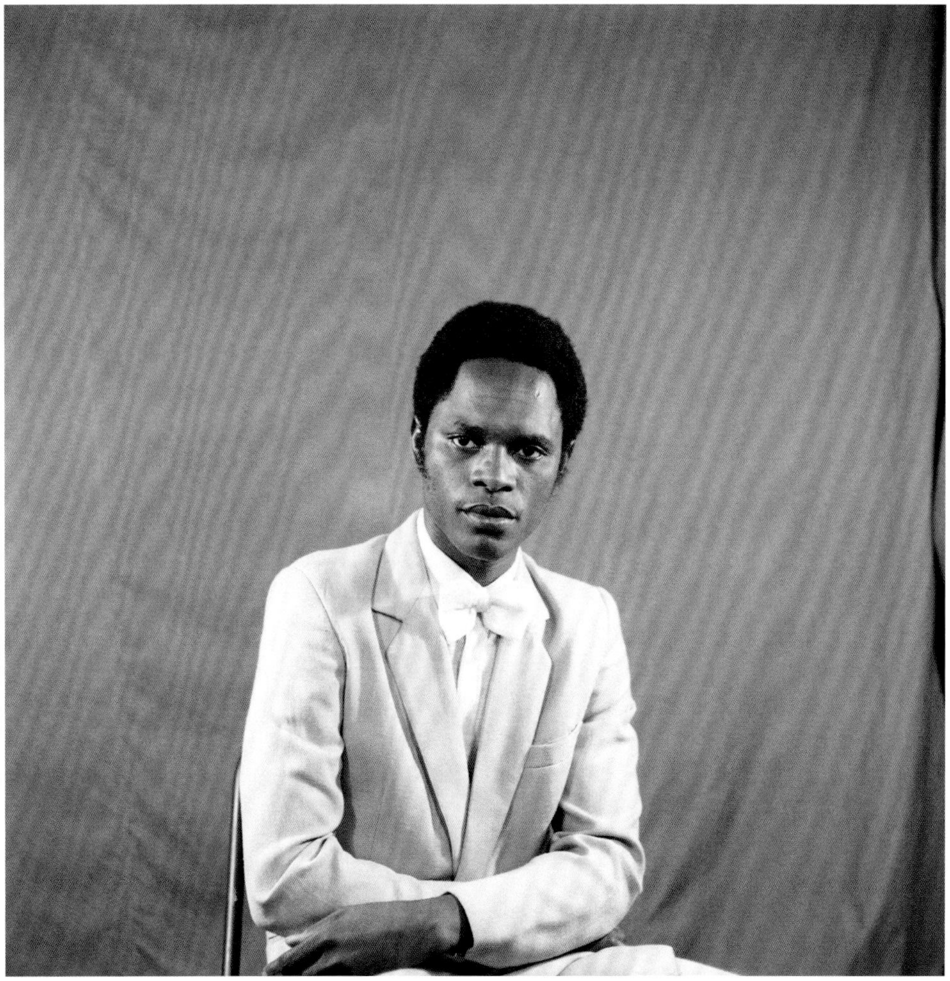

their works for the first time. This was an epiphany for him: 'I came to understand my process was an asset I shouldn't overlook.'[3]

Fosso's first exhibition in Paris took place the following year (alongside Martin Parr), and in 1997 he was commissioned by Tati, the Parisian department store, to create a series of images to celebrate their seventy-fifth anniversary. If Bamako was a revelation personally, the *Tati* series established Fosso as an artist on an international level. He has continued to exhibit all over the world, including a 2002 touring retrospective starting in the place where it all began, Bamako, and a BBC documentary was released the same year. Most recently, a 2017 survey of his work was held at the National Portrait Gallery, London.

After 1994, Fosso's self-portraits began to project a greater sense of purpose. In his 2008 series *African Spirits*, Fosso turned his attention to political and cultural figures from Africa and its diaspora, meticulously restaging original photographs of these icons, now working with the help of a team of make-up artists and stylists. He posed as Angela Davis, Haile Selassie and

Nelson Mandela; he referenced a famous 1968 *Esquire* cover image of Muhammad Ali impaled by arrows and made his own version of a mugshot of Martin Luther King Jr. *African Spirits* was a follow-up to the *Tati* series that speaks of a unified Black culture and history, this time by creating a hall of fame of the figures who shaped the Black image in the twentieth century in an exploration of the idea of Négritude (the founders of the movement, Aimé Césaire and Léopold Sédar Senghor, also feature in the series). By re-photographing photographs, Fosso also highlights the power of photography to shape and take ownership of collective and individual identities and histories.

In a more recent work, *SIXSIXSIX* (2015), Fosso created 666 large-format Polaroid self-portraits, shooting every day over an intense period. The images stand out from his previous work, with no make-up or costumes and a plain red backdrop framing only the head and shoulders in identical poses. These are not the dynamic full-body shots Fosso usually produces. For Fosso, *SIXSIXSIX* is an in-depth study of subtle nuances of mood and expression, without artifice: 'When you look at my works, it's my body that is looking at me. It's my way of seeing.'[4]

Photography for Fosso is a way to mark our existence, for now and for the future. As a child, he never had his photograph taken, as was customary at the time – his parents didn't commission one because of his childhood paralysis. By portraying himself, time and time again over the decades, Fosso has said that he wanted to make up for that absence. As he explained to Okwui Enwezor in his monograph *Autoportrait*, 'When you ask me why I privilege my self-portraits, I believe the answer is rooted in the condition of my life and the meaning of self-representation.'[5]

Autoportrait (The Liberated American Woman of the 1970s) **from the series *Tati*, 1997**
In this highly stylized, kaleidoscopic and satirical self-portrait, Fosso poses as the titular liberated woman, wearing a panama hat, heels and an ornately patterned trouser suit, with strings of beads. Though every detail is carefully staged in this tableau, its artifice is also apparent – this 'woman' may not be as liberated as she would like to be. According to Fosso, the image projects 'a dream that narrates slavery, segregation, and the desire to be free, to get revenge, to be independent from whites, from men, to be economically independent, to make a career for herself'.[6] In 1997, Fosso's masquerade was a radical act: just by wearing women's clothes, he was making made a bold statement about the intersection of race, gender and sexuality.

The image, one of the most famous in Fosso's widely acclaimed series *Tati*, was originally a commission for the French department store in 1997. The retailer had invited Fosso, together with Seydou Keïta and Malick Sidibé, to create a series of self-portraits using the characteristic backdrops, styling and props of West African studio photography. While Keïta and Sidibé shot in their trademark black and white, Fosso decided to experiment with colour, shifting the studio photograph once again in a new direction.

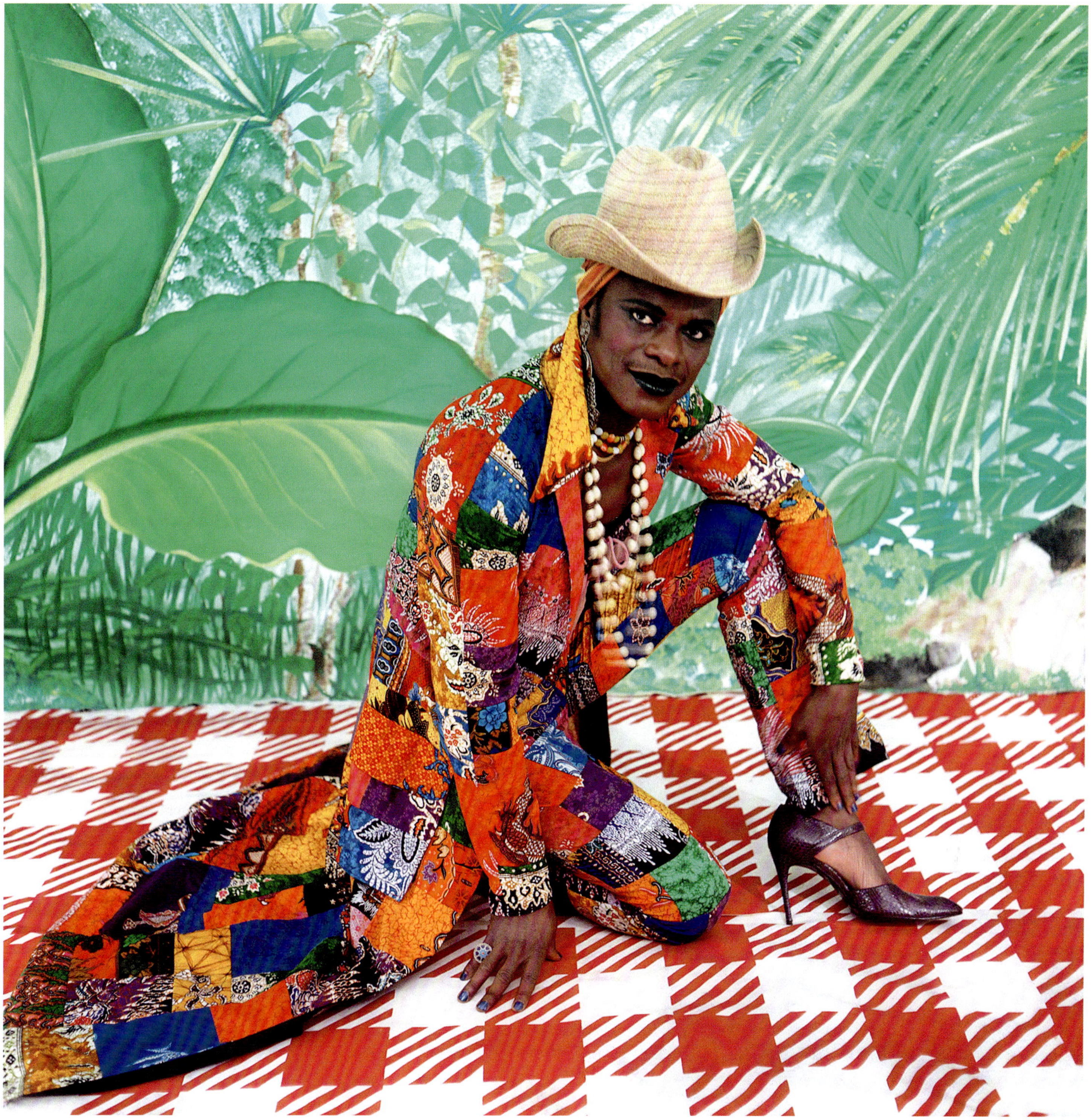

Rahima Gambo

How might photography exist as a physical act? Rahima Gambo's radical reinvention of photography uses its perambulatory aspect to create images, but without a camera. She sets off on city walks and, rather than taking photographs, she responds to her surroundings by collecting items that catch her interest along the way. Then, with these found objects, she constructs a 'picture' of her experience back in the studio, or at the site of an exhibition, using the photographic process to come up with an entirely different result. In these multisensory installations, which include sculptural assemblages and are accompanied by video essays that narrate the paths she has taken, Gambo's own body becomes the medium, replacing the camera.

Born in Nigeria in 1986, Gambo studied anthropology and sociology before becoming a visual artist. She describes her ongoing series *A Walk* (2018–) as a 'psycho-geographical survey'[1] that maps her inner world as she encounters the external environment. Gambo first began to experiment with this approach after thinking deeply about the rise of female suicide bombers in Nigeria's north-eastern region, and the ways women's bodies move through public spaces and interact with landscapes, and the relationship between the suicide bombers' bodies and her own. 'I felt a void in linear photographic language in capturing these horrific incidents,' she reflects.[2]

Before she began to conceptualize her photography as walks, Gambo's practice was aligned more closely with photojournalism. She became well known for her photographic research project with schoolchildren in Borno and Adamawa states, Nigeria, where schools were being subjected to violent attacks by Boko Haram, culminating in April 2014 in the abduction of hundreds of schoolgirls from Chibok.

However, photojournalism was becoming a genre with which Gambo felt increasingly uncomfortable and she now sees it as a construct that has unavoidable negative consequences. 'We always seem to forget, whenever we're dazzled by beautiful images and well-written stories, that journalism is an extractive industry – it's a business that mines the peripheries of the world, or the peripheries of knowledge, to own that information and transmit it back into the world in a highly manipulated way,'[3] she says. 'It gets even more problematic the further away it is from local models (where local news is created by locals to enlighten and move forward the local community). The chances are slim that it ever benefits the person at the other end of the camera. I also think that not everything needs to be

***Collage VI* from the series *A Walk*, 2018. Digital print on matt archival paper. 63.5 x 88.9cm (25 x 35in)**
Millennium Park is a popular public park in Abuja, where Gambo lives. It is frequented by photographers who make a living taking portraits there, printing them on the spot. During her walks in the park, Gambo found many of these photographs torn up and thrown away – discarded when the printer didn't work properly or the results were unsatisfactory. 'I started to think of the connection between photographs and plants, both light-sensitive and light-dependent materials, and what happens when a photograph is left in the grass for so long,' Gambo explains. Instead of 'taking' photographs, she began to collect them – 'picking them up like seeds and flowers. I felt more like a gardener during this process and latched on to botanical and plant biology concepts. I started to think of the photo-collages I was making as a sort of cross-pollination and dialogue with the materials I was encountering.'[6]

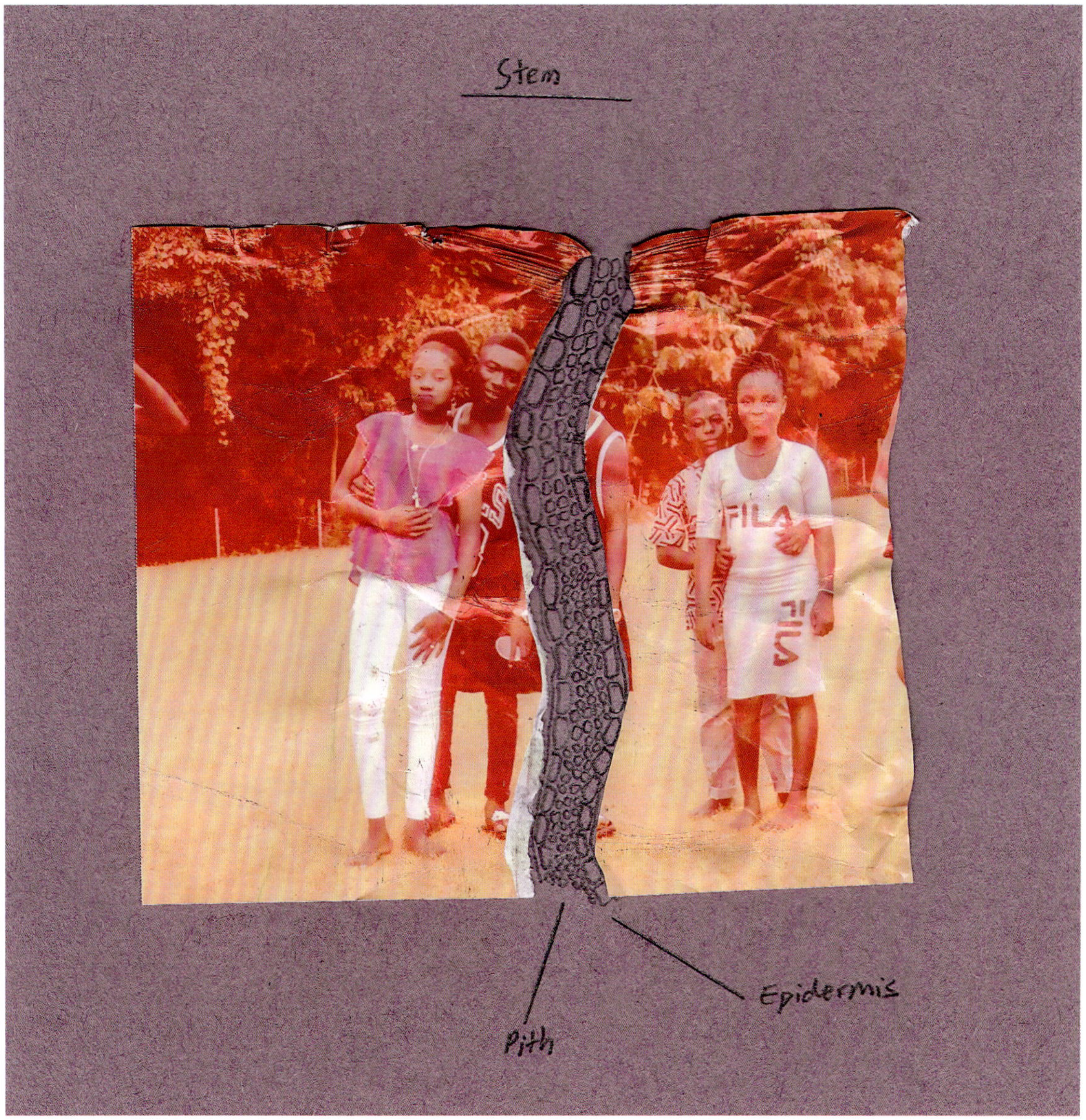

exposed, seen and known; that perhaps it's not for us to see and we should respect that boundary.'[4]

In 2017 Gambo embarked on a collaboration with young women students at the Shehu Sanda Kyarimi Government School in Maiduguri, Nigeria, as part of her evolving series *Education is Forbidden* (2016–), the title of which is the literal translation of 'Boko Haram'. As schools remain targets for terror, with many students killed or missing, she says that she realized 'how someone is affected is hard to measure or even visibly see'.[5] Gambo led storytelling workshops with female students aged between seventeen and nineteen in which still images, videos and performances made with the students allow them to talk in their own language, with no attempt to speak directly of or interpret the trauma of the Boko Haram conflict in any traditional or informative way. She named the project Tatsuniya, meaning 'riddle' or 'fable' in Hausa. One of the standout images catches a group of young women students in motion, dressed in their uniform of pink hijabs, as they perform a choreographed sequence created during a workshop. The Tatsuniya project, which has evolved and continues, is fundamental to Gambo's approach to being an artist: 'I'm starting to see my role as a sort of facilitator, convener or even a teacher, as providing alternative space for them to "play" and be together outside of their normal routines.'[7] She describes the Tatsuniya workshop as 'an experiment and unlearning of what it means to narrate something outside of myself and to stay with this open-ended enquiry. In a way it is also a rehabilitation, regeneration and alchemy of my previous work as a photojournalist and documentarian focusing on students.'[8]

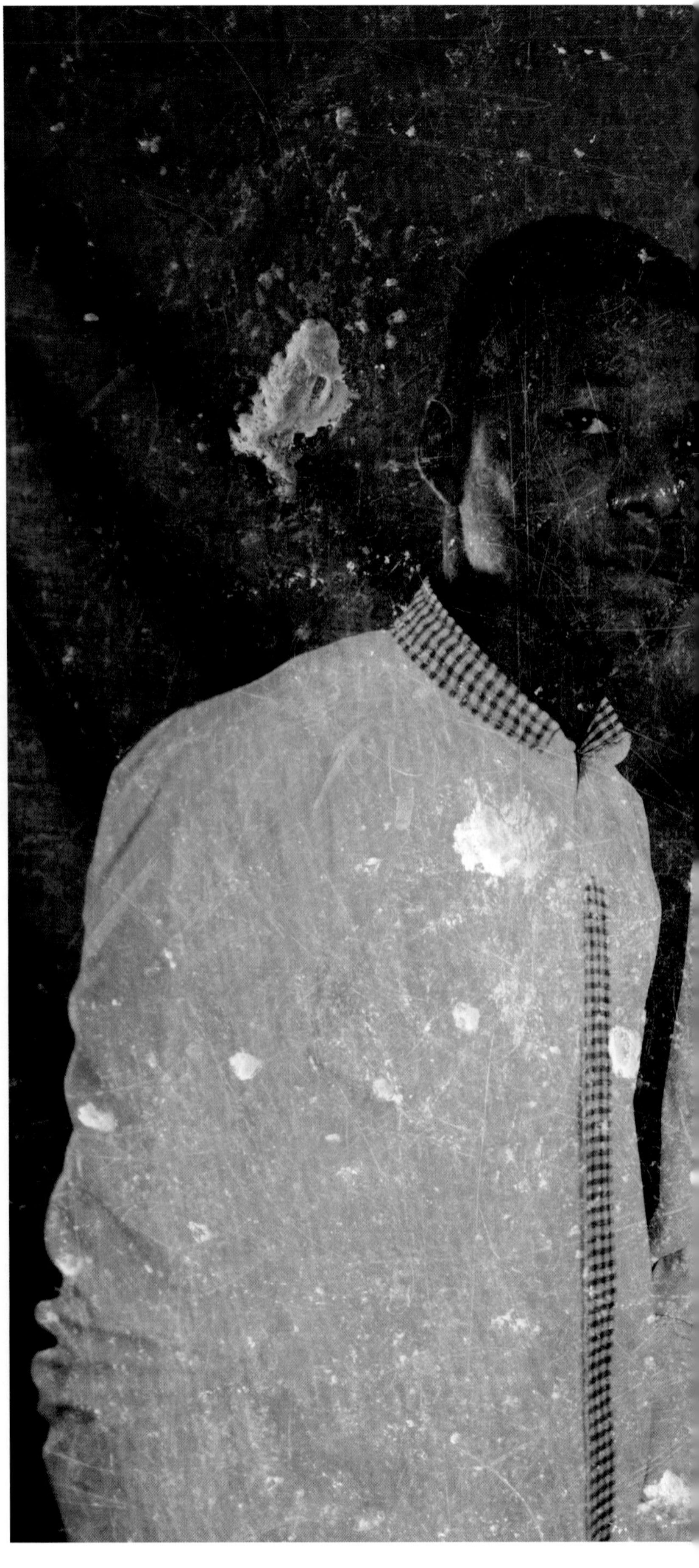

***Three boys from Shehu Sanda Kyarimi Government School, Maiduguri, Nigeria* from the series *Education is Forbidden*, 2016. Digital print on matte archival paper, 33 x 45.7cm (13 x 18in)**
This photograph is a portrait of three students taken during Gambo's first visit to the Shehu Sanda Kyarimi Government School in Maiduguri. The double-exposure image shows the boys overlaid with an image of a classroom blackboard chalked with Arabic writing – when the regular school day ended, the classrooms were used to give lessons in Islamic studies. The photograph forms part of Gambo's *Education is Forbidden* series in which she attempts to envisage the gap between the experiences and accounts of students and daily life at the school in the aftermath of a terror attack that took place there in 2013.

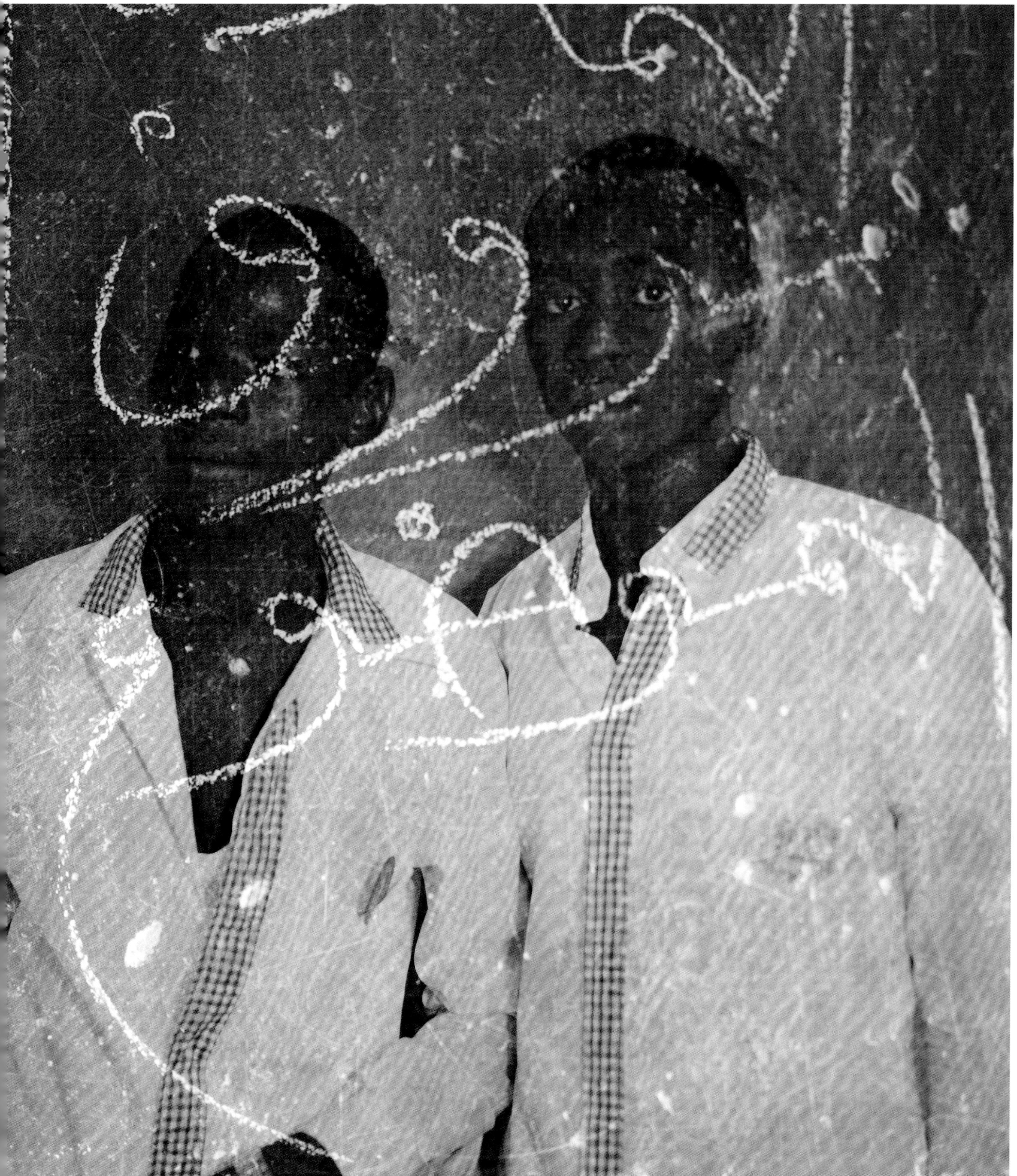

Nan Goldin

In the twenty-first century, photography has become less about capturing the 'decisive moment', as Henri Cartier-Bresson once termed it, and more oriented towards a stream of moments, emotions and experiences, individually inconsequential but definitive in retrospect. One of the first photographers to realize this significant shift in the way we experience photographs, some decades before social media would affirm it, was Nan Goldin.

Born in 1953 in Washington, D.C., Nan Goldin began to take pictures at the age of fourteen, after leaving home. She spent some years living in foster homes and with friends before attending the School of the Museum of Fine Arts in Boston and then, in 1978, moving to New York. Her work has always dealt with her close contact with addiction, abuse, violence and sickness in the 1970s and 1980s, but also with her experiences of love, friendships, sex, euphoria and escape. Goldin's early work was remarkable in that she made her own world and the people in it – friends, lovers, biological and chosen families – the centre of her images, moving the art of photography into a new era where it no longer had to find some kind of objective truth.

The people Goldin portrayed – those she lived with, partied with, slept with – had previously been invisible in the mainstream media, overlooked and existing on the edge. Early on, Goldin believed in the power of the camera as a way of seeing the world and being recognized – universal human themes that transcend the intimate borders of her work. The urge to make the invisible visible, to visualize what is felt, had come much earlier, after Goldin's older sister, Barbara, committed suicide at the age of eighteen. 'I saw the role that her sexuality and repression played in her destruction,' Goldin has said.[1] She was just eleven at the time Barbara took her own life and she has since dedicated several works to her sister.

Goldin was also among the first artists to plunge us into a world experienced photographically. Since her breakthrough work, *The Ballad of Sexual Dependency*, was included in the Whitney Museum of American Art's biennial in 1985, Goldin has created slide show installations compiled of hundreds of deeply personal photographs, hyper-emotive snapshots of her life and 'tribe', that the artist describes as 'a diary I let people read'.[2] *The Ballad of Sexual Dependency*, published as a book in 1986, has become one of the most influential artworks of its era, a contemporary classic that has continued to be referenced by artists and photographers ever since, prefiguring the way we see photographically in the social media age.

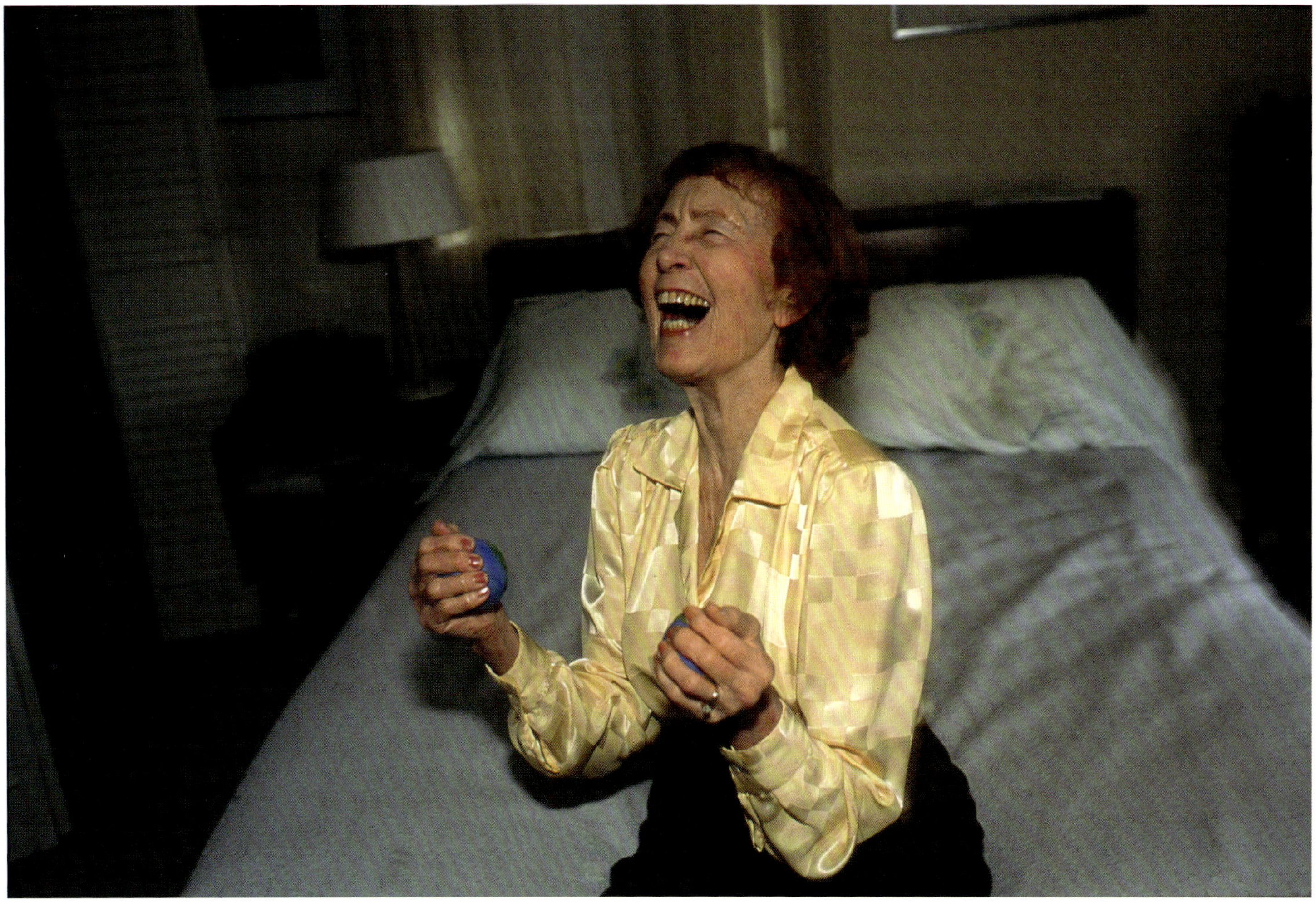

***Lil laughing, Swampscott, MA, 1996*, 1996**
This image presents an enduring theme in Goldin's work: joy. Although she is known for her searing portraits of pain, both physical and emotional, her work follows a cyclical drama of dualities in which rock-bottom lows coexist with euphoric highs. Goldin's interest in sexuality is related to her interest in joy, in transcendence and out-of-body experiences, whether through intoxication with drugs, sexual climax, love, laughter, or even in squeezing stress balls, as her mother Lil does in this image. Goldin had a difficult relationship with her family when growing up and left home at a young age, but this image finds laughter in the darkness. Goldin has said that it is 'empathy and love' that motivate her work.[3]

The Ballad of Sexual Dependency's operatic overture comes from the way the installation of the 700-image slide show unfolds to a soundtrack. Goldin has used this technique in other monumental slide-show works, such as *The Other Side* (1994; taking its name from a famous Boston drag bar Goldin used to frequent), *Scopophilia* (2010; commissioned by the Musée du Louvre) and *Memory Lost* (2019), her most ambitious slide show to date, a 24-minute avalanche of emotions set to a musical score composed by Mica Levi. The audio track undoubtedly influences audiences' responses to the visual material; the viewing pace is carefully controlled, allowing us to stay with each photograph for only a few seconds.

Photography can be an attempt to preserve the fleeting, to record things that might be forgotten or will inevitably cease to exist. Memory, loss and death are never far from the frame in Goldin's work. The artist was a heroin user in the 1970s and 1980s, and while she recovered, many of her muses – close friends – did not, losing their lives to addiction or disease. The photograph acts as both memory and memorial, moving between the celebratory and the wistful.

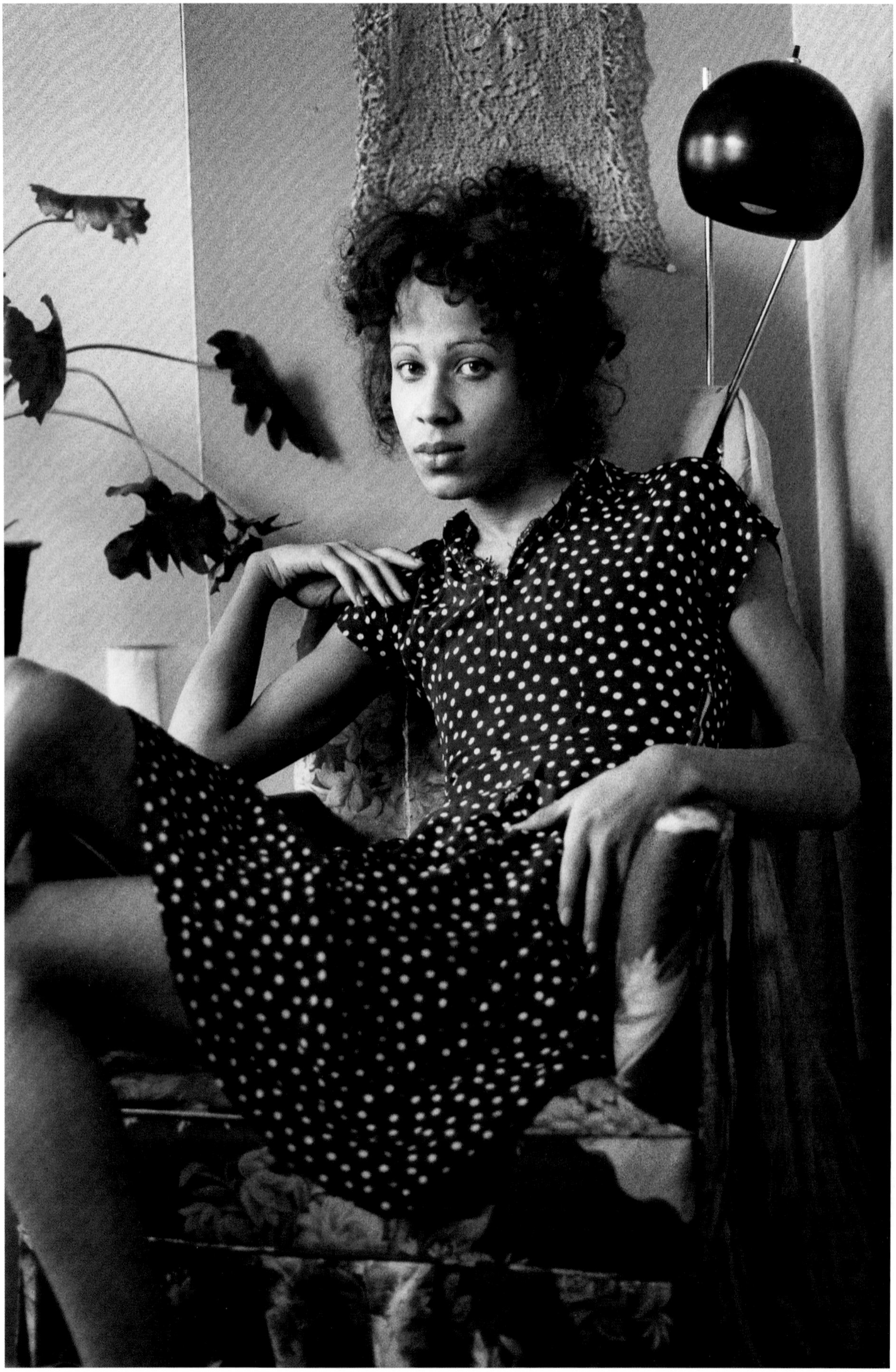

These losses have impelled Goldin to make increasingly activist works about addiction and its impact on individuals. Her 2019 exhibition at the Marian Goodman Gallery in London showcased *Sirens*, a call to arms about the heartbreak of addiction, as well as campaign pamphlets and materials produced by P.A.I.N. (Prescription Addiction Intervention Now), an advocacy organization Goldin founded in 2017 to lobby against the Sackler family, owners of Purdue Pharma LP, which manufactures the opioid painkiller OxyContin. The Sacklers are known for their large donations to public arts institutions. Goldin, who is herself in recovery from OxyContin addiction, has staged protests outside the Metropolitan Museum of Art and the Guggenheim in New York, and the Victoria and Albert Museum in London, demanding that they refuse Sackler money. In 2019 Goldin famously turned down a solo exhibition at London's National Portrait Gallery while they were considering accepting a donation from the Sacklers – which was eventually turned down.

In a 2016 *New Yorker* profile of Goldin, the critic Hilton Als speaks of the feeling of hope that emanates from a rare photograph of Goldin's sister Barbara, a kind of 'hope that the voodoo of love can make a difference'.[4] Ultimately it is perhaps because Goldin cherishes her life and recognizes its fragility and ephemerality that she photographs it for posterity. It's only by remembering what we no longer have that we learn not to take things for granted.

***Bea in her chair, Boston 1972*, 1972**
In the 1970s Goldin shot exclusively on black and white film, making this period of her work distinct from her later, colour-rich photographs. This portrait is of Bea, a drag queen and Goldin's flatmate and friend, who appears in many of her pictures in the 1970s. The tenderness and exchange of a soft gaze in this image suggest the affection shared between subject and photographer.

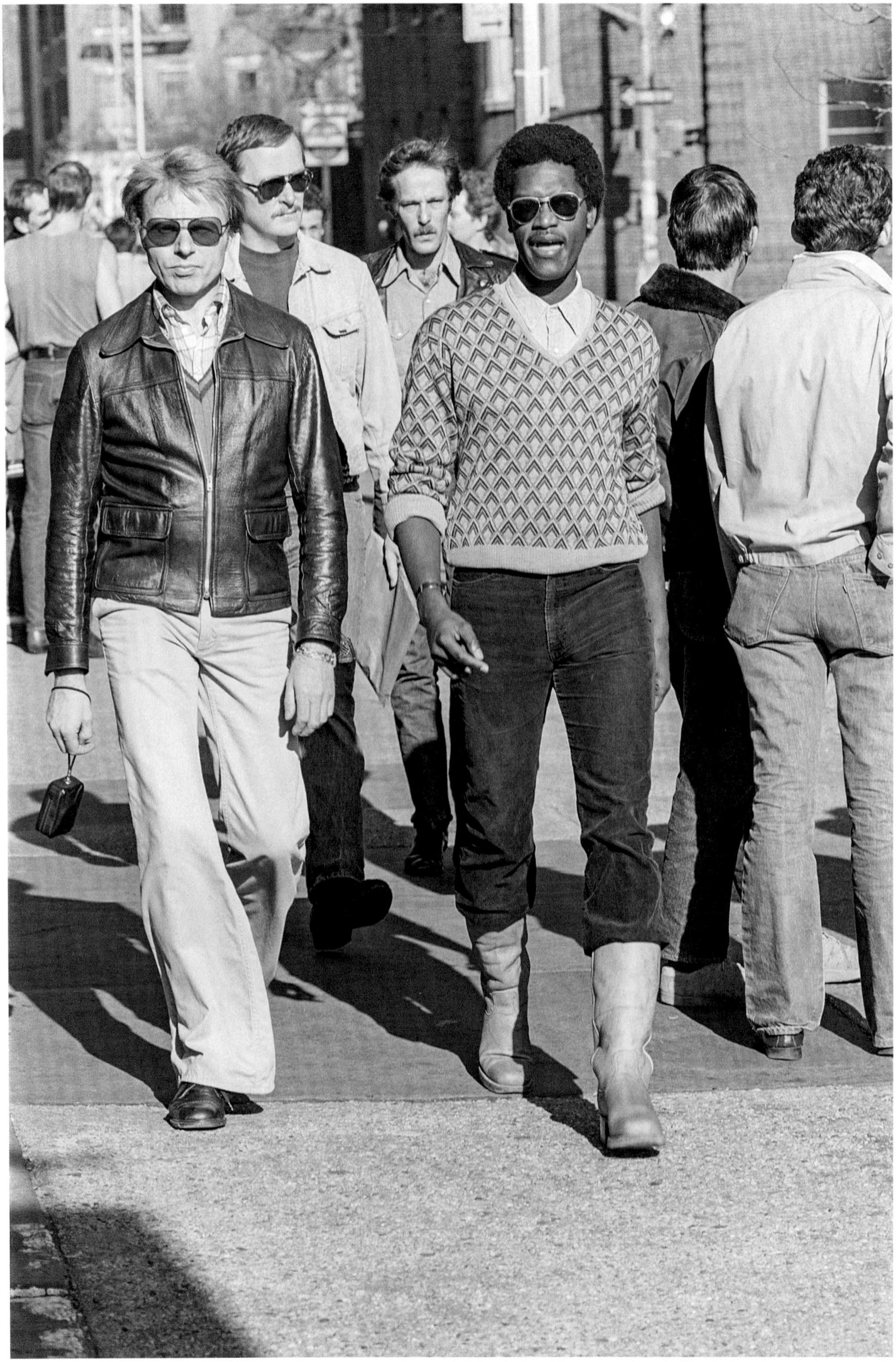

Sunil Gupta

Untitled #8 **from the series** ***Christopher Street, New York, 1976*****, 1976. Archival inkjet print, 28 x 19.1 cm (11 x 7 ½ in). Edition of 5 plus 2 artist proofs**

Gupta has experimented with different photographic modes and languages throughout his career, but street photography has always been at the centre of his art. His first series of work, *Christopher Street, New York, 1976*, is an archive of images of the gay community taken on and around this famous street in Manhattan shortly after the artist moved to New York. The image here captures what has become another constant theme in Gupta's work over the years: interracial relationships and the intersections between the lives of gay men of colour in the Western countries where he has lived (the USA, Canada and the UK) and his birthplace, India.

Whether curating, writing, teaching or creating, Sunil Gupta sees photography as something between a personal document and a form of social critique, and as a conduit for community – somewhere diasporic identities can come together. Photography has been a way to confront conflicts in Gupta's own life as a gay man of colour who lives with HIV, and to raise awareness about ongoing prejudice against and persecution of LGBTQI people in both the East and the West.

Gupta was born in Delhi in 1953 and moved to Canada with his family in the 1960s, aged 15, at a time when gay people and people of colour were mostly invisible in the visual culture of the West. He became actively involved in the Gay Liberation Movement after moving to New York in 1976. It was a time of cultural revolution and rebellion, and photography's place in the world was also changing. This was the halcyon era of gritty New York street photography. Jack Garofalo's pictures of Harlem in summer, Meryl Meisler's documents of the nightlife at Studio 54 and Martha Cooper's reports on the emerging graffiti scene stirred a heady excitement around the medium as a way to observe the city's subcultures.

Gupta enrolled on a course at the New School for Social Research taught by the prolific street photographer Lisette Model, who also trained Diane Arbus and was an early supporter of Gupta's work. He would spend weekends strolling on Christopher Street in the West Village, the centre of gay counterculture and protest. Gupta did not know then that the casual photographs he took there and developed in his bathroom at home would become an important record of an unprecedented time, as New York's gay and transgender community began to establish a public voice in the aftermath of the 1969 Stonewall Riots and before the AIDS crisis. They also comprised his first body of work as an artist.

Gupta has been conscious of the camera as a powerful tool for activism and advocacy ever since. In 1977 he relocated again, this time to London, where he continued to study photography, completing an MA at the Royal College of Art. In 1988 Gupta was one of the founders of the non-profit photography association Autograph ABP, which was established in London as a way to promote and support the work and careers of artists from diverse cultural backgrounds who had been omitted from British institutions, galleries and collections. The establishment of Autograph was an exciting moment for Gupta and many artists involved in the wider Black Arts movement in the UK in the 1980s. This high was followed by what Gupta describes as one of the lowest points of his life, when in 1995 he was diagnosed as HIV positive. The diagnosis inspired the video work (*A World Without*) *Pity* (2003), which was filmed in India, about the specific impact of HIV there and the way it is treated both medically and culturally.

From London, Gupta began to look back at and visit his place of birth, and turned his focus in particular on gay rights in India and his position as a gay Indian man living in the West. In *Exiles* (1986–7) he photographed gay men – homosexuality was still illegal at the time in India – next to famous Indian public monuments. It was not until 2017 that it became legal to express your sexual orientation as a LGBTQI person in India; consensual gay sex was legalized only in 2018. In texts that caption each image, Gupta gives voice to the hidden inner lives of the men in the photographs. He returned to live in India in 2004, staying there until 2012, and revisited *Exiles*, creating a new series of portraits of the queer community he became a part of, entitled *Mr Malhotra's Party* (2007). Gupta's photographs – and the people who appear in them – are therefore part of a brave act of defiance and activism, a vital statement about the right to exist and to be seen in public.

***Jangpura* from the series *Exiles*, 1987**
The first series Gupta made in India was *Exiles*. At the time, since homosexuality was a crime and culturally taboo, gay men led clandestine lives. A nuanced work, it includes portraits of gay men whose identities are protected, often featuring Delhi's prominent public monuments as a backdrop. Here, a man stands alone in a domestic setting in the Jangpura neighbourhood. The juxtaposition of local and historic sites with the subjects' personal reflections creates a tension that speaks of post-colonialism and the clashes between traditional values and modern life, conformity and self-expression, and being both inside and on the margins. A painful discord between the private and the public often emerges, while the inability to live and love freely, out in the open, is evoked with sensitivity and inflected with moments of humour.

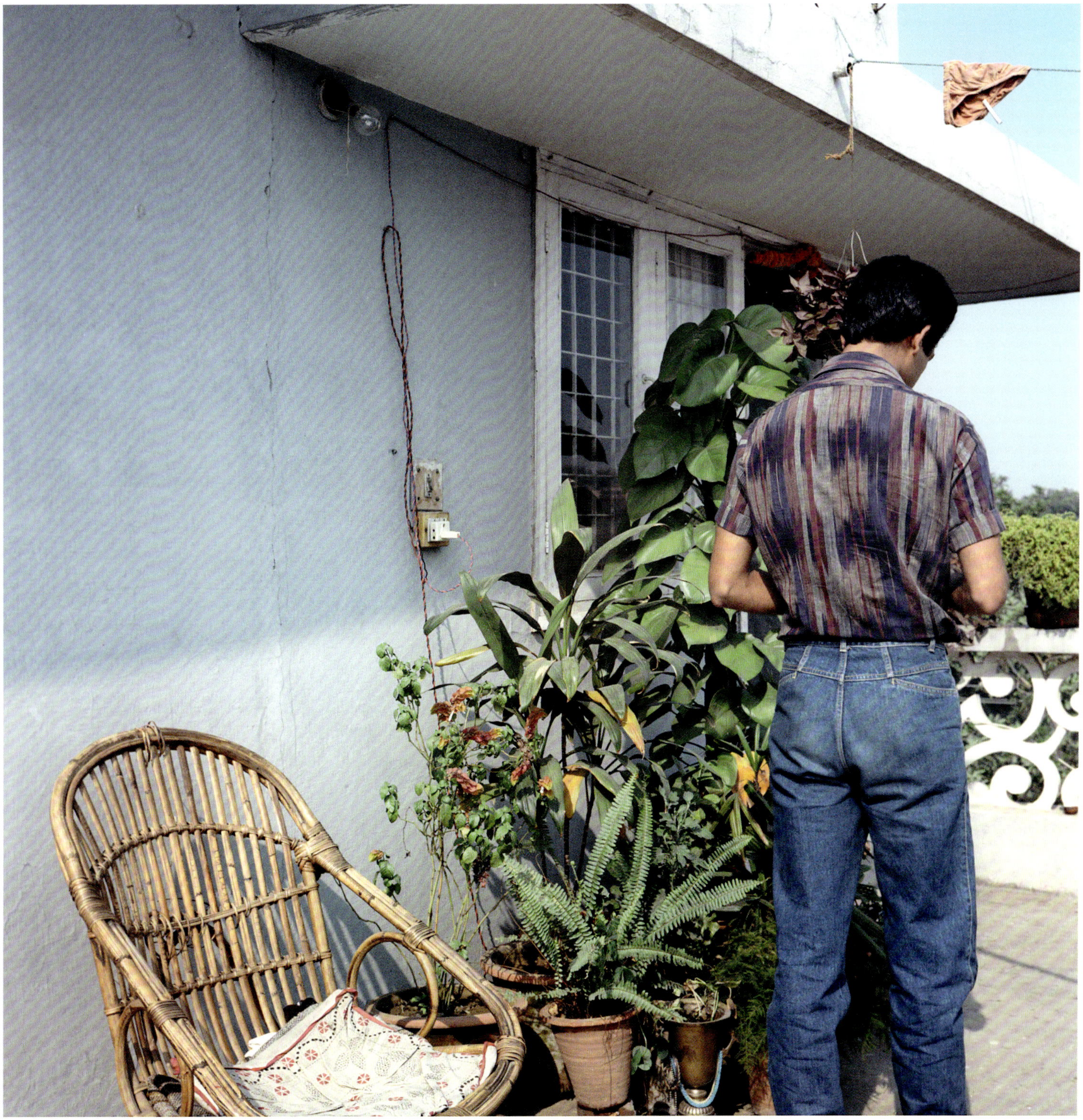

Jangpura
I am tired of being alone with no prospect of meeting anyone I like. I'm nauseated by the party and park scene.

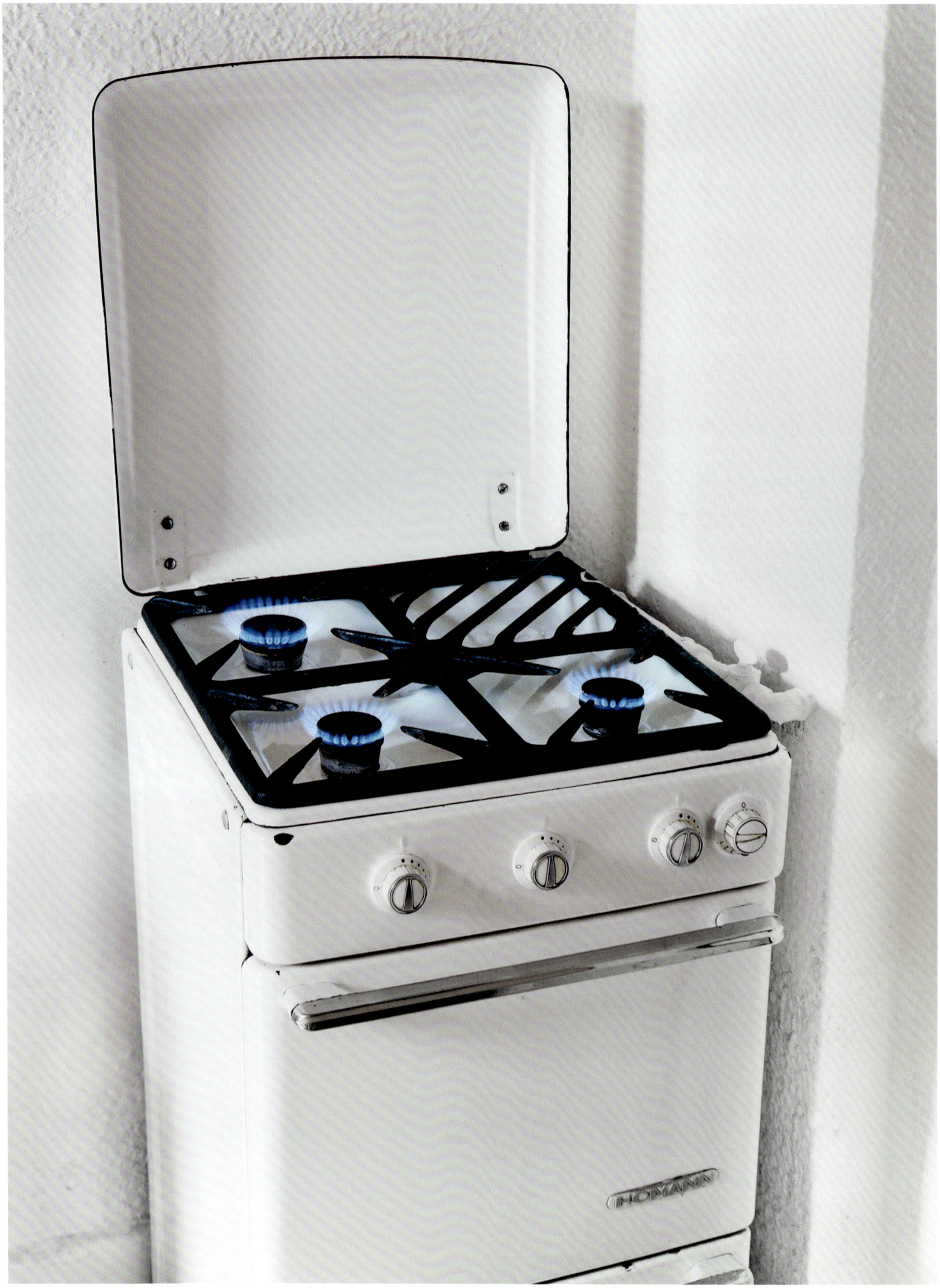
HOMANN

Andreas Gursky

Are there things a photograph can do that we cannot? Andreas Gursky suggests that photography might be more intelligent than we are. In a capitalist society where we are constantly bombarded with products, information and images, our understanding of the vast global systems within which we live may be limited. Gursky uses photography to make sense of 'how the world fits together', according to Ralph Rugoff, the director of the Hayward Gallery, London, where the artist had a major retrospective in 2017.

Gursky was born in Leipzig in 1955 but his family relocated to West Germany in 1957. He grew up immersed in photography, as his parents ran a large commercial studio in Düsseldorf, which prospered in the post-war economic boom. Gursky has recalled the orange glow of the darkroom, the smell of chemicals and the shriek of the lab clocks. He used one of his father's Linhof cameras to shoot his early landscape pictures, although as a student at the Kunstakademie Düsseldorf in 1980, the Plaubel was the preferred camera.

Gursky arrived at the Kunstakademie with technical prowess, thanks to his father, but his aesthetic would be informed by Hilla and Bernd Becher and their influential ideas as the founders of the Dusseldorf School. The Bechers trained Gursky to adhere to a strict set of pictorial paradigms: flat lighting conditions to eliminate shadows, a uniform raised vantage point, a full-frontal view and standardized crop and distance. 'I was able to appropriate this compositional template and have internalized it to such an extent that I often return to it.'[1]

Salerno (1990) marked a change of direction in Gursky's work on a number of levels. Shot on a 4 x 5 in broad daylight – against the Bechers' teachings – the sweeping aerial view of the port of Salerno with its flattened composition creates a 'balance between great scale and a huge amount of sharp detail'.[2] Soon after, Gursky began to work digitally, opening up new opportunities as he concentrated on 'finding' images, and using photography to construct them. *Salerno* marked the beginning of this approach to sites where the industrial, the global and the masses meet – airports, supermarkets, warehouses, crowds at concerts and stock exchanges – in an attempt to visually conceptualize the sheer scale of international systems of trade, commerce and consumerism.

***Gas Cooker*, 1980**
This deceptively simple photograph of the lit gas cooker in Gursky's home in Düsseldorf was taken after the artist had been cooking. Dating from the same year Gursky began to study at the Kunstakademie Düsseldorf under Hilla and Bernd Becher, *Gas Cooker* was the first photograph he published. It already bears many of the hallmarks of Becher's teaching: the balanced light with little shadow, the slightly elevated viewpoint and the centred perspective. The minimal composition emphasizes geometry and line, while the monochrome palette gives the image a deadpan austerity. While this contrasts with his later work, which focuses on increasingly complex collections of objects, it nevertheless heralds themes that have continued to preoccupy the artist concerning everyday commodities and the machinations of capitalism in all their strange and compelling guises.

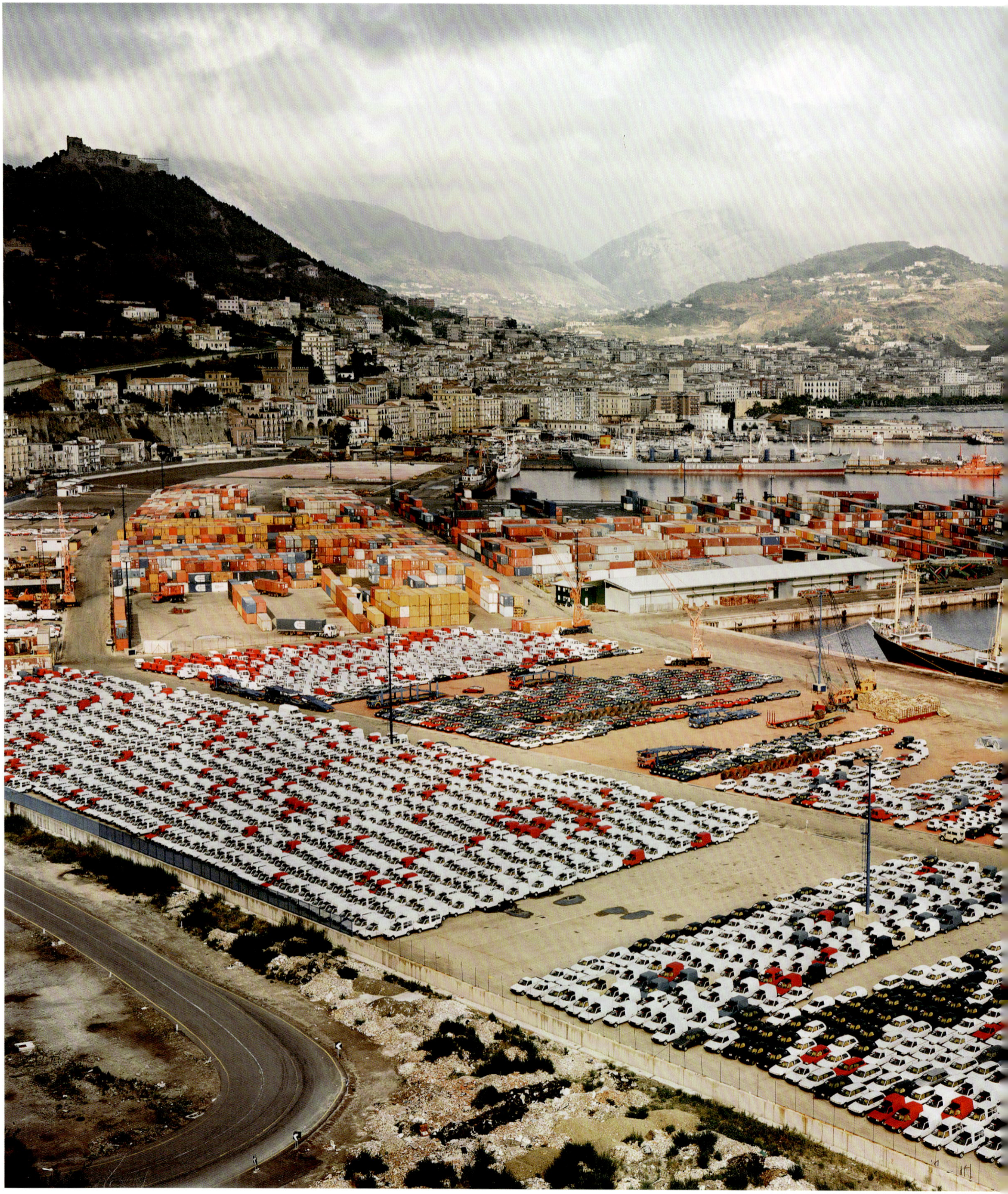

'My images are a lot about space, but that doesn't mean it's space that is unlimited,' Gursky has explained. 'Space for me is a metaphor for the way we as mankind travel through space at home and on our planet. And the universe is huge and we are so limited in our perception and this is one of the things I want to show in my images.'[3] The composite form of his images, printed on an enormous scale (another trait of the Düsseldorf School of Photography, with which Gursky is associated), embodies these ideas and the 'epic sights'[4] – as Rugoff called them – of our time.

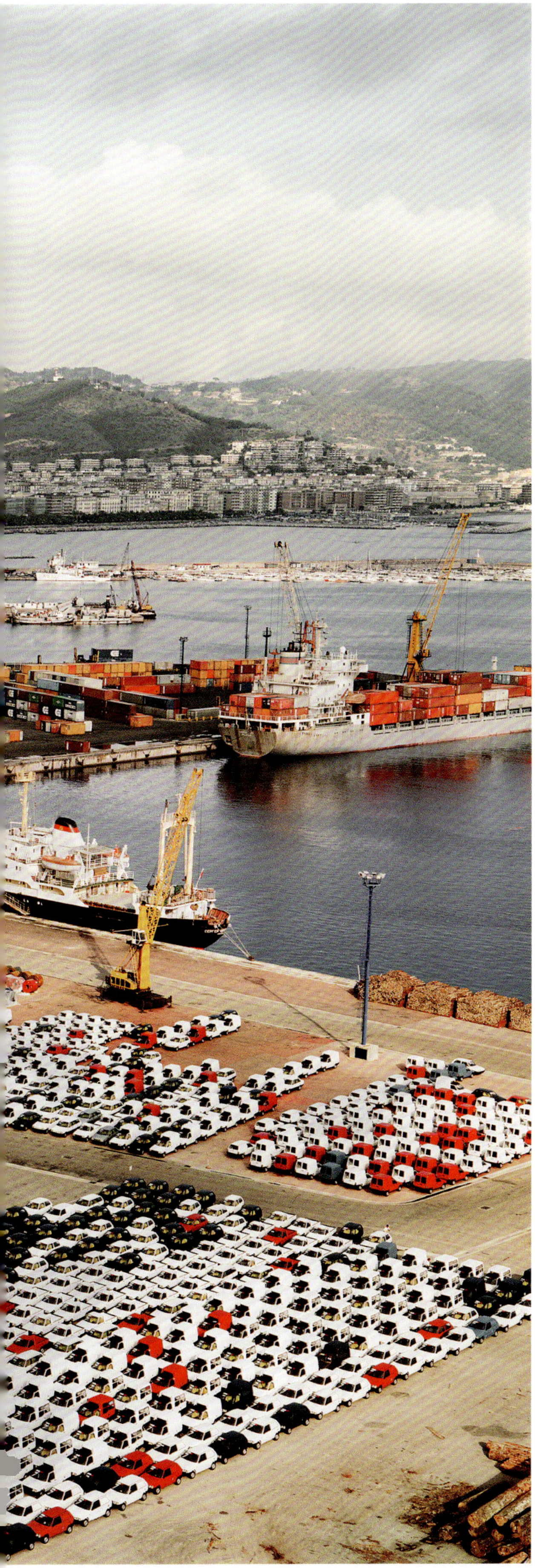

***Salerno*, 1990**
Gursky has described this image as heralding a new phase in his work. By moving back from what he was photographing and shooting with a telephoto lens, he achieved a 'more abstract point of view'.[5] The artist has said that he was travelling in Italy with his family when he was struck by this panoramic scene of the industrial port of Salerno. The sun was already setting but Gursky set up his tripod and took just four frames: 'There was no time to weigh up if it was worth it or not.' As it transpired, it was worth it. 'It opened up a new sense of possibility, stylistically and thematically' he reflected.[6]

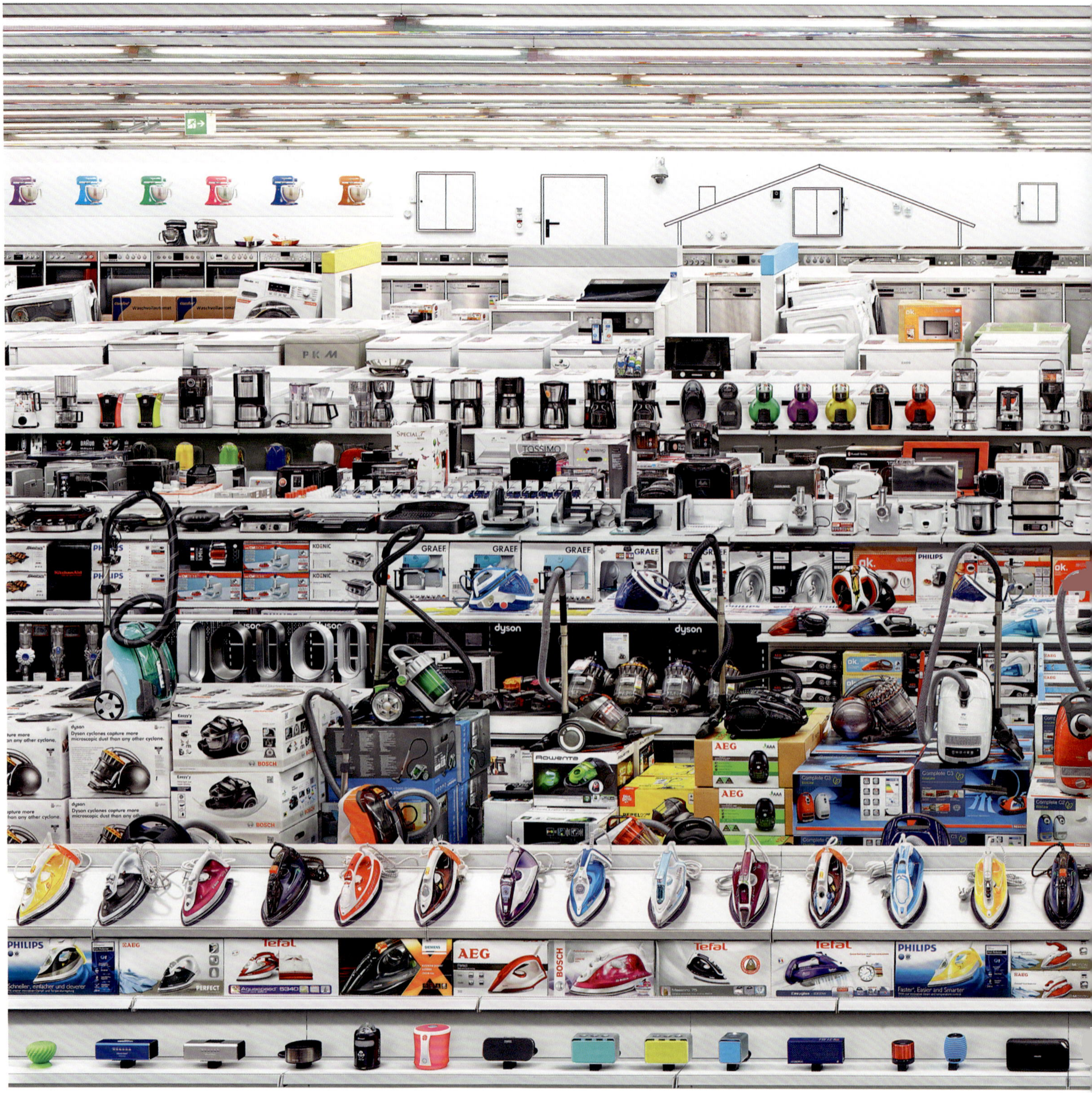

***Mediamarkt*, 2016**

This photograph is the consummate Gursky image. The vast, undulating image, photographed in the town of Neuss and printed large-scale, is almost overwhelming. It is so big we can hardly take it in, yet as we move back the image begins to disappear altogether, a blur of lines and colours. Up close, myriad details reveal themselves, submerging us in another way – an apt metaphor for how we are affected by consumerism.

When this photograph was presented as part of his 2016 exhibition *Not Abstract II* at the Gagosian Gallery in New York, it was accompanied by an audio installation by DJ Richie Hawtin that had been made in response to the images, bathing them in experiential sound.

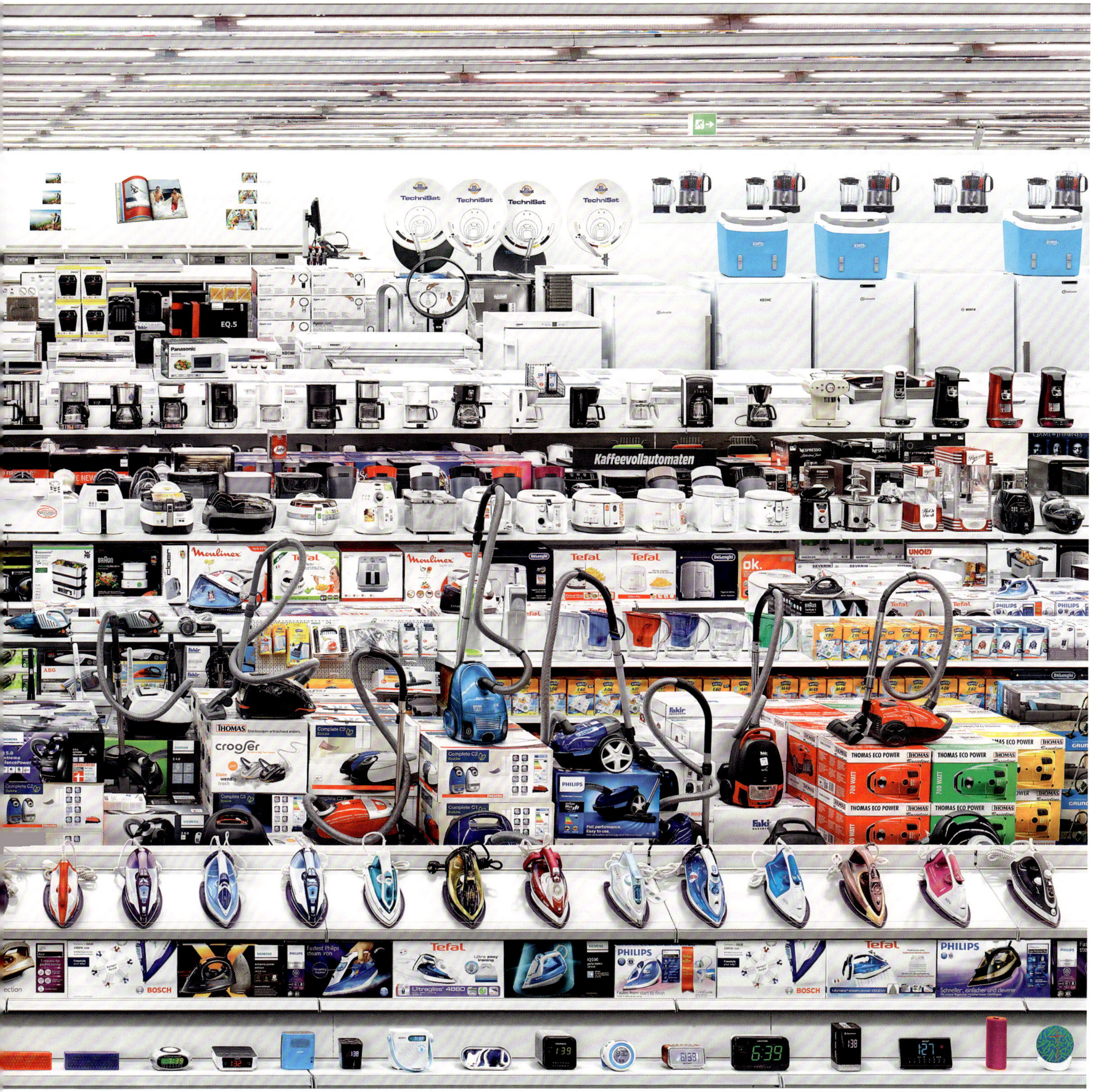
TechniSat
Kaffeevollautomaten
Moulinex
Tefal
THOMAS ECO POWER
PHILIPS
BOSCH
6:39

Eric Gyamfi

When we look out at the world, we are often looking for ourselves. For Eric Gyamfi, photography began as a process of exploring his own identity, and the ways in which our relationship to ourselves is shaped by society and conditioned by culture.

Born in Ghana in 1990, Gyamfi completed a BA in Economics and Information Studies in 2014 before embarking on a career as an artist, then later studying for an MFA in Painting and Sculpture at the Kwame Nkrumah University of Science and Technology. All these interests converge in his multilayered artistic practice, which centres on photography but incorporates technical and physical elements from his previous training, such as sound, printmaking and installation. For three consecutive years he participated in the Photographers' Master Class in Khartoum, Sudan, 2016; Nairobi, Kenya, 2017; and Johannesburg, South Africa, 2018. He is also a member of the Nuku Studio in Ghana, a photography collective committed to telling the stories of Ghana, Africa and the diaspora in a responsible fashion. In 2016 Gyamfi's nascent talent was recognized when he was awarded the Magnum Foundation Fund, and in 2017 he was a participant in the World Press Photo Foundation Masterclass: West Africa.

Self-portraits were among Gyamfi's first works and he has returned to them over the years, using the camera as a tool for introspection. In *Fixing Shadows; Julius and I*, for which Gyamfi received the 2019 Foam Paul Huf Award, the artist makes undulating visual connections between his own image and that of the pioneering late American minimalist composer Julius Eastman by overlaying their faces and reprinting them as one, as cyanotypes and silk screens. When the work was presented at Foam, Amsterdam, the artist compiled a score of WhatsApp voice notes reflecting on the images that filled the walls. Using different materials and methods is a purposeful part of Gyamfi's engagement with photography. He often installs his photographs as a kind of diary, with handwritten notes, but they are stories that unfold in an enigmatic way, denying the viewer a single straightforward narrative. If photography has been a way to fix and define us, then Gyamfi's work is an attempt to free us from the frame – to make the static image fluid and shifting by giving us multiple ways of seeing simultaneously.

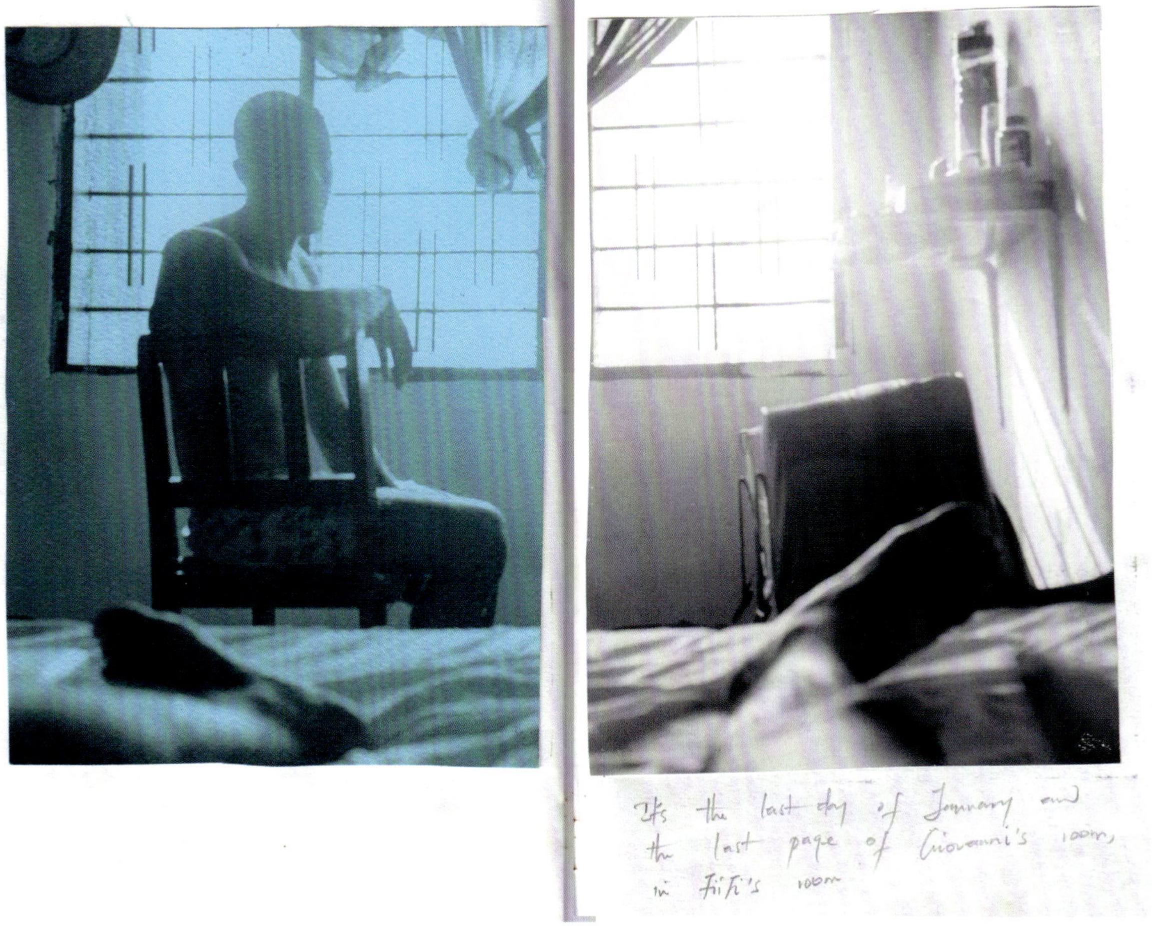

Untitled from the series _A Certain Bed_, 2017
Between February 2017 and January 2018 Gyamfi was homeless. This image comes from the photo collage series *A Certain Bed*, a personal rumination on the meaning of home and belonging, and how memories are made through images. Presented as a diaristic installation where the images unfold in a desultory way into each other between personal scribbled notes, *A Certain Bed* is a semi-autobiographical account of Gyamfi's experiences after being forced to leave his home, the camera acting as his constant companion, a coping mechanism for dealing with dislocation and displacement.

In Gyamfi's acclaimed, poignantly titled series *Just Like Us* (2016), we see love, warmth and togetherness as the binding common threads of humanity. The series features people from the queer community Gyamfi belongs to, whom he refers to as 'participants' rather than 'subjects' – the photograph being an act of willing collaboration, not of intrusion or 'othering'.[1] These are real people: friends, lovers, friends who used to be lovers. Gyamfi doesn't look for spectacle for the straight eye; he searches for the ordinary things that bring us closer. Full of joy and optimism as the images are, there is an undertone of tension that comes from the stark reality of strict laws on homosexuality (in Ghana, same-sex relationships are illegal) and the more insidious impact of cultural expectations. Gyamfi questions the internationalist view of LGBTQI issues and activism, and the implicit role of colonialism in the way sexuality is policed in Ghana at present.

Just Like Us is undoubtedly an important document of and for queer people in Ghana, marking moments and events in a shared, local history. It also speaks of what Gyamfi has declared as his mission, which is to actively create history through his photography. His works tell stories about contemporary life in Ghana that go beyond time and place, using black and white film as a kind of subterfuge to create ageless images. Gyamfi unifies the gaze, closing the distance the camera can impose, looking for the point that 'them' becomes 'just like us'.

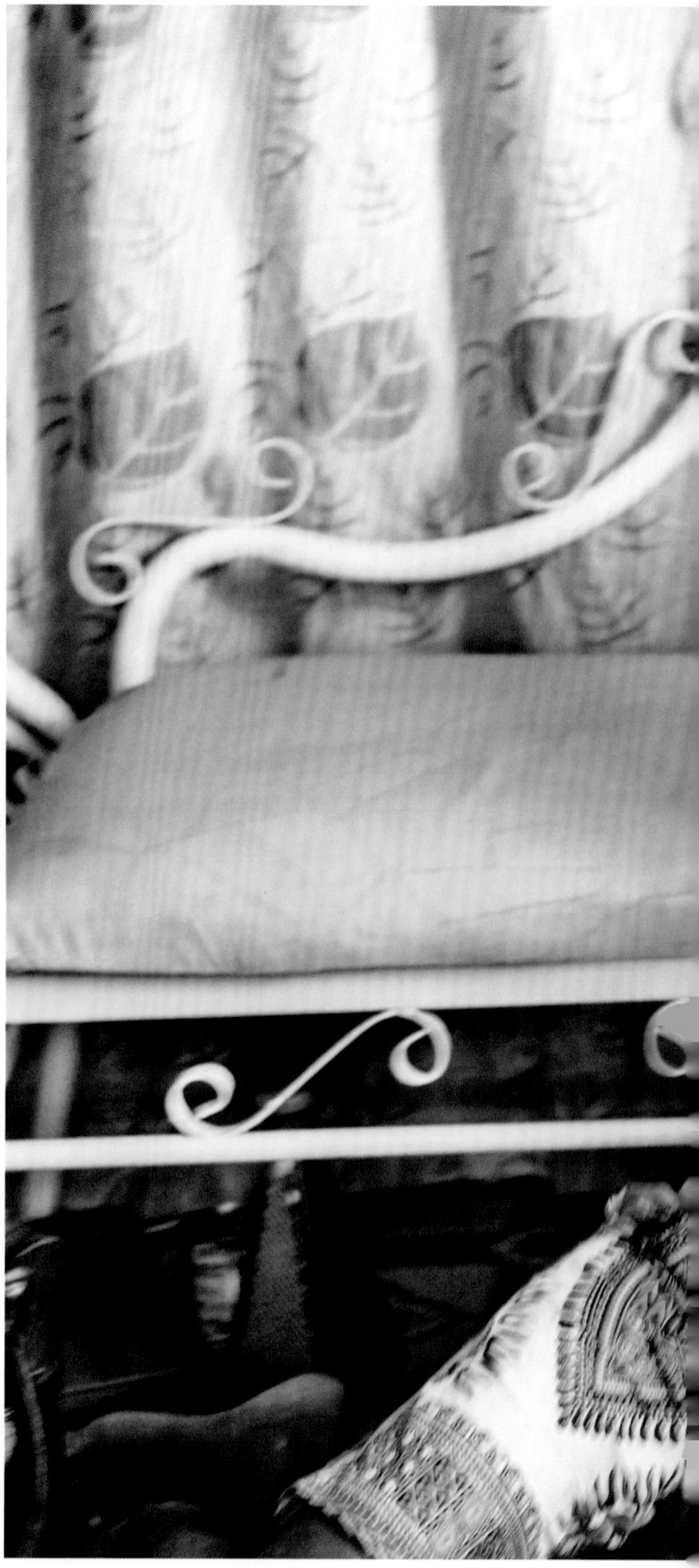

***Henry and Mingle at Home* from the series *Just Like Us*, 2016**
The series of which this photography is a part presents different stories about family life, domesticity, love and sexuality. Here, Henry and his boyfriend Mingle are caught in motion, laughing, and the photographer seems complicit in their joke. Happy, harmonious and at ease, they create the perfect family photograph. Other images in the series reveal less straightforward situations. One portrait depicts a friend of Gyamfi's sitting alone with a pensive expression. Although he is gay, he is soon to be married to a woman who has been chosen for him by his family, so that he can fulfil their wishes for him as well as his own desire to become a father.

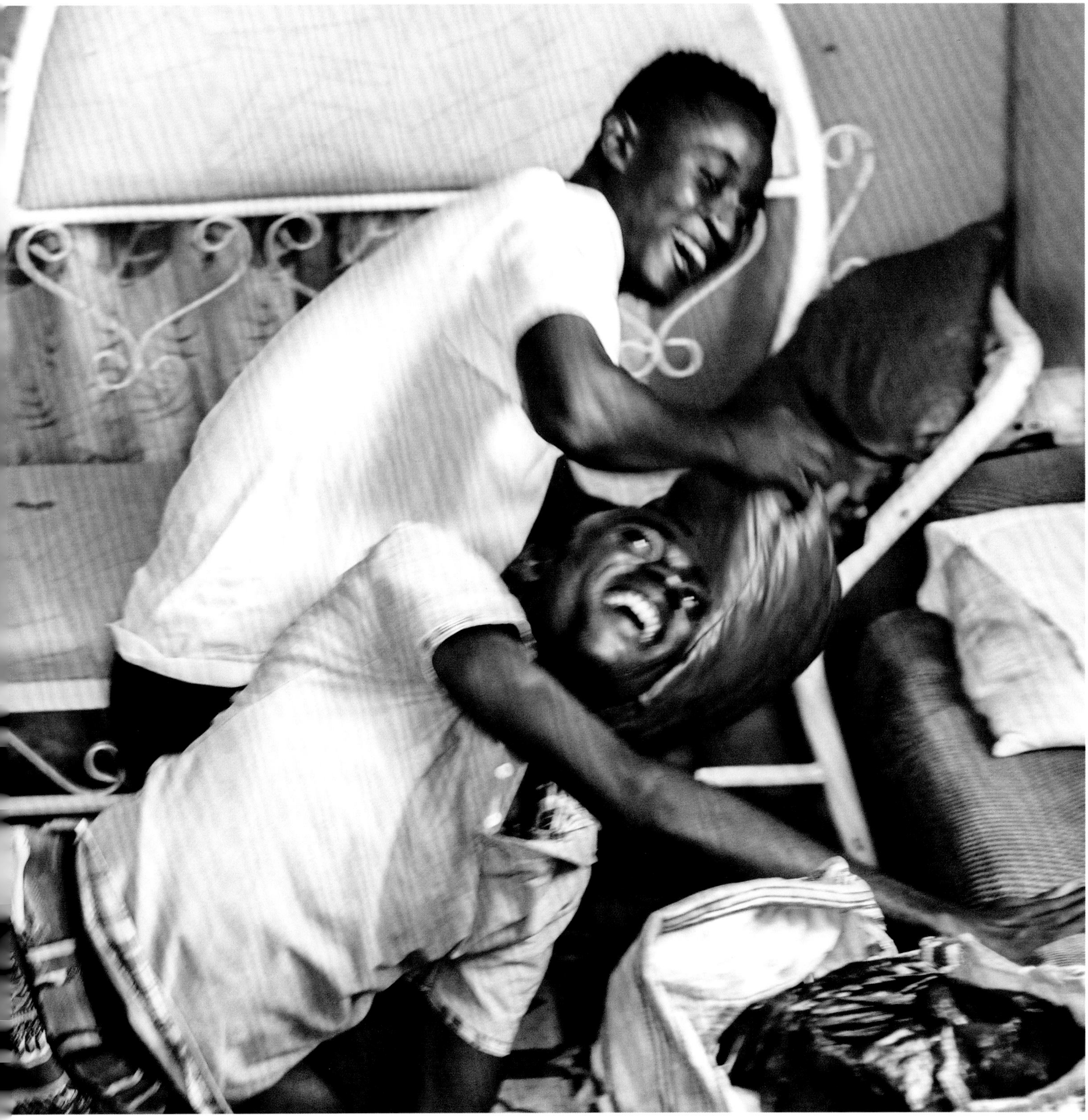

Hassan Hajjaj

Hassan Hajjaj was born in the small coastal town of Larache, Morocco, in 1961. From an early age, he was making necklaces and other items to sell to tourists on the beach. When his family came to London in 1973 to join his father, who had moved there soon after Hajjaj was born, this way of connecting by creating became even more important because he found the transition tough. He spoke little English and struggled to find his place. Growing up in west London's immigrant community, living in one room with five siblings and his parents, it was a psychological need as much as a physical necessity to make his own space.

Space, or the lack of it, has since become a fundamental aspect of Hajjaj's practice, in which installation, design, photography and film are all meshed vibrantly into one. His photographs use every bit of space, with no hierarchy between the vertical and the horizontal, and are packed with patterns. His subjects are styled in tailor-made clothes designed by the artist and their images are hung in customized frames that incorporate products from Morocco, from canned food to zellige tiles, with their branding in Arabic script as prominent as that of Louis Vuitton, Coca-Cola or other Western brands that are recognized around the world.

Equally important are the small shop spaces Hajjaj runs, where many of his photographs are also taken and many of his props and products are piled high, like a stall in the souk. He opened his first shop in Covent Garden, central London, in 1984, selling his streetwear brand R.A.P, and in 2005 he relocated to the emerging arts scene of east London, where he has run a shop in Shoreditch ever since. In 2006 he opened Riad Yima, in the heart of Marrakech's medina, where local artisans are just as likely to stop by for tea as some of the artist's famous clients. In London and in Marrakech, Hajjaj has created a community around these spaces: they are places to drink tea while seated on stools fashioned from crates, to see and buy art, to listen and talk. The spaces invariably become locations for his photo shoots, as he rolls out a textile backdrop onto the street, surrounded by a crowd of friends, collaborators and curious spectators. A fusion of people and objects, Hajjaj's vibrant, multi-functional spaces are the living, breathing dimension of his photography.

This set-up is vital to understanding what Hajjaj does and why he has had such an impact. The enterprising, inventive street spirit that he learned in Larache and brought to London – working as a trader at Camden Market and as a streetwear designer and

***Kesh Angels*, 2010. Frame: wood sprayed white gloss with empty and clean car paint tins; print: metallic lambda on 2mm dibond. 94 x 130cm (37 x 51in)**
The women who appear in this image, one of Hajjaj's best-known portraits, are friends of his, henna artists who work in Marrakech's lively, touristic Jemaa el Fna square. Shot in Marrakech in 2010, the group pose on their motorbikes and in veils, wearing sunglasses Hajjaj picked up in the souk. The unexpected fusion of religious dress and fashion, tradition and modernity, is what makes this image so definitive of Hajjaj's vision of the hybrid nature of contemporary life in the Moroccan city. *Kesh Angels* also addresses the Western-centric tendencies of pop culture by creating a self-defined pop language rooted in North African and Arabic styles.

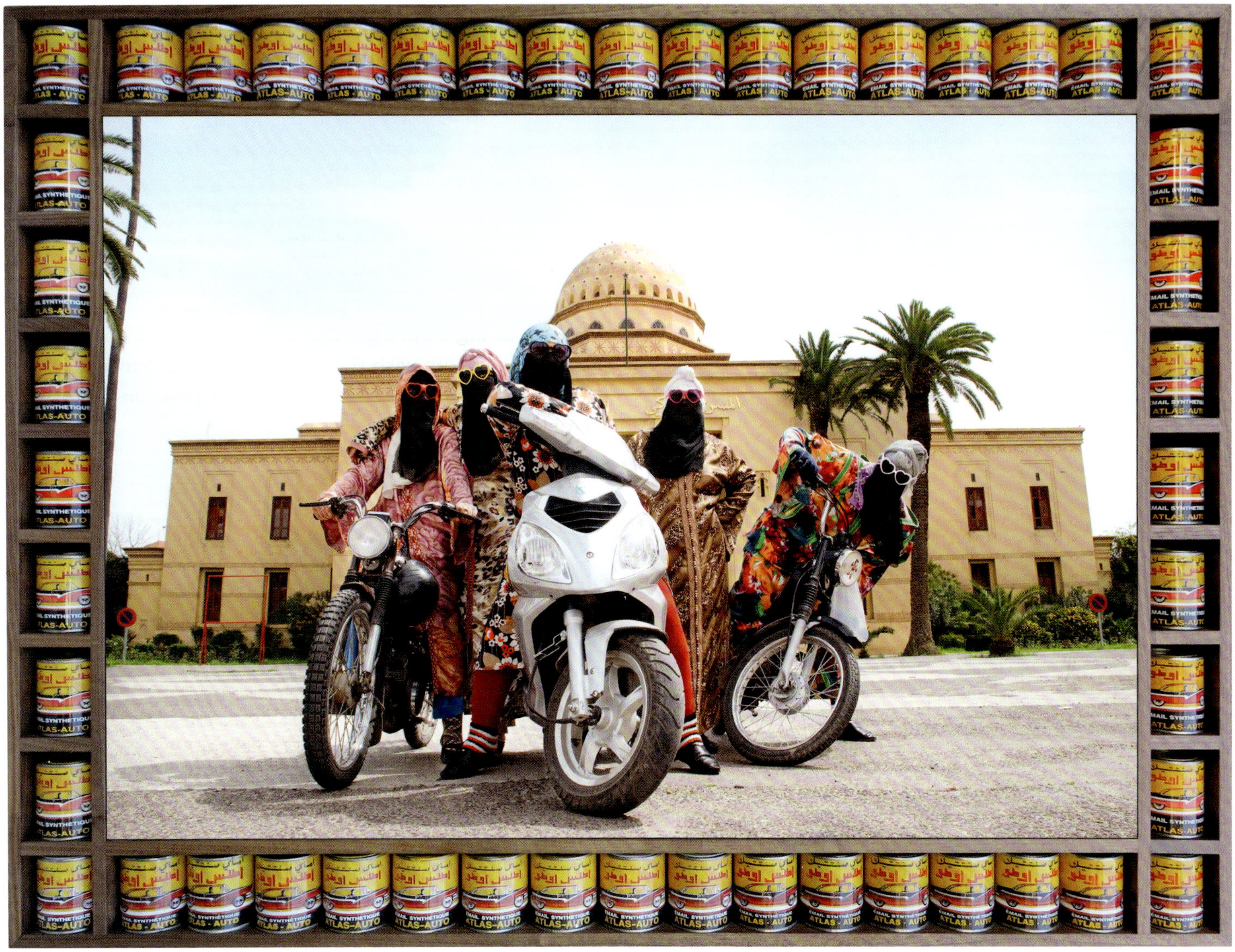

music promoter – is what has made Hajjaj's work so appealing for a wide audience. In 1993 he went back to Morocco for the first time in more than a decade, and the visit had a profound effect. Seeing his homeland with the fresh eyes of a foreigner and the soul of a local, he was inspired.

It is in Marrakech that Hajjaj has met many of his subjects, such as belly dancers, henna girls, market sellers and traditional musicians. 'It's about taking this Orientalism vibe and saying, "OK, let's take ownership of it" – me being Moroccan, you being a Moroccan subject, let's take that kind of thing, and do it in our way,' Hajjaj said in an interview in 2019.[1] The interplay between modernity and the cosmopolitanism specific to the city became a source for the first artworks Hajjaj brought back to London. The late 1980s and early 1990s were the beginning of the neoliberal era and the start of a new wave of multiculturalism in the UK capital. Emerging as part of a golden era that brought in Britpop and the

YBAs, Hajjaj completely reinvented the image of Morocco with his photographs and installations. In this way, his work aligns with that of West African commercial studio photographers, who defined the image of African independence from the centre of marketplaces in Bamako, Ségou, Dakar and Lomé in the 1960s and 1970s. For these photographers, working in the post-independence years, the studio/shop itself – much like Hajjaj's own – was an intrinsic part of the work, where having your photograph taken constituted a social ritual. Continuing the legacy, Hajjaj shoots in an improvised, informal way, using the dynamism of the market and a collaborative spirit to create images that speak of pride and self-determination.

***Hamid's Back*, 2000. Frame: wood with Arabic Sprite cans; print: digital C-type photograph. 136 x 93cm (53.5 x 36.6in)**
This image, taken in Marrakech in 2000, depicts Hamid, a Gnawa musician. A former music promoter who worked in nightclubs in London for more than a decade, Hajjaj frequently features musicians in his photographs and films. For him, the hypnotic, trance-like Gnawa music is a constant source of inspiration. It is a central component of Gnawa culture, which originated in the Moroccan and Algerian Maghreb region and draws on classical Islamic Sufism and African traditions. The musician's traditional dress is framed with Sprite cans, a playful juxtaposition that Hajjaj often employs to connect the local and the global as part of his glorious, nomadic melting pot.

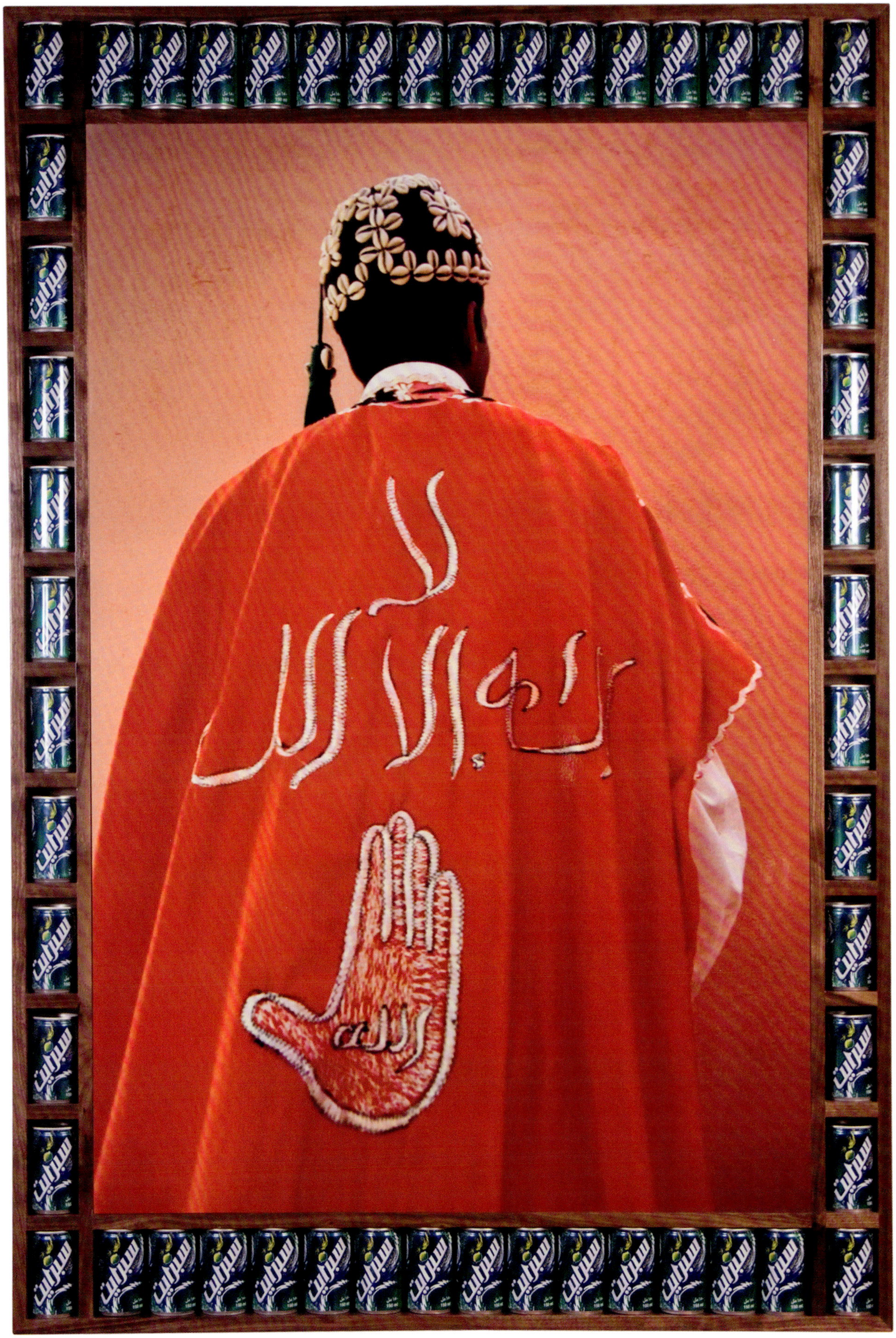

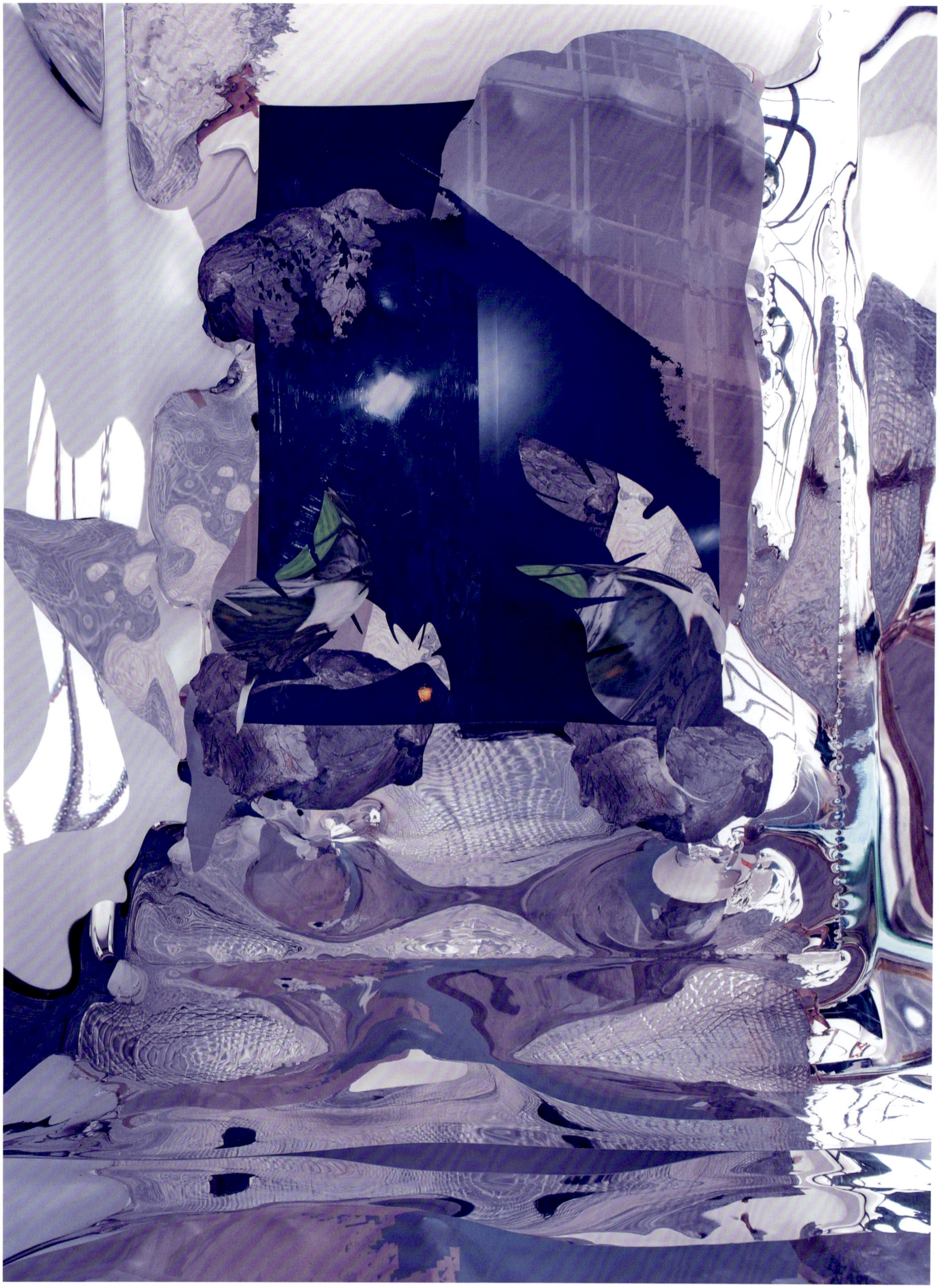

Felicity Hammond

In 1970 the Museum of Modern Art in New York put on *Photography into Sculpture*, the first exhibition exploring 'photographically formed images used in a sculptural or fully dimensional manner'.[1] Curated by Peter C. Bunnell, then curator of the museum's Department of Photography, this groundbreaking group show identified a first generation of mostly North American artists who had turned photography into sculptural forms, using newly available technologies.

Over the intervening decades, the physical material of the photograph has all but disappeared into data, becoming files that flow into a digital stream, but a new generation of photographers continues to carve out a physical space for photography. Key among them is Felicity Hammond, who was born in 1988 and grew up in Birmingham, UK. For Hammond, photography is both content and material: while she contends with the traditional idea of the flat photograph, she brings the unreality of digital imagery into the tangible, three-dimensional realm of craft and sculpture.

To what extent do we 'buy into an image', even knowing, as we do, that it is not real? There are parts of Hammond's work that look instantly familiar – house plants, slabs of sleek marble, delectable slices of citrus fruit – but something bizarre has happened to them. As though steamrolled flat, they drip over their three-dimensional platforms and hang like sodden towels.

The digitally rendered visual language of luxury design and living – so prevalent in cities everywhere – is Hammond's main source material. Moving to east London shortly before the 2012 London Olympics, she witnessed at first hand the rapid changes being made to the urban landscape as old buildings and neighbourhoods were demolished, invariably to be replaced by megalithic residential blocks. Hammond naturally became concerned about the socio-political impact of these profit-driven developments on the local community. Increasing inequality in urban areas is often reinforced by advertising through rendered photography, these simulations playing an important part in the homogenization of architecture and interior design towards a global aesthetic. Hammond perceives this as leading to an urban identity crisis.

In 2015 the artist's first experiment with these themes was the monumental photograph *Capital Growth*.

***Fragment #6* from the series *Arcades*, 2016. Inkjet vinyl print**
This image from *Arcades* demonstrates Hammond's unusual methodology. It is composed of an installation image of a previous work, which itself used imagery printed onto objects; this was then printed onto reflective acrylic, vacuum-formed, rephotographed and reprinted. This laborious process mirrors the way urban spaces are continually redesigned and the interplay between the computer-generated architectural image and its realized, built counterpart.

Comprising a composite of computer-constructed, photoshopped images taken from digital architectural renderings or real estate developers' hoardings and tacked onto a large-scale wooden structure, it is reminiscent of slick billboard advertising. These photo-based sculptures and installations, amalgams of simulated images, make us query the function of photography as a kind of commercial propaganda where, as the artist puts it, 'capital is held in the virtual depiction of space rather than the physical structure itself, and where properties are bought and sold based solely on their digital representations.'[2]

Hammond's photo-based sculptures have become increasingly complex and ambitious over time, turning into illusionistic installations that bathe the spectator-viewer in muted hues of blue or pink, creating the eerie sense of a dystopian future in which progress has halted. Often incorporating industrial materials such as steel, concrete and rubber, these objects occupy a space between function and obsolescence – much like the non-existent built environments represented in corporate marketing.

Hammond builds on a legacy of photographers who have interrogated the photograph's material function. Manipulations have a special significance in her work, addressing themes around urbanization and concepts of progress, and the role of computer-generated imagery in creating a homogeneous, cosmopolitan urban ideal. Working like an archaeologist, Hammond strips away layers to reveal the contradictions that are entangled in these images of aspirational non-places.

***Surface Treatment*, installation view, 2019**
The image opposite is a site-specific photo-collage installation at Cleveland Pools, Bath, the UK's oldest surviving outdoor public swimming pool. Bath is a city that reveres the healing powers of water and has constructed its civic identity around the image of its ancient Roman spa. *Surface Treatment* points to the irony of its predilection for the eponymous Bath stone, a water-permeable building material largely unsuitable for the aquatic nature of the historic city, where there is a constant threat of flooding. Partly submerged in water, Hammond's sculpture could be either sinking or emerging.

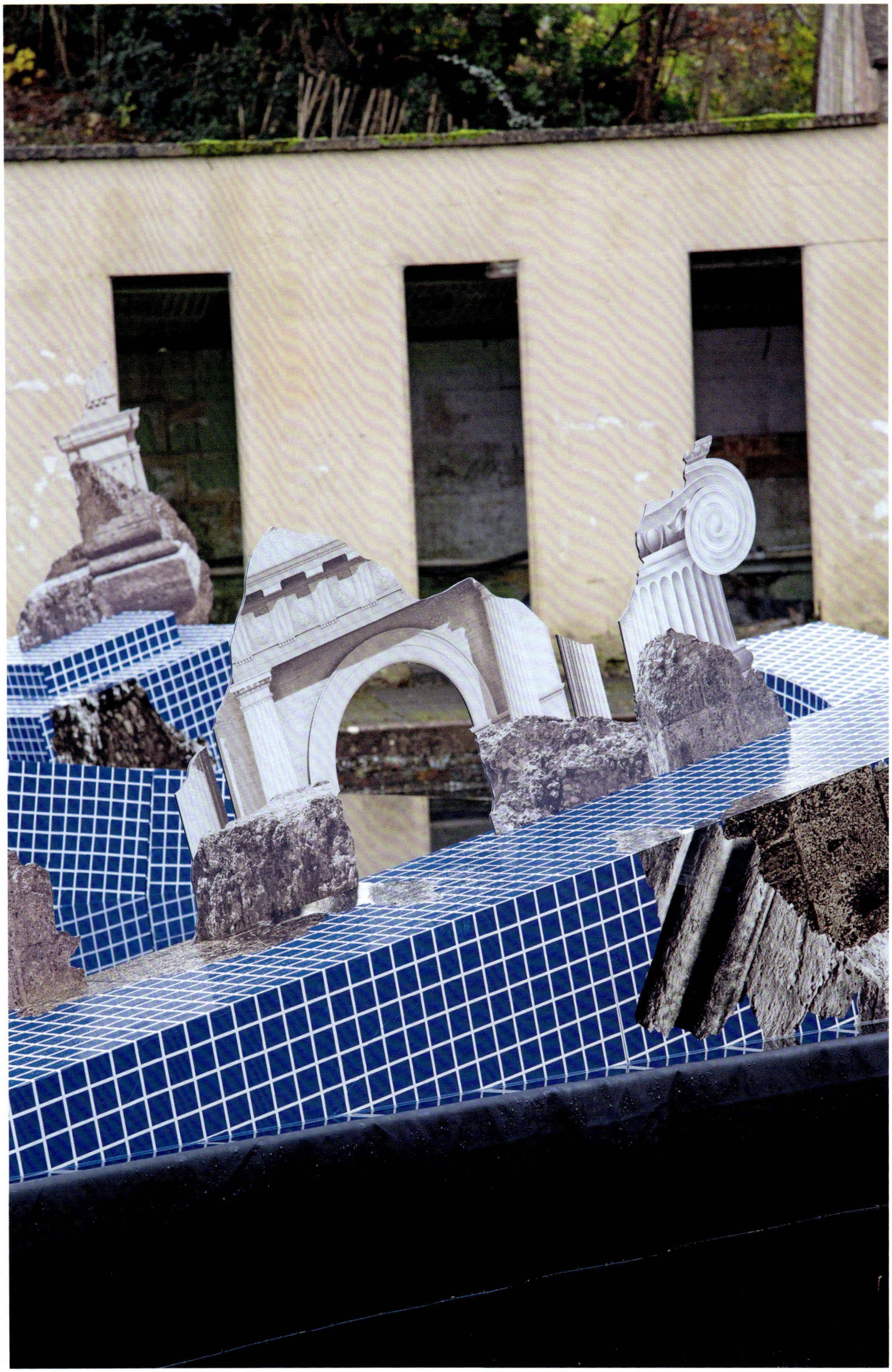

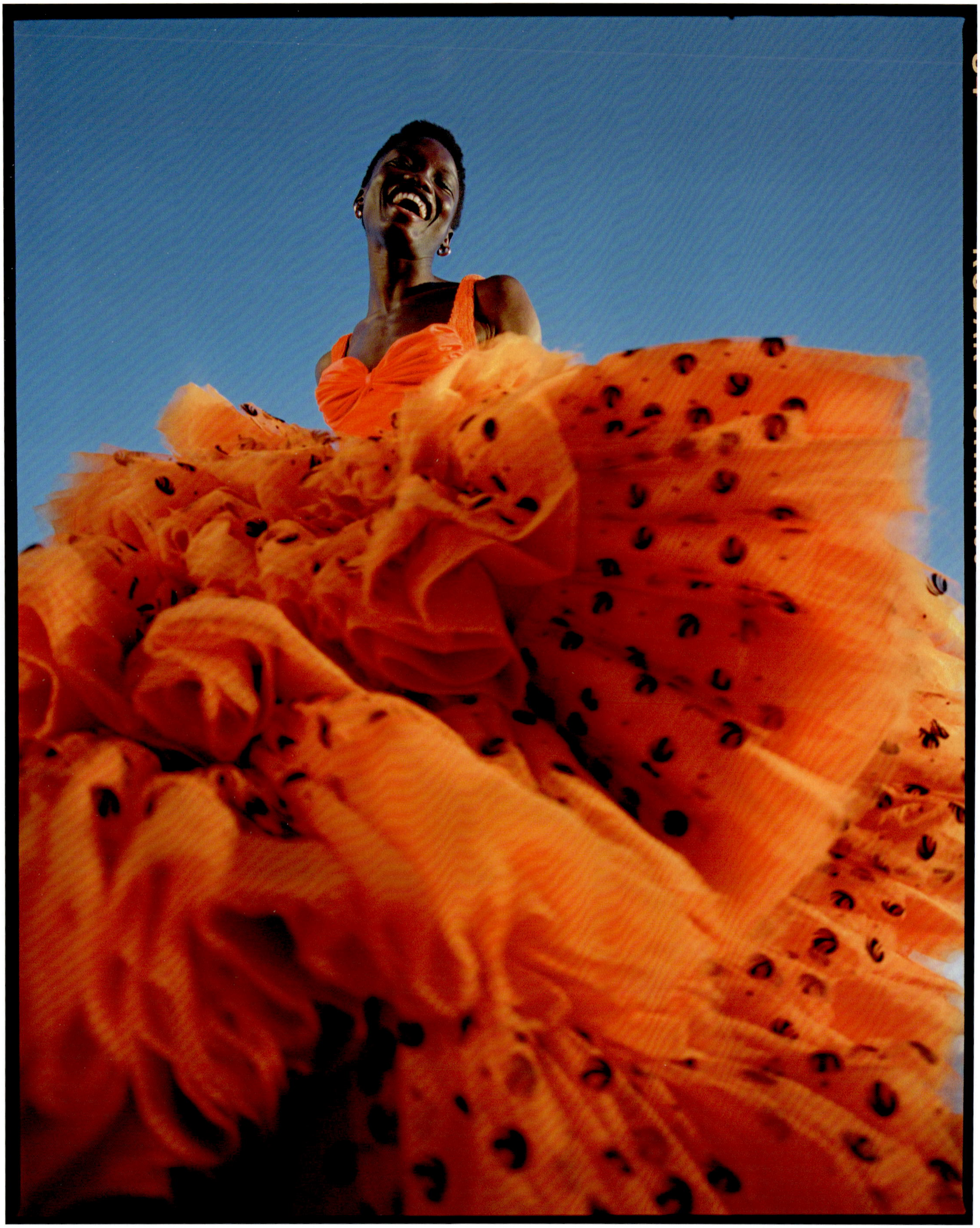

Nadine Ijewere

At the age of twenty-six, Nadine Ijewere made history when she became the first woman of colour to shoot a *Vogue* cover. When the image appeared on the January 2019 issue of British *Vogue*, her place in the history of visual culture was confirmed. It also marked Ijewere's perspective as a leader in fashion photography; by the end of that year she could claim her rank among world's leading fashion photographers.

Growing up in the multicultural metropolis of London in the late 1990s and 2000s with Nigerian and Jamaican heritage was part of Ijewere's daily lived experience – yet the obvious ethnic diversity she saw around her was not reflected in the mainstream media. Vexed by the fashion industry's narrow representation of beauty, and the feeling of dislocation that comes from not seeing yourself reflected in the world, Ijewere quickly adopted the attitude that in order to create change, you have to be able to see change.

Instagram was a tool for Ijewere early on in her career, as a platform for asserting her personal vision of the beauty of people of colour, who have been underrepresented in fashion and visual culture. Major global brands started to take notice and success followed soon after Ijewere graduated from the London College of Fashion, with commissions to shoot campaigns for Stella McCartney, Dior, Nike, Gap, See by Chloe, and Valentino, as well as editorials for American *Vogue*, *Garage* magazine, the *Wall Street Journal* – and another cover for British *Vogue*.

For the Stella McCartney campaign, Ijewere travelled to her paternal grandparents' place of birth, Lagos, where she street-cast models and explored different aspects of contemporary everyday life in the city through fashion and self-expression. Some of the photographs also appear in the series *9-ja_17* (2017), illustrating the way Ijewere introduces her personal story and vision within her work, and in an industry that has historically erased the individuality of both women and people of colour.

Ijewere's models are part of her strategy to subvert a system controlled by exclusionary standards. Casting has become increasingly important for a new generation of socially conscious fashion photographers, and a fundamental aspect of Ijewere's practice is her mix of muses – professional models as well as those she casts from the street or Instagram. She has repeatedly emphasized, however, that she does not want to simply create new ideals for beauty or construe new stereotypes and that celebrating difference should not devolve into

Fashion editorial for *i-D* magazine, published September 2018
This image embodies the spirit of Ijewere's fashion work, where the status quo is confidence and happiness is the prevalent mood. Being comfortable in your own skin is not easy when facing systemic racism and prejudice, but Ijewere creates a space for people of colour to celebrate their identity and feel good. Bursting with infectious energy, this picture also demonstrates many of the stylistic signatures for which Ijewere has become known: shooting exclusively on film, using minimal backdrops and maximizing the contrasts between colours.

dictating dialectics of taste. It is impossible to categorize the kind of person Ijewere photographs, beyond the fact they are people who have not been included in the language of fashion before. In 2020, in acknowledgement of all of these achievements, the International Center of Photography in the US named Ijewere as an Honoree of its prestigious Infinity Award.

While embracing the fantasy and pleasure of illusion that are always present in fashion photography, Ijewere also proves how important the medium is as an arbiter of social norms and culture. As a genre of art it remains relatively overlooked by academics, but fashion photography has a pervasive influence and appeal, and Ijewere has shown it to be one of the most dynamic forces for reinvention in contemporary popular culture.

***Untitled* from the series *Tallawah*, 2019**
In 2019 Ijewere visited Jamaica for the first time, which gave her an opportunity to look at the connections between her own heritage, the Jamaican diaspora and contemporary life on the Caribbean island. This image comes from the series she shot in Port Antonio, Ocho Rios and south-east London in collaboration with the hairstylist Jawara Wauchope. The photographs explore expressions of identity across different generations through hair. The title of the series, *Tallawah*, is patois for strong-willed and fearless, both qualities that Ijewere believes are intrinsic in the Jamaican community.

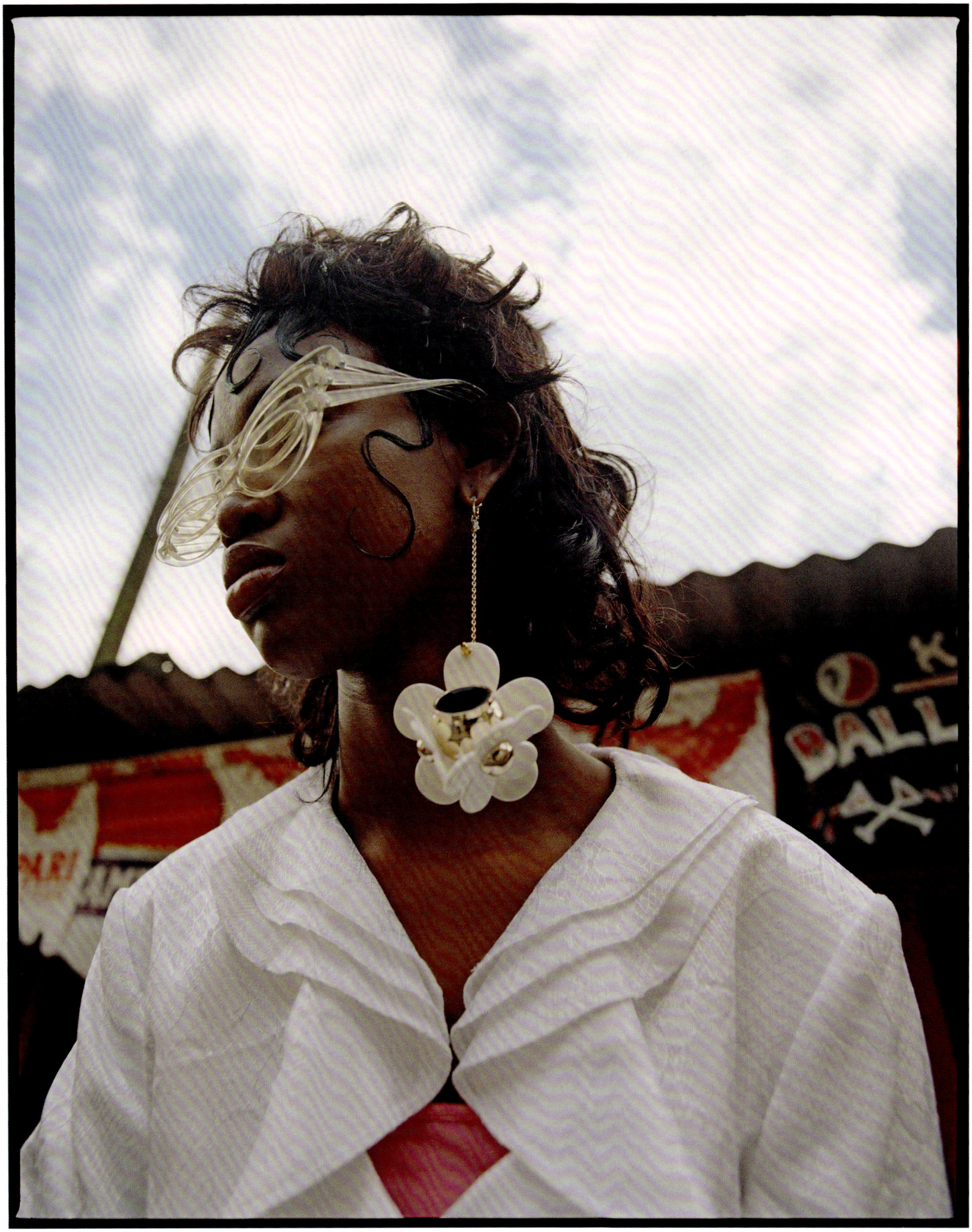

Graciela Iturbide

'I do not like Mexican stereotypes, but unfortunately many photographers who come from abroad and who have not understood my country fall into this error,' Graciela Iturbide once said.[1] Undoing the damaging stereotypes created by the camera has been a constant motivation for Iturbide, whose work spans more than five decades.

Iturbide herself has come to understand her heritage through a long and profound exploration of her country. She began on the streets of Mexico City, where she was born in 1942 and raised, the eldest of thirteen children in a conservative Catholic family. She then went on to live with indigenous communities of Seri Indians in the Sonoran Desert and Zapotec Indians in Juchitán de Zaragoza, Oaxaca, whom she spent a decade photographing, between 1979 and 1988, along with the Mexican migrant community of East Los Angeles. The camera, according to Iturbide, has been a pretext for learning and discovery. Her vast body of work – vignettes of life not only in Mexico but also in Panama, where she took photographs in working-class communities in the aftermath of the military coup in 1968, Ecuador, Cuba, Argentina and Venezuela, as well as India and the USA – is an intricate study of mystery and surprise propelled by enduring curiosity.

Iturbide initially studied film-making at the Centro Universitario de Estudios Cinematográficos. In 1972 she found a job as an assistant to the influential modernist photographer Manuel Alvarez Bravo and her passion for photography began there. Iturbide became one of the founding members of the Mexican Council of Photography, which was established in 1976 to forge a collective vision for Latin American photography through events, discussions and exhibitions. Although she has been a leading figure in Latin American art, Iturbide's work has been less celebrated in the USA and Europe. Despite a solo exhibition at the Centre Pompidou in Paris in 1982, it was only in 2008 that she was recognized with the Hasselblad Foundation International Award in Photography, becoming the first Mexican woman to receive the prestigious accolade. Her first major exhibition in the USA, at the Museum of Fine Arts, Boston, was in 2019 and focused on the pictures of Mexico taken between 1969 and 2007. The exhibition opened at a time of increased political tension and anti-Mexican rhetoric in the USA, serving as an important reminder of the danger of stereotypes and as a counter to heightened racism directed at Mexicans.

***Mujeres Seris, Desierto de Sonora, Mexico* from the series *Los que viven en la arena*, 1979**

The depiction of women is a major theme in Iturbide's photography. She has redefined the way indigenous women are seen, showing the importance of their role within different communities, and depicting them with majesty, power and grace. This photograph of a group of Seri Indian women, taken in the Sonora Desert in 1979, is part of one of Iturbide's best-known series. She spent a month and half with the semi-nomadic community of five hundred people in Punta Chueca, close to the US border, commissioned by the National Indigenous Institute. At the time, the Seri's traditional way of life was changing under the influence of capitalism from the USA, yet they were also determined to keep their independence and sense of community. This is captured in the dress of the women, contrasting with the car and the can of fuel.

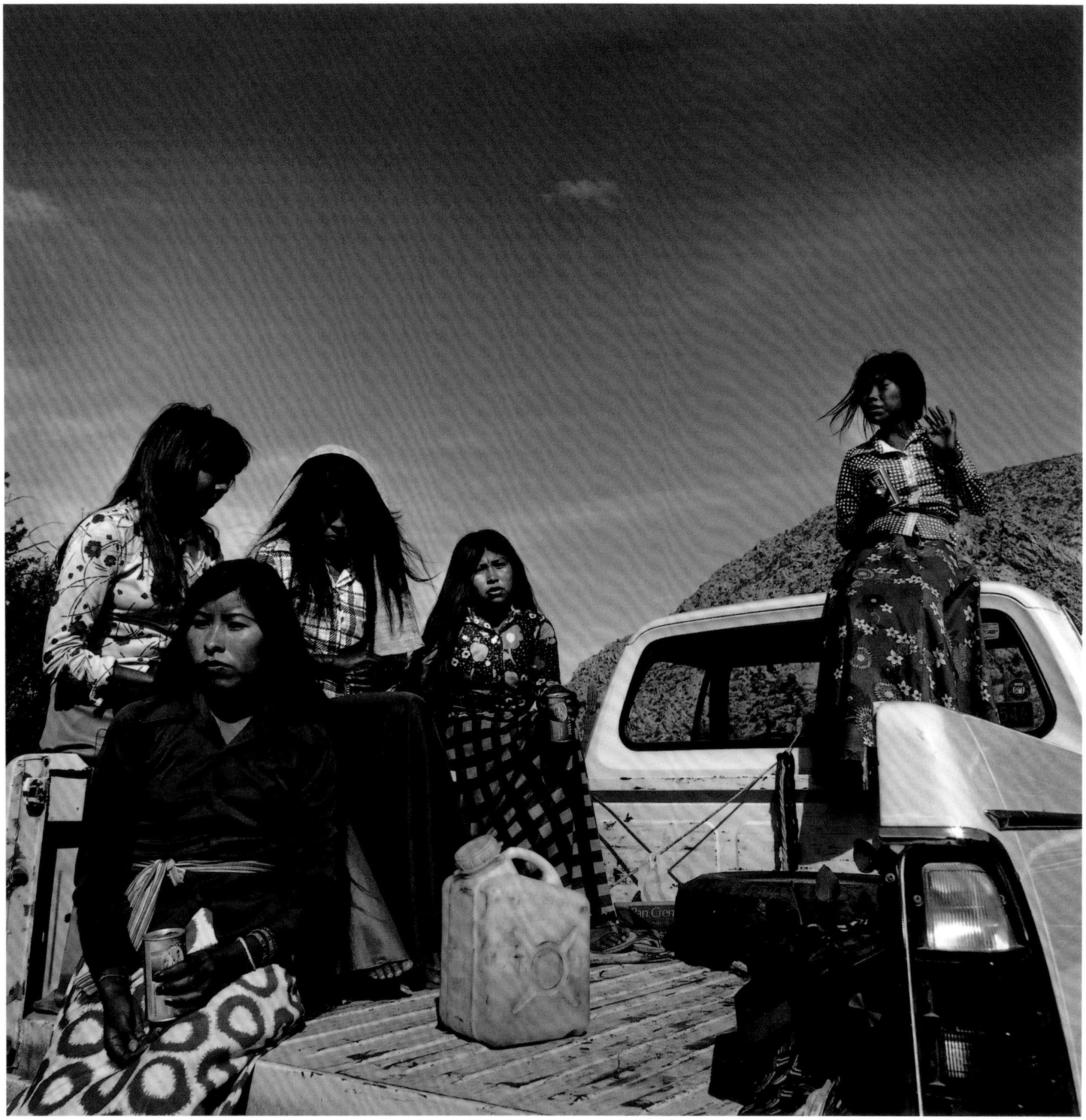

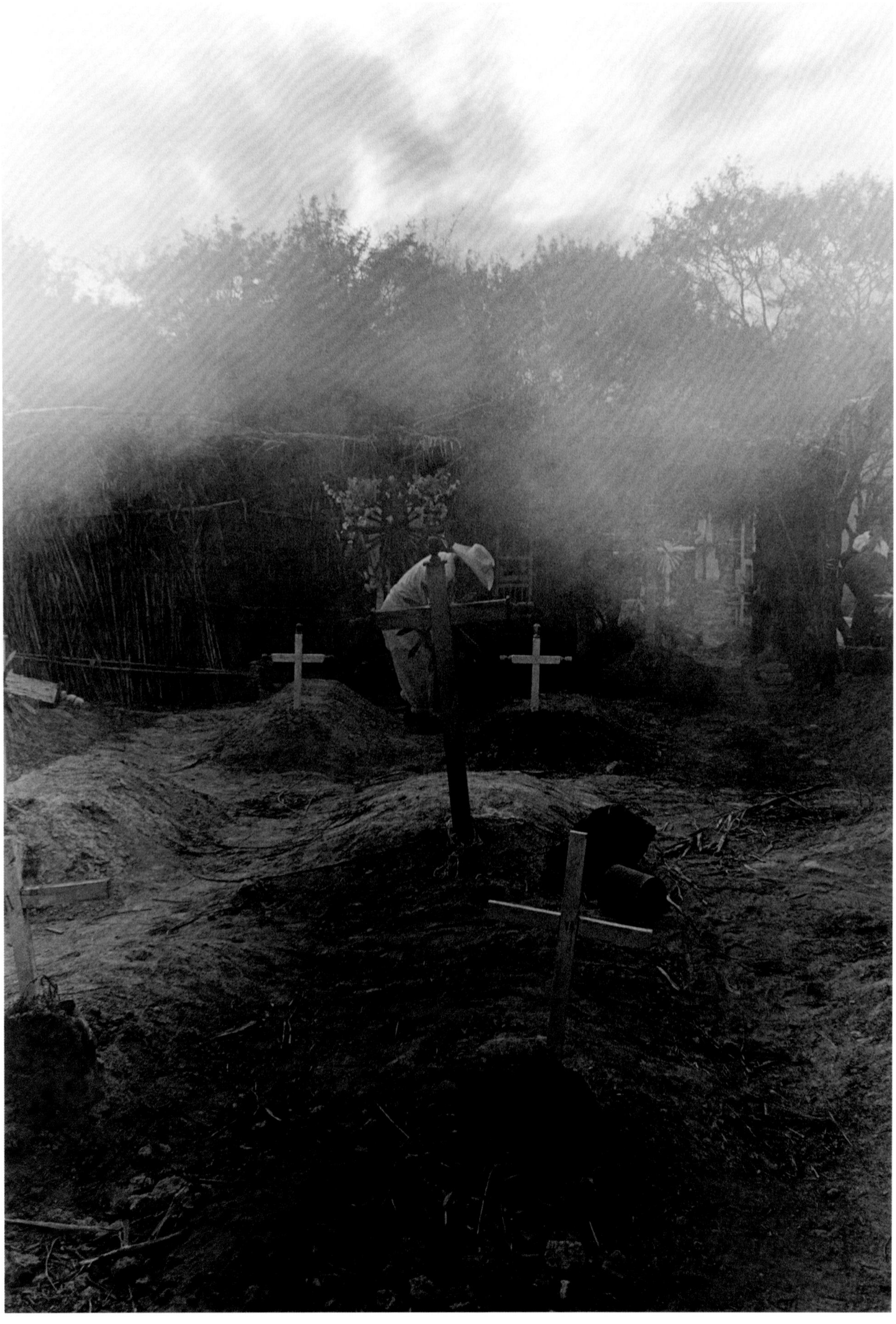

From her earliest works, Iturbide has been interested in uncanny associations and in creating her own symbolism through recurrent motifs, reflecting her interest in ritual, religious practices and customs. Her religious upbringing instilled a profound fascination with the performative aspects of spiritualism. The sudden death of her second daughter, Claudia, at the age of six compounded Iturbide's interest in how cultures deal with mortality in particular.

Iturbide's composite portrait of Mexico shows a place that is not monolithic but instead is geographically vast and ethnically diverse, a hybrid of ancient indigenous and colonial cultures, rich with symbolism and contrasts, where life and death are present in every moment. Iturbide addresses stereotypes about Mexico – Day of the Dead ceremonies, Frida Kahlo, folklore and fiestas – but never from the expected point of view. Dignity is another quality that Iturbide has frequently emphasized. The immense respect she shows for her human subjects is clear. She doesn't avoid political subtexts, such as the poverty and hardship experienced by many of the people she photographs, but her subjects are proud, not pitiful, autonomous and independent.

Iturbide has also always chosen to shoot on black and white film, giving all of her works a sense beyond time and place that contends with the colourful exoticism associated with Mexico. As she moves between portraits, landscapes and street photography, in a dance that is dreamlike and macabre, the black and white film unifies all of her subjects and encourages a different kind of engagement, moving away from social documentary towards a deeply personal and transcendental 'poetic vision'.[2]

***Día de Muertos, Chilac, Puebla, Mexico, 1992*, 1992**
Death plays a central role in Mexican culture and is ever-present in Iturbide's photographs, in particular the pictures she has taken in Mexico. Iturbide has continued to document the different ways of dealing with death across the country, through funeral rites, burial ceremonies and traditions. The importance of symbolism and iconography is also apparent in this photograph, taken at a cemetery in Chilac, Puebla. Whether looking up at the sky or down to the earth – as we do in this picture – we are reminded of the proximity of this life to the next.

***Mexico quiero conocerte* from the series *Muerte*, 1975**
A human skull, wearing a helmet adorned with a swastika, grins back from behind a shop window. Next to it, a stuffed animal stands rigid on the floor. The silhouette of a pair of legs belonging to a passer-by is reflected in the glass. A banner stuck to the top of the window reads, 'MEXICO… ¡quiero conocerte!' ('Mexico … I want to get to know you!') In this apparently desultory display, photographed in 1975 in Chiapas, Iturbide captures her vision of Mexico in a single image: what is dead appears to be alive, spirits and flesh cross paths, and everything is imbued with an unmistakable air of mystery.

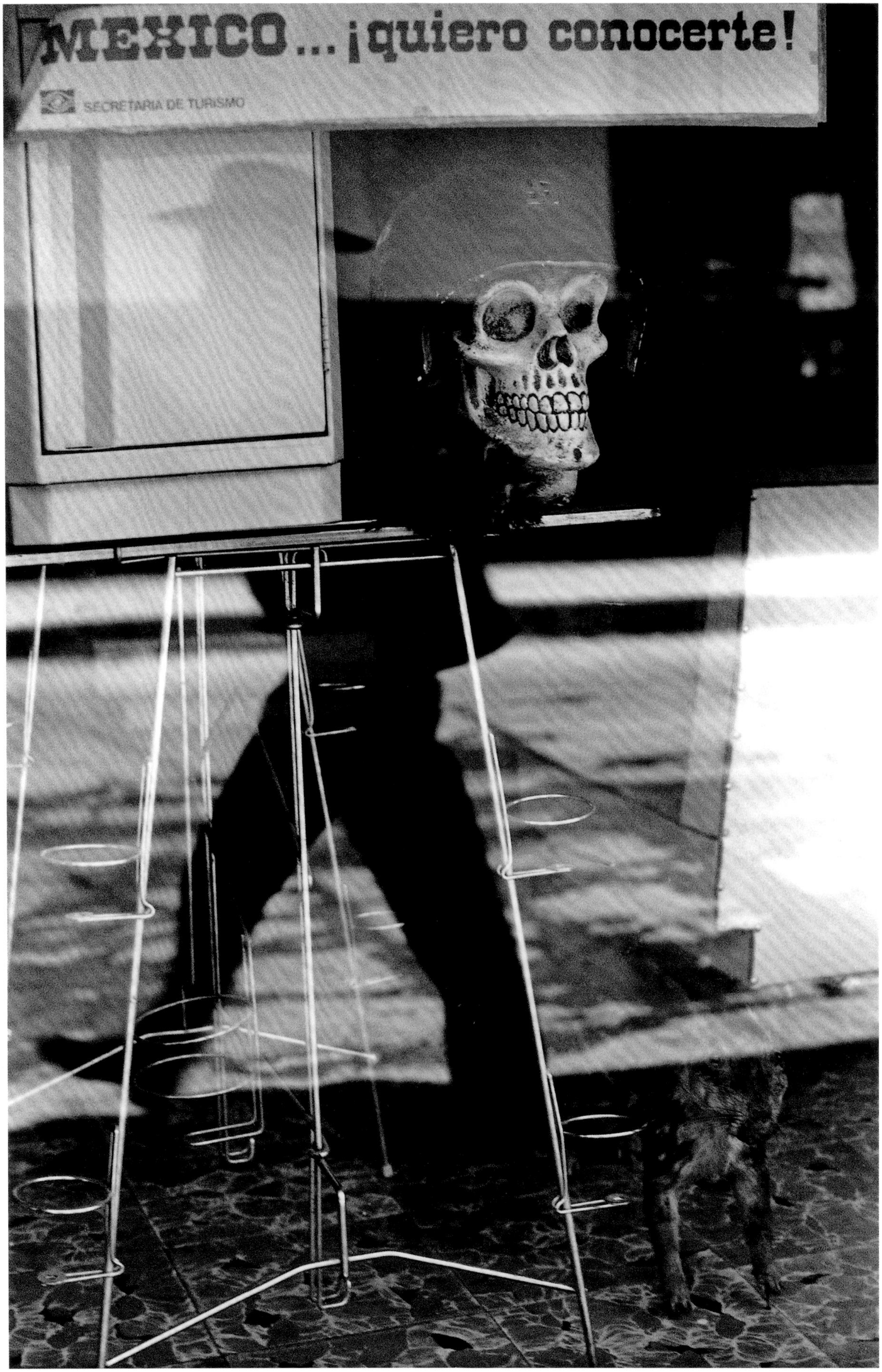
MEXICO... ¡quiero conocerte!
SECRETARIA DE TURISMO

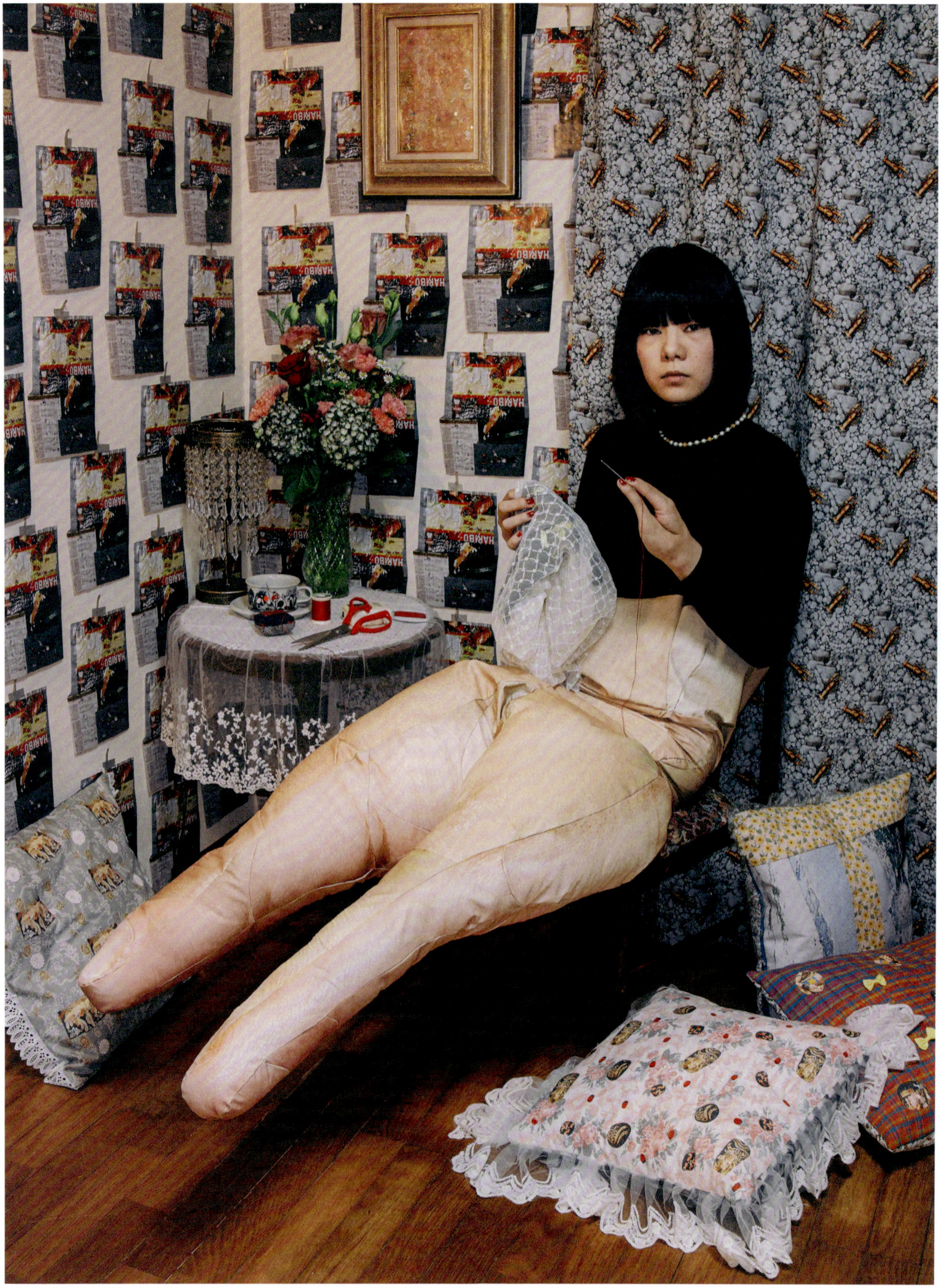
HARIBO

Mari Katayama

bystander #014 **from the series** ***bystander*****, 2016**
This self-portrait, one of a series taken in Katayama's childhood home, reveals various aspects of the artist's practice. She poses with a needle as she creates one of the many *objets d'art* that appear in her work, while wearing a costume she has made – a large, soft sculpture representing her cleft left hand, worn as legs. Although she spent many years confined to this space while growing up in order to escape the bullying she suffered at school, it was during this time that she learned the craft skills that would provide her with solace and a way to connect with the outside world.

At the beginning of the TED talk she gave in Kobe, Japan, in 2015, Mari Katayama spent five minutes on the stage fixing custom-made high-heeled shoes to her prosthetic legs. The gesture was a statement not about her disability, but about her creativity. The high heels that she had specially manufactured in Tokyo gave her confidence, she explained, in art as a way to connect with others like her, a tool to bridge the impossibility of communication and the disconnect between the physical and our individual sense of self. She has been successful at doing just that, for her art has received acclaim in Japan and abroad. At sixteen, she was awarded first place in the Gunma Biennale for Young Artists, and in 2012 she was the recipient of the Grand Prize at the Tokyo Marunouchi Art Award. Her inclusion in the group show *My Body, Your Voice*, at the Mori Art Museum in Tokyo in 2016, brought international attention to Katayama's work, and she has since exhibited at museums and galleries across Europe and the USA. In 2019 she participated in the 58th Venice Biennale.

Katayama was born in 1987 in Saitama with a rare condition known as tibial hemimelia, which affects the development of the bones in the lower leg. Aged nine, she decided to have both legs amputated to enable her to walk with prosthetic limbs. Her limbs, decorated, reconstructed or bare, have become her preferred material, but she emphasizes that neither disability nor diversity is the subject of her art: 'I just want to present the experiences that I have through my body, meaning the way I see the world, society, and the atmosphere around us.'[1]

The relentless bullying Katayama experienced while growing up, she has said, shaped her practice more profoundly than her disability. The perceptions and prejudice that made it impossible to establish relationships drove her deep into the world of the visual, beyond the pain of words and being misunderstood. She began to seek non-verbal ways to express her inner world by making things. Used to sewing her own clothes from a young age, Katayama was already skilled at crafting. When she began to stage her first self-portraits in her bedroom for sharing on MySpace, she introduced her own handmade props and designs, which have remained an intrinsic part of her practice ever since, whether configured within installations or photographs.

While Katayama's early works dealt more directly with her childhood memories, and feelings of isolation, anxiety, pain and vulnerability, her later works, such as *you're mine* (2014), *bystander* (2016) and *cannot turn back the clock* (2017), characterize themes of fragility, love, identity and motherhood in a wider cultural context, reflected in part by placing her body in outdoor settings (and often, symbolically, between land and water, a reference to both her star sign, Cancer, and her feeling of belonging to an in-between space). Fantasy and role play are important aspects of Katayama's self-portraits, allowing her to reclaim the carefree games of a childhood she could never enjoy and to construct her own identity. Katayama's hands-on objectification of her body – dismantling it, decorating it, rearranging it – allows her to re-present her identity without limits and in limitless ways, uniting the disparate parts of herself into an emboldened celebration of her own body, not restricted by the way the world defines her.

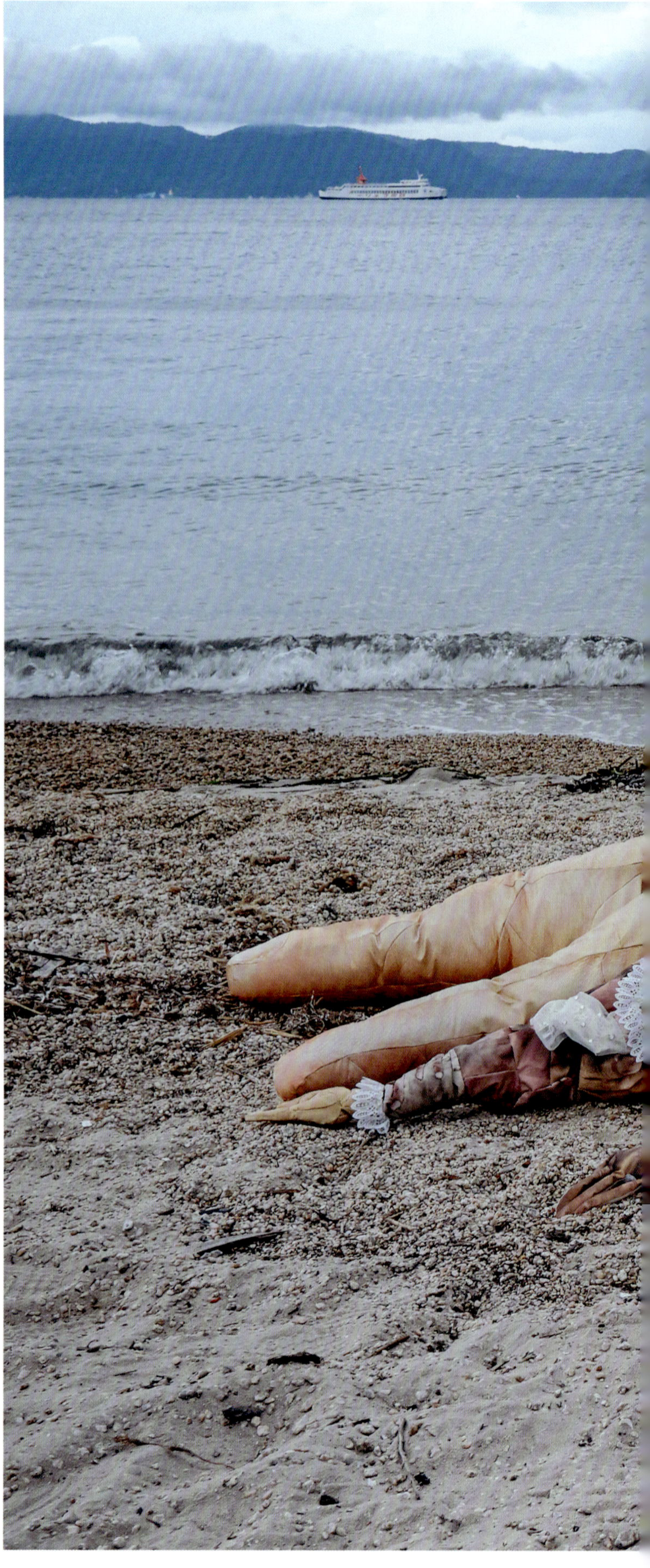

shadow puppet #014 **from the series** ***shadow puppet*****, 2016**
A residency on the island of Naoshima in the Seto Inland Sea brought Katayama into contact with the traditional, all-female puppet theatre Naoshima Onna Bunraku. As the large folk puppets typically used in productions do not have legs, Katayama became interested in the hands and began to create her own troupe of stuffed, sewn arms. In this image she is seen reclining on a beach in Naoshima in a classical pose that recalls Botticelli's *Birth of Venus*, while the arms are arranged around her like tentacles. With its erotic atmosphere, the photograph may also be read as a reimagining of Hokusai's iconic *The Dream of the Fisherman's Wife*, an exploration of the multifaceted nature of desire and female sexuality.

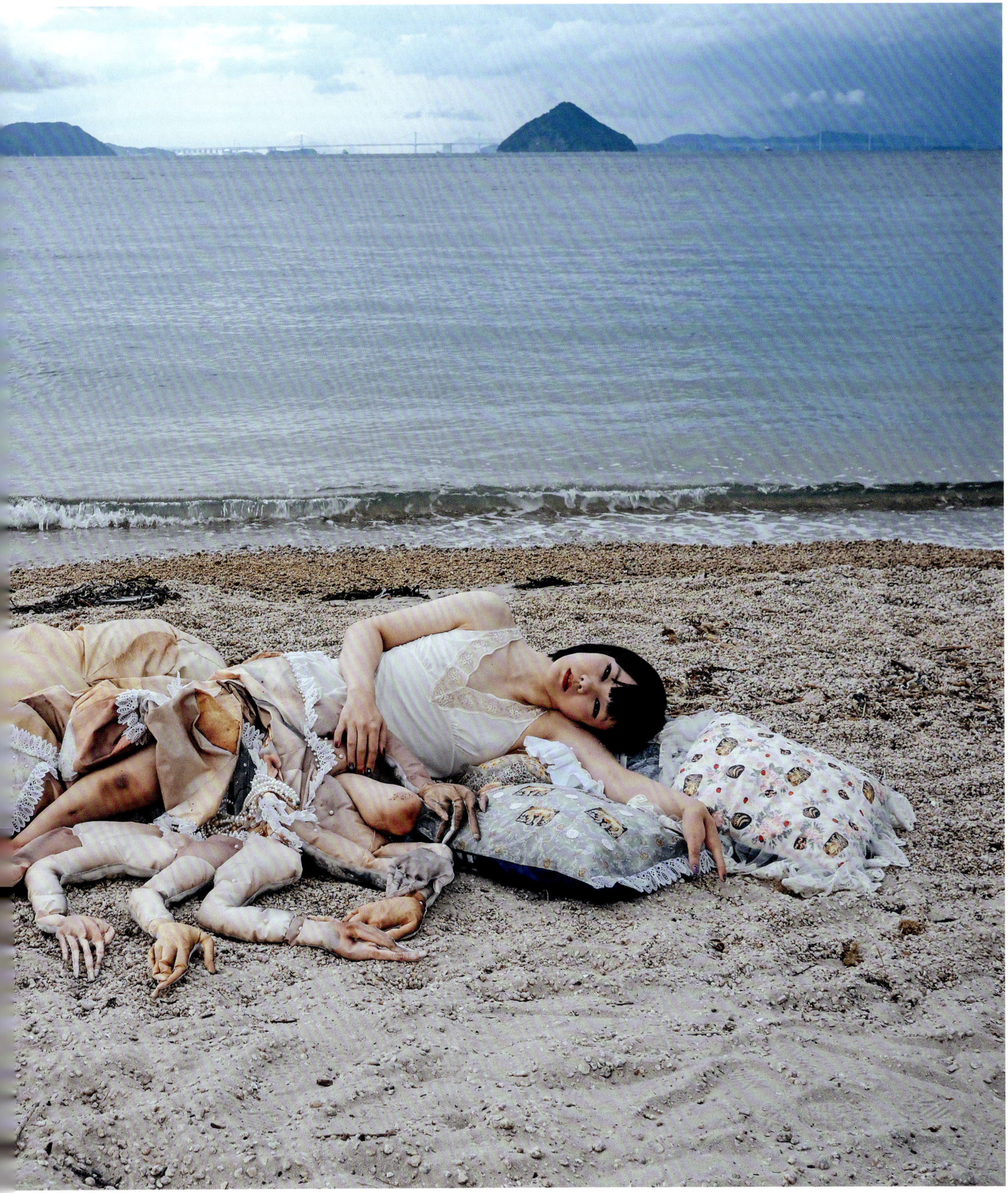

Keyezua

'I take a risk in creating images that are often not following my society's ideal, but somehow I became fearless,' Keyezua reflects.[1] Femininity, feminism, the physical body and the way it is controlled by social attitudes and custom are themes foregrounded in the artist's striking photographs. Keyezua, who was born in Luanda in 1988, finds in her work a freedom that does not always exist in the real world.

One of the artist's earliest works was *Stone Orgasms* (2015), a response to the genital mutilation of more than 200 million girls and women worldwide. In the photographs, the various layers of the digital palimpsest are left visible to reflect the way a woman's identity is imposed upon. The classical poses of statues and portrait paintings represent the ideal woman according to art history; their faces are covered by stones and rocks to connote the weight of oppression, while superimposed medical depictions of internal organs allude to the way women's bodies are being dismantled through physical abuse.

The intrusions of culture and custom on the physical body have continued to be a theme in Keyezua's work since she graduated from the Royal Academy of Art in The Hague in 2015 and returned to live in the Angolan capital. In *Fortia* ('Force'), a 2017 series of performance-based portraits of a masked character in a voluminous red dress, Keyezua wanted 'to visualize empowering images of life after physical disability. I wanted to create images that were not obvious and that would not give the viewer the pleasure of being right about their assumptions.' The work was inspired by her father, who suffered from diabetes, had both legs amputated when Keyezua was a teenager and died soon after. 'His disability felt like the end of the existence of my father as a strong man,' she has reflected.[2] *Fortia* deals with notions of physical strength, power and their relationship to perceptions of masculinity, subverted through an imagined ritual journey undertaken by an anonymous female figure. Every material detail in these pictures has a specific meaning and history: for example, the handmade masks were designed and created by a group of disabled men who practised traditional crafts in Luanda. The protagonist's poses were also informed by these men and the artist's conversations with them about how they move, so that the series interweaves their stories with her father's in a unique and empathetic way.

Paramount in Keyezua's work is her position as an African woman who enacts her own narratives that seek, by addressing stereotypes, to empower those who have been 'othered'. Her works imagine an Afro-positive future that aligns with contemporary discourses on pan-Africanism, 'an ideology that supports the solidarity of Africans worldwide', as political activist Thomas Wakiaga defined it.[3]

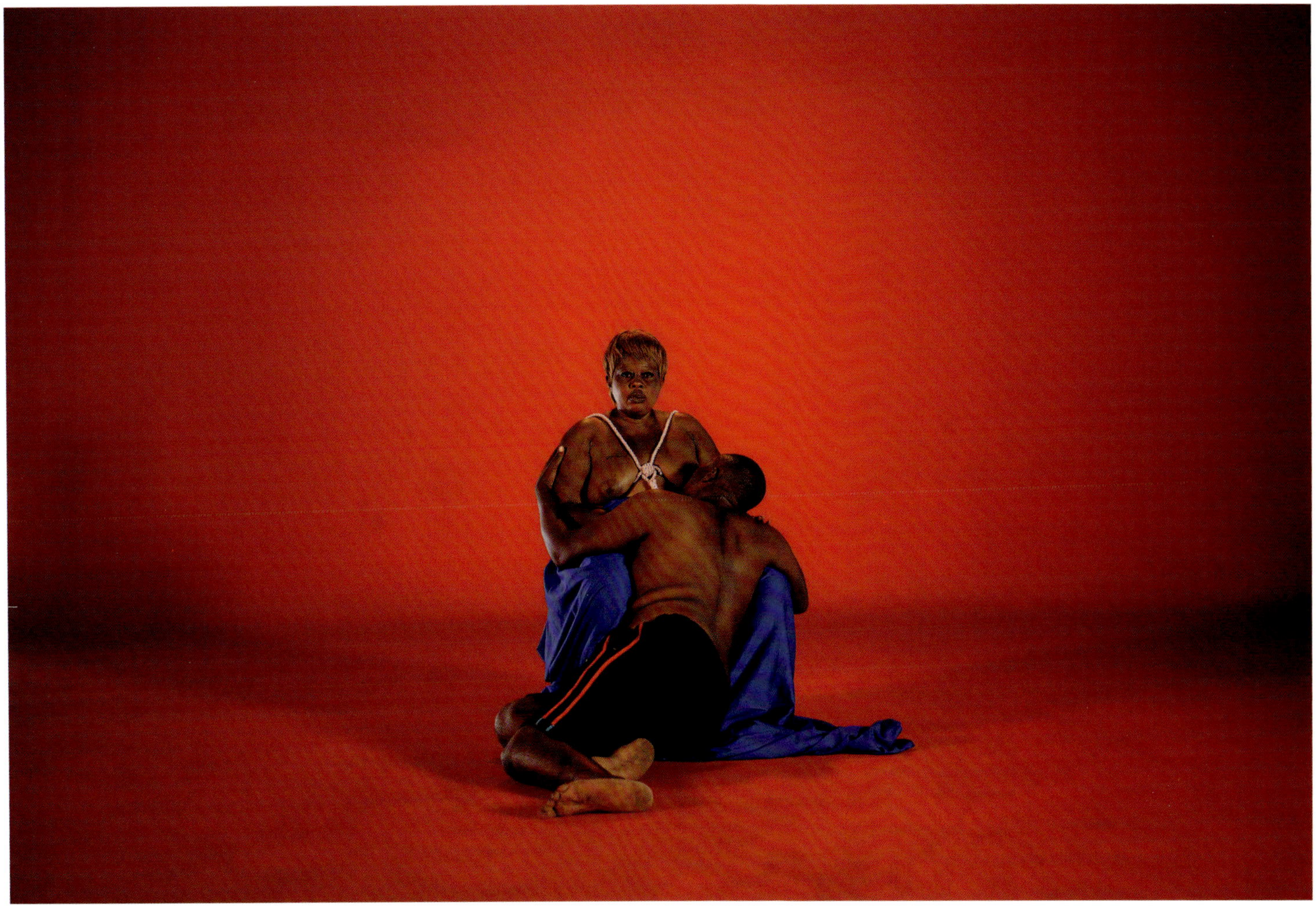

From the series *Floating Nightmares*, 2018
'We nurture the men that start wars with our bodies and we survive to tell our stories,' says Keyezua of this image,[4] part of her series *Floating Nightmares*. It is an extended piece of research into the lives of refugee women commissioned by BredaPhoto and curated by Azu Nwagbogu. The constructed images respond to a world dominated by men in which the female body is abused and brutalized, and used as a weapon in war. In this image, the artist asked a woman to pose with a man she appears to be breastfeeding, to reflect on the role of women in a patriarchy where men will later dominate their bodies.

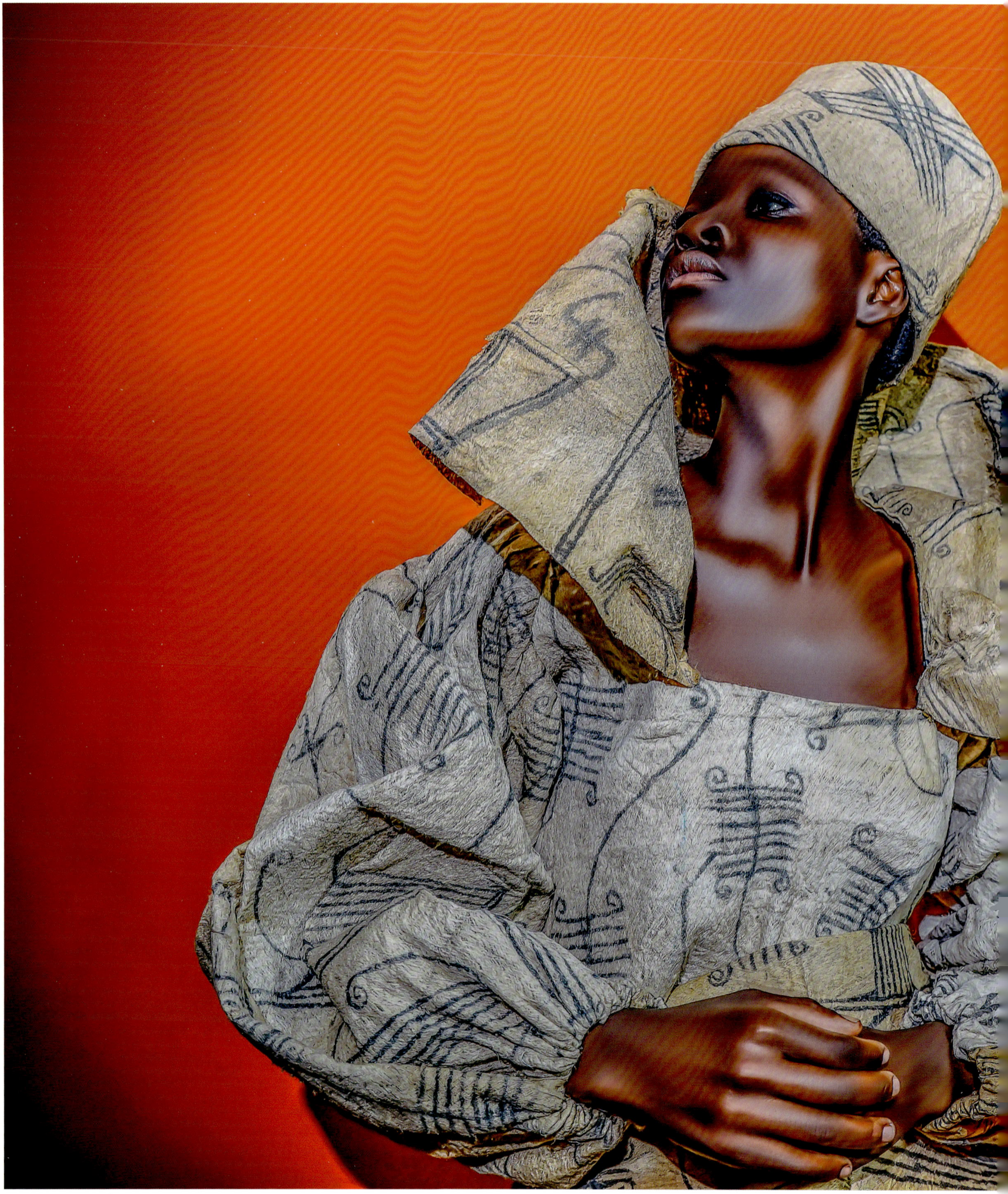

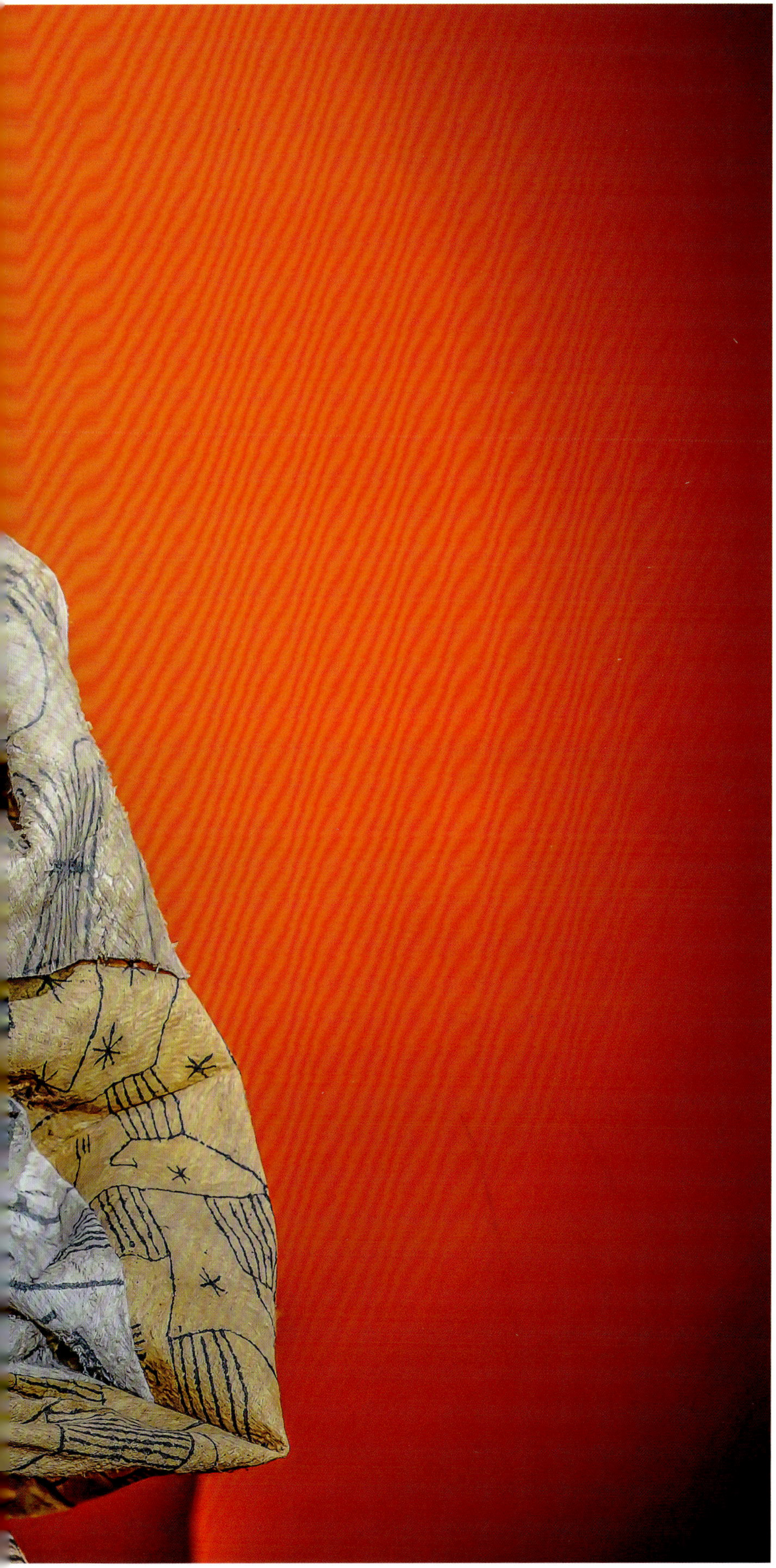

Royal Generation 02 **from the series *Royal Generation*, 2016. Giclée print on rag baryta paper, 84.6 x 118.9cm (33⅜ x 46⅞ in)**
In this image, a female model wears clothes made using ancient Angolan basket-weaving techniques and fabric prepared in the traditional way from fig tree bark. The image shows Keyezua's ongoing dialogue with Angolan craft and design, incorporating elements of both into her photographs. *Royal Generation* is both a celebration and a critique, for, as the artist notes, many African designers incorporate textiles manufactured by companies such as Vlisco, the Dutch firm established in the mid-nineteenth century that appropriated and has since profited from designs inspired by Africa – promoted as the 'new Africa' in a colonial narrative. It is important, Keyezua explains, to reclaim these narratives about production and creativity. As she says, 'Africa always had enough resources to reinvent and tell their fashion stories without any influence from the West.'[5]

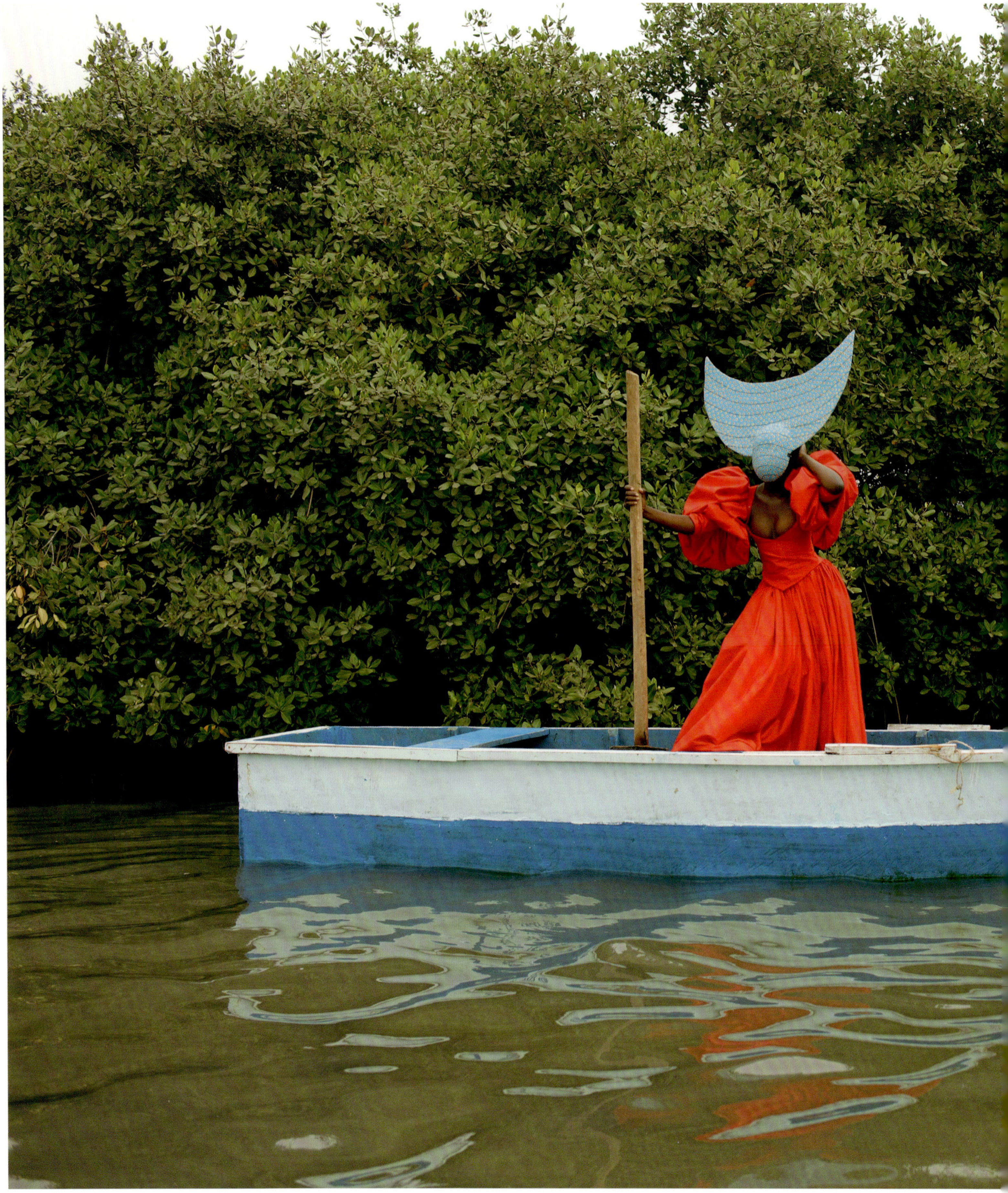

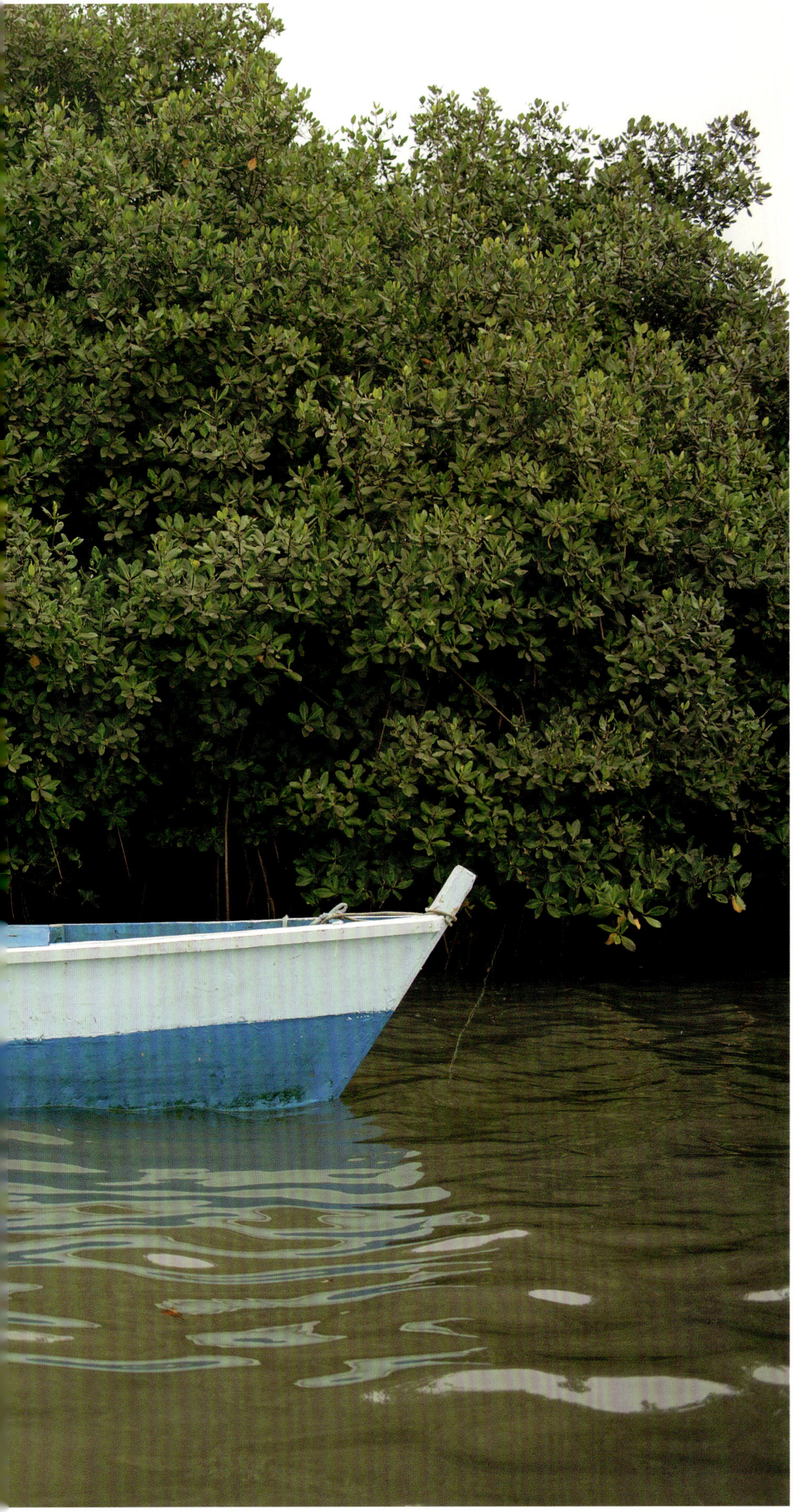

***Sailing Back to Africa as a Dutch Woman, 2017* from the series *Fortia*, 2017. Giclée print on Hahnemühle bamboo paper, 29.5 x 44cm (11 ⅝ x 17 ⅜ in)**
This image is taken from the part performance, part photographic work *Fortia*, in which Keyezua deals with themes around the body and disability and confronts her own personal journey, following her father's death and her migration to the Netherlands and back to Angola. The shape of the mask worn here refers to the traditional Dutch head covering worn by a *melkmeisje* or milkmaid. The image speaks of integration, the adaptation of immigrants and the process of social acculturation.

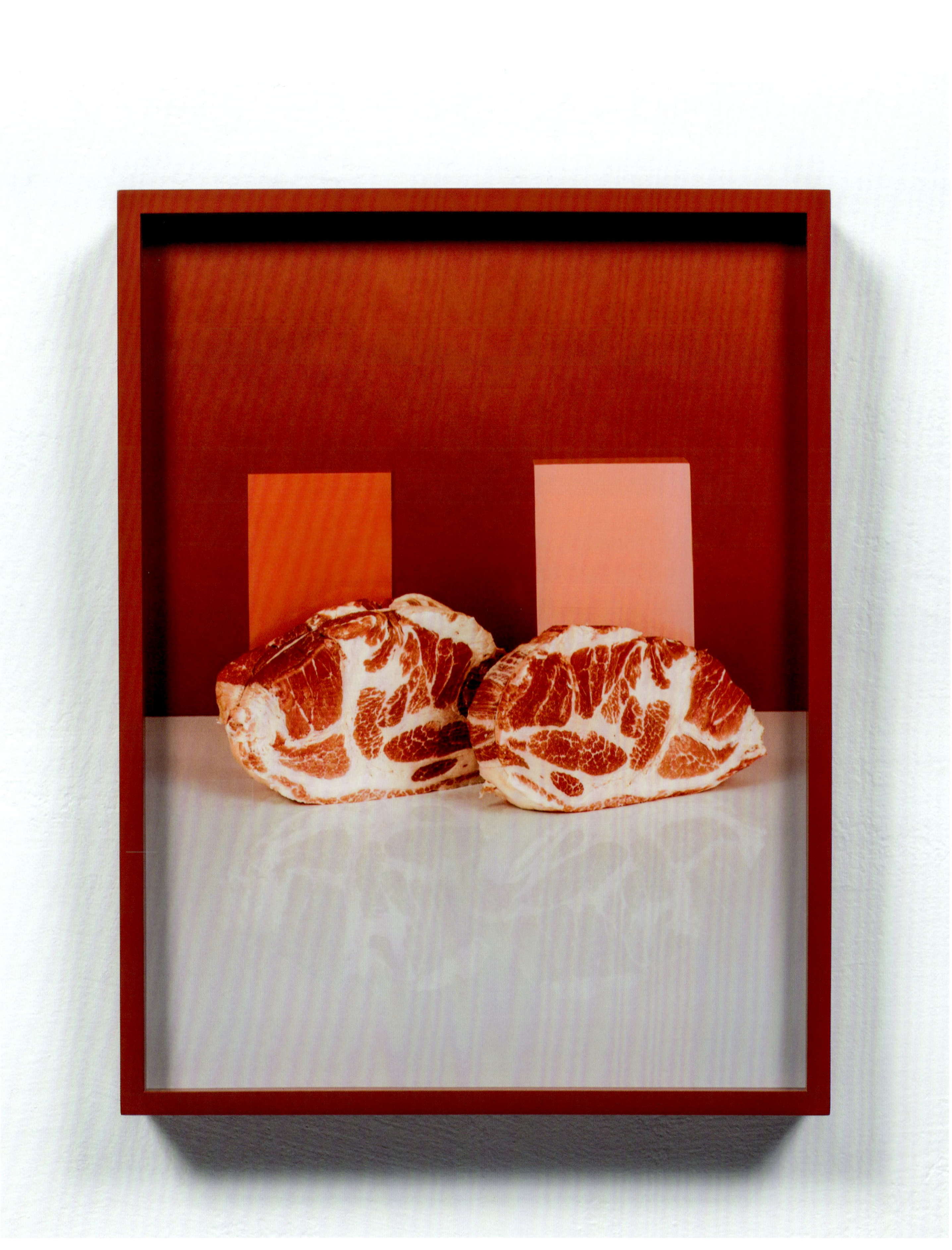

Elad Lassry

What does a picture mean now? Elad Lassry has been asking this question for more than a decade, using the most ubiquitous, familiar and everyday photographs as his source material in order to examine the place of photography today. When is a photograph an object and when is it an image, and does the object or the image have more control over our viewing experience? Lassry's enquiries into image-making have taken him right to the heart of the relationship between objects and their representation, and the way we are made to look. The artist explains his motivation thus: 'I started making photographs mostly interested in what they are not.'[1]

It is not easy to do something new with a photograph of a mushroom or a pork chop, but that's where the magic lies in Lassry's work. Lassry might not even be a photographer at all – as he said in a 2015 interview, 'Whether it's photography or not isn't exactly what's at stake for me.'[2] Rooted in a postmodernist approach, he revisits the things we may feel we have seen a thousand times before – still lifes of food, celebrity portraits, household utensils, cats, birds, beauty products – and reinvents them. To his mind, the more generic and clichéd they are, the better. His aim is to wrest the picture from the ways it has always been viewed – 'a subject fighting its history',[3] as he describes the process. Where he feels that subjects have been exhausted but 'deserve another chance' or 'need another circulation',[4] Lassry might turn to the moving image to perform his investigations. He asks us to start over again with these pictures, to embark on a new relationship with what we see, where authorship and place are ambiguous and surprise can surface in the photographic non-space.

Born in Tel Aviv in 1977, Lassry moved to the USA at the end of the 1990s to study film at the California Institute of the Arts and completed an MFA at the University of Southern California, where he was taught by Sharon Lockhart. The proximity of the movie industry and his exposure to the pictures generation and American conceptualism led to his fascination with visual storytelling, particularly in pop culture. Although his sources are incredibly wide-ranging, Lassry's work is immediately identifiable, typically he has used the same size of 29.2 x 36.8cm (11½ x 14½in; portrait or landscape), and hung the prints in coloured frames that mimic the dominant colour of the image, becoming an extension of the picture itself – moving out of the virtual and into the physical realm. The glossy patina of his pictures recalls the way contemporary commercial photography

***Boston Shoulder Roasts*, 2012. C-print, painted frame, 36.8 x 29.2 x 3.8cm (14½ x 11½ x 1½ in)**
What are the differences between still life and abstraction, between photography and sculpture? Lassry poses these questions when he gives us this image of two perfect slabs of raw meat, poised and posed, fleshy and formal at the same time. The aligned papers that look like colour swatches behind the meat seem to nudge us away from its physicality and towards seeing it as an image. Food features often in Lassry's work, perhaps because, as a visual category that is so generic and universally evocative, visceral and idiomatic, it makes us question the nature of how we see and how we relate to images as opposed to physical objects.

manipulates context and colour, whether working with vegetables, ornaments or shoes posed prodigiously on plinths. But these aren't comments on advertising, or deconstructions of it. What Lassry is interested in is the status of the picture.

His large library of pictures combines found imagery with photographs shot in the studio, but shown side by side, whether created or appropriated, performed or artless, and stripped of their context, Lassry makes it impossible to tell what comes from where. The pictures simply exist here, suspended.

His works have always oscillated between two and three dimensions; he has even described them as sculptures that 'happen to be photographs'.[5] Lassry has continued to add materials that protrude from his flat pictures and to create structures they can inhabit. At his 2020 exhibition at the San Francisco Museum of Modern Art, he presented new works that take different types of picture-making as their material: there were collages of archival negatives from sales catalogues, amateur photographs of nature and the outtakes from a fashion shoot. Lassry then created sculptures to sit with the photographs. The point of all this is to destabilize what a photograph is: 'My whole practice raises the question of whether the work's existence is image-based or object-based, or whether it can be both. It becomes a struggle between the image and the presence or physicality of it in space.'[6]

***Untitled (Costume) A*, 2013. C-print, walnut frame, 4-ply silk, 36.8 x 29.2 x 3.8cm (14 ½ x 11 ½ x 1 ½ in)**
For his 2013 solo exhibition at the 303 Gallery in New York, Lassry made a series of small works that dressed up photographic images in 4-ply pleated silk. Wrapped around a walnut frame, the various silks created a deliberately sensuous curtain that partly conceals and partly reveals the image underneath, leaving us guessing as to its original context and message. For example, in this work we see the bottom half of two people, one dressed in a flamboyant costume, the other in nondescript black jeans and shoes. Their positioning suggests they are conversing and their setting seems to be an urban street. But Lassry poses other questions here: do the tactile suggestiveness of the fabric and our experience of the physical quality of the photo-object influence how we interpret the image?

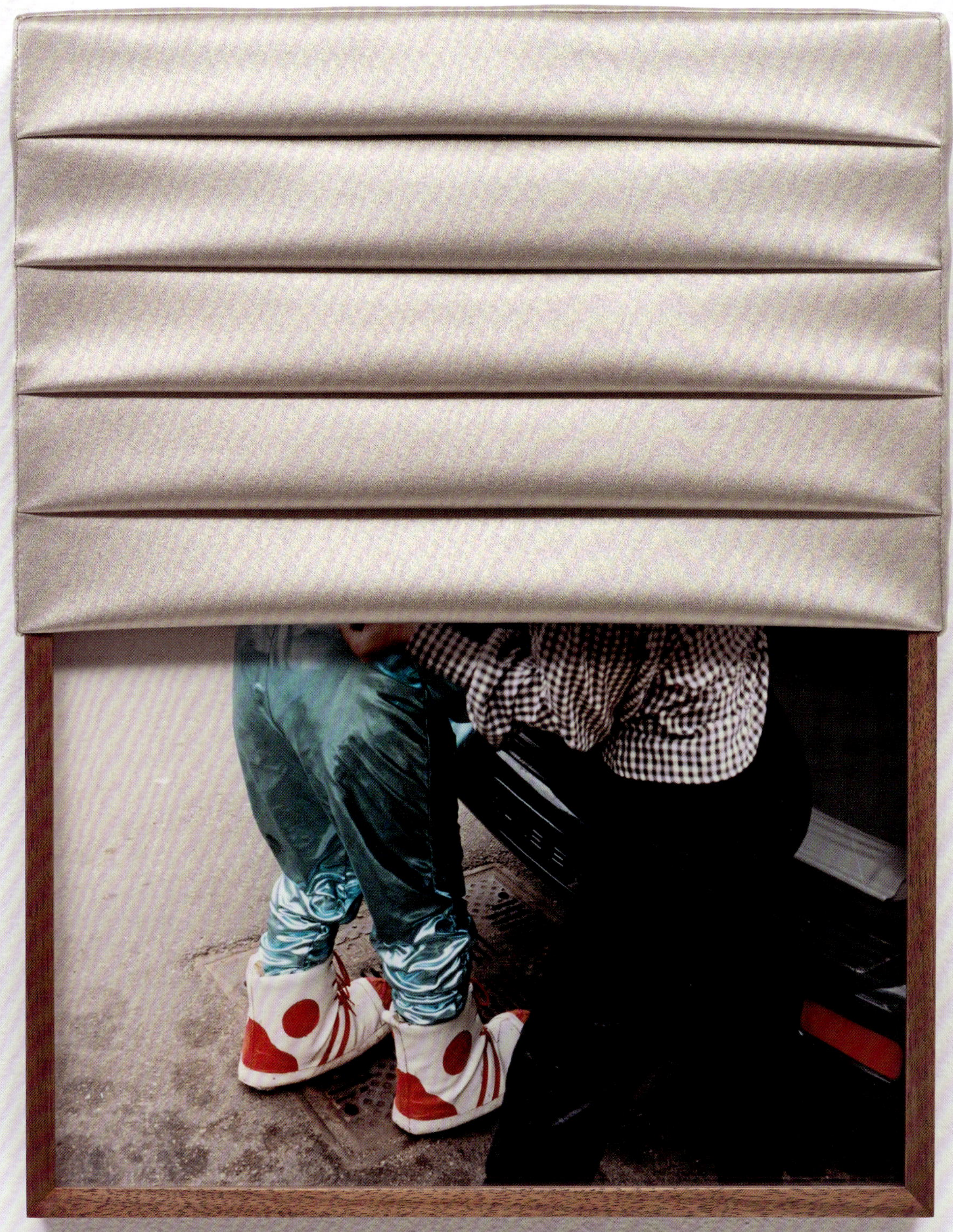

Deana Lawson

Deana Lawson has described her path to photography as destiny. Born in 1979, she was raised in Rochester, New York, the home of Kodak. Her father comprehensively chronicled the family's life in photo albums that Lawson continues to revisit and pore over, 'images of my family in all their glory and in the everyday'.[1] Those pictures have had a profound effect on her. The combination of brilliance and banality, in addition to a sense of identification with her subjects – people she has referred to as 'family', though most of them are strangers – runs through all her work. She began taking pictures in the early 2000s, graduating from Rhode Island School of Design in 2004.

At first, Lawson's pictures appear to be documentary, but they are in fact meticulously staged realizations that she creates by casting strangers in locations (typically homes) and shooting them using medium- and large-format cameras that produce richly detailed prints. Every element of the composition is directed by Lawson, from the pose of her subjects and the thrift-shop clothes they wear to the positioning of props. As she has explained, when she has an image in mind 'it burns so deeply that I have to make it and I don't care what people are going to think'.[2]

Lawson has described being influenced by the paintings of her ex-husband Aaron Gilbert, who depicted scenes of family life, and also cites Diane Arbus as an important reference. From her first portraits, her approach has been similar to that of a painter setting up a scene. The primary power of Lawson's portraits lies in the people depicted, and the energy she draws out from them. Her subjects are always black and predominantly from working-class backgrounds: 'my choice feels natural because it's a reflection of the people and forces I grew up around in Rochester,' she has said.[3] The author Zadie Smith has written that all Lawson's subjects 'seem to occupy a higher plane, a kingdom of restored glory'.[4] Their poses are proud and self-possessed, whether they are clothed or nude; these are people who command the space, confronting the camera with a direct look that makes time stop momentarily – 'a gaze so intense that it's the viewer who ends up feeling naked,' as Smith describes it.[5]

It is a force that is present throughout Lawson's images, presented against a backdrop of shared domestic settings, whether the homes are in Port-au-Prince, Haiti or Brownsville, Texas. Recognizable elements emerge in the scenery, such as curtains and couches, all signalling a common way of using and

***Barbara and Mother*, 2017. Pigment print, 175.3 x 139.7cm (69 x 55in)**
Lawson met the two women who appear in this photograph – Barbara and her daughter – in a dollar store in Charleston, South Carolina. Lawson was fascinated by the polished toenails on Barbara's prosthetic leg. Yet, that is not what you notice first in the portrait. Positioned in the centre of the frame and directed by Lawson to pose with hands on hips, the women mirror each other, smiling with confidence. The sharp focus of Lawson's lens allows the surroundings to be seen in detail – the wall patched up with tape (a leitmotif in Lawson's photographs), the Bible, the stereo, the vase of fake flowers and the kitsch lampshade – giving hints at their everyday lives. The photograph shows Lawson's continued interest not only in people and their ability to transcend their working-class context but also in describing black aesthetics and finding similarities in the domestic space across the diaspora.

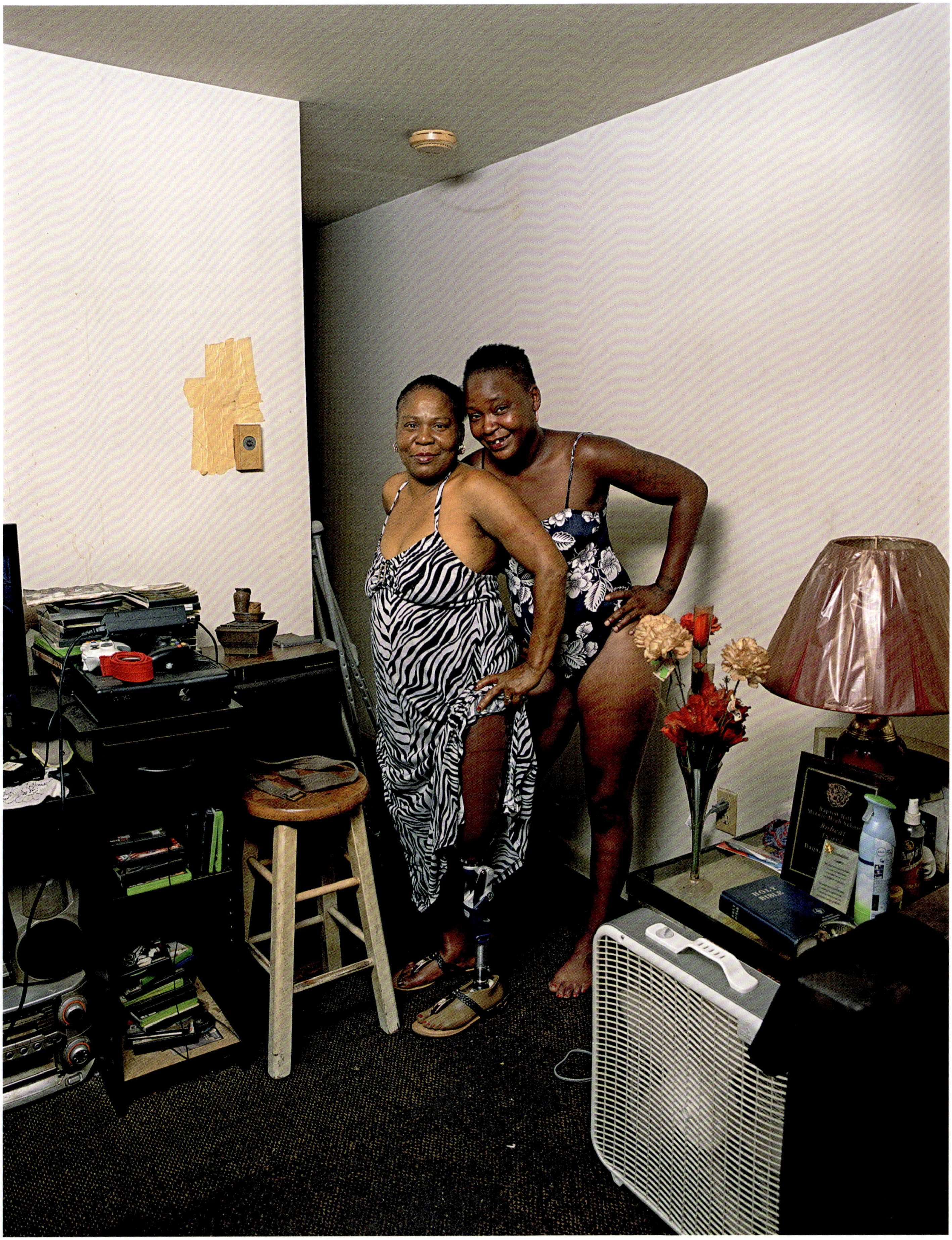
HOLY BIBLE

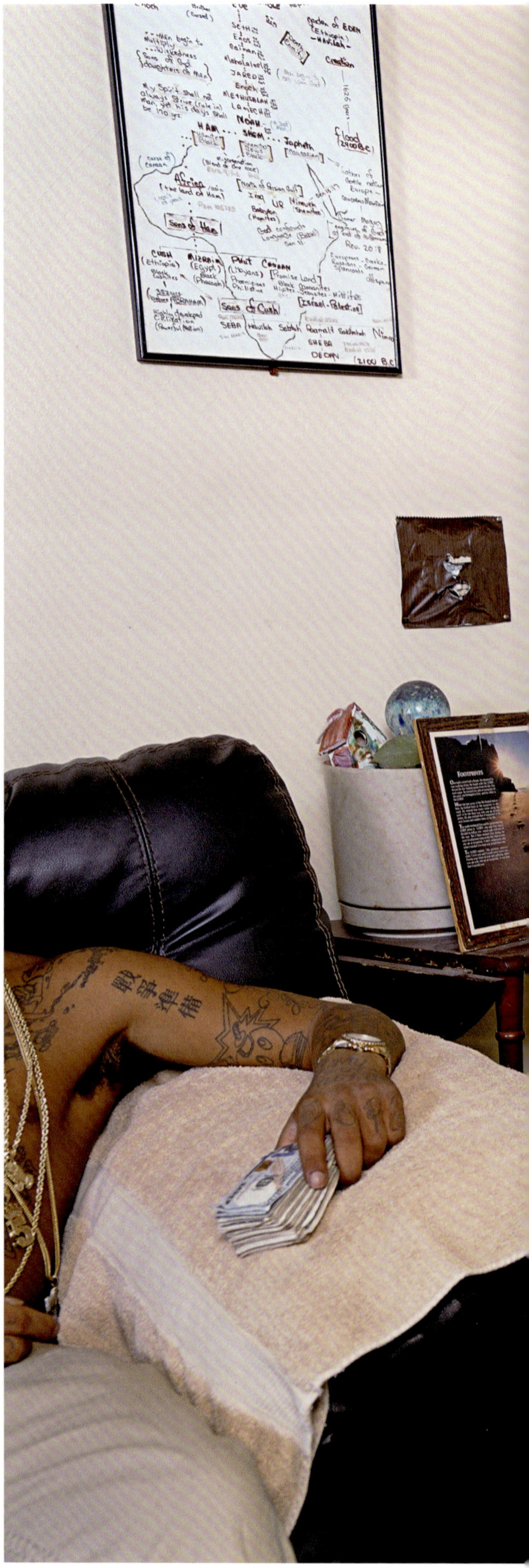

Sons of Cush, 2016. Inkjet print, 109.2 x 137.8cm (43 x 54 ¼ in)
Lawson's vision is so precise that sometimes it takes a long time to get the image she wants. She attempted to shoot *Sons of Cush* in Michigan, and then in the Democratic Republic of the Congo, before eventually settling on Los Angeles. The final image was initially conceived as two separate pictures. The hand holding a stash of cash at the edge of the frame was going to be shot separately, but Lawson decided to connect it with the muscular, tattooed man who holds his two-month-old daughter. The fourth 'character' in the photograph is the setting – a home Lawson had scouted previously. The space is crammed with furniture and laden with details, such as the whiteboard tracing the evolution of the word 'Cush': originally referring to a biblical character, the son of Ham, it is now slang for a type of cannabis. The young man at the centre of the image is intentionally photographed with passion and desire: 'I realized it's rare to look at desire and sensuality in pictures through the gaze of a heterosexual black woman,' Lawson has said, reflecting on the image.[6]

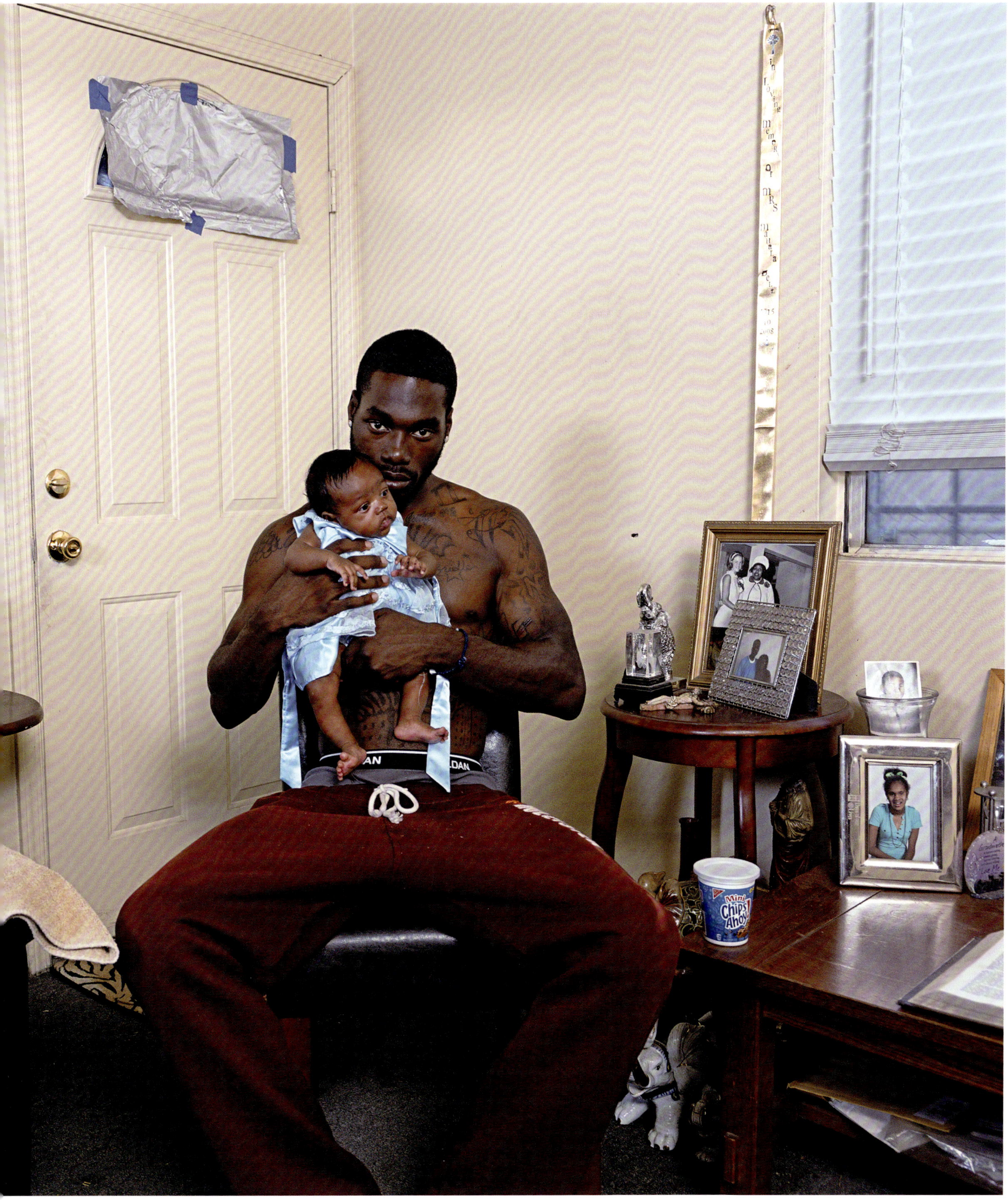
Mini
Chips Ahoy!

thinking about private, intimate spaces. Lawson is interested in the rites, rituals and ceremonies that take place in these environments, in moments of communion and togetherness. These are much like the occasions recorded in a family album and are photographed with the same familiar regard for her subjects.

Lawson allows the familial, the erotic and the spiritual to reside side by side in her images. From the first nude she took in 2005, *Ashanti*, which showed a woman reclining in a classical pose on a bare mattress, to her many portraits of couples embracing, exuding sexuality, Lawson plays with being seen and seeing – particularly for her female subjects, who often meet the viewer's desirous gaze and appear to welcome it. However, the staged environments and the acts of a private fantasy project remind us that being seen is complicated.

In Lawson's works, people are vessels. Emanating an aura of consecration, they transcend the fraying edges of their cheap clothes and cramped homes; even their own skin seems hardly able to contain them. They are, as Lawson puts it, 'creative, godlike beings. I don't feel like we carry ourselves like that all the time, or that we know how miraculous we are. I try to locate the magnificent and have it all come through in the picture.'[7]

***The Beginning*, 2008. Inkjet print, mounted on Sintra, 76.2 x 107.3cm (30 x 42 ¼ in)**

'I see photographs as visual testimonies. Familial relationships, sexuality and life cycles are repeated motifs,' Lawson has said of her work.[8] This photograph shows her interest in examining the lives of women and in the maternal, reframing black mothers as the root of the universe and portals to the future. Depictions of childbirth in contemporary art are rare and Lawson's raw image is taken at a moment of high drama just as the baby has emerged, the camera positioned to show both the baby's first sight of the world as it is lifted towards its mother and the pain, exhaustion and relief etched onto its mother's face.

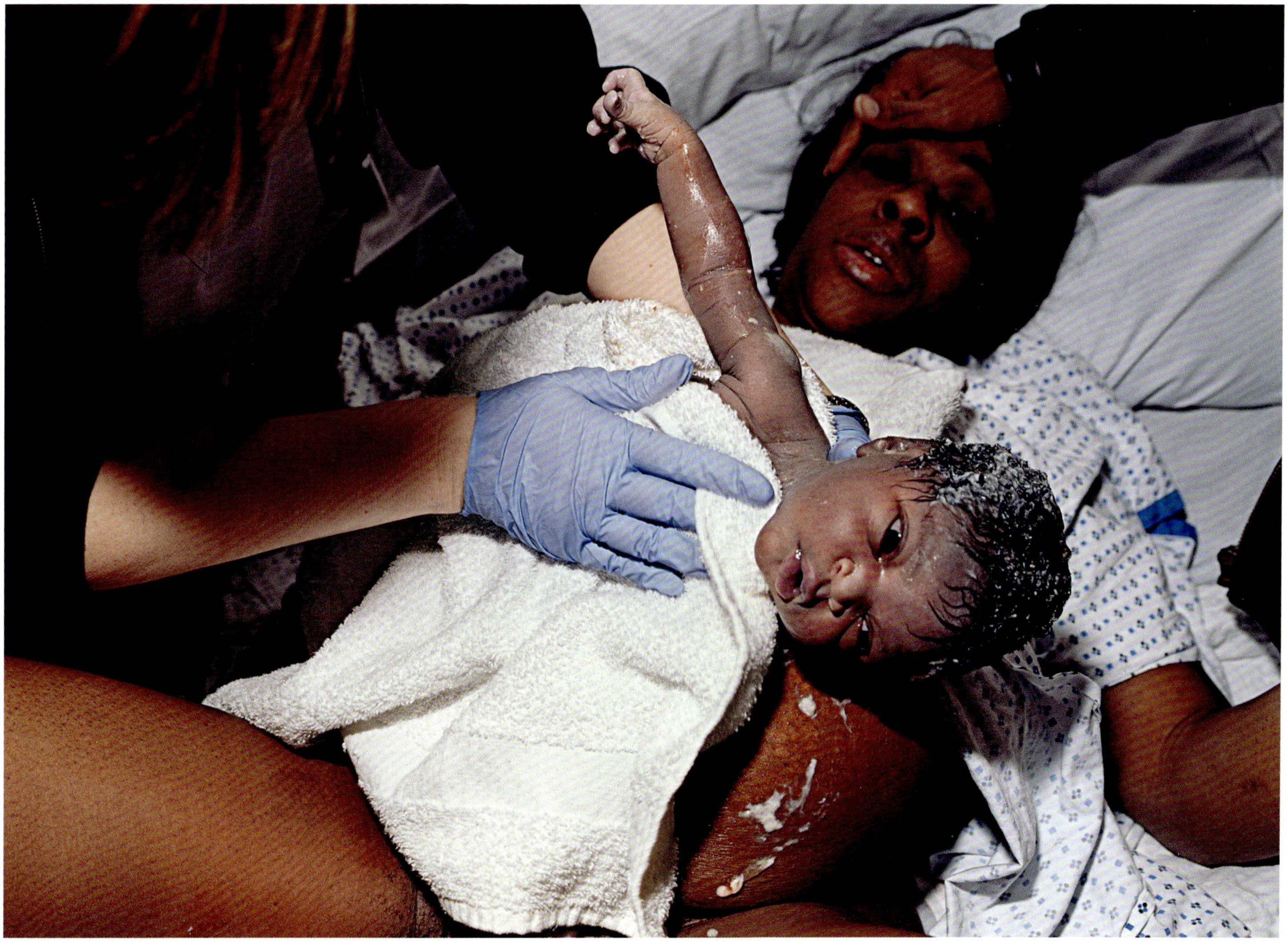

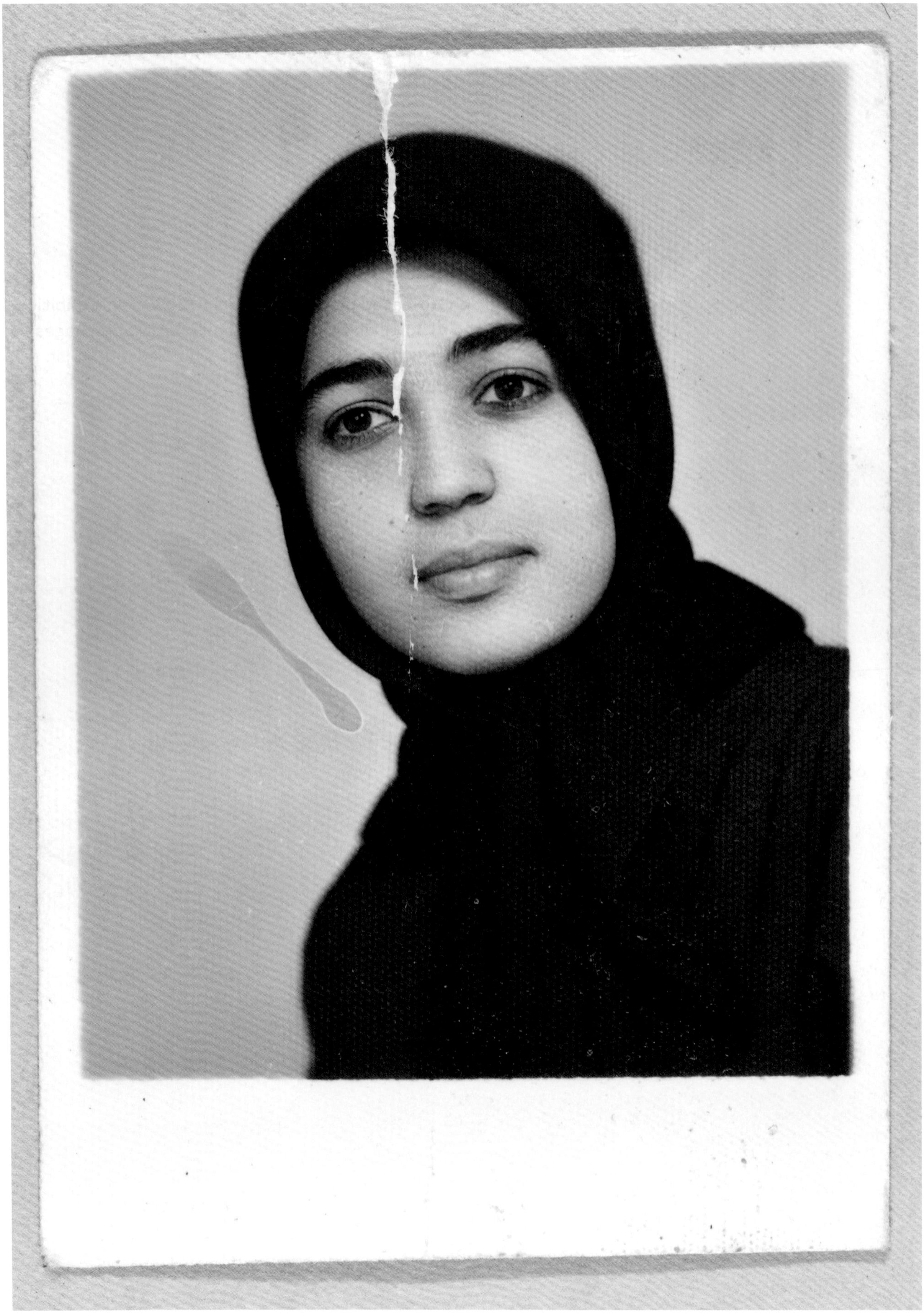

Amak Mahmoodian

'Photography is a way of talking,' Amak Mahmoodian has said.[1] For the Iranian-born artist, this means communicating with both the living and the dead. Real and imagined conversations between people, and between people and pictures, are a recurrent theme in her photo-based projects. In *Zanjir* (2020), an exhibition at the Arnolfini in Bristol, she used poetry and images to converse with a Persian princess who died in 1936; in another project, *Kodaki* (2006–7), she spoke with Iranian schoolchildren, asking them to write down their thoughts when looking at archival images of Iranian children taken in the nineteenth century. Mahmoodian's purpose is to use text and images not to illustrate one another but to create new dialogues and stories between them, bridging the perceived void between the visual and the verbal. Writing appears to represent the fluid inner world of thoughts, dreams and desires, while the historical photographs she incorporates seem to have a formal, authoritative presence, fixing an image or an idea. Mahmoodian sees her role as more of a medium, or a translator, than a photographer: 'I listen to my photographs and allow them to speak.'[2]

Born in Shiraz in 1980, Mahmoodian recalls asking herself the most profound of questions at a young age: 'Who am I?' According to Mahmoodian, women in Iran exist on the edges of society. As a consequence, as she herself is aware of experiencing, there is a chasm between public and private identities. Her work recognizes this split, dealing with the contradictions between the cultural ideals and the identity imposed collectively on women, in this case by Iranian and Islamic culture, and the women's personal expressions of their individuality in the private realm, through their own accounts, documents and diaries. *Zanjir*, the outcome of two years' extensive research in the Golestan Archives in Tehran into early portraits of the women who lived in the palace during the Qajar dynasty, digs deeper into the differences between their official identity recorded in photographs and their private, everyday lives as reflected in personal journals and poems. *Zanjir* gives these faces from the past a contemporary context, as Mahmoodian asked members of her family to hold the historic pictures over their own faces.

Although rooted in Iran, the disorienting effect of this fissure between projection and perception as

***Farid* from the series *Shenasnameh*, 2016**
Shenasnameh (which refers to Iranian birth certificates) is a series Mahmoodian began over a decade ago after reflecting on how she and her mother were represented in their official ID documents. For these images, women must cover their hair and wear minimal makeup, eradicating their individuality. Mahmoodian was struck by the similarity between the images of herself and her mother, but their fingerprints different. She gathered images and fingerprints like these from different women in Iran, each one unique and with its own story to tell. This photograph belongs to a friend of a friend; her image is paired at random with a fingerprint that might belong to her, but might belong to any of the other woman in the series.

experienced through photography is widespread among the internet generation, used as they are to creating different versions of the self to inhabit different contexts simultaneously. 'Which is the truest version?' is the question to which Mahmoodian constantly returns.

'Isn't the review of one's personal history the best undertaking in the world?' reads a line in an imagined exchange with the radical princess Zahra Khanom Tadj es-Saltaneh in *Zanjir*. Mahmoodian has often described her work as autobiographical 'chapters' and each new project begins with a photograph of herself, her mother or her grandmother. She assumes the role of the observer and the observed, the photographer and the subject, looking inwards and out at the same time, by using these personal photographs as a point of departure to situate herself and find connections with other women, and the way they have been represented by the camera.

***Exotic* from the series *Mohr*, 2008**
In the 2008 series *Mohr*, Mahmoodian is both the observer and the observed. The texts that accompany the images are from the perspective of a non-Iranian writing about Iranian women. The artist collected these texts in the UK and, when she returned to visit Iran in 2008, merged them with images of the daily life of women living there. In a number of the photographs, the writing is shown on a mirror 'because the mirror is a symbol of purity and light'.[3] This photograph was taken in the house of a woman called Goli in Karaj, a suburb of Tehran. Mahmoodian describes the encounter: 'We met in the afternoon. She made tea for us and we talked. She asked me to translate the words I had with me, pointed to the mirror, gave me her red lipstick. She chose "Exotic".'[4]

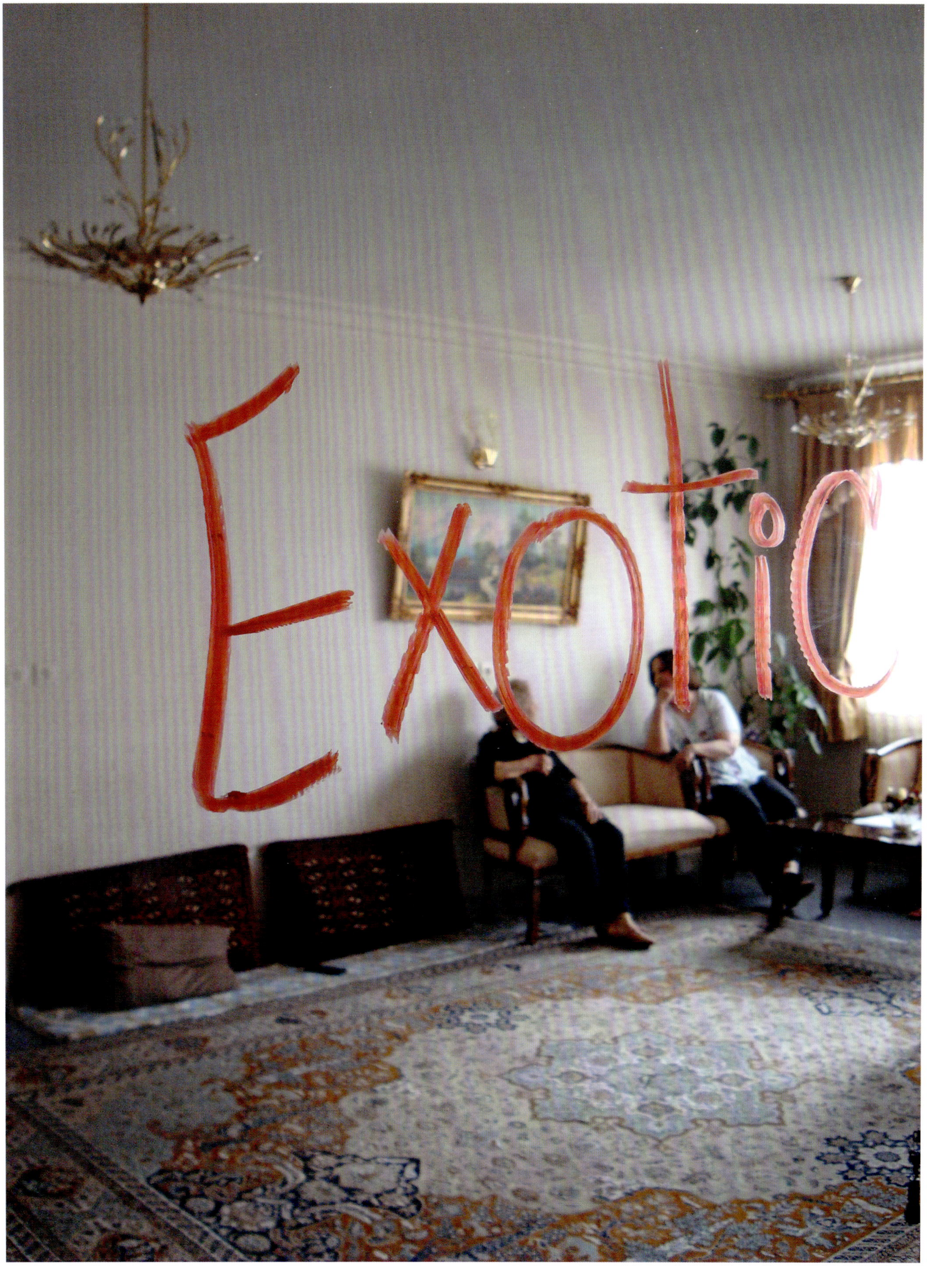
Exotic

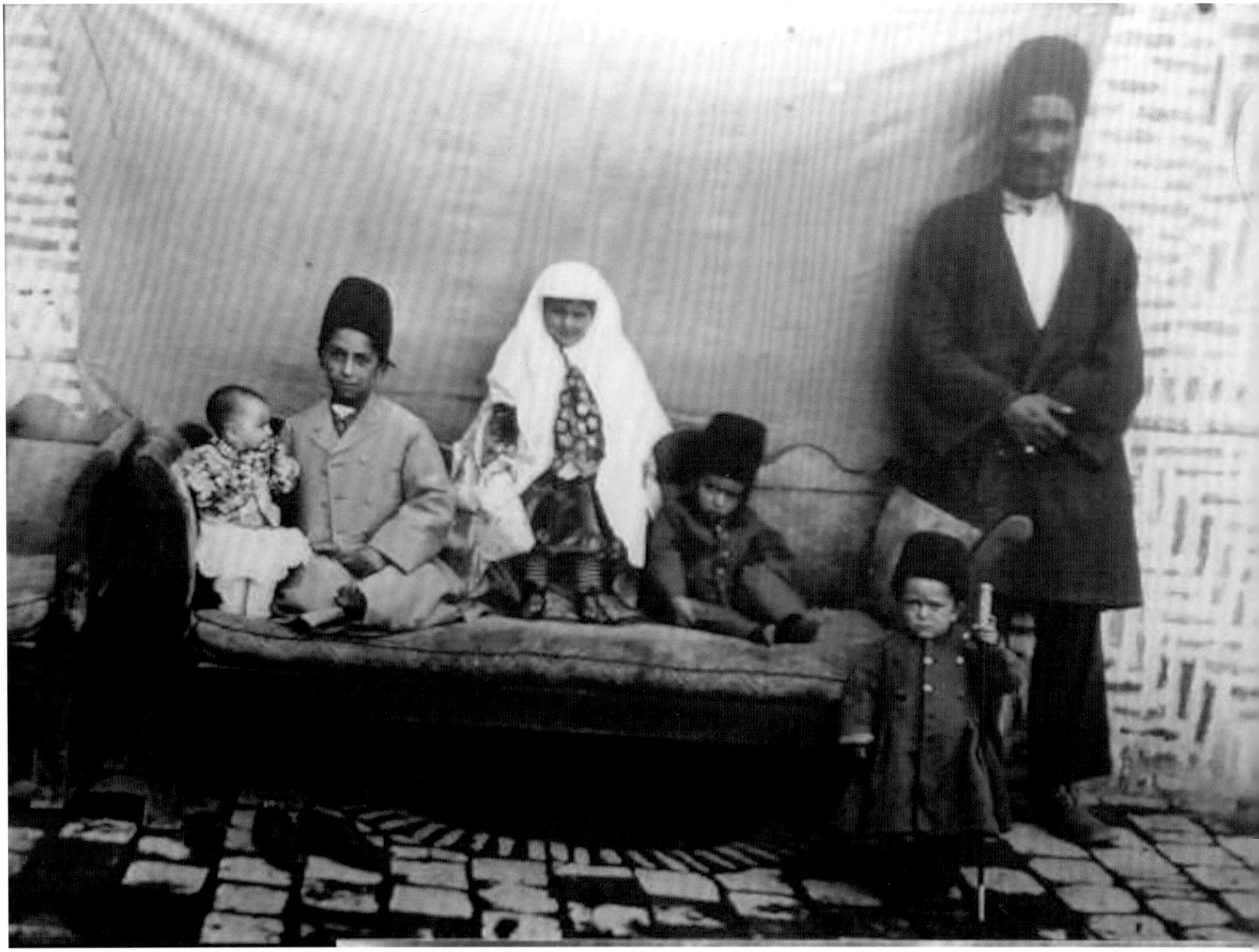

From the series *Kodaki*, 2007
In *Kodaki*, Mahmoodian asked children aged nine to study photographs from the Golestan Archives, Tehran, that were taken between 1850 and 1896, the period when photography first arrived in Iran. She wanted them to share their reactions to the images. Their handwritten responses to these nineteenth-century portraits of children are included with the photographs. This passage (above right), written in particularly beautiful handwriting by one boy from Tehran, translates as: 'From this photograph I understand that it shows me a very, very long time ago, compared to these days. In those days they wore such beautiful coats, trousers, hats... The kind of decoration, on the wall, sofa and floor, shows how traditional their life was... How lucky they were. I wish I was living in the past time.'

از این عکس می فهمم که این جا زمان خیلی، خیلی قدیم را نشان می دهد که در آن زمان چه لباس ها، کوت و شلـ
و... زیباتری از حال داشتند؛ چه طرح هایی بر روی دیوار، مُبل یا زمین آن وقت بود؛ چه آداب و رسومی
داشتند و... خوش به حال آن زمانی ها؛ کاش من هم در آن زمان بودم.

Alix Marie

Orlando, installation view, 2014
This large-scale, sprawling sculpture is not your typical romantic statement, but this work concerns Marie's most intimate relationship at the time, that with her lover Orlando. He is reimagined as a heap of fleshy boulder-like photo-objects that allude to the veined marble of classical sculptures as much as to the human form as they tumble towards you. Marie dipped prints of close-up photographs of Orlando's body parts in wax, then crumpled, scanned and reprinted them. 'I have always felt teased by the similarities between skin and the photographic print: both surfaces, both fragile, both ungraspable,' she has said.[4] This is desire represented as raw, messy, gender-free – with a nod to Virginia Woolf's novel *Orlando* – and just a little bit gruesome.

Born in Bobigny in 1989, Alix Marie was raised on cinema. The first film she watched, at two years old, was not a Disney classic but F.W. Murnau's *Nosferatu* (1922), the classic silent horror film about a vampire interested in buying a new property – and in his estate agent's beautiful wife. Marie has said in an interview that this early encounter with the grotesque has informed her highly unusual works, in which she sculpts photography into something fleshy and visceral.

As a student at Central Saint Martins and then the Royal College of Art in London, Marie has developed a practice that fulfils her desire to be able to both see things and touch them. Frustrated with the flatness of photographs but nonetheless enthralled with image-making, she concentrates today on photo-based sculptures and installations that envelop the viewer. The physical aspect of Marie's work is just as important as the visual, not only in the way she fills space but also in the treatment of her recurrent subject matter: bodies. 'The practice of photography can be so clinical; it did not fit me as a messy sculptor. But that was kind of my obsession – to work out how to give the medium a body,' she has explained.[1]

Throughout its history, photography has established a hierarchy of bodies, representing aspirational forms and perfect physiques for men and women, whether in advertising campaigns, publications or pornography. To eschew this heteronormative gaze on binary bodies, Marie prefers to create layers that merge different parts of differently gendered bodies, surfaces that often conceal the source material or trick us into seeing something that is not there. She used X-rays of classical sculptures from the Victoria and Albert Museum's collection in London, cast her own body, and printed biceps and torsos onto Perspex boxes filled with water and heated by lamps, making the pictures look as if they are perspiring. For Marie, 'The way I photograph is claiming a place for genuine depiction of our bodies, in opposition to the impossible ideal we are fed everyday through advertising and mass media.'[2]

Metamorphosis and hybridity are core components in Marie's work. A starting point is often classical mythology, together with archetypes of femininity and masculinity and assumptions about ideal bodies, all of which are ways to speak about the

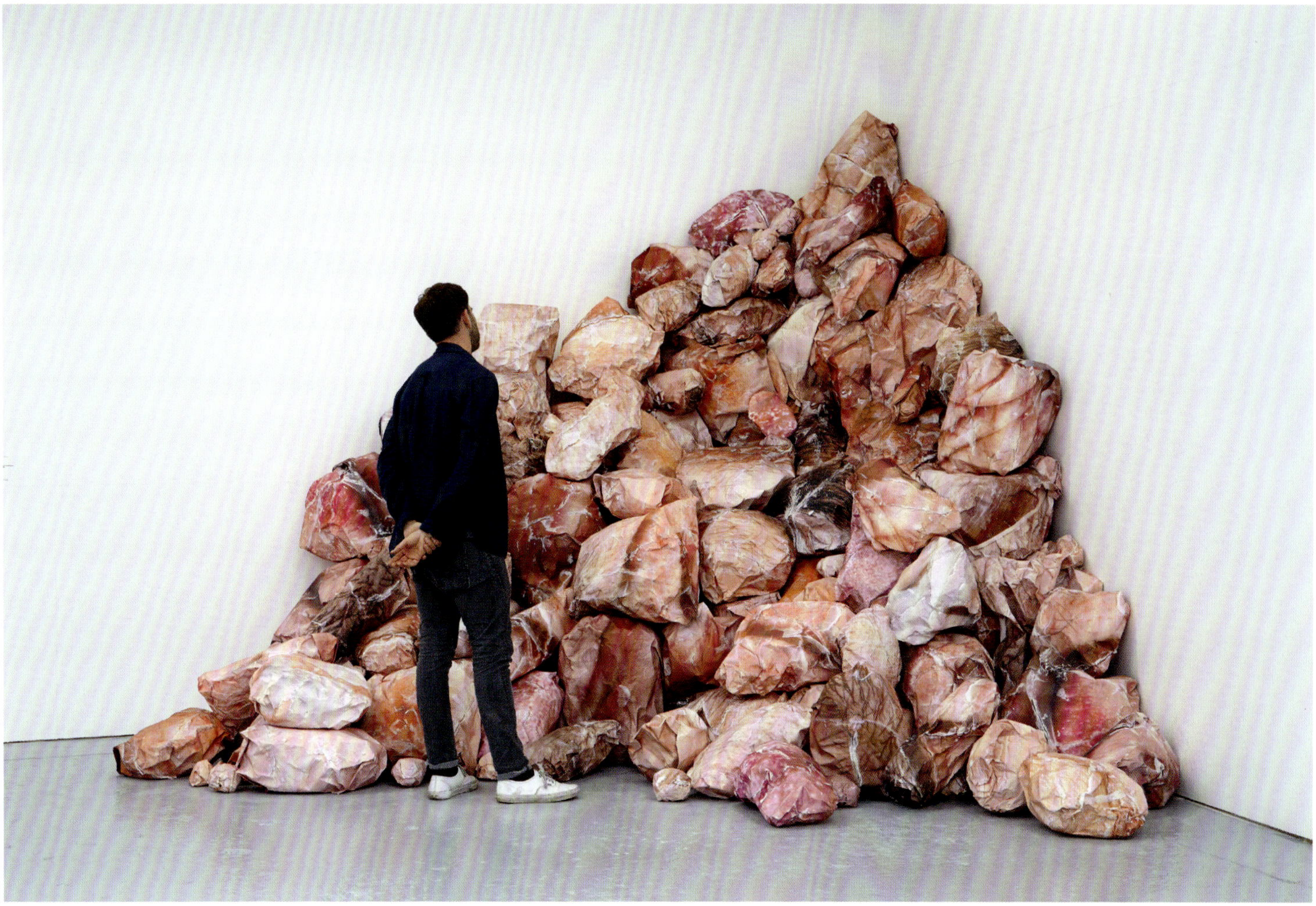

construction and performance of gender and identity in the contemporary context.

In tandem with explorations of exaggerated feminine qualities, Marie has investigated displays of masculinity that date back to ancient Greek athletes. In her trio of works *Flex* (2017), *Shredded* (2018) and *Olympians* (2019), she examines this specifically through bodybuilding, using found images from bodybuilding magazines like *FLEX*, Swedish porn and the profiles of bodybuilders she has met on Instagram. With its posturing and posing, often in skimpy outfits and in front of an audience – not unlike a striptease – bodybuilding for Marie represents a clash of camp and heteronormative hypermasculinity. It is also a subject that has an established history with the camera, both as a way to record athletes' accomplishments and physiques, and as an area of fascination for artists such as Robert Mapplethorpe, Camille Vivier and Bill Dobbins. Marie articulates the analogy thus: 'Bodybuilding is about image and aesthetic, the performance of strength rather than physical strength itself, and it sits in between science and art, in which it relates to photography.'[3]

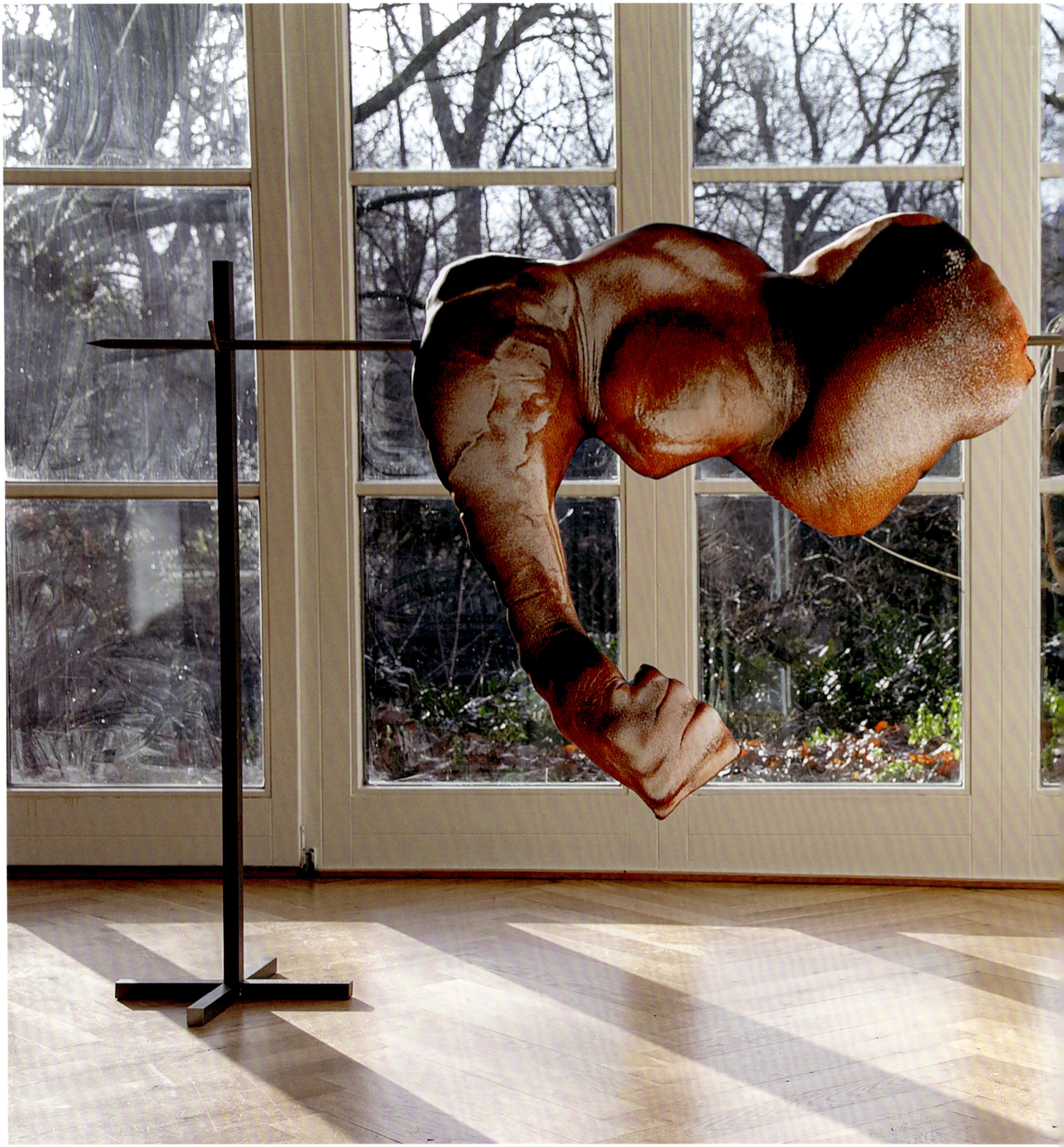

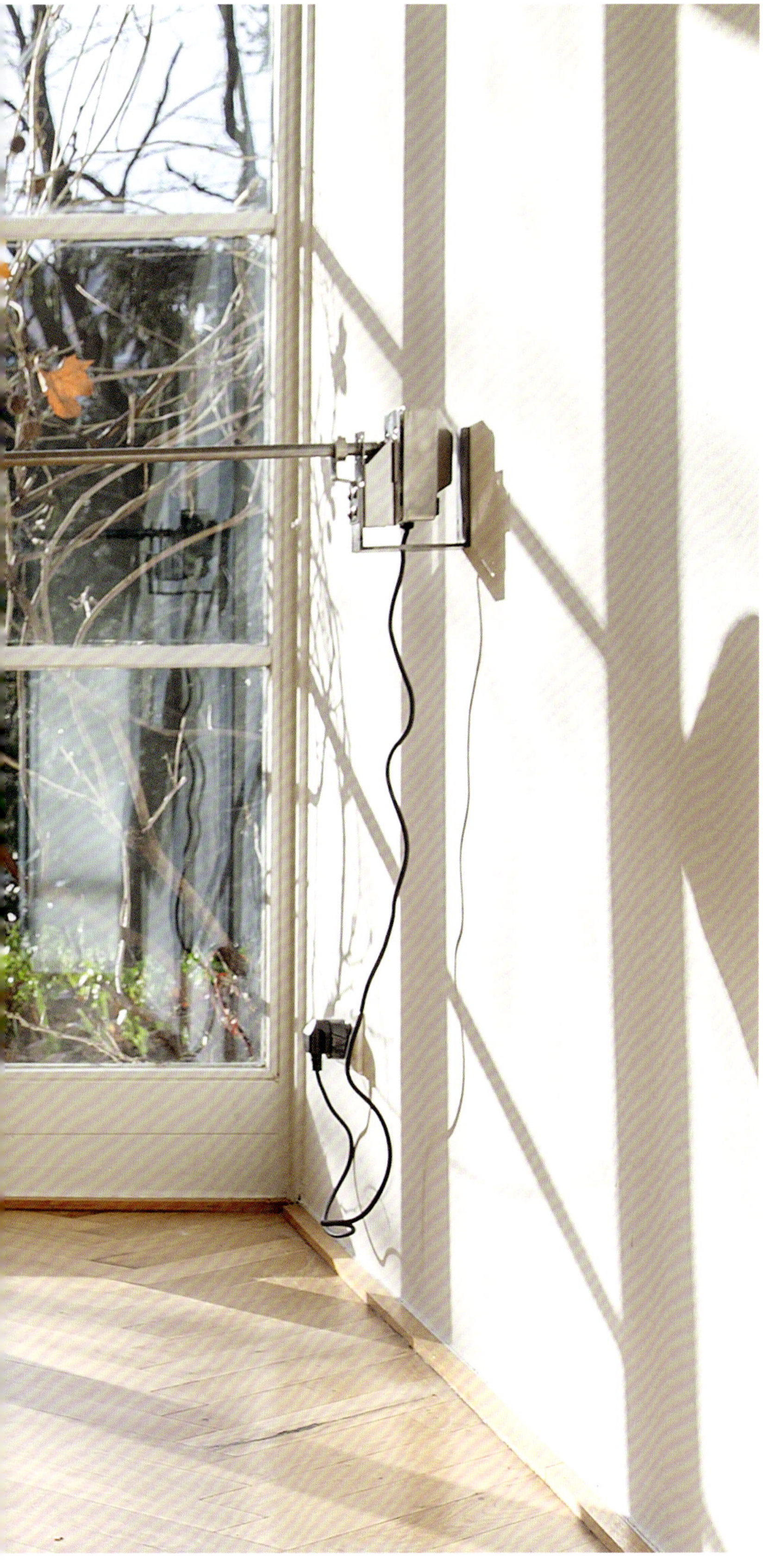

***Héraclès 3*, installation view, 2018**
Using a dye-sublimation printing technique, Marie printed close-up photographs of bodybuilder's arms onto cushion-like objects. There is a playful tension here between softness and the apparent hardness of the biceps, machismo turned into something decorative. She then skewered the photo-objects so that they turned on rotary barbecues, pushing the objectification of these bodies, valued for their meaty muscularity, to an absurd, cannibalistic extreme.

Ryan McGinley

Perhaps no one has defined what it meant to be an American youth in the late 1990s and 2000s better than Ryan McGinley. The recurrent subject of his photographs is, in his own words, 'the evidence of fun'[1]: the freedom, hedonism and carefree abandon afforded only to privileged young people. McGinley's idea of fun is naked bodies, running, jumping and swimming through picturesque American landscapes that can barely contain their wild energy, beauty and verve. More than a decade before Instagram, McGinley gave us a vision of youth culture filtered through dreamy sunsets; tattoos, cigarettes and caresses were his props. He imagined what America's youth wanted and how they wanted to be seen, and his aesthetic has remained an important reference for a whole new generation of young, upcoming talents he has helped nurture, from Petra Collins (whom he met in a bar in Toronto and who became one of his model-muses) to Sandy Kim and Michael Bailey-Gates.

McGinley has achieved a kind of mythological status in the USA, and especially in New York, where he has lived and worked since he moved there in 1998. At that time, while still a student at Parsons School of Design, he took Polaroids of everyone who came to his apartment, describing his relationship with photography as obsessive. McGinley's remarkable rise to fame came only three years after his first solo exhibition in an abandoned space in SoHo in 2000, when he became the youngest artist in three decades to have a solo exhibition at the Whitney Museum of American Art in 2003. By the age of thirty, he had been named Photographer of the Year by *American Photo* magazine and had won the International Center of Photography's Young Photographer Infinity Award.

At first McGinley trained his lens mostly on his peers, the graffiti writers, skateboarders, artists, musicians and revellers he was spending inconsequential days with, including the artist Dan Colen and the late photographer Dash Snow. After the Whitney exhibition, however, he changed the way he worked, moving from the autobiographical, casual and spontaneous documenting of friends towards a more directed, intentional style. He would engineer events by inviting models to his home or on the summer road trips he began to organize in 2005, choosing locations and even giving his models references for poses. His photographs became more purposeful and deliberate, but with the same aim of creating a feeling of communal joy. Laughter, jumping, holding hands – these gestures are trademarks of McGinley's work and point to his interest in finding natural states of euphoria.

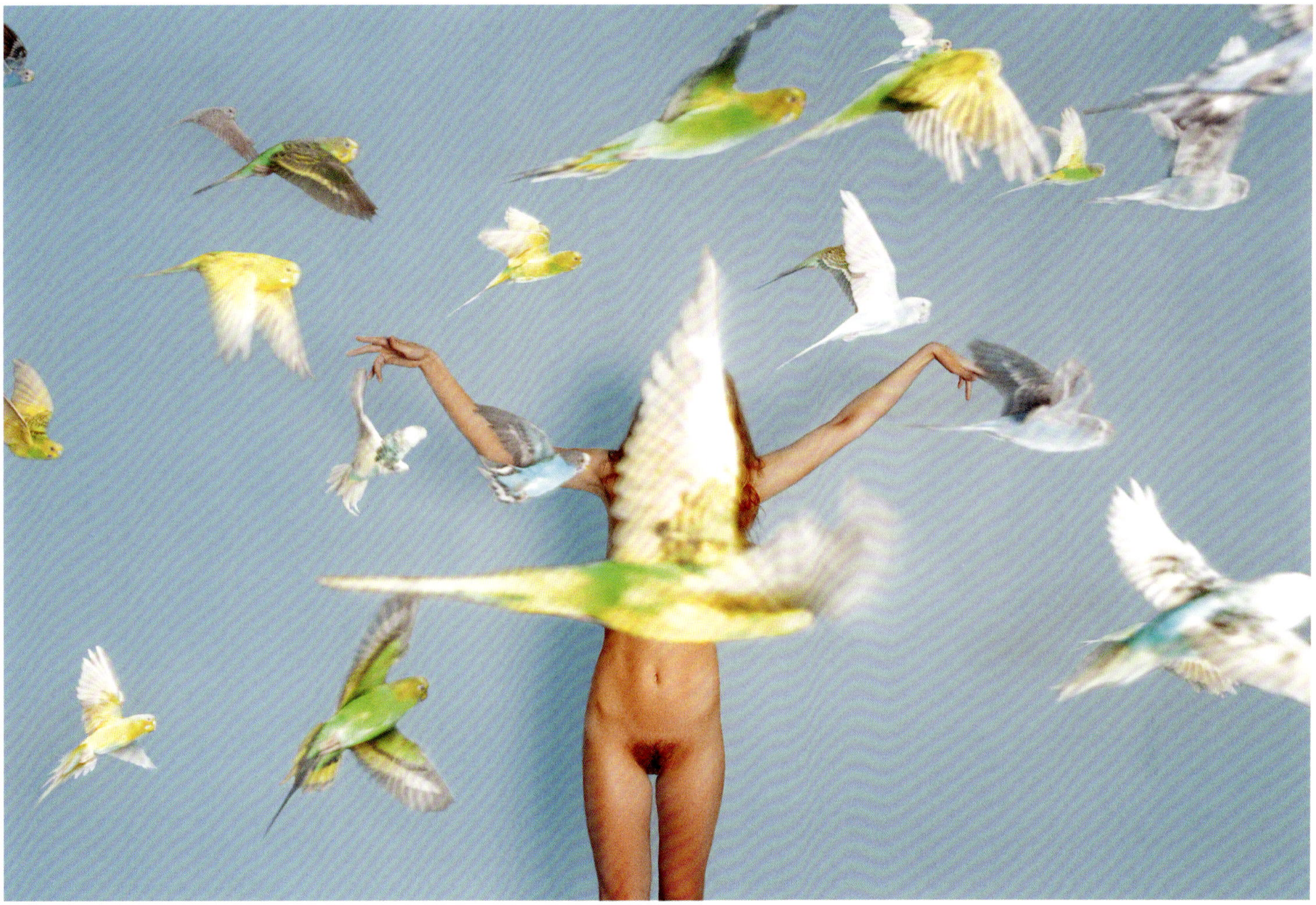

***Parakeets*, 2011**
This soaring, euphoric image shows McGinley's ongoing interest in movement: his figures are rarely static, more often depicted running, jumping, swimming or diving. Here, a young female figure is obscured by a flock of colourful birds, their flight a metaphor for freedom. With its bright, minimal backdrop and sense of playfulness, McGinley also mimics the aesthetics of advertising and commercial photography. As is typical in his work, the subject is young and unclothed. But McGinley sees nudity not as sexual but as a way to represent figures in their most natural, neutral and honest state.

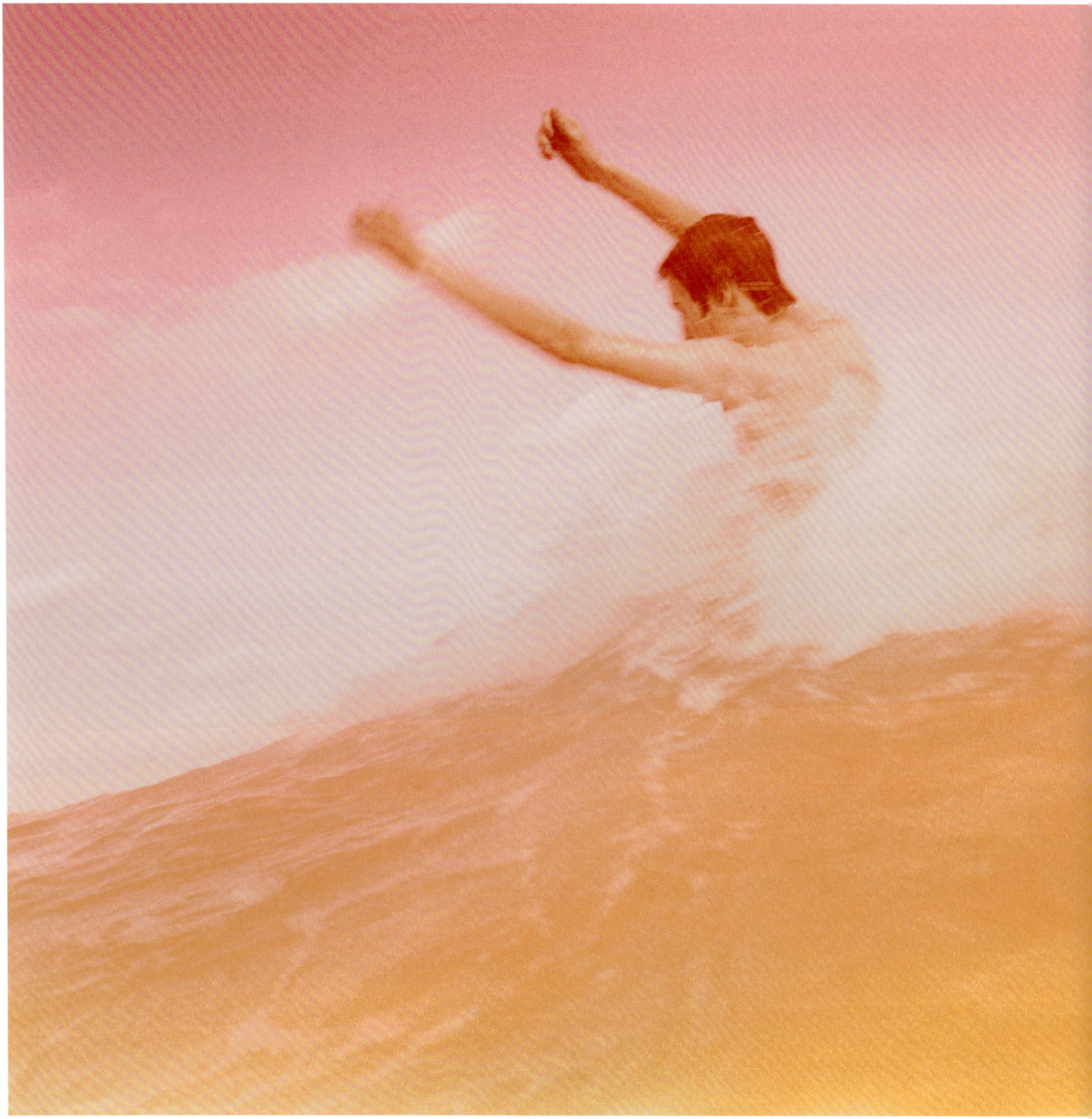

This sense of the communal goes back to his childhood. Born in 1977, McGinley grew up in an Irish Catholic family of eight children in the suburbs of New Jersey. The youngest by eleven years, at the age of eight he found himself alone at home with his parents and missing the sense of community and constant activity he had previously enjoyed. His siblings were also influential in that they opened the door for him onto the world of New York culture; one older brother in particular, who passed away from complications related to AIDS when McGinley was seventeen, introduced him to the art of Manhattan's downtown – in particular, paintings by Keith Haring and Jean-Michel Basquiat. McGinley was his brother's main carer at home and he has said that the experience has informed his art more than anything else. A year after his brother died, McGinley came out to his family and moved to downtown Manhattan himself, where he could create a new family through his photographs.

McGinley's place in contemporary photography is also significant because he represents the last generation of pre-internet photographers. His prolific way of working – he is known to shoot up to thirty rolls of film a day during his road trips – and his belief that editing is as important as shooting prefigure the way we use photography in our day-to-day lives now. As is true for his predecessors, Nan Goldin and Larry Clark, the youthfulness of his subjects, his voyeurism and his queering of the gaze have made him both fashionable and an outsider. His importance is nonetheless unquestionable as he continues to create a vast body of work that constitutes an open, comprehensive study of the spirit of rebellion and the desire to be free.

***Wade Wave*, 2004**
'I have absolutely no interest in creating depressing images,' McGinley once declared in an interview.[2] Here, a male figure leaps in a crashing wave, capturing a moment of pure unalloyed joy. Water, open fields and sky are natural motifs that recur across McGinley's oeuvre, serving as metaphors for an open mind and spirit, in symbiosis with the bodies of his models. This image also typifies his influential style in terms of colour and light, the magenta and orange hues giving a dreamy quality.

Susan Meiselas

Susan Meiselas was born in Baltimore in 1948 and began her professional life as a teacher at an elementary school in the South Bronx, where she introduced photography to her classes. Using the camera as an educational tool has remained an important part of her work ever since. In 2007 she established the Magnum Foundation, a non-profit program supporting diversity in documentary photography, to set out new models for visual storytelling on social issues and human rights around the world by future generations. Her photojournalism has won many prestigious awards and accolades: a MacArthur Fellowship in 1992, the Hasselblad Award in 1994, the International Centre of Photography's Infinity Award in 2005 and a Guggenheim Fellowship in 2015. In 2019 she was awarded the Deutsche Börse Photography Foundation Prize for her retrospective exhibition *Mediations*, held at Jeu de Paume in Paris.

Meiselas did not originally see herself as a photographer, but after a chance encounter with Gilles Peress while on an assignment for *Harper's* at the 1976 Democratic convention, she ended up joining the Magnum cooperative. The same year she published *Carnival Strippers,* a work that would define her as a photographer. The photographs, arranged as a visual essay, told the story of the women who performed striptease across New England, photographed at country fairs over three summers.

One of the most groundbreaking aspects of *Carnival Strippers* was the close involvement of the women themselves. Her subjects were involved in shaping their own images, and the portraits were a powerful way to define themselves. In the book, Meiselas also includes accounts by the strippers, together with comments from male spectators overheard in the crowds. Sometimes these comments reveal entrenched misogyny and sexism, at other times, unexpected empathy, but all of the divergent voices serve to interrupt the male gaze on the women.

In June 1978 Meiselas arrived in Nicaragua, where 'everything was about to erupt'.[1] Shortly after her arrival, Meiselas witnessed the Insurrection, the beginning of the Sandinista revolution that would overthrow the regime of Anastasio Somoza DeBayle, seizing power a year later. She initially spent six weeks documenting this definitive moment in the nation's history, and in the process created one her most outstanding bodies of work. She returned to Nicaragua for over a decade, continuing to photograph different aspects of the conflict and of daily life, side by side, as they happened. She documented the

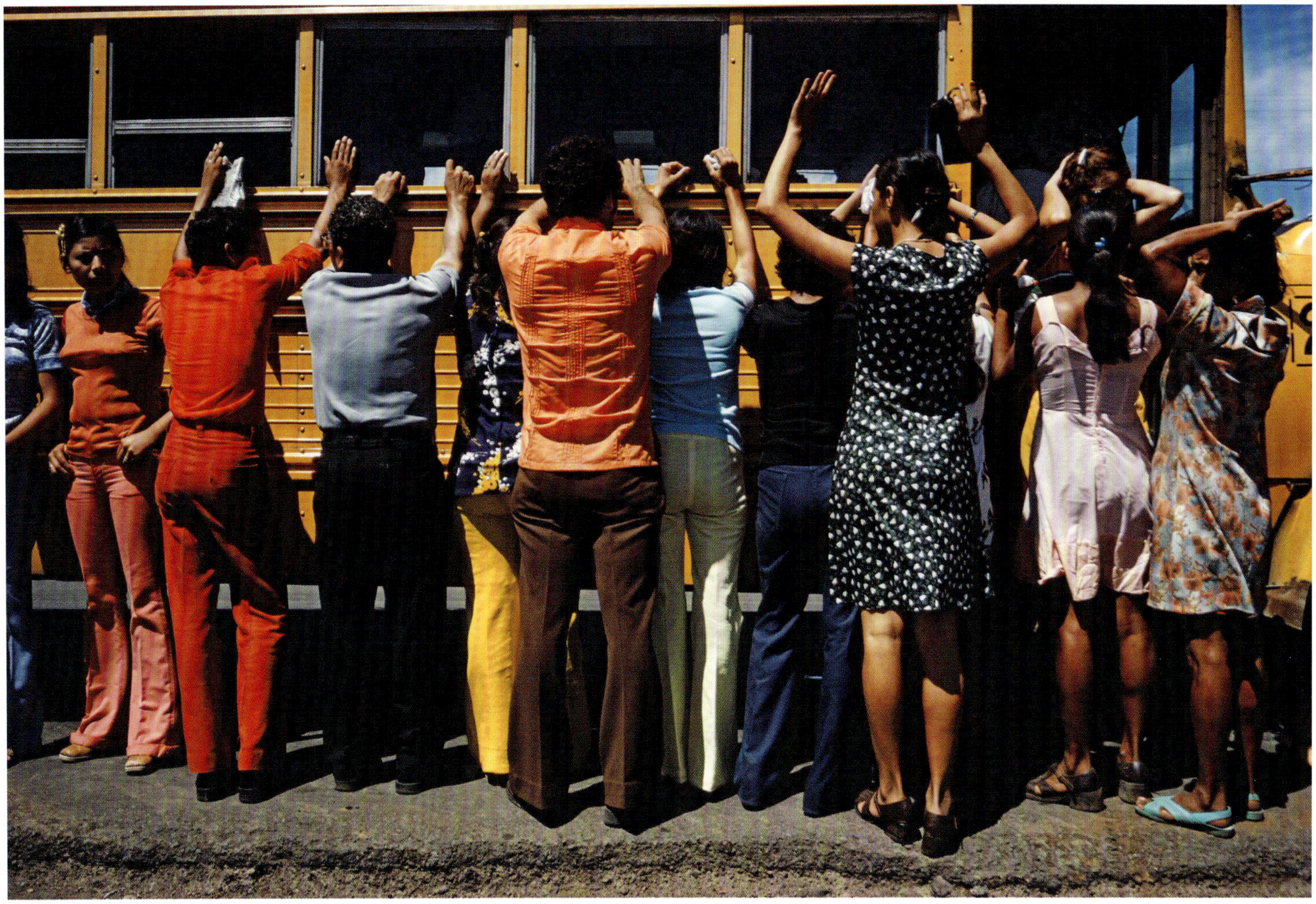

***Ciudad Sandino, Nicaragua, 1978. Searching everyone traveling by car, truck, bus or foot*, 1978**
This photograph was taken on the highway to León, Nicaragua, in 1978. It shows what had become a daily reality for many Nicaraguans during this time of political turmoil, to be routinely stopped and searched by the military. As is often the case with Meiselas's pictures, it is what we do not see, but know is there, that heightens the tension. We cannot see the soldiers, who are out of the frame, nor can we see the expression on the passengers' faces here; their body language and actions provide the only clues as to what is happening. The image demonstrates Meiselas's belief in the role of the photograph to 'act as testimony'.[4]

grisly mutilation and violence, but also the moments of respite, resilience and repair. This was a time of hope, but simultaneously the beginning of another turbulent period in Nicaragua's history. Meiselas was one of few women at the time to photograph war, but she did not consider herself a war photographer in the traditional sense, as she was 'really interested in how things come about, and not just in the surface of what it is.'[2] In 2004 she returned to Nicaragua once more and installed nineteen public murals of the images she took between 1978 and 1979, working with local communities. One of them was installed where the photograph was taken, on a hillside outside Managua, known as a place where assassinations were carried out. It depicts the dead body of a man, already picked apart by vultures, the limbs scattered and spine gruesomely exposed.

Meiselas spent over a quarter of a century photographing human rights issues across Latin America and recognizes the importance of standing 'for and with those who can't always speak for themselves'.[3] She has always acknowledged her role as an outsider, and as an American photojournalist documenting political situations

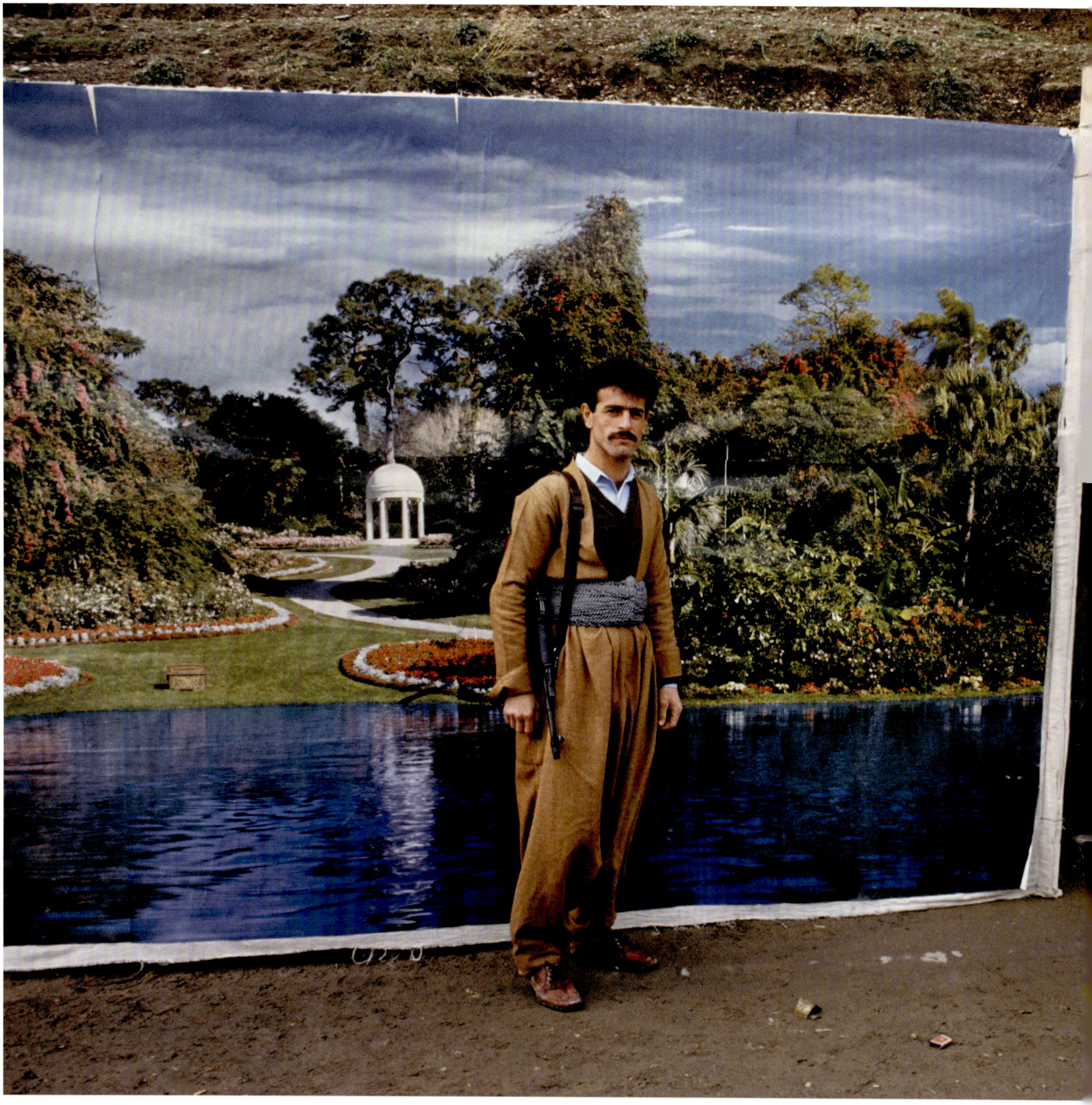

that the USA was often implicated in. She may not be able to resolve this dilemma in her work, but many of her photographs have been used by the people she has photographed, such as her famous *Molotov Man* (1979), capturing a revolutionary hurling a Molotov cocktail in a Pepsi bottle in the street, which was later used as a recruitment poster for the Sandinista movement.

A photograph, according to Meiselas, is a chance to bear witness, to make a claim for the future and to galvanize moves for change. In a career that now spans more than five decades, she continues to ask, 'What can photographs do now?'

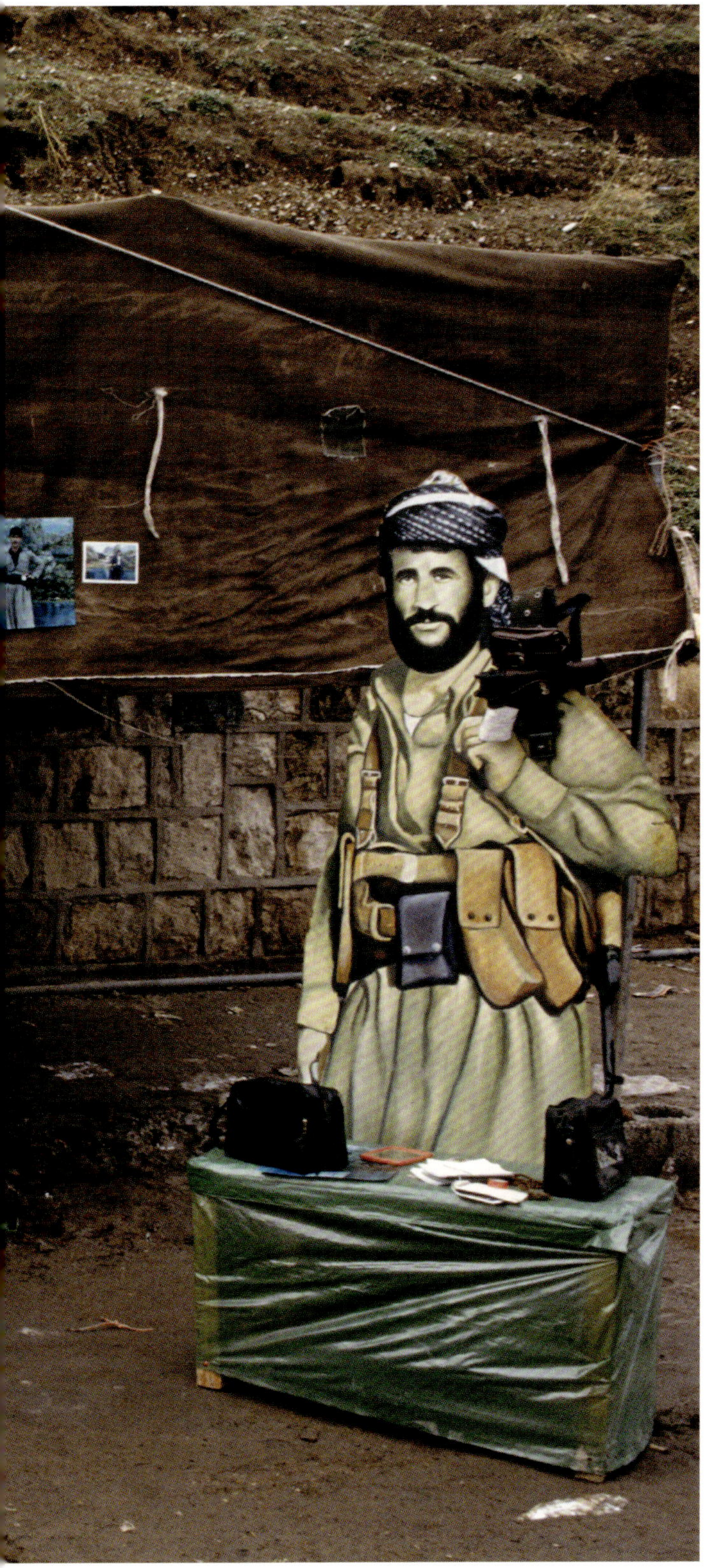

***Kurdistan, Iraq, 1991. A proud Peshmerga soldier pays to have his photograph taken on the streets of Arbil*, 1991**
This image of a Peshmerga soldier, who has paid to have his photograph taken in the town of Arbil, was taken when Meiselas first arrived in the northern Iraq to document the Anfal genocide of the Iraqi Kurds. Over the next three decades, realizing the complexity of the situation, her project changed and she began not only to take photographs but also to collect them from the people she encountered. The resulting body of work, *Kurdistan: In the Shadow of History* (1997), explores collective memory through visual materials and documents, photos from family albums, maps, drawings, newspaper cuttings and archival imagery, creating an ambitious retelling of the history of the Kurdish diaspora.

Zanele Muholi

Karabo Sebetoane, Parktown, Johannesburg, **2012, from the series** ***Faces and Phases*****. Silver gelatin print, 76.5 x 50.5 cm (29 ⅛ x 20 in)**
Karabo Sebetoane is a survivor of sexual violence who was raped because of his sexual orientation. When the mainstream media covered his story, Sebetoane has said, they emphasized his sexuality rather than the attack. His account highlights not only the ongoing threat for LGBTQI people in South Africa, but the role and responsibility of the media in educating and changing attitudes. This portrait is the first of two Muholi took of Sebetoane; the second was in 2016.

'A true and worthy ideal frees and uplifts a people,' wrote W.E.B. Du Bois,[1] the prominent pan-Africanist polymath who fought against racism in the early twentieth century. Du Bois helped put together The Exhibit of American Negroes, a collection of more than 500 photographs, archive material and documentation that was shown at the 1900 Paris Exposition with the aim of representing, reinforcing and revering the place of African Americans in the world. The visual activist Zanele Muholi has likened what they do to Du Bois's project, having worked tirelessly for over two decades to foreground the importance of self-representation, documenting the lives of the black lesbian, gay, transgender and intersex people in their community in South Africa and its diaspora.

Muholi was born in Umlazi and studied at the acclaimed Market Photo Workshop in Johannesburg before completing their MFA at Ryerson University in Toronto. Having been raised in apartheid South Africa, their relationship with photography began in its aftermath. The camera was a tool to negotiate some of the complexities of the post-apartheid era, including telling the stories of LGBTQI people in a democratizing state where, in spite of legislation, the right to live equally is undermined by the persistence of hate crimes, rape, assault, abuse and homophobia. Muholi's earliest work, *Only Half the Picture* (2003–6), was a series of intimate photographs in which the stereotypes, taboos and stigma that confront LGBTQI people living in a heteronormative society are visualized through images of bodies. Intimate but never sensationalized, the cropped and close-up frames convey ambiguity, while the black and white film creates a kind of distance in time and place. Muholi has rejected the term 'artist' in favour of 'visual activist' to describe their practice[2] and with *Only Half the Picture* they established that intent: to insist on being seen, and on seeing, on their own terms.

In *Faces and Phases*, the storied and unprecedented series that followed in 2006 (and is still ongoing), Muholi began not only to record the lives lost to violence and the pain inflicted on individuals by discrimination, but to elevate and celebrate the subjects, showing them in a way they had never been viewed in public spaces. Muholi described the portraits as 'at once a visual statement and an archive, marking, mapping and preserving an often invisible community for posterity'.[3]

Faces and Phases now comprises more than 500 portraits. The portraits are united by their direct look back at the camera – at Muholi, whom they clearly trust.

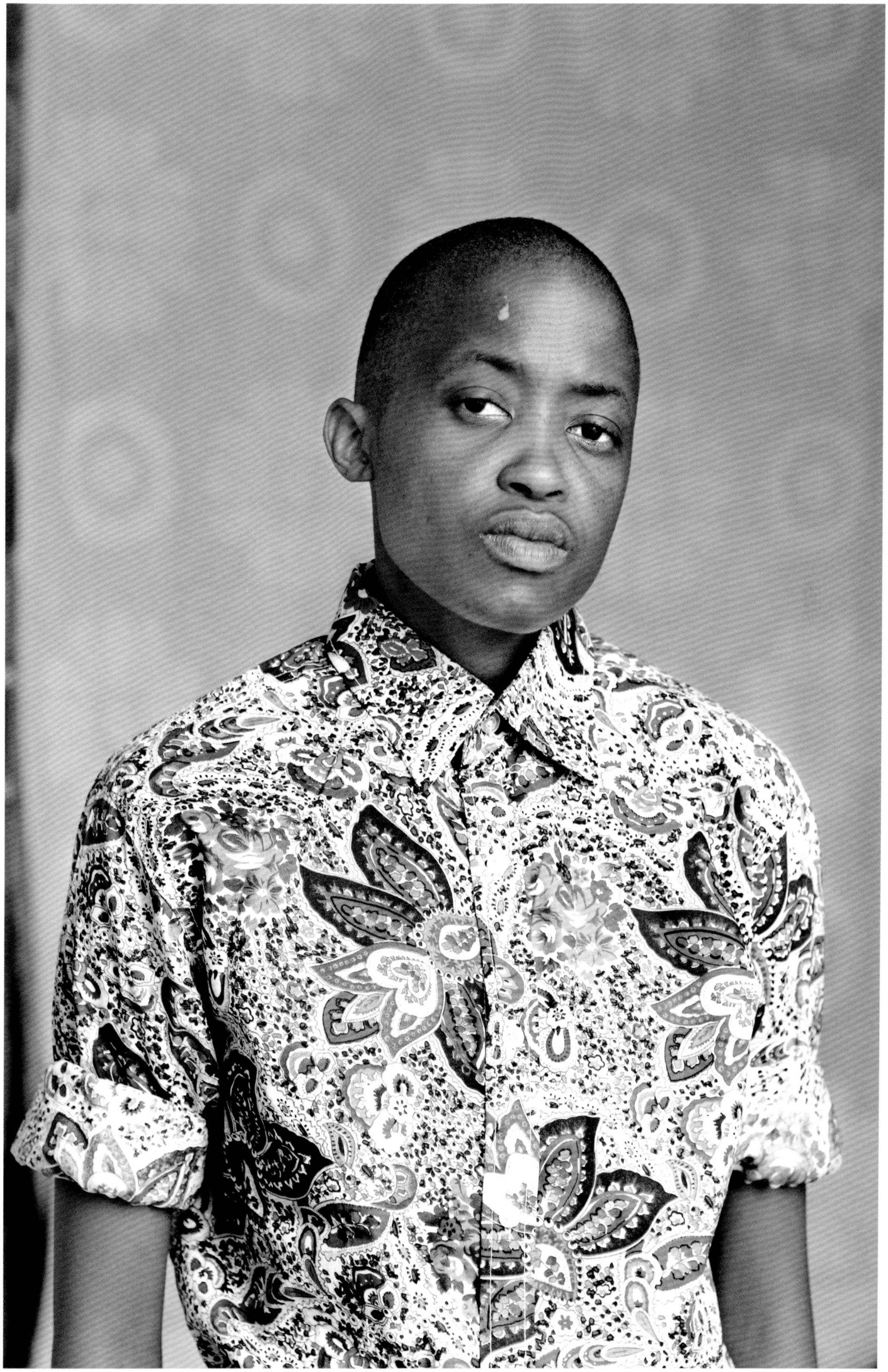

As Tate curator Kerryn Greenberg, who worked on Muholi's 2020 mid-career survey at London's Tate Modern, remarks, Muholi's work is fundamentally about 'rediscovering beauty'.[4] In the context of South Africa's apartheid history and politics, where beauty standards have been not only racialized but institutionalized by legislation, Greenberg adds, reclaiming beauty is a bold political stance as much as an aesthetic aim.

Representing so many people, however, is a heavy responsibility. International success in recent years means that Muholi is often on the road, as their work has been widely exhibited at festivals, museums and galleries across Europe and the USA. They also regularly give talks, lectures and interviews about their work – another fundamental aspect of Muholi's practice of visibility, which is essential in order to ensure that the purpose of the portraits is understood and endures.

This idea underpins Muholi's most recent series, *Somnyama Ngonyama: Hail the Dark Lioness*, which started in 2012 and now comprises more than 200 images. The photographer inhabits different characters, staging re-enactments of personal encounters and experiences with racism and homophobia in both their own and a collective history, some of them responses to unpleasant episodes while travelling in the West and entering white-dominated spaces. In portraits taken in locations all over Europe, the USA and Africa, Muholi's body becomes a canvas on which the blazing oppositional gaze that was employed in *Faces and Phases* here reflects Du Bois's notion of a 'double consciousness', one directed towards white, Western prejudices and projections about blackness and queerness, while at the same time emphatically embracing their own selfhood and claiming their history.

***Balindile II, The Square, Cape Town*, 2017 from the series *Somnyama Ngonyama: Hail the Dark Lioness*. Silver gelatin print, 50 x 35.1 cm (19 ¾ x 13 ⅞ in)**
The title of this self-portrait photograph translates as 'they are waiting'. The bag of produce wrapped in a thin plastic sheath balances on the figure's head, recalling the way heavy domestic items and food are traditionally carried by women throughout the country. Muholi refers to what they wear in this series as 'material' rather than props so as to force the viewer to rethink the connotations and history involved. Muholi also heightens the contrast in the series of performative self-portraits to emphasize their skin tone. This image is striking in its simplicity and minimalism, with the focus falling on the direct gaze back at the camera/viewer, which is, as always in Muholi's work, paramount: 'I looked directly at the camera in order to create a sense of questioning or confrontation which could be read by viewers in different ways.'[5]

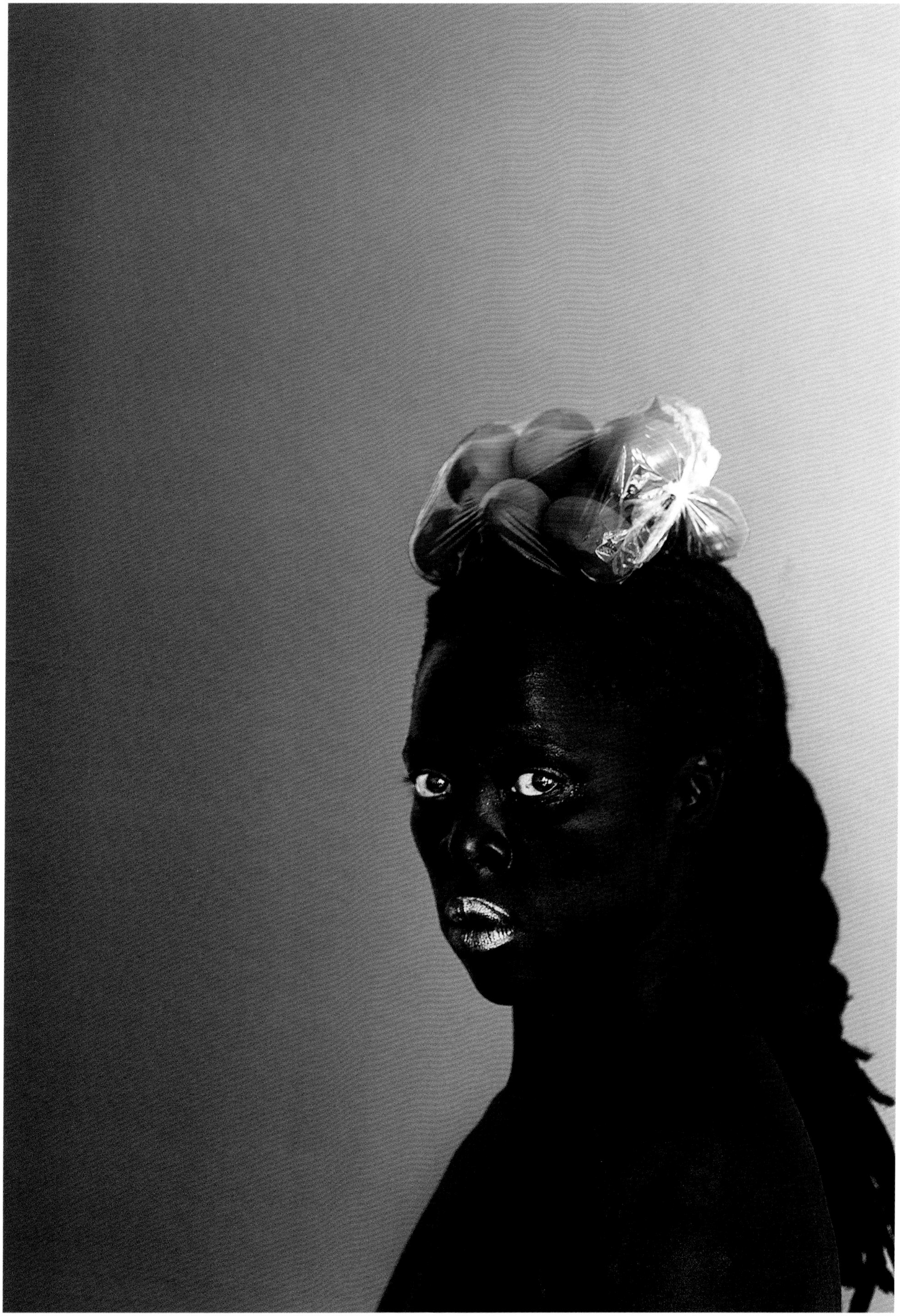

Shirin Neshat

Born in 1957, Shirin Neshat left Iran in 1975 and was studying art in the USA when the Iranian Revolution of 1979 erupted. Witnessing what was happening in her homeland from abroad and seeing how events played out in the media in the West affected her deeply, but it was only after she briefly returned to Iran in the early 1990s that she began to make artworks about the subject. This was a disorienting visit, as she encountered the country she had known through her memories and images as an entirely new and changed place, after not only the revolution but also the war with Iraq. She described the effects of her visit as profound, but it marked something of an epiphany too, because when Neshat returned to New York she embarked on a new path as an artist. Years later, Neshat remains in exile in New York, having been banned from entering Iran in 1996, and although she does not know if she will ever be able to return, she maintains a strong connection with the country, which continues to shape her work in different ways.

The experience of oscillating between two countries – especially two countries that are culturally and politically opposed – has been a constant theme in Neshat's films and photographs right from her breakthrough work, *Women of Allah* (1994–2015). Inspired by the newspaper images of armed Iranian women that were widely published during and after the revolution, the black and white self-portraits of veiled women – religious martyrs – are inscribed with Farsi calligraphy taken from poems on the subject of martyrdom. This series was, and remains, a groundbreaking investigation of the relationship between femininity, Islamic fundamentalism and militancy in Iran, subjects sensationalized widely in the West. Placing herself in front of the camera in *Women of Allah* was also a way for Neshat to navigate her ambiguous and discordant feelings and relationship to Islam and Iran, as an artist and a migrant living abroad. After using herself in early works like *Women of Allah* and *Soliloquy* (2000), Neshat began to cast other women in her place, but they closely resemble her, both in appearance and in spirit. This has become one of the signatures of her work, indicating its profoundly personal subtext.

Women of Allah was also the beginning of an enduring relationship with black and white, now instantly recognizable as part of Neshat's visual language, whether in static or moving images. As the artist explains, 'When I decided to do photography, the subject was the Iranian Revolution of 1979. Colour was really irrelevant because I felt the subject was so severe and so much about

***Untitled* from the series *Women of Allah*, 1994–2015. Silver gelatin print and ink, 152.4 x 107.3cm (60 x 42 ¼ in)**
In this performative self-portrait from Neshat's most prominent photographic opus, *Women of Allah*, the artist poses as a *shaheed* ('martyr'), wearing a black *chador* and holding a rifle, her hands draped in cloth and not visible. The skin of her neck is inscribed with Farsi calligraphy, from a poem by Tahereh Saffarzadeh, recalling tattooing traditions in Middle Eastern cultures. The figure's soft, contemplative gaze is apparently at odds with the threat of violence implied by the gun, exploring the paradox between stereotypical femininity, beauty and passivity, and cruelty, militancy and religious martyrdom among women in Iran. Deliberately ambiguous, Neshat does not offer a critique or comment on the Muslim women who devote their lives to religious extremism. Instead she explores the ways a 'woman's body has been historically a type of battleground for various kinds of rhetoric and political ideology'.[4]

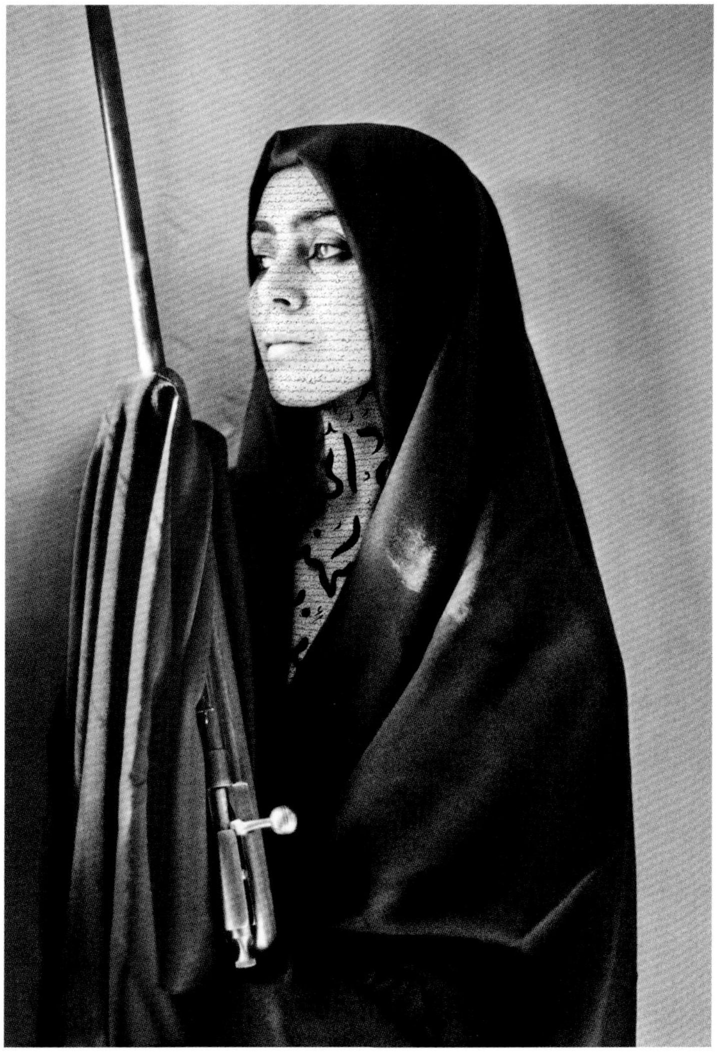

opposites.'[1] The starkness of the black and white emphasizes Neshat's fascination with dialectics: male and female, East and West, Islam and secularity, landscape and architecture, the subconscious and the rational, body and spirit. 'The black and white always seems to emphasize that sense of duality,' she notes.[2]

Although she trained as a painter, Neshat has always gravitated towards the camera for its immediacy, intimacy, drama and realism. Her films are in some way an extension of her photography, carefully choreographed and directed, with monumental constructed scenes, but with the addition of sound and movement. Her first video installation, *Turbulent* (1998), continued to explore the binaries and divisions inherent in the position of Muslim woman in a contemporary context. It places footage of a veiled woman, her back to the viewer, on one screen, facing a man, who sings in Farsi to an all-male audience; when his performance ends it is the woman's turn, but her song is wordless.

Neshat always keeps the viewer conscious of the camera in her works, through careful and deliberate framing, or by using narratives that incorporate the film-making or photographic process. Her 2017 biopic *Looking for Oum Kulthum*, co-directed by her husband, Shoja Azari, follows an Iranian film-maker living in exile who begins to make a film about the eponymous celebrated Egyptian singer. More recently, Neshat's three-part *Land of Dreams* (2019) included two short videos and a selection of portraits. The first video follows Simin, a young Iranian photographer who travels across the USA knocking on strangers' doors, taking their portraits and recording their dreams. In the second video, Simin's documents are analyzed by the Iranian government. The photographic component comprises more than a hundred portraits taken across New Mexico, captioned with Farsi calligraphy.

Combining political satire, surrealism and portraiture, *Land of Dreams* gives a complex view of contemporary US society under the Trump administration, a radical reimagining of the American dream. The camera in works like *Land of Dreams* acts as a vessel, a way to navigate fraught and complex relationships, allowing Neshat and her protagonists to enter spaces where they may not feel welcome or comfortable. 'I play with the idea of being a woman, an artist, a photographer – how photography captures human beings,' Neshat reflects.[3] In recognition of her innovative approach to image-making, she was awarded the 2020 Master of Photography Award by Photo London.

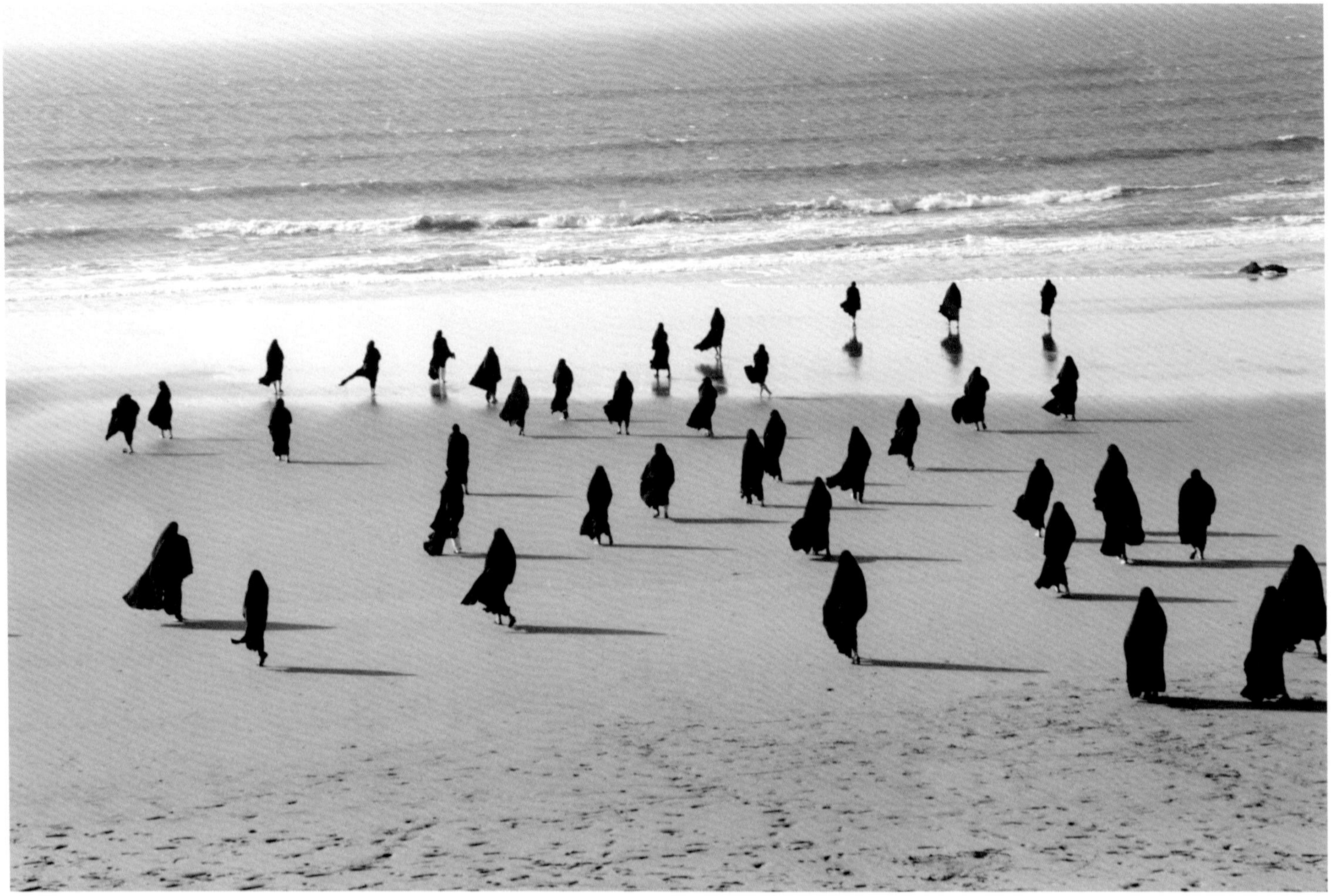

From the series *Rapture*, 1999. Gelatin silver print
These striking images are from Neshat's early two-channel video installation *Rapture*, an allegorical examination of the ways Islamic law in Iran affects gender politics and everyday life. Shot in her trademark black and white on 16mm film, the split-screen installation positions the viewer between two contrasting views: one shows a group of women, dressed in black *chadors*, on a beach; the other, a group of men dressed in suits, in front of an imposing fortress. Deeply symbolic, *Rapture* examines the ways architecture, culture and religion can divide and dislocate, not only in Islamic society, but everywhere.

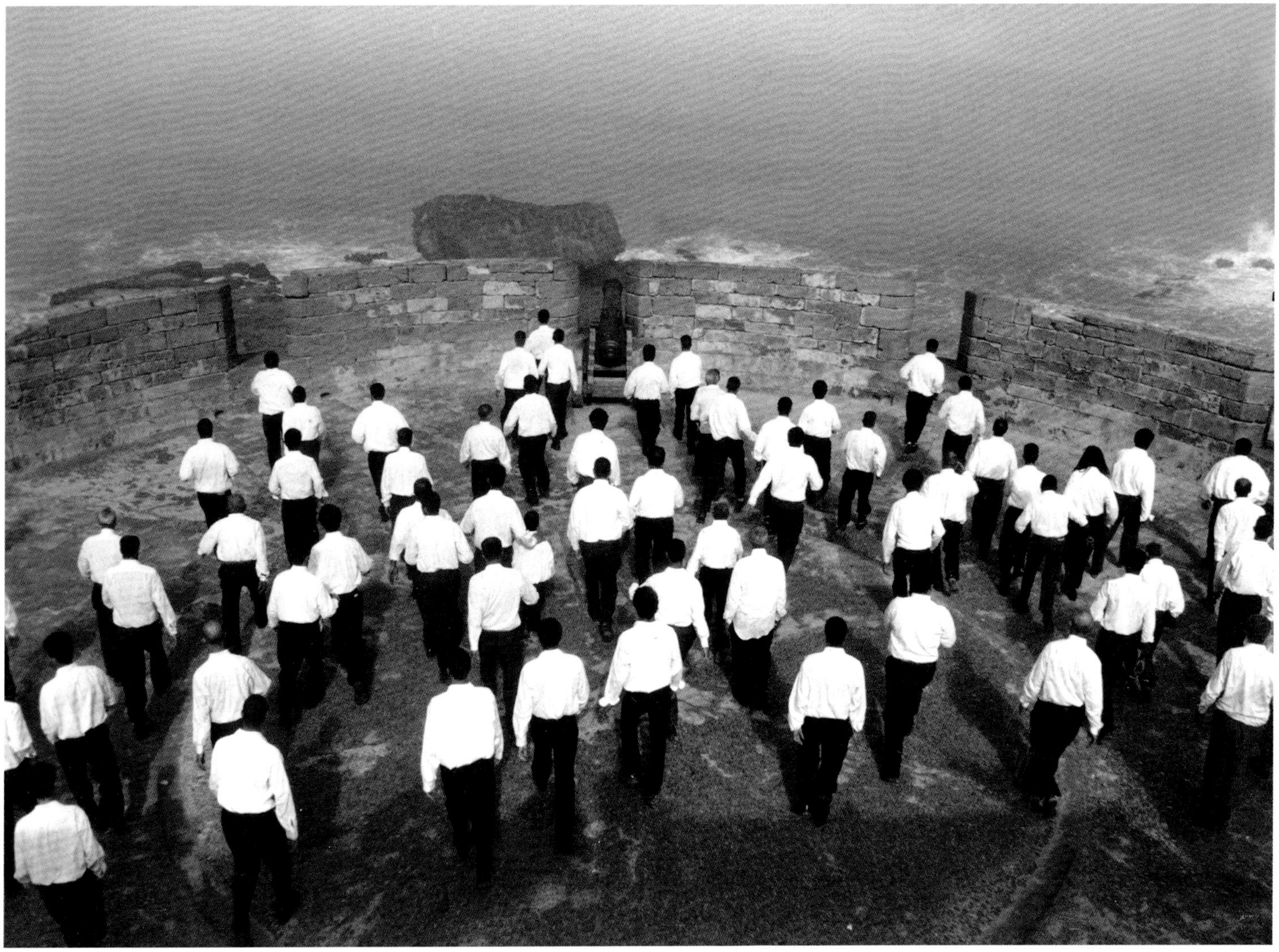

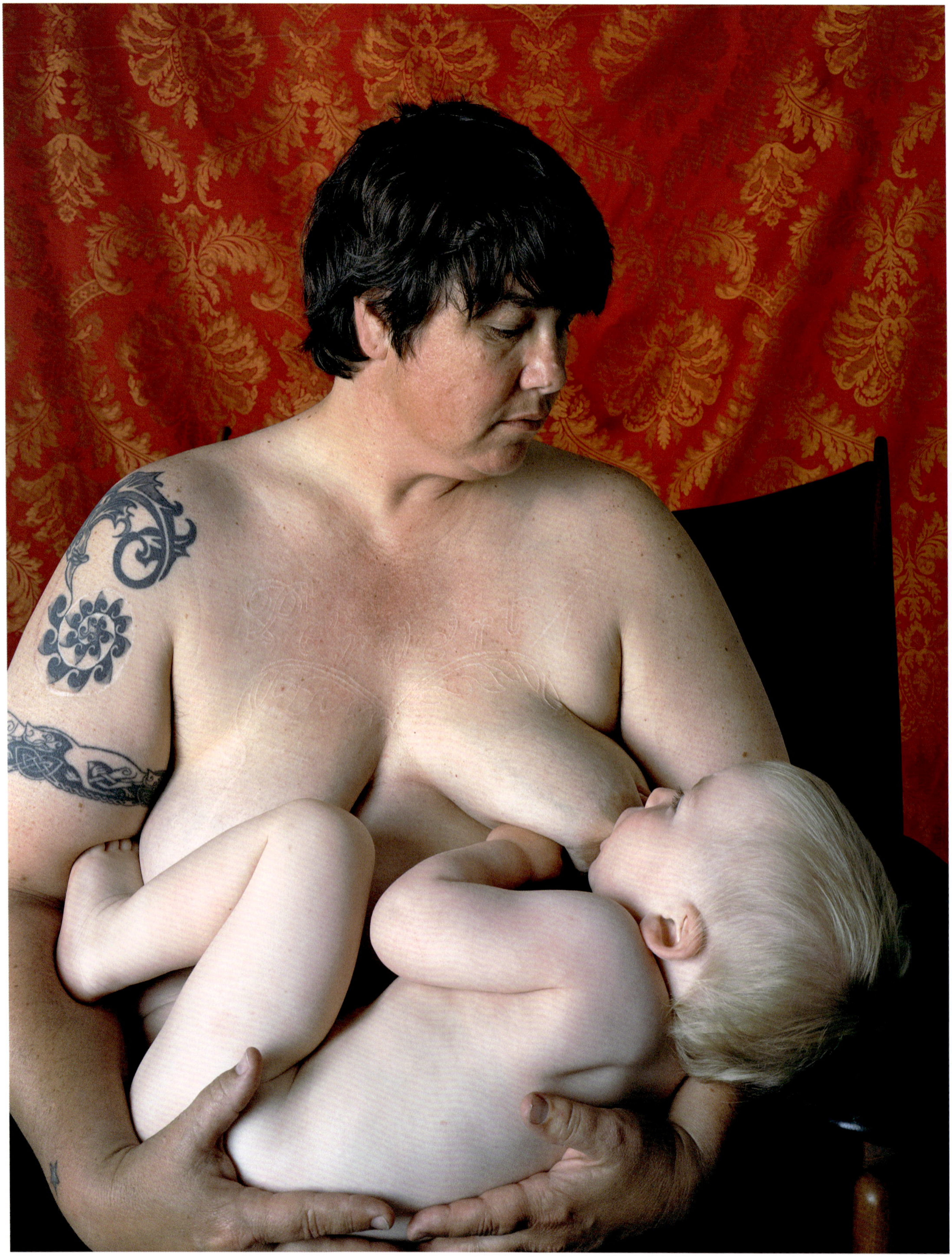

Catherine Opie

Can you be a traditionalist and a transgressive at the same time? One of Catherine Opie's most memorable works, *Self-Portrait/Cutting* (1993), made when she was in her thirties, suggests that you can. In it she had the idyll of a happy family carved into her back with a knife and then, while the blood was still dripping from her bare flesh, displayed the results to the camera. During three decades working in photography, Opie has moved between the radical and the regular, with portraits from high schoolers to world-famous artists, with images from masochism to motherhood, from the World Trade Center to Lake Michigan and Yosemite Falls. Her oeuvre constitutes a prolonged stare at contemporary America in which nothing is excluded, in which icons are overturned and new idols are created. 'The most important thing to do is to begin with an idea that tries to answer some questions,' was Opie's reply when asked what compels her to shoot a subject.[1]

Opie's life story is often related as a background to her work, though she rarely ventures too deeply into the personal – her son, Oliver, for example, makes only a few appearances in her portraits. Born in 1961, Opie grew up in Ohio, where she started taking pictures aged nine. Her childhood was spent roaming outdoors, but at home family life was fractured and chaotic – her parents would eventually divorce. When Opie was thirteen, the family moved to California. Her first forays into 35mm film came at around the same time that she realized she was attracted to women; later, when studying at the San Francisco Art Institute, she came out. It was then that she became involved with the leather-dyke scene and began taking photos for the lesbian sex magazine *On Our Backs*. An active member of the BDSM scene in Los Angeles, she featured many of the people she met there in her portraits in the 1990s. But, as Opie has emphasized, for her it was always more about community and feminist discussion than about sex. The emphasis is reflected in a series such as *Portraits* (1993–7), which is distinct from the works of predecessors, such as Robert Mapplethorpe, in that she is rarely explicit in her treatment of sexuality.

Opie presented *Being and Having* – her first widely influential work – at her first solo exhibition in 1991. This series established the foundations of her signature studio portrait style: bold, brightly coloured minimal

***Self Portrait/Nursing*, 2004. C-print, 101.6 x 81.3cm (40 x 32in)**
Compared to the number of portraits she has taken, Opie rarely uses herself as a model – but when she does, it is usually with intent and purpose. *Self-Portrait/Nursing* is Opie's answer to classical Madonna and Child depictions, a deeply personal reimagining of one of art history's most universally resonant images. Here she breastfeeds her son, Oliver, against a red and gold backdrop that refers to Renaissance art. Opie casts herself as a new kind of Madonna – in her forties, butch, with tattoos and scars (the traces of 'Pervert' on her chest recall an earlier BDSM self-portrait), nothing about her body conforms to the traditional portraits of maternity. Yet, as the image shows, she is no less able to nourish, protect and love her child. Once again, Opie was ahead of her time in offering an alternative perspective to the idealized, heteronormative images of motherhood we are constantly exposed to in the mainstream.

backgrounds, an interest in shape and lighting, closely observed details that suggest intimacy with the subject without exposing them. *Being and Having* paved the way for a new photographic approach to the politics of bodies and gender: in staged self-portraits, Opie, dressed in different guises as an alter ego named Bo, appeared alongside portraits of lesbian friends, all of them with fake moustaches and macho expressions. The work is both playful and trenchant, setting a precedent for what is now a popular idea in photography, and visual culture in general, that gender is only a performance.

Gender and sexuality have remained a recurrent theme in Opie's work, but she has never limited herself in terms of her subject – or her audience. Opie is known for referencing canonical works of art history, from Baroque painters and Renaissance old masters, Hans Holbein to Monet, Eugène Atget to August Sander. A major mid-career survey at the Guggenheim in New York in 2008 was entitled *Catherine Opie: American Photographer* and perhaps this remains the best description for her. Ultimately, Opie's most ardent muse is America, with its multifaceted, endlessly complex physical and social structure, its natural and man-made geography and its infinite variety of residents: from freeways to sweeping lakes, and from the private residence of Elizabeth Taylor or underground sex scenes to surfers in Malibu waiting on the waves.

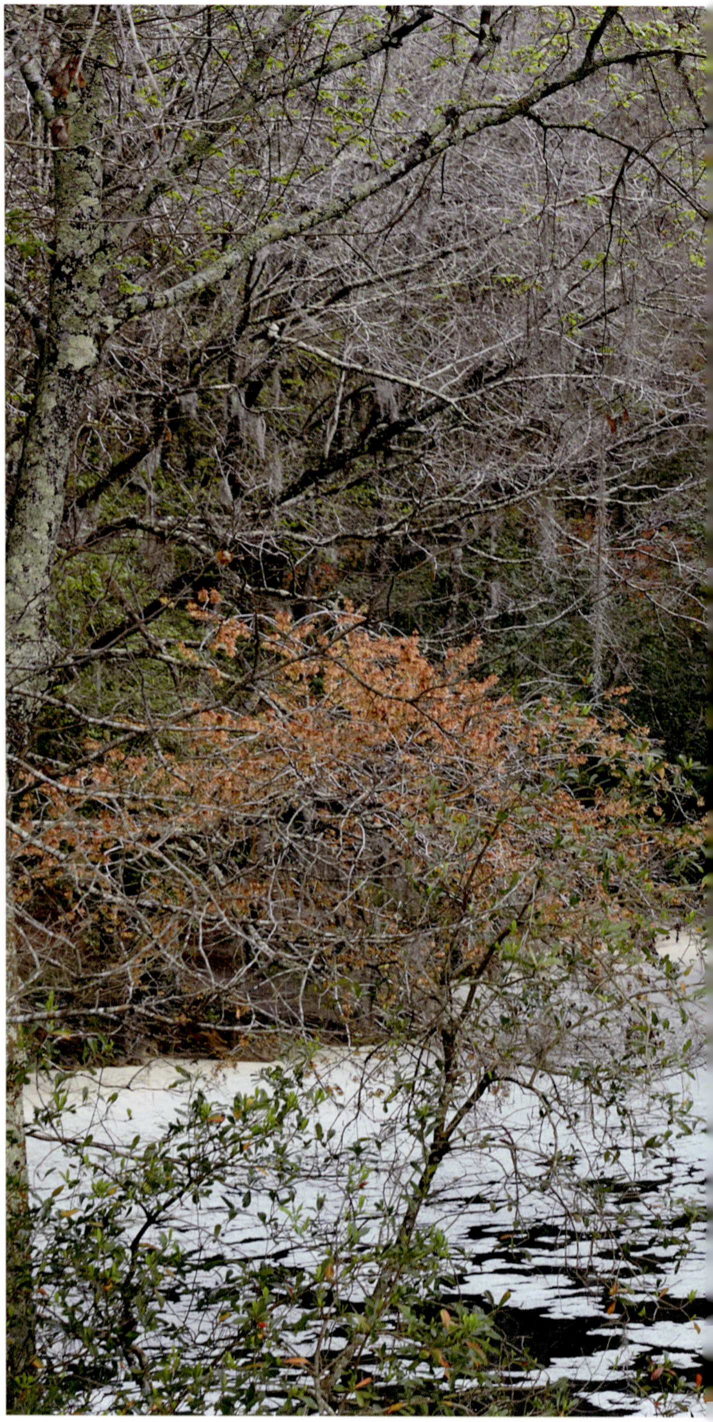

***Untitled #8* from the series *Swamps*, 2019. Pigment print, 101.6 x 152.4cm (40 x 60in)**
Opie has got to know her home territory well over the last thirty years, documenting its diversity not only through the various communities she has photographed but also through its natural landscapes and built environments. Her landscape photographs – often printed on a vast, immersive scale – are another way for her to enter into a dialogue with art history. In *Swamps*, Opie visited the wilds of the American South, a contested area that has been mythologized in American history and culture but that appears in her work as empty and uninhabited. In a play on words, the swamps evoke the American political metaphor of 'draining the swamp' manipulated by Donald Trump, yet they also remain one of the last undeveloped ecosystems facing the effects of climate change and human development.

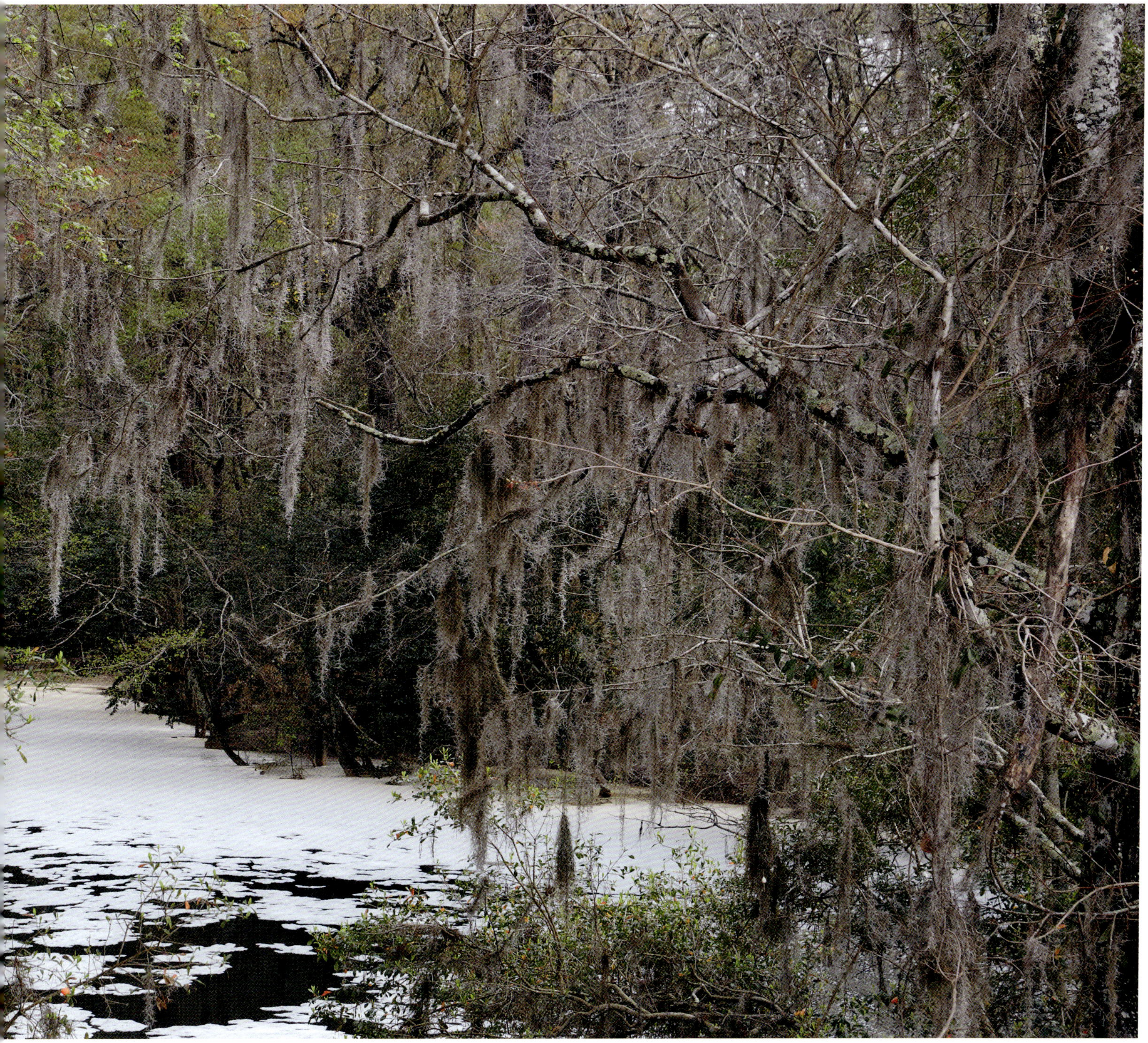

Martin Parr

No other photographer has dedicated as much attention to the UK as Martin Parr. Born in Surrey in 1952, for the last forty years he has trained his lens on his home country, its banalities and eccentricities, forgotten customs and glaring stereotypes. From beaches to Butlin's, to food, fetes and families, he has said 'there's nothing I don't want to photograph.'[1] Inevitably, these photographs reflect class, identity, social habits, landscapes and politics, so with the passage of time they give an unprecedented insight into the changes that have led to the UK of today.

Parr was interested in photography from an early age, encouraged by his grandfather, and he went to study at Manchester Polytechnic (now Manchester Metropolitan University). He graduated in 1973, though famously almost failed the course. When Parr started out in the 1970s, black and white photography was considered the only serious form of expression and his earliest works, using a 35mm lens, conformed to this standard. But when he moved to Liverpool in 1982, he began to shoot with colour film on a new medium-format camera, a Plaubel Makina with a 55mm lens and on-board flash. The shift was revelatory and Parr's use of saturated colour – his confidence bolstered by American photographers Stephen Shore and William Eggleston – has remained one of the defining characteristics of his photographs ever since.

In 1985 Parr published his most celebrated and collected work, *The Last Resort*. The publication is currently in its eighth edition and the images are featured in several museum collections. The series of photographs focused on the seaside resort of New Brighton, on the Wirral Peninsula, near Liverpool. *The Last Resort* captured the quintessence of British culture in the mid-1980s: a vibrant jamboree of pets, babies, perms and deckchairs, unglamorous but good old-fashioned fun.

After *The Last Resort* was shown at the Serpentine Gallery in 1986, it launched Parr's career and also one of his central themes: leisure. It is leisure, Parr believes, that really defines who we are. He soon began to document this in other parts of the country, capturing larger-than-life characters at beaches, piers, amusement parks, promenades and parties, eating, drinking and dancing. The south-west of England was the focus of *The Cost of Living* (1987–9), in part a portrait of the rise of the middle class under Thatcherism. From the late 1980s he began to look more globally, first in *Small World* (1987–94), then in *Common Sense* (1995–9), at the effects of

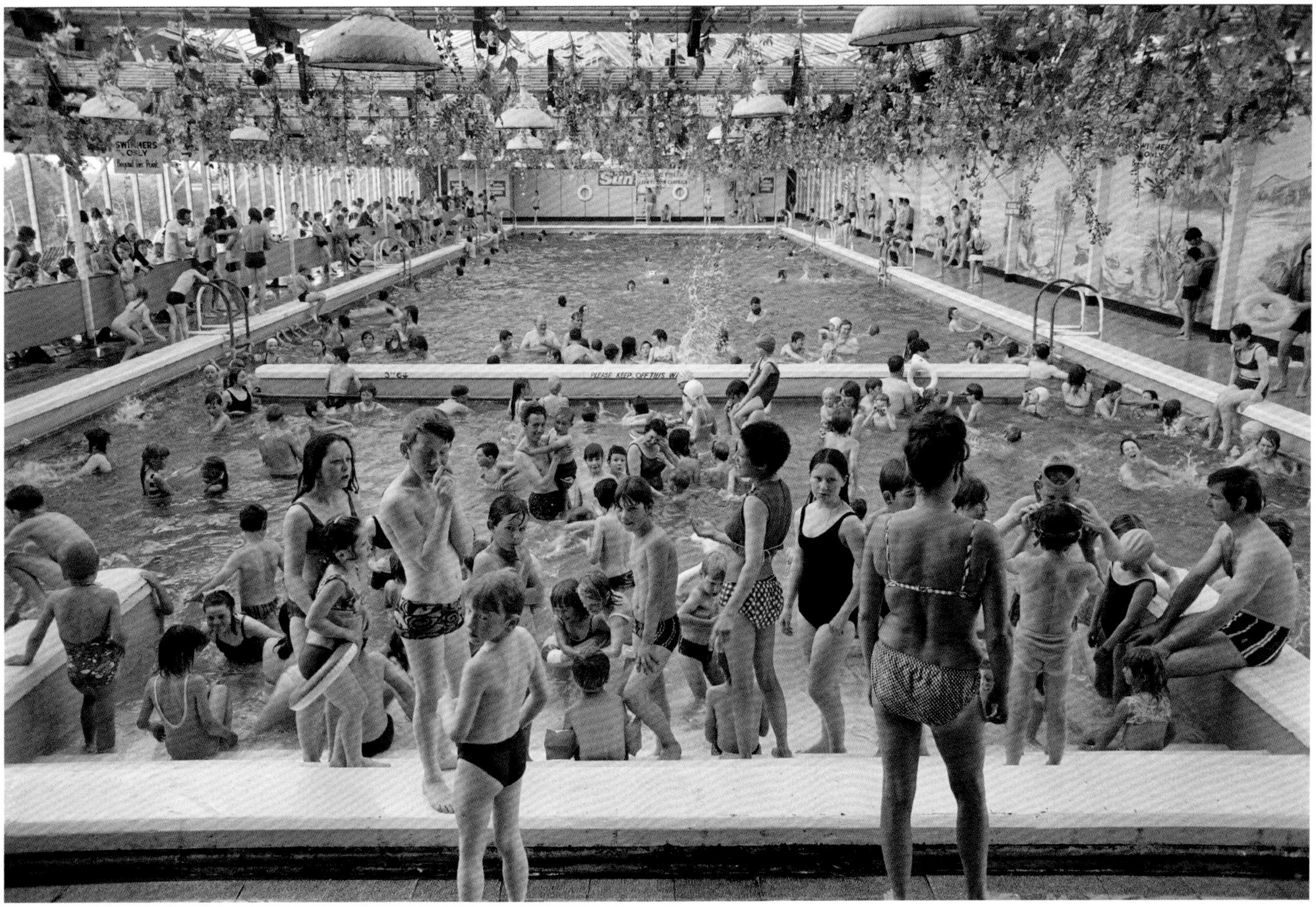

Butlins, Filey, North Yorkshire **from the series *Early Works*, 1972**
Parr was only twenty and still a student at Manchester Polytechnic when he took this picture in Filey, North Yorkshire, depicting a pool scene. He was working as an official photographer at Butlin's by the Sea, as a way to earn money, but his observations of British people at play during that time would go on to shape his interests as a professional photographer later. Long before the 'staycation' was a marketing tool, Parr captured families enjoying themselves close to home at weekends and during the summer holidays.

mass leisure culture and consumerism. To date, Parr has produced more than a hundred photobooks of his own work. Unlike many photographers who document changing times, he isn't nostalgic or sentimental about the shifts he has seen: 'I've as much got an eye on the future as the current time.'[2]

Not only is Parr one of Britain's most important documenters – as illustrated by a major 2019 exhibition at the National Portrait Gallery, London – but he has been a prominent and active collector, curator and archivist of photography and its practitioners, particularly those working within the documentary genre. From 2014 to 2017, he was the president of Magnum Photos International, having been a full member since 1994. In 2017 he opened the Martin Parr Foundation in Bristol, dedicated to collecting and exhibiting photobooks and photographs both about Britain and by British photographers.

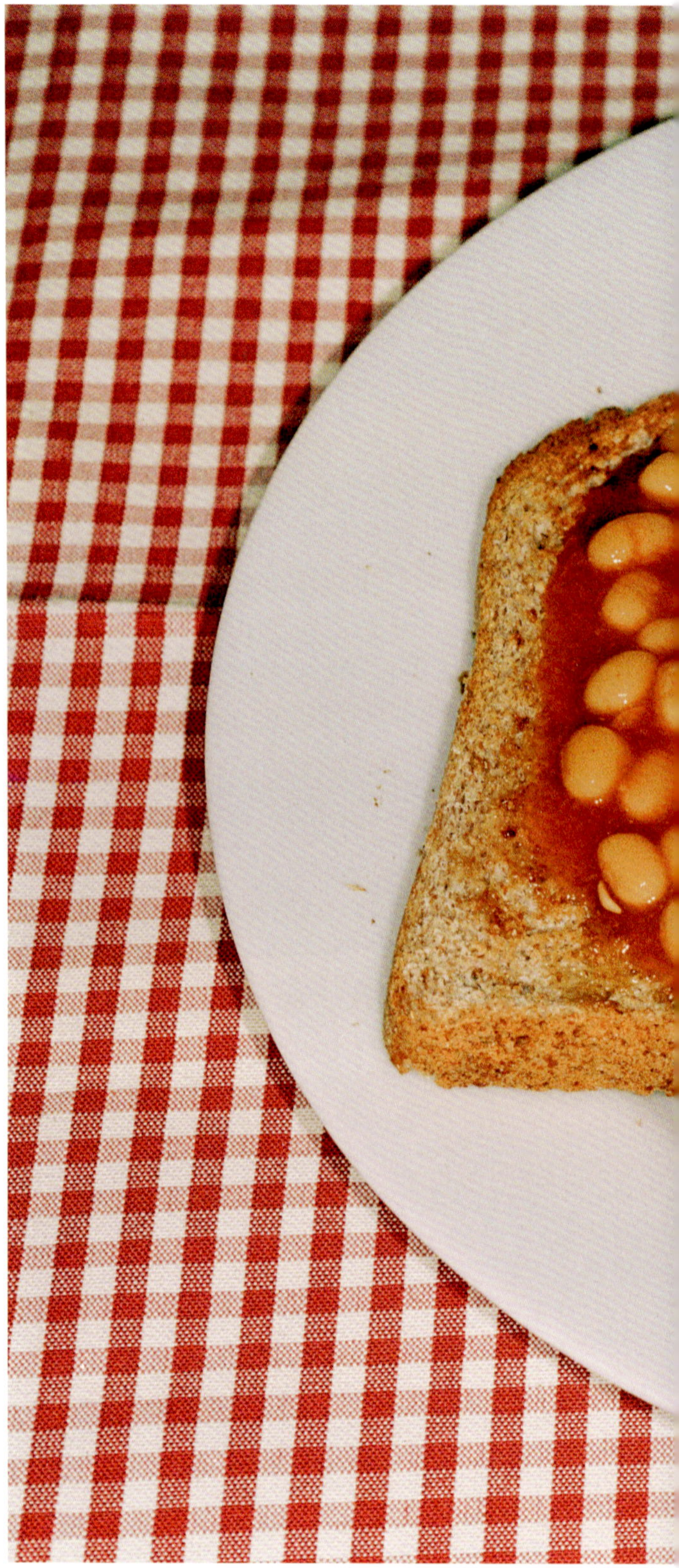

***Bristol, England*, 2005**
Food is one of the themes that Parr is best known for – cheap, no-frills, unpretentious and unequivocally British food. This image immortalizes the iconic dish of beans on toast, recognizing its central place in contemporary British identity, a synecdoche of sorts. Shot in close-up in Parr's typically loud and cheerful colour, his version of beans on toast shows just how emotive food can be and how intrinsic it is to culture.

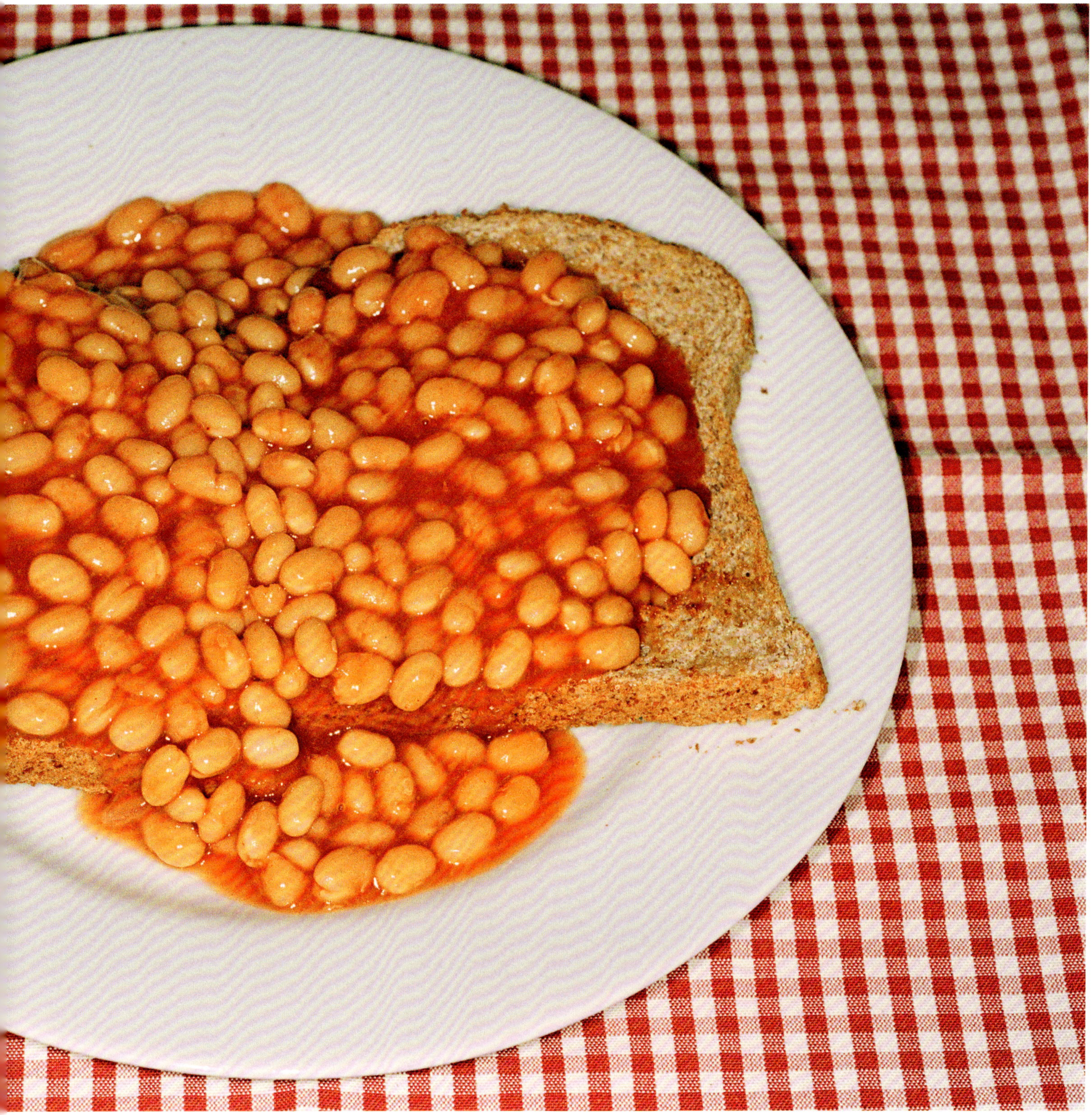

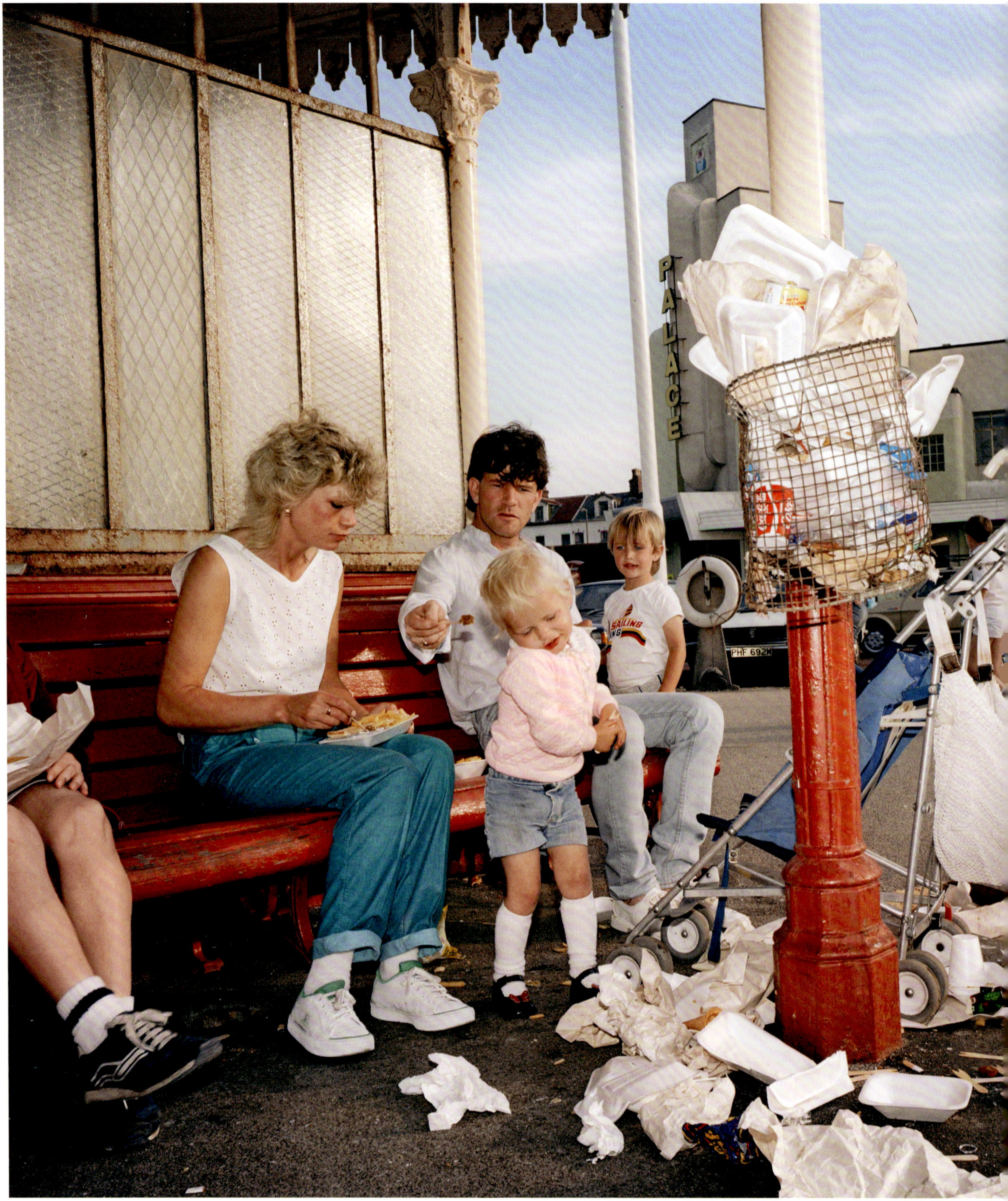
PALACE
SAILING
PHF 692M

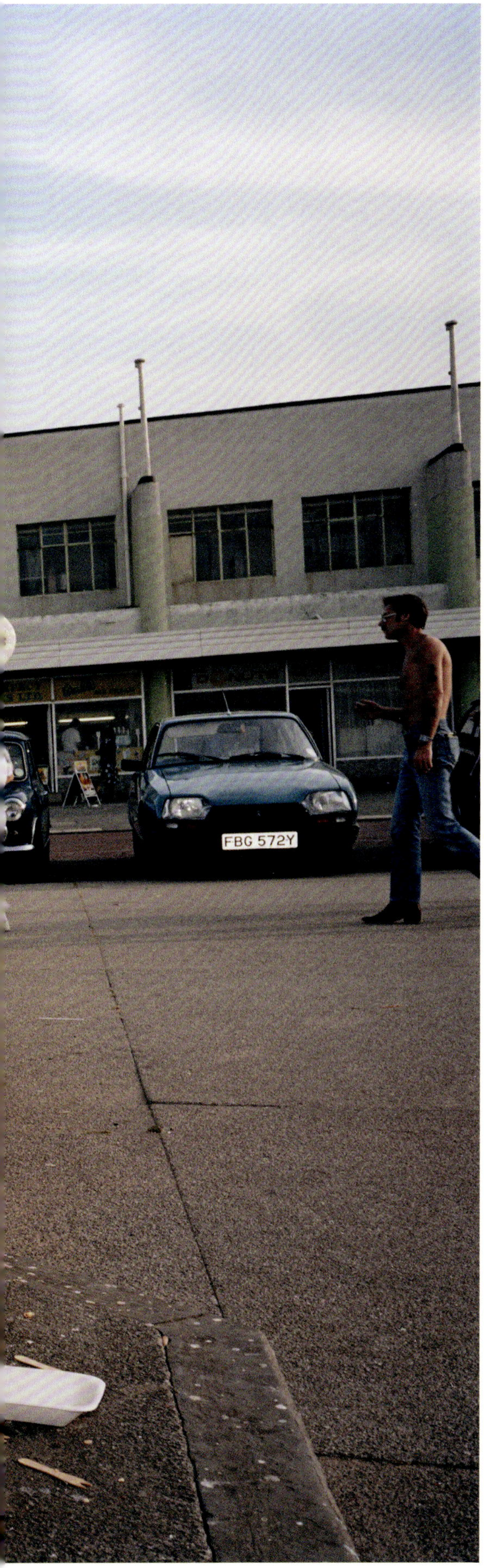

***New Brighton* from the series *The Last Resort*, 1983–5**
During the period 1983–5 Parr travelled to New Brighton, near Liverpool, on sunny days to shoot the seaside town. This image forms part of *The Last Resort*, the pivotal body of work which was published as a book in 1985. It shows Parr's desire to 'make a picture that's going to be entertaining and good to look at, and also one that relates to people's lives'.[3] The work initially elicited some criticism, with claims that it mocked his working-class subjects by showing them in an unflattering manner. Parr riposted that the work was not about class but rather about the things we share no matter who we are, the simple pleasures and the screaming infants.

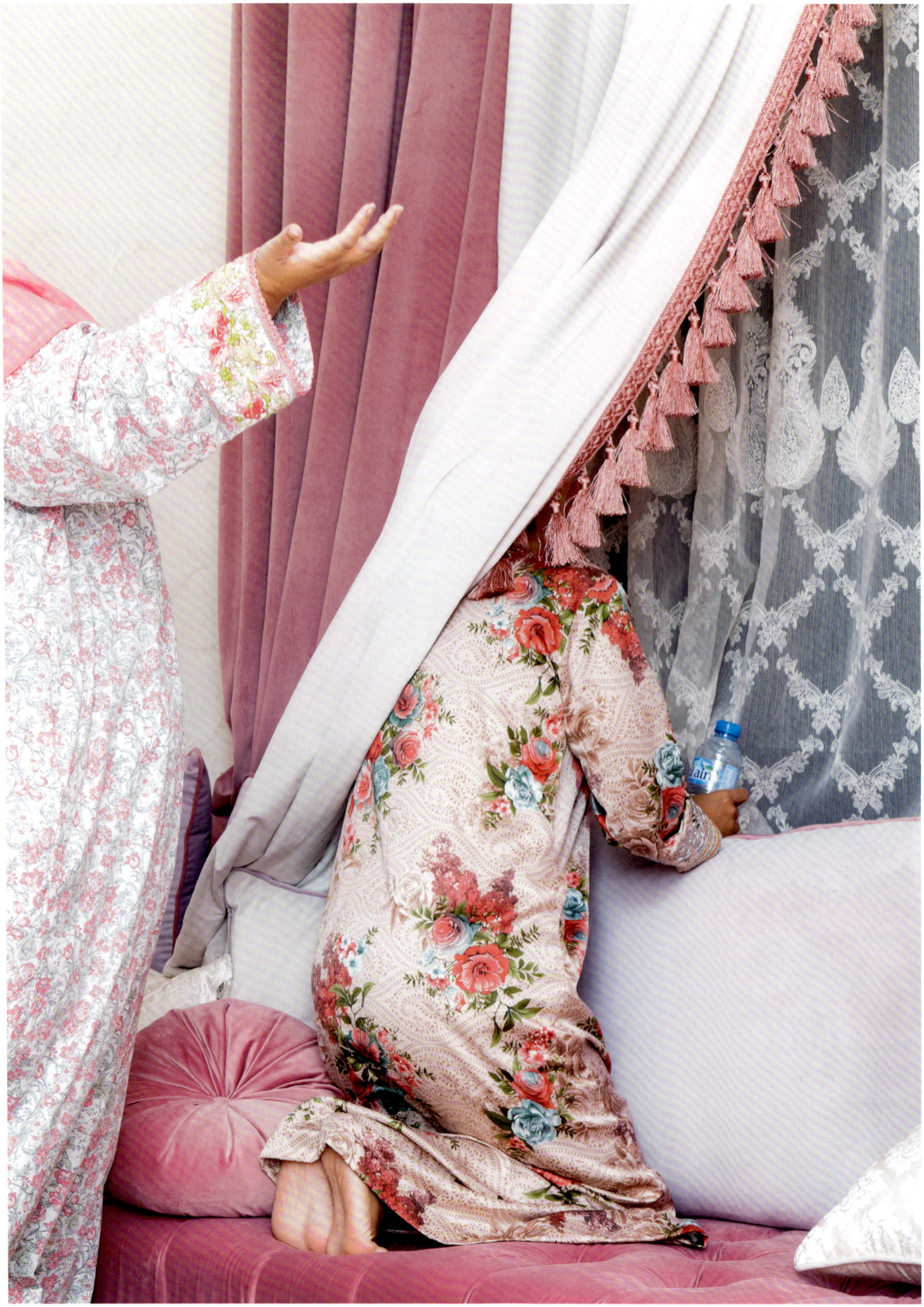

Farah Al Qasimi

After Dinner 2 **from the series** ***Arrival*****, 2018. Archival inkjet print, 66.7 x 89cm (26 ⅜ x 35in)**
Arrival is a work in two parts, with a series of photographs providing static moments that relate to scenes in Al Qasimi's forty-minute horror-comedy film, which was inspired by jinn folklore. Jinn are supernatural creatures from pre-Islamic Arabian mythology which were later incorporated into Islamic theology. The word 'jinn' itself derives from the verb meaning 'to hide' and some translators note a specific meaning, 'beings that are concealed from the senses' – which seems an apt way to describe Al Qasimi's photographs, in which nothing is ever fully visible. Like the jinn, the characters in these cinematic vignettes are ambiguous and can be read as innocuous or malevolent – it is up to the viewer to interpret the gestures, objects and adornments.

One of the first people to capture Abu Dhabi in photographs was the German explorer Hermann Burchardt, who arrived in 1904 for a tour of the Middle East. While there, he took the earliest known photograph of the ruler Sheikh Zayed the Great. More than a century later, this famous picture has been endlessly reproduced and continues to be one of the defining images of the eastern Arabian peninsula.

Abu Dhabi has had a vibrant twenty-first-century rebranding with the work of Farah Al Qasimi, whose photographs wrest her home city and Arab culture from the supremacy of the Western eye and Orientalist representations. Al Qasimi was born in Abu Dhabi in 1991 and spent her formative years there before moving to the USA to study at Yale. Her vision of contemporary urban life in the United Arab Emirates couldn't be more different from the sombre black and white glass plates Burchardt made in the early twentieth century. Inspired by the brightly coloured fabrics, fashions and domestic interiors of the Emirati capital, Al Qasimi presents the culture of the Arabian Gulf and its diaspora in a vivid and playful way.

One of the subjects she returns to constantly is masculinity, and in particular racialized ideas about Arab men as articulated through images. In her 2018 exhibition *More Good News* at Helena Anrather in New York, she displayed a series of portraits – including ones of her father – that reveal a vulnerable side to Arab and South East Asian men in order to directly subvert prevalent associations with threat and violence. These portraits are presented alongside still lifes – an important part of Al Qasimi's work – that overturn symbols of masculine authority and patriarchal power, sometimes literally: a heavy volume on US treaties and international agreements seems about to fall from a shelf; a dog looks up forlornly at the camera from underneath a table on which a dish of raw meat, several guns and bullets are enigmatically scattered.

Enigma, concealment and disguise are tools Al Qasimi uses again and again, and to great effect; she once even found a doppelgänger via Instagram to stand in for her in one performance work. Her photographs, films and performances depend on the dialectic tension between fear of the invisible and the desire to manifest it. Cloaks, shrouds and camouflage are cleverly deployed to resist straightforward readings of people and their identities, inverting the portrait form. 'There's often this conversation about visibility being the highest goal,' the artist explains. 'I like to find beauty in other places.'[1]

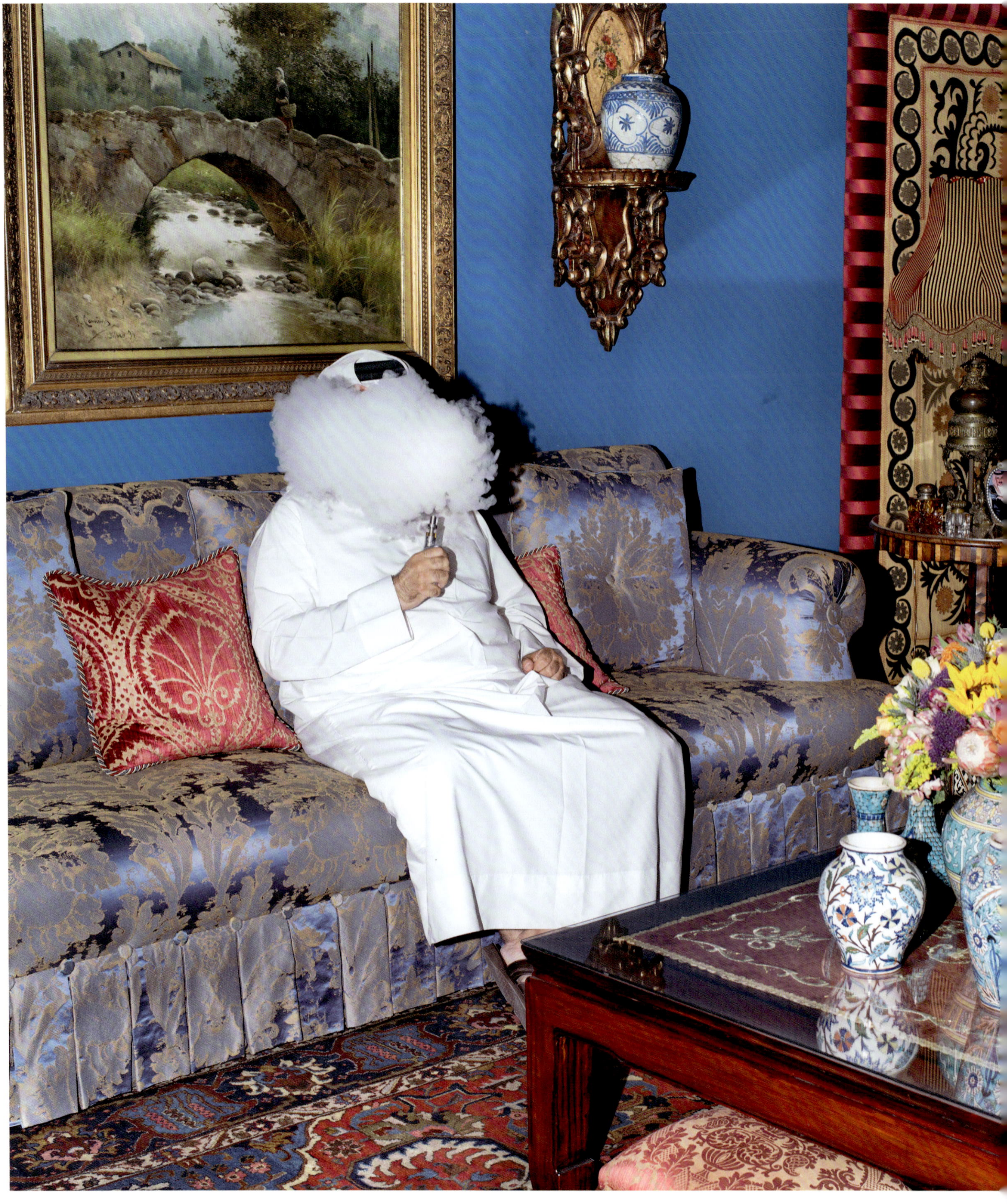

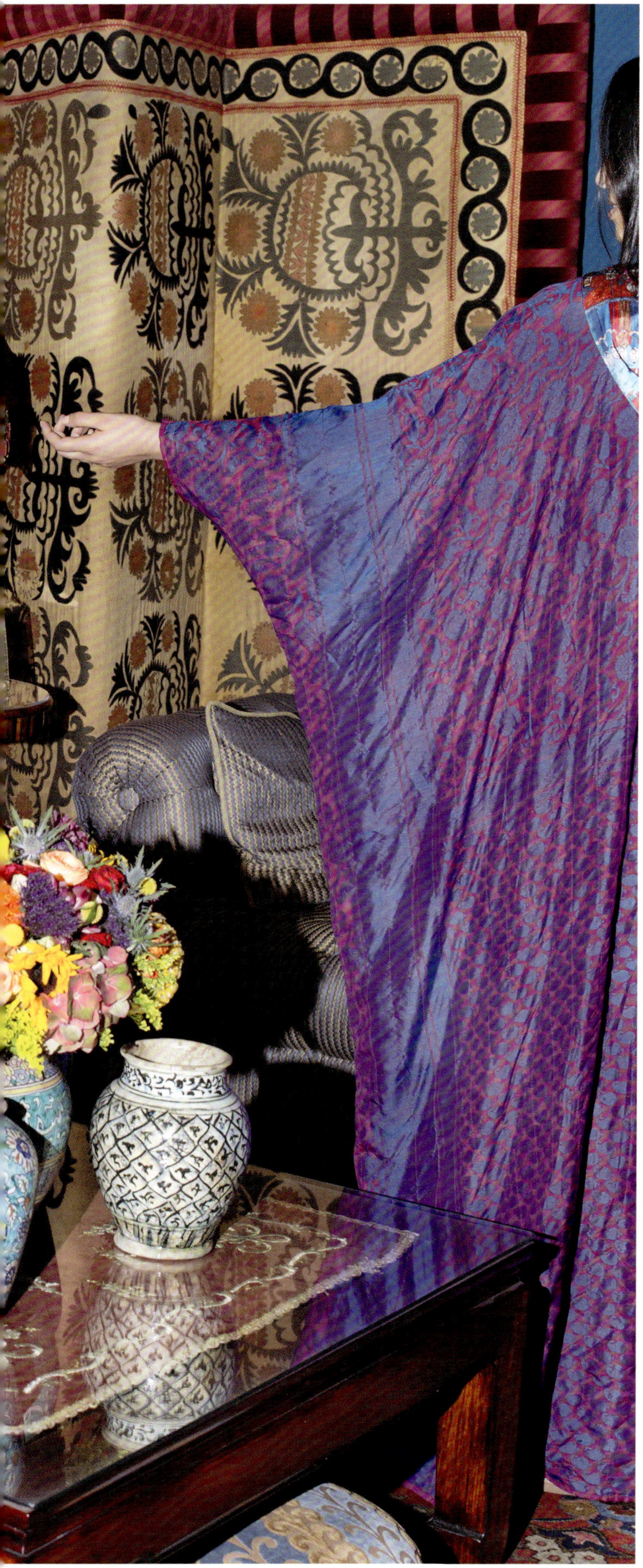

***Living Room Vape* from the series *More Good News*, 2017.**
Archival inkjet print, 52 x 102cm (20 ½ x 40 ¼ in)
In this enigmatic photographic work from Al Qasimi's series *More Good News*, which was exhibited in New York in 2018, a man sits in a domestic setting, a cloud of vapour engulfing his face and rendering it invisible, while a female figure, who edges into the right of the frame, appears to be moving in the middle of a dance. This cryptic scene is seductive and strange, while the absence of the gaze makes us travel the surfaces of the room to understand who is here and what is happening. As art consultant Marina Iordan has written, 'Many of Farah's photographs contain a looming sense of dread or entrapment, even as the world they depict is full of color and cheer.'[12]

This need is an important part of Al Qasimi's interest in finding a new kind of language for portraiture in photography – one in which the face and the body do not have to appear, creating more complex and nuanced meanings for the figure. How can you depict someone through gesture, clothing, objects and expressions? How can you represent the body, or even transcend it as the anchor of identity? The artist took these questions further in seventeen photographs, *Back and Forth Disco*, which were pasted up at bus stops all over New York in 2020. Commissioned by the Public Art Fund, the series was inspired by the women who featured in the sort of advertising that Al Qasimi had grown up with in the UAE. The photos, which she took in locations across New York, show not only people, but also streets, interior scenes and surfaces – all ways of envisioning the individual through diverse forms of display, interwoven with the fabric of the city.

***S Eating Watermelon* from the series *Arrival*, 2015**
The critic Murtaza Vali called this photograph 'Caravaggesque',[3] and it is easy to see why. The striking photograph is loaded with dramatic tension, and as with many of Al Qasimi's images, it has a certain opacity, so it could be read in many ways: the eyes are cropped out of the frame, we don't know where – or at whom – the woman might be looking. Is the gesture threatening or seductive? Watermelons symbolize fertility and sexuality, and the appearance of their fleshy pink innards is certainly provocative here. Or, with her tongue just at the tip of the blade, is this mysterious figure, 'S', simply enjoying the sweet taste of the fruit?

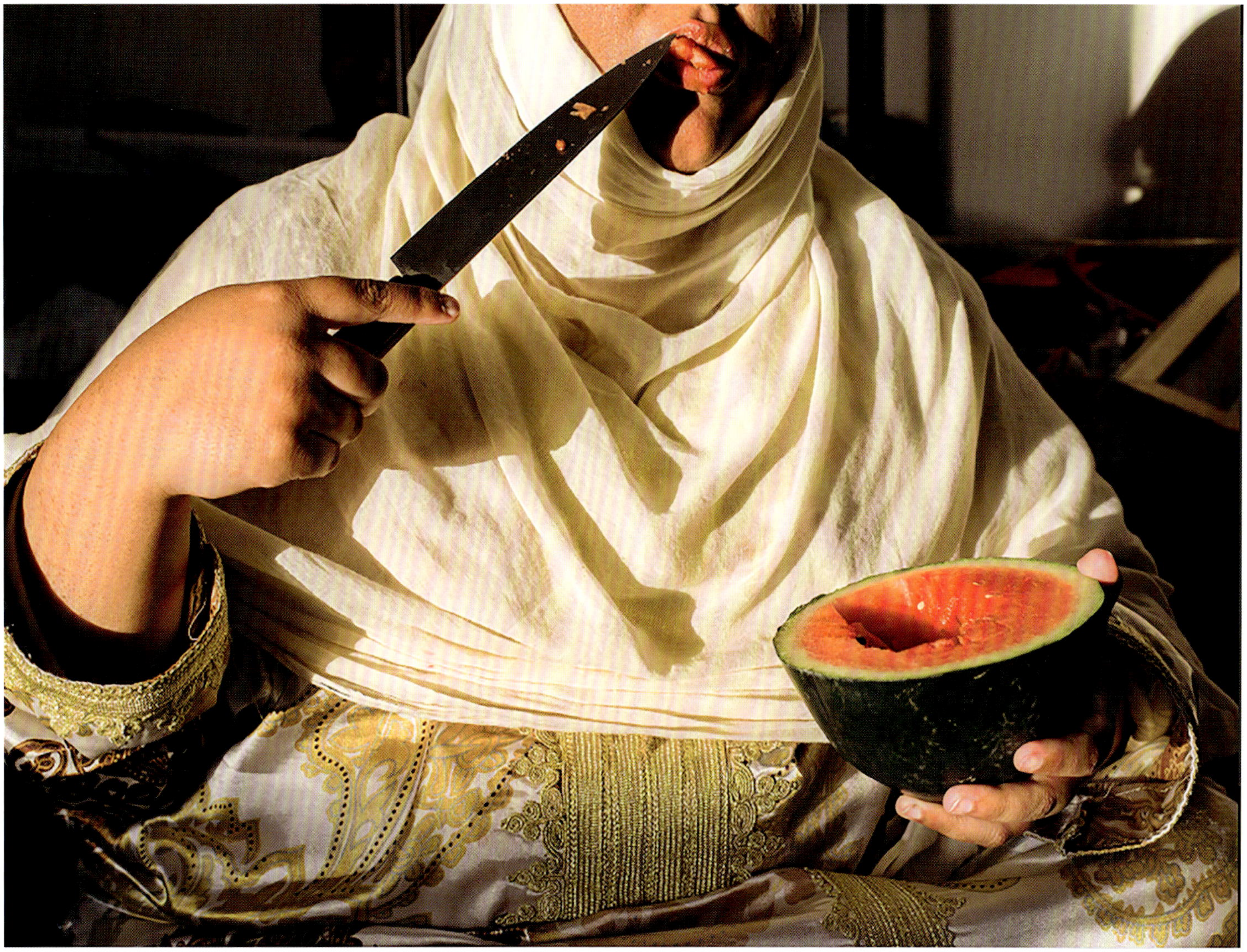

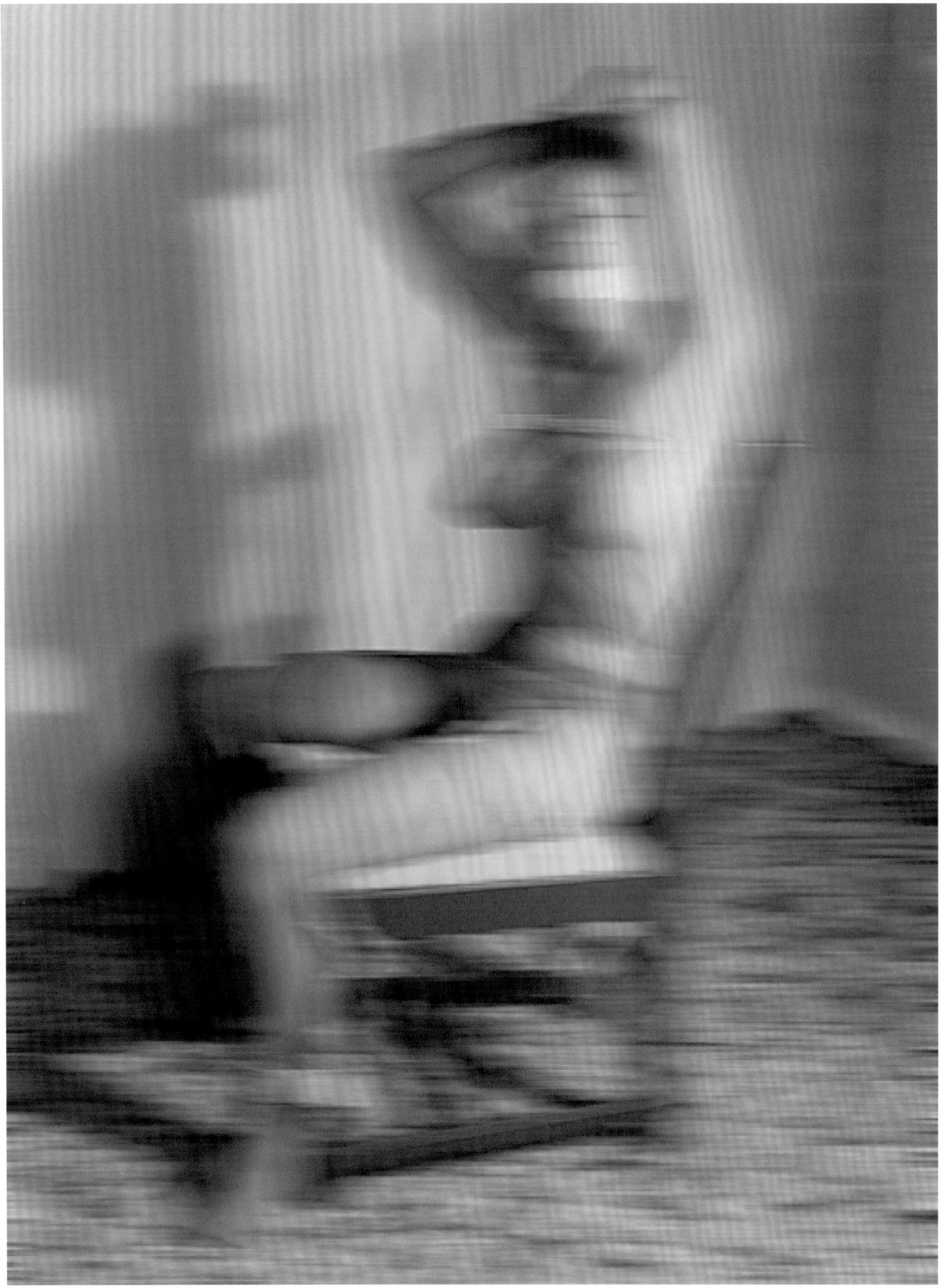

Thomas Ruff

Nude NK12 **from the series** ***Nudes*****, 2000. Colour coupler print, 39.4 x 29.2cm (15 ⅝ x 11 ½ in)**
The source material for *Nudes* is pornography, but Ruff's approach stakes a more intellectual claim over the image. Inspired by the way Gerhard Richter dealt with the nude in his paintings, Ruff turned to the 72-pixel, sexually explicit images that dominate the internet. Altering the images and removing certain elements, he then printed them large-scale once again. In the resulting series, of which this image is a good example, with its origins blurred but its purpose still identifiable, 'sex slips into something ravishingly, optically comfortable', as art critic Jerry Saltz wrote of the series in 2000.[2]

What if a photograph's purpose was not to communicate but to obfuscate? Thomas Ruff is a masterful manipulator who, since the 1970s, has been altering the DNA of photographs, whether found or created, making it difficult to see beyond the surface. His materials have included satellite photographs of Mars and Saturn, low-resolution porn images pulled from the internet and illustrations cut from newspapers and magazines. By distorting, enlarging, retouching and erasing elements of a photograph's structure using different technologies and techniques, Ruff queries the ever-changing relationship of photography to the world.

Born in West Germany in 1958, Ruff was undoubtedly influenced by his academic training. His teachers at the Kunstakademie Düsseldorf in the mid-1970s were the redoubtable Bernd and Hilla Becher, who taught him – alongside fellow students Andreas Gursky, Candida Höfer, Axel Hütte and Thomas Struth – to use strict conceptual parameters, with a propensity for viewing the built environment in a matter-of-fact, objective way. Ruff became part of the movement known as the Düsseldorf School of Photography, which was widely influential in Europe and beyond.

He broke away from his peer group by turning to portraiture: he moved swiftly on from an early series on domestic interiors – shooting the empty homes of friends in a straightforward, simple way – to portraiture, and from 1981 to 1989 shot a series of sixty photographs of people he knew in his studio. Reminiscent of passport pictures in their number and repetitive frontal framing, blank expressions and backgrounds, they indicate uniformity rather than individuality. *Portraits* made Ruff a name in the art world. As he has said, 'At that time the portrait had almost disappeared from this part of contemporary art, so I wanted to try a new minimalistic contemporary portrait.'[1]

Ruff's photography has often brought attention to different ways of taking pictures, from obsolete machines and analogue methods to advanced new digital technology and 3D software. In fact, his work could be said to be photography about photography, a way of preserving and innovating within the medium. At his presentation for the German Pavilion at the Venice Biennale in 1995, he created other *Portraits* series by means of a little-known device called the Minolta Montage Unit, which had been used by East German police in the 1970s to generate composites of suspects to show witnesses. Each of these photomontages was composed of four different faces, making a non-face that destabilized any notion of an objective photograph, thus emphasizing Ruff's ongoing interest in the structure and construction of images through different kinds of apparatus.

Although Ruff has explained that he is not interested in authorship, there is a personal aspect to his work. He has revealed that he is compelled by images that unnerve him or pique his interest, such as those showing the 9/11 terror attacks – the starting point for *Jpegs* – or astronomical images of Saturn and Mars downloaded from NASA's website, which form the basis for his series *Cassini* (2009) and *ma.r.s.* (2010–13). In certain contexts these images could be spectacular, but Ruff removes the shock or sensation and by doing so creates a new hierarchy that encourages us to look at the surface before the image. This, he has suggested, brings us closer to understanding how we really see: 'I believe that vision has little to do with our eyes and more to do with our brain. The brain sees, not the eyes.'[3]

Porträt (C. Kewer) from the series Portraits, 1988. C-print, 201 x 165cm (79 ¼ x 65in)
Since Ruff has worked in series since the 1970s, stating that you cannot explain a whole work in a single photograph, it is uncommon to view his images individually. This 1988 portrait of C. Kewer belongs to a series of sixty passport-style, frontal portraits he began to take of young friends and colleagues in his studio in 1981. The series would undergo several refinements before he hit upon the magic format, printing them 2.1 x 1.5m (7 x 5ft) in size, which is how this photograph was presented when it appeared in exhibitions such as Ruff's 2011 survey at the Museum of Contemporary Art, Chicago. Portraits remains one of Ruff's most revered bodies of work and the monumental scale of his photographs has remained a staple of his practice, dwarfing the viewer in the gallery or museum in a way that photographs now rarely do.

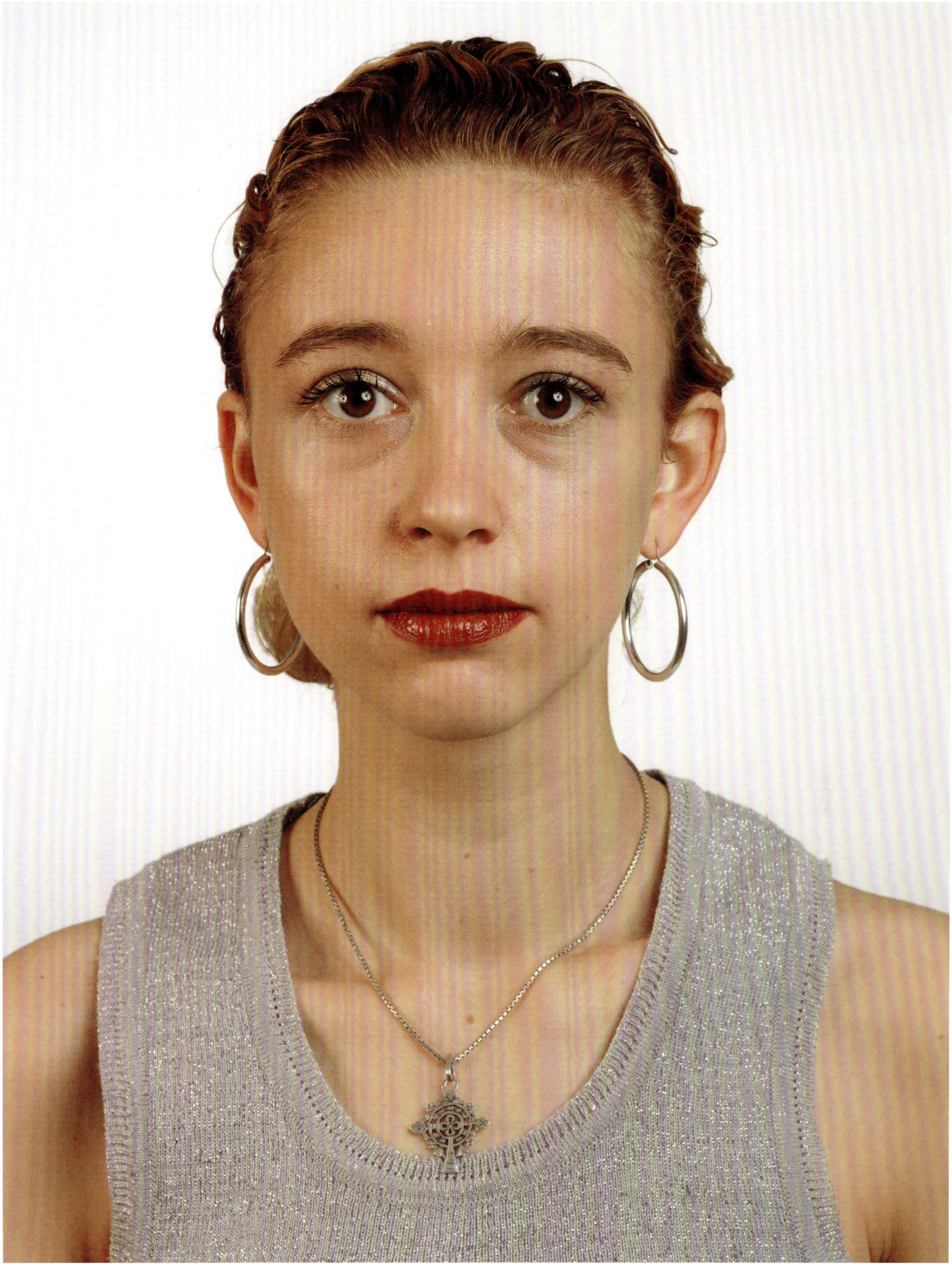

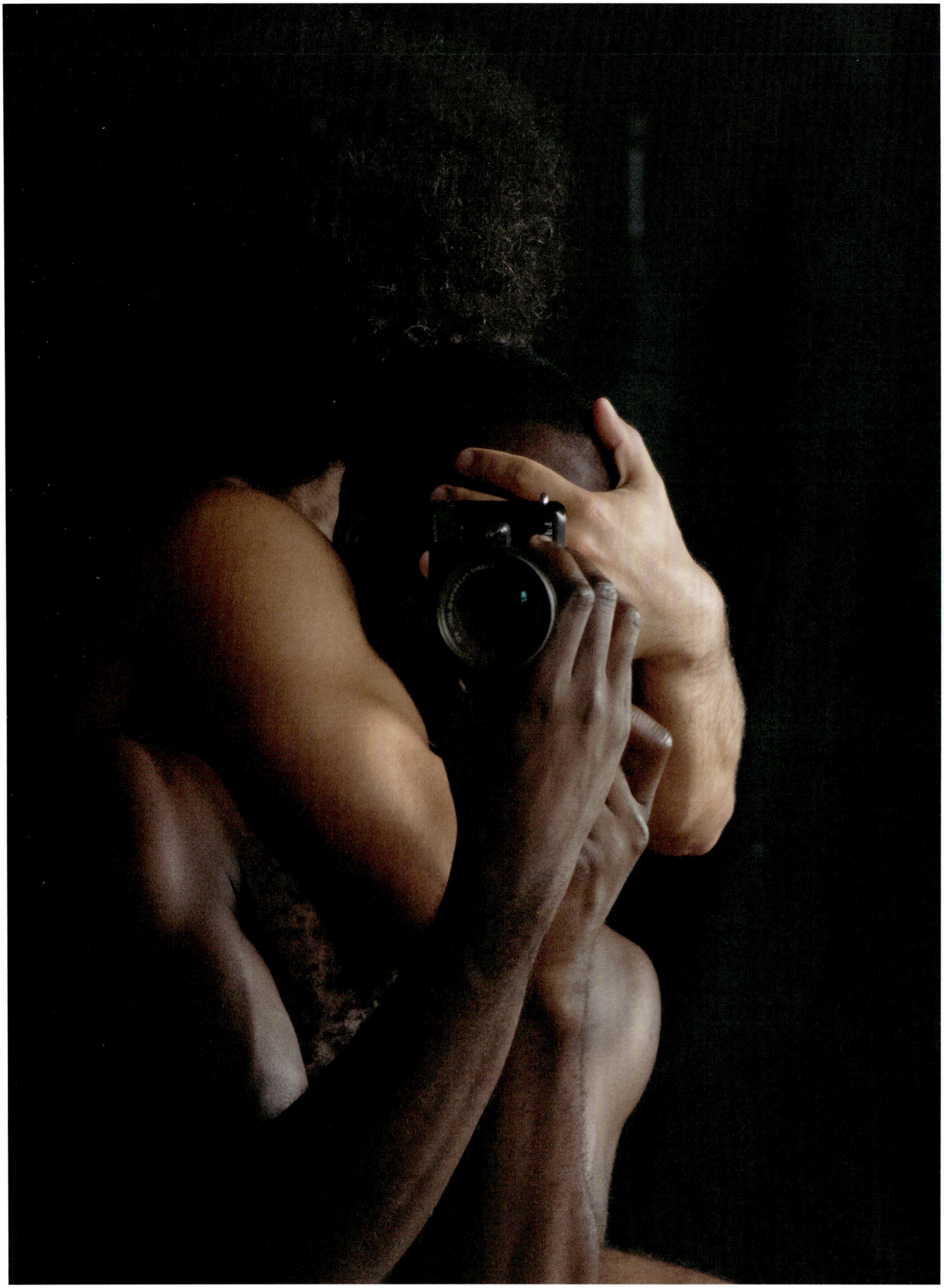

Paul Mpagi Sepuya

Photographic apparatus and cameras are the primary focus of Paul Mpagi Sepuya's photographs. The studio is the main, recurrent subject and setting: lighting and lenses, tripods and clamps, mirrors and curtains – the props of traditional studio photography – all become conspirators in a play of concealing and revealing. The studio for Sepuya is a queer social space, a generative place with limitless potential for creativity and a safe environment for expression and liberation from patriarchal norms.

Born in California in 1982, Sepuya initially made traditional portraits, publishing some of them in an underground queer zine called *Shoot*. Portraiture is still the foundation of his practice: 'There can be no fragments without portraits,' the artist notes[1]; 'fragments' referring to one of the recurring and defining features of his works – carefully staged elements that dissemble his own photographs and body. He does not make works that classify people by their image since he believes that 'the photograph can't tell you really anything about the person.'[2] That is to say, a person's private, shifting, identity cannot be captured by the camera.

Moving away from traditional portraiture around 2010, Sepuya began to use devices to fragment, deconstruct and conceal the figures – himself and his friends – so that they are no longer the central focus of the work. None of these images is manipulated digitally, however, and everything that is present in the photograph existed in the real, optical space. Sepuya skilfully arranges compositions made up of fragments, frames and torn strips of prints he has discarded; from 2016 he also introduced mirrors, with fingerprints and smudges left visible on the glass. This is not about subterfuge. 'I'm not making tricky pictures,' he emphasizes.[3] He even titles his works with their DSLR file names or their film roll and frame numbers (he has worked with both analogue and digital formats) to demonstrate that there is nothing hidden in the making – these are all single shots. That also goes for the cameras and apparatus we see, so that if a hand is holding a camera, then a picture has been taken. We might be looking at the final image, or the image that is taken might be in the process of evolving into another work, in another form.

According to Sepuya, 'What my work is about is the openness of queer and homoerotic social structures,

***Darkroom Mirror (_2070386)* from the series *Darkroom Mirror*, 2017. 61 x 81.3cm (24 x 32in)**
This image from the acclaimed *Darkroom Mirror* series depicts Sepuya and an unnamed friend. Sepuya holds a Panasonic Lumix camera, pointed at a mirror – and ultimately at the viewer – taking the picture we see. The process of taking the picture becomes the final work, which supports Sepuya's thesis that photography is 'a medium of construction and desire, of looking and knowing we are being looked at'.[4]

where there are slippery and less rigid boundaries between platonic, creative and sexual relations.'[5] Each photograph explores a relationship to another person, the particular exchange that making an image together stimulates, and the dynamic between a photographer and his collaborators, mediated by the camera and the architecture of the studio.

Sepuya's work has been included in seminal group exhibitions in recent years – the Museum of Modern Art's *Being: New Photography 2018* and the 2019 Whitney Biennial in New York; *Masculinities* at the Barbican in London in 2020 – confirming the contribution his work has made to the history of portrait photography in particular, and the way it pushes the conversation into the present. Sepuya was also included in *Mapplethorpe Now* at the Guggenheim Museum in 2019, exploring the legacy of the late artist.

As his photographs deconstruct and reflect the physical processes of image-making, Sepuya sees his work as 'insisting on the materiality of blackness and subjectivity of queerness as essential to the emergence of photography'.[6] Blackness is vital to the execution of a photographic image, and the making of a photograph is always inseparable from an articulation of desire.

***Study for B.H. with Five Figures, 2013–15 (0602)*, 2015.**
152.4 x 206.2cm (60 x 81¼in)
At the centre of Sepuya's studio the camera is on a tripod, staring back at the viewer and, we assume, the artist taking the picture. This photograph seems to be emphatically about the process of image-making – the various stages that result in the finished work. It is part of a 2015 series of studies of the artist's studio in which Sepuya is organizing material from 2011. By 2013 he had begun to assemble snapshots, printouts and unresolved work in progress as *Some Recent Pictures* – what we see on the studio wall in the background here. Once again attempting to resolve these unfinished works, he arranged them for the purposes of this photograph – but they will eventually end up elsewhere, possibly in a book.

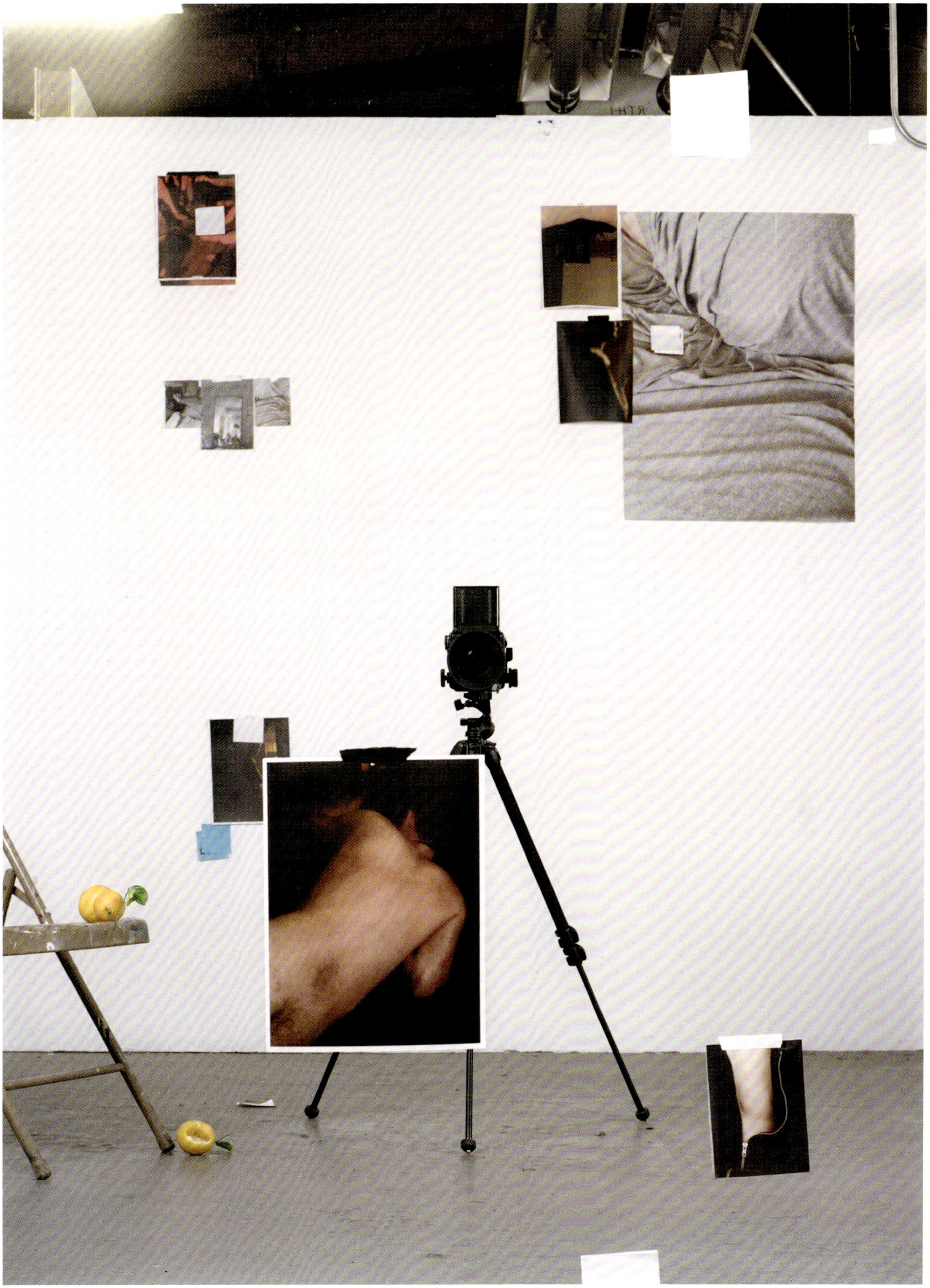

Cindy Sherman

Untitled #363, 1976/2000. Gelatin silver print, 18.3 x 12.7cm (7 ¼ x 5in)
Bus Riders is one of Sherman's earliest series of photographs. Made the year she graduated from art school, the photos were not seen for more than two decades, until Sherman printed them for an exhibition in New York in 2000. All fifteen of the characters she recreated in the series were based on passengers seen on or waiting for the bus. The origins of many of Sherman's enduring interests as an artist can be observed in *Bus Riders*, including the way she uses dress, props and pose to signal identity, and leaves small details to hint at the fact we are looking at a construction. In this image, for example, the cable connecting to Sherman's shutter is visible, with the release pedal underfoot and markings on the studio floor, while another foot appears at the side of the frame.

'I'm not sure we'd know what a selfie is in the same way without Cindy,' said the art critic Hal Foster,[1] referring to the phenomenon that is Cindy Sherman. For four decades, the American artist – who is not only a photographer but also a set and costume designer, director, model and performer – has made herself a tabula rasa, exclusively using herself as the model for any number of characters, all of them familiar but at the same time faux, satirized and scrutinized. Through these performances as other people, Sherman has undoubtedly changed the way we see portraiture – and the way we see ourselves through it.

'It's really about obliterating myself within these characters,' Sherman has emphasized,[2] correcting a common misconception that her photographs represent her innermost desires. Although she always appears in her images, it is never really Sherman we see. Even after forty years she remains relatively undercover, reticent about analyzing her photographs or getting into 'theoretical bullshit'.[3]

Born in 1954, Sherman was raised in suburban Long Island, a solitary child who was much younger than her four siblings and a self-confessed TV addict. She moved to New York to attend the visual arts programme at Buffalo State College in 1972, and her interest in television and cinema would shape her photography from the start, as she emulated their codes and cues in astutely observed stagings. Her first major work after graduating was *Untitled Film Stills* (1977–80), a series of seventy black and white images in which she poses as the female protagonist in what would appear, as the title suggests, to be recreations of scenes from B-movies or film noir classics. However, these are faked film stills, and as such they reveal how emotional responses are manipulated by construction and archetype – a concern that has continued to underpin Sherman's oeuvre.

Sherman makes portraits about portraiture, revealing its multifarious and sometimes insidious functions. Portraits, more than any other art form, speak about our 'contemporary way of being, and the fact that photography is very complicit in the way in which identity is manufactured today,' as Eva Respini, curator of Sherman's 2012 retrospective at the Museum of Modern Art, New York, explained.[4]

Untitled Film Stills situated Sherman as a key exponent of the pictures generation, a group of young, New York-based artists who had grown up, like Sherman, on TV and were interested in 'understanding the effect of these mass cultural images', as Hal Foster put it,[5] by

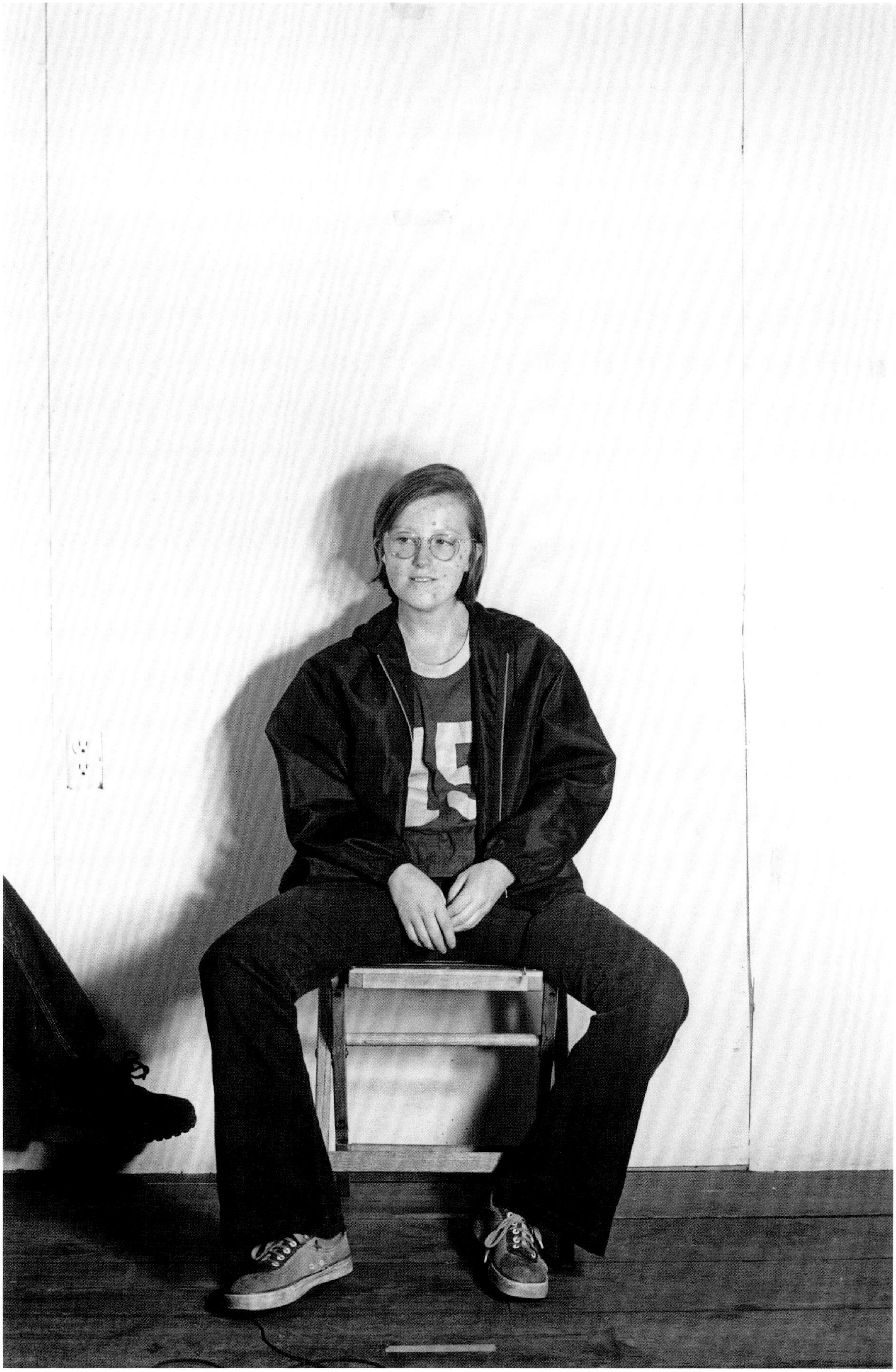

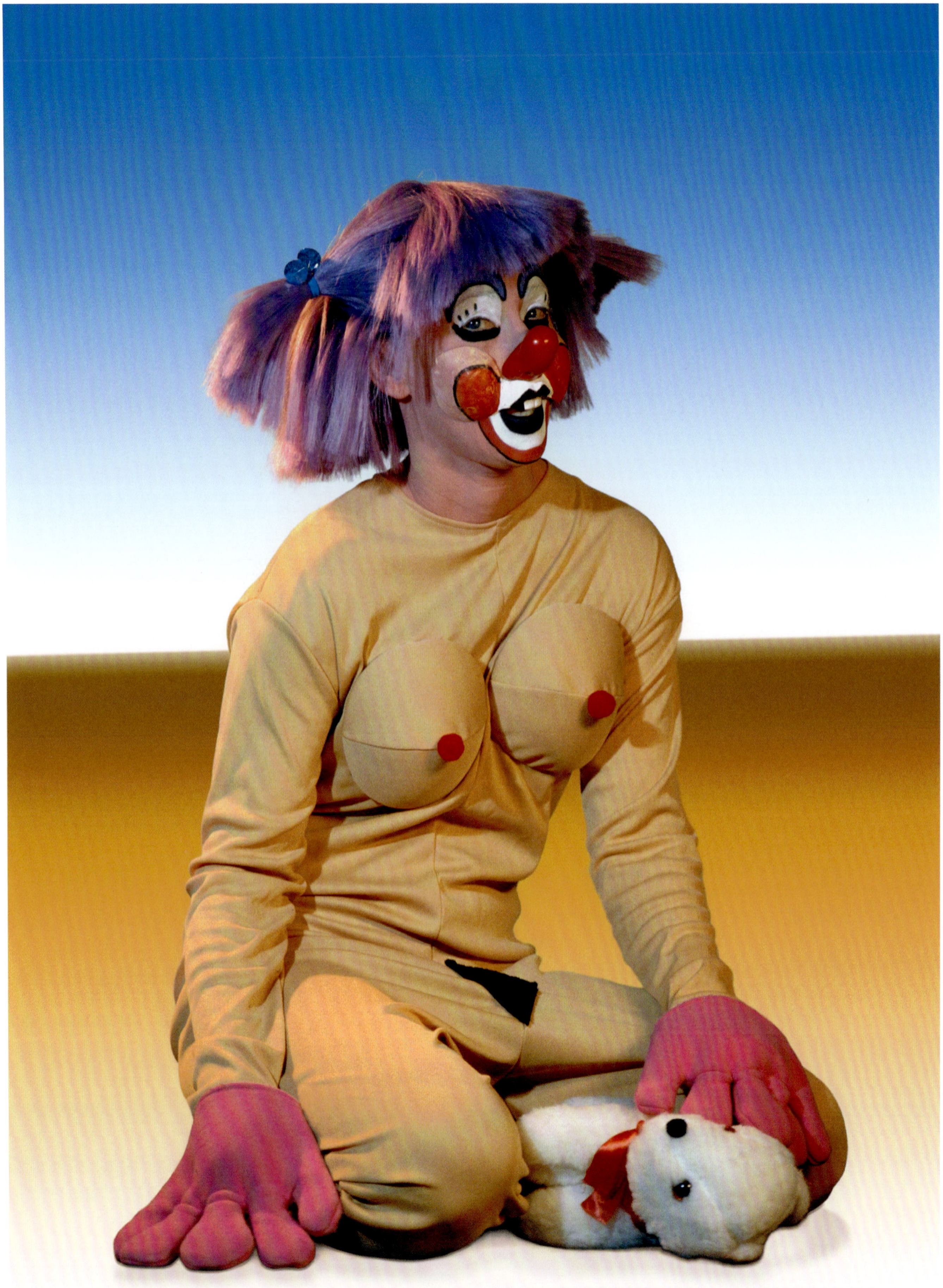

'critique and complicity' with them. There is a deep ambivalence in Sherman's work towards the subjects she parodies. She is enthralled by them but is also brutal in her treatment of them; the women she depicts often appear to be vain, conceited, brash or supercilious, clichés of conformist femininity, but who are also victims of a patriarchal society.

To a younger generation, the large-format, Cibachrome photographs Sherman has made since the 1980s are often better known. The monumental size of her portraits and her use of colour work together to reveal the all-important details in the composition. The effect of these photographs hinges on the tension between the image as a whole, as we first encounter it, and the glaring imperfections that emerge on closer inspection, when the mask slips away and we see, say, the crude application of make-up to try to cover up age, the cheapness of a dress intended to show off status, or a protruding prosthetic nose. A master of the grotesque and black comedy, Sherman produces images that are the stuff of disturbed dreams and dark corners, haunting viewers long after they have left the gallery.

***Untitled #419*, 2004. 166.4 x 122.6cm (65 5⁄8 x 48 3⁄8 in)**
This image from the *Clowns* series (2003–4) – lurid, garish and nightmarish – typifies Sherman's mastery of colour for dramatic effect as she makes a crude connection between female sexuality and the exaggerated masquerade of a clown. Sherman has said of her motivation in making these clown pictures, 'I'd been going through a struggle, particularly after 9/11. I couldn't figure out what I wanted to say. I still wanted the work to be the same kind of mixture – intense, with a nasty side or an ugly side, but also with a real pathos about the characters – and [clowns] have an underlying sense of sadness while they're trying to cheer people up. Clowns are sad, but they're also psychotically, hysterically happy.'[16]

***Untitled #216*, 1989. C-print, 221.3 x 142.6cm (87 ¼ x 56 ½ in)**
The series of images known as *'History Portraits'* is one of Sherman's most copied works and constitutes a series of copies in itself. This photograph restages a 1450 diptych by Jean Fouquet of the Madonna and Child. In Sherman's 1989 version, it is the details that give the game away: the Madonna is as risibly fake as the baby Jesus she holds; her breast, with its blanched-out nipple, is obviously prosthetic; and her gown and crown look as if they have come from a fancy-dress shop. Sherman has said, 'When I was in school I was getting disgusted with the attitude of art being so religious or sacred... That's the reason why I wanted to imitate something out of the culture, and also make fun of the culture as I was doing it.'[7]

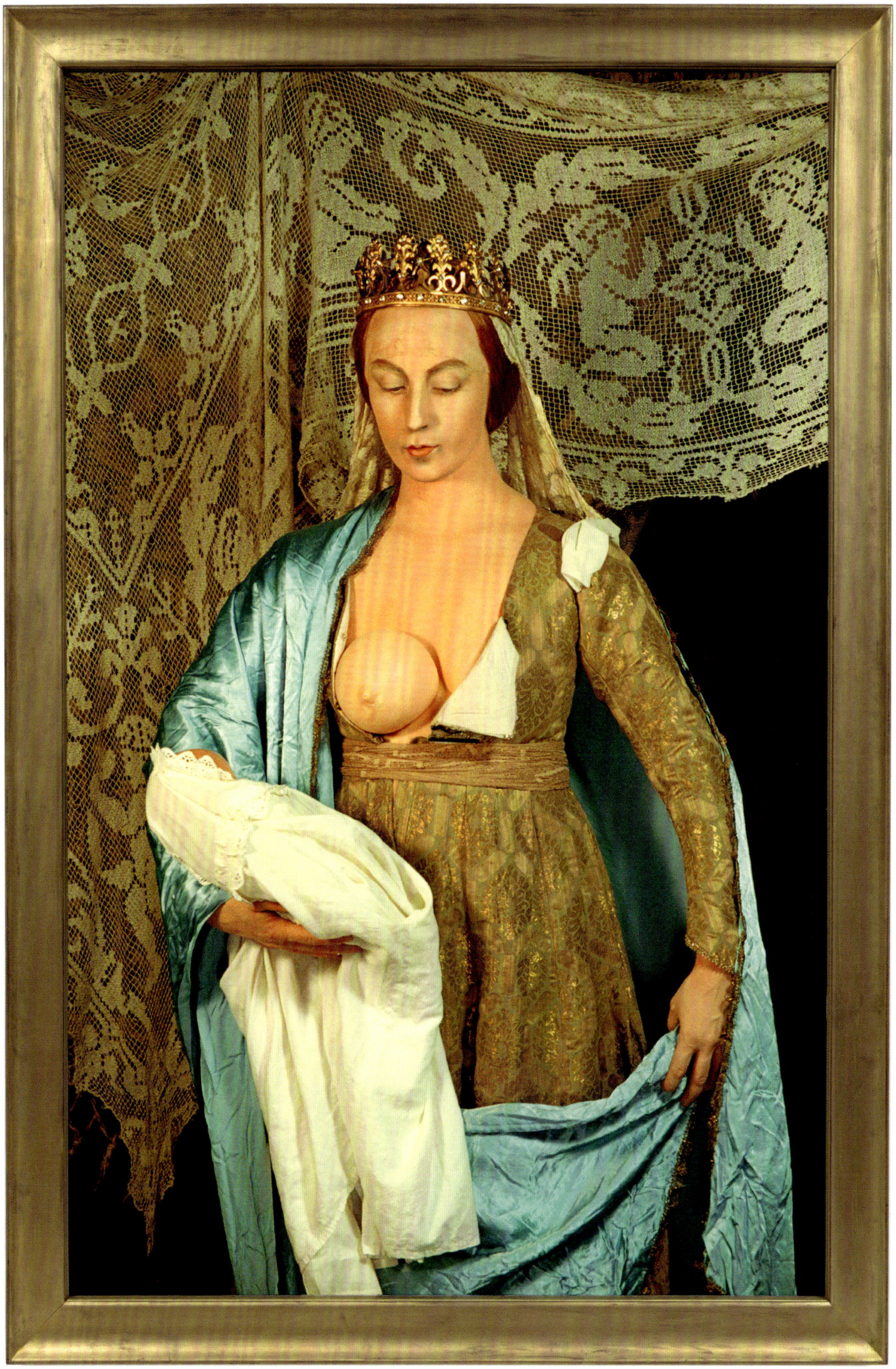

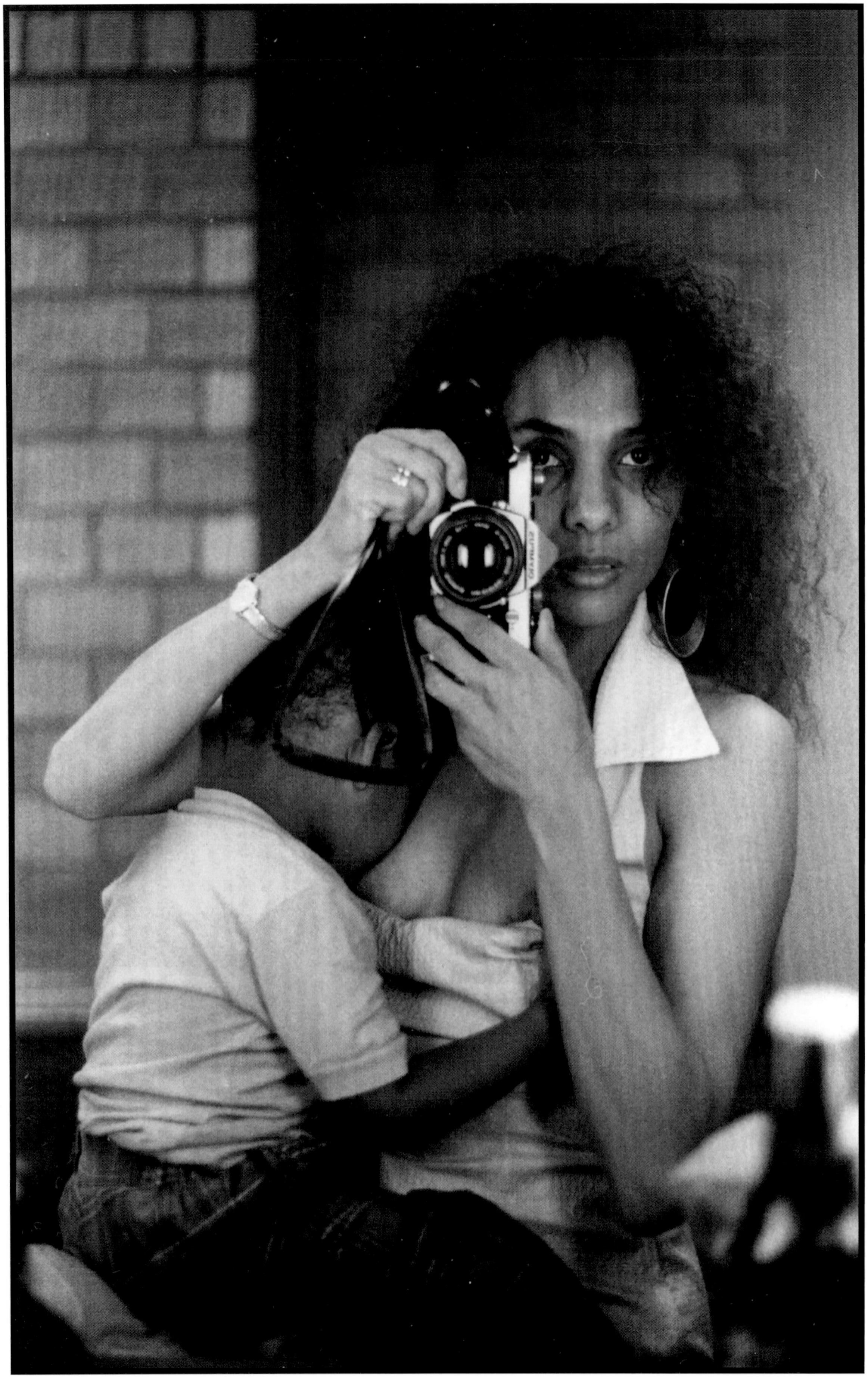

Ming Smith

'Photography saved me,' Ming Smith has said. For the best part of four decades the American photographer was overlooked by the art world, but she never stopped taking pictures. 'It was about getting through the struggle, the negativity, the violence and pain. It was my struggle and the camera was my friend.'[1]

Smith was born in 1947 in Detroit and raised in Columbus, Ohio. A shy, self-conscious child, she was always observing and first picked up her mother's Brownie aged seven to take a picture of her school class. After graduating from Howard University in 1973, Smith moved to New York, where she worked as a model because it paid better than any other job she could get at the time. Despite the efforts of the Black Power and Women's Liberation movements in the USA in the 1960s, Smith faced an art world that was dominated by white men and in which photography was not considered an art form.

In 1972 Smith joined a group of older, more established, all-male photographers known as Kamoinge; their members included Gordon Parks, Louis Draper and Roy DeCarava. They were emphatic in 'defining themselves as photographers', not artists, Smith recalls.[2] She participated in a Kamoinge group show at the Studio Museum in Harlem the same year as their first and only female member. Though the group eventually disbanded, Smith was fundamentally shaped by them. 'It was about owning our own image,' she said, 'making our own images about Black people, working against the stereotypes created by the people in power.'

In 1978 Smith made history when she became the first black woman photographer to be acquired by the Museum of Modern Art in New York. But there are details of the story as Smith tells it that frame the moment as less than a complete triumph: when she submitted her portfolio, she was mistaken for a courier, and the museum paid only 'around $300'[3] for the two works purchased for the collection. Despite this apparent early success, Smith's career was not changed in the way she anticipated either. 'Nothing happened for forty years after that,' she has said. And even at the time, she was hesitant about selling her work, knowing that the offer wasn't right. 'I was quiet and not confrontational, but I was political, and I had the fight in me,' she recalled.[4]

***Self Portrait (Total)*, 1986**
Smith finds elegance in the everyday and locates the extraordinary in the familiar. The bond between a mother and child, particularly during the act of breastfeeding, captures both; it is mysterious and magical, yet primal and universal. This photograph depicts Smith with her son Mingus, taken spontaneously while on the road taking pictures; she has said that photographing and nursing came in that order. Asked about her experience of motherhood, Smith recalls that when Mingus was about four or five he asked to borrow $20, which Smith didn't have. His reaction was, 'What is the point of being in the Museum of Modern Art if you don't even have $20?'[5]

Over the years, a number of exhibitions – mostly group shows – did take place, and after 'a few bad experiences'[6] with publishers, Smith began publishing her own photobooks in the 1990s. Her breakthrough came in 2017, when she took part in major exhibitions at the Brooklyn Museum, the Detroit Institute of Arts, Tate Modern and Nottingham Contemporary, and she collaborated with Arthur Jafa for his show at London's Serpentine Galleries. In 2020 Aperture released a monograph of her work.

There is a duality in Smith's work that reflects her interest in the microscopic and the monumental. She is always interested in the possibilities of light and the ethereal – a summer breeze lifting curtains against a window, the glow of a television screen, a mother sharing a moment with her child. She often returns to solitary figures, to moments of contemplation and transcendence, whether through prayer or music, or a child thrown up in the air with sheer delight. There is a prescient joy in many of these photographs, a sense of awe at life's mysterious effervescence. 'It is like God working through me,' Smith has said. 'I really feel that.'[7]

***August Blues (Invisible Man), Harlem, New York*, 1991**
This semi-abstract photograph presents a different and equally important facet of Smith's practice: her concern with visibility, both literally, and as a metaphor, for the position of Black people in American society. Smith often plays with effects of the light and movement to create an atmosphere rather than an image; we cannot always see exactly what we are looking at, as if we are looking with peripheral vision. The picture belongs to her *Invisible Man* series – the name is taken from the 1952 Ralph Ellison novel. Although this is a scene shot on a street in Harlem, it is radically different from the documentary street photography of the day and demonstrates how pioneering Smith has been throughout her career.

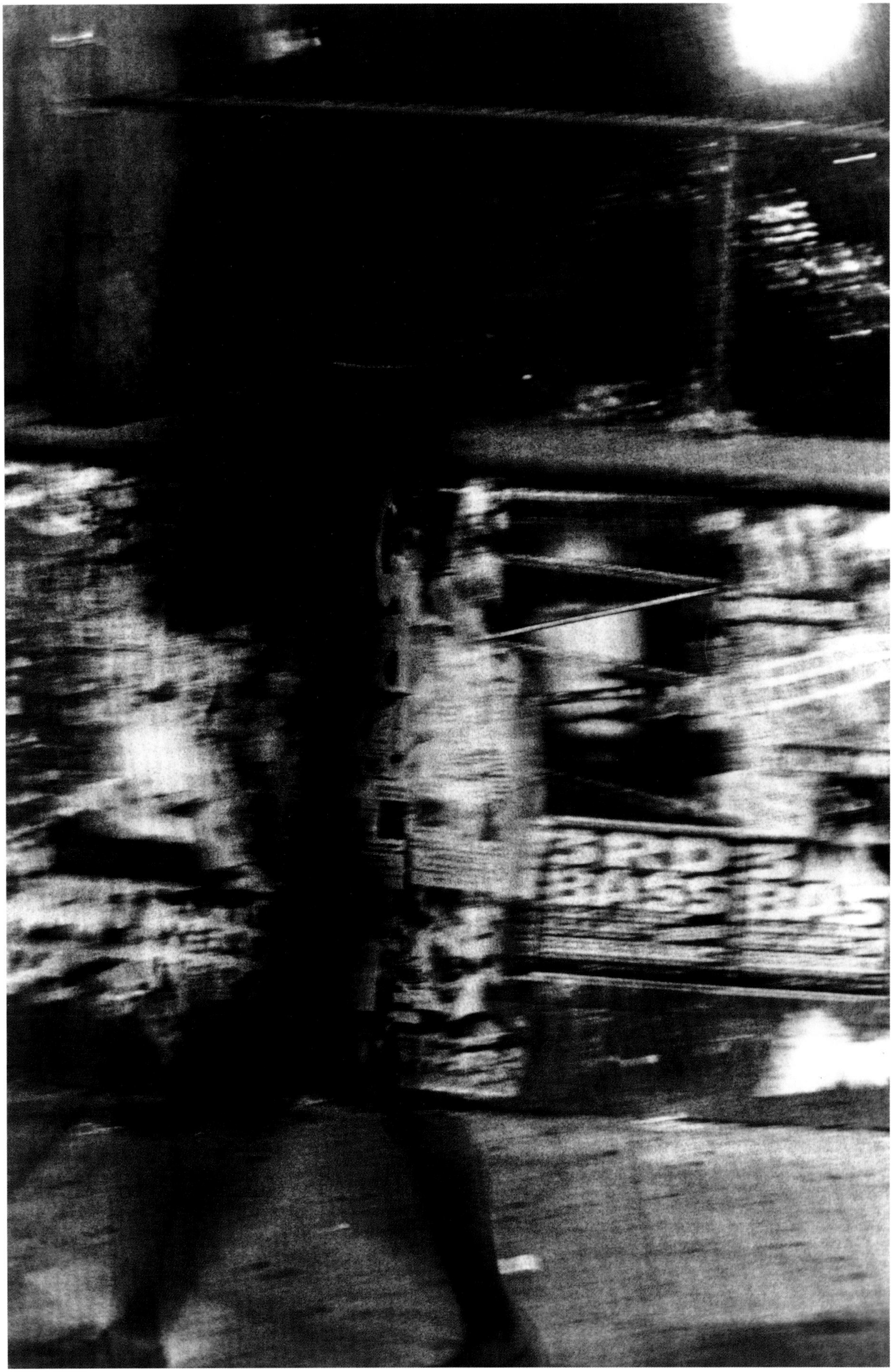

Mikhael Subotzky

Sometimes, even when a photograph is taken with respect and the best of intentions, it causes a deep, unavoidable feeling of disquiet. Born in 1981, Mikhael Subotzky began his career as a documentary photographer in his native South Africa in 2000, but the pictures he took later provoked a profound crisis about the implications of photography and his own gaze as a white man. Exposing his gaze and acknowledging the way images are consumed, Subotzky has come up with a stance that is radically self-critical and approaches an understanding of what active anti-racism might mean. 'As a white man, the question of my own presence in my work has been a tension for a very long time,' he explains.[1] Over the years, this questioning has become the work itself, re-examining his relationship to the subjects he has photographed and challenging the purpose and function of his photography in relation to and within dominant social, political and economic narratives.

Subotzky's first major work was *Die Vier Hoeke* ('The Four Corners') (2004), a panoramic portrait of South Africa's penal system and, in particular, life at the notorious Pollsmoor Maximum Security Prison, where Nelson Mandela spent some of his twenty-seven years' incarceration. On South Africa's Freedom Day in 2005, Subotzky exhibited the photographs of the prison in situ. Two series, *Umjiegwana* ('The Outside') (2005) and *Beaufort West* (2006–8), followed *Die Vier Hoeke*, a continuation of Subotzky's documentation of disenfranchised communities across South Africa only a decade into the aftermath of apartheid.

His first monograph, *Beaufort West* was presented in 2008 at the Museum of Modern Art's *New Photography* exhibition, making Subotzky an international name. The attention the work attracted also forced the artist to consider what happens to such photographs when they are presented to the public and become objects of spectacle. How could the photographer write his own responses, his own subjectivity and, especially, his own whiteness back into these pictures? How could he close the sense of separation and expose his own complicity in the structural problems he observes, not only in the image-making but in how he lives his life?

A collaboration with the British artist Patrick Waterhouse was a pivotal moment in Subotzky's practice. *Ponte City* (2008–14) took six years to complete as the duo photographed every single door, television and the view from every window in the eponymous fifty-five-storey 1970s skyscraper in Johannesburg – the tallest residential

***Howl (or Jacaranda)* from the series *Massive Nerve Corpus*, 2018. Ink on found book pages**
Howl (or Jacaranda) forms part of *Massive Nerve Corpus*, which juxtaposed historical perspectives of white men in South Africa and Subotzky's personal reflections and records in the present day. The starting point for this image was Subotzky's book collection and one volume in particular: Gerald Hamilton's 1961 memoir *Jacaranda*, in which the author recounts his travels in South Africa in the 1950s and his admiration for the Nationalist leaders. Having spent years trying to take the perfect photograph of the jacaranda tree, here instead Subotzky returned to the book cover, horrified by the 'very particular form of British liberal racism'[2] it exhibited in its language. Subotzky disassembled the book and flattened the pages to create backdrops to print on. The first of two resulting *Jacaranda* works, this image depicts an anonymous disabled man of whom Subotzky says, 'his expression brought to mind Ginsberg's *Howl* in the context of my attempts to dismantle white masculinity throughout the works of *Massive Nerve Corpus*.'[3]

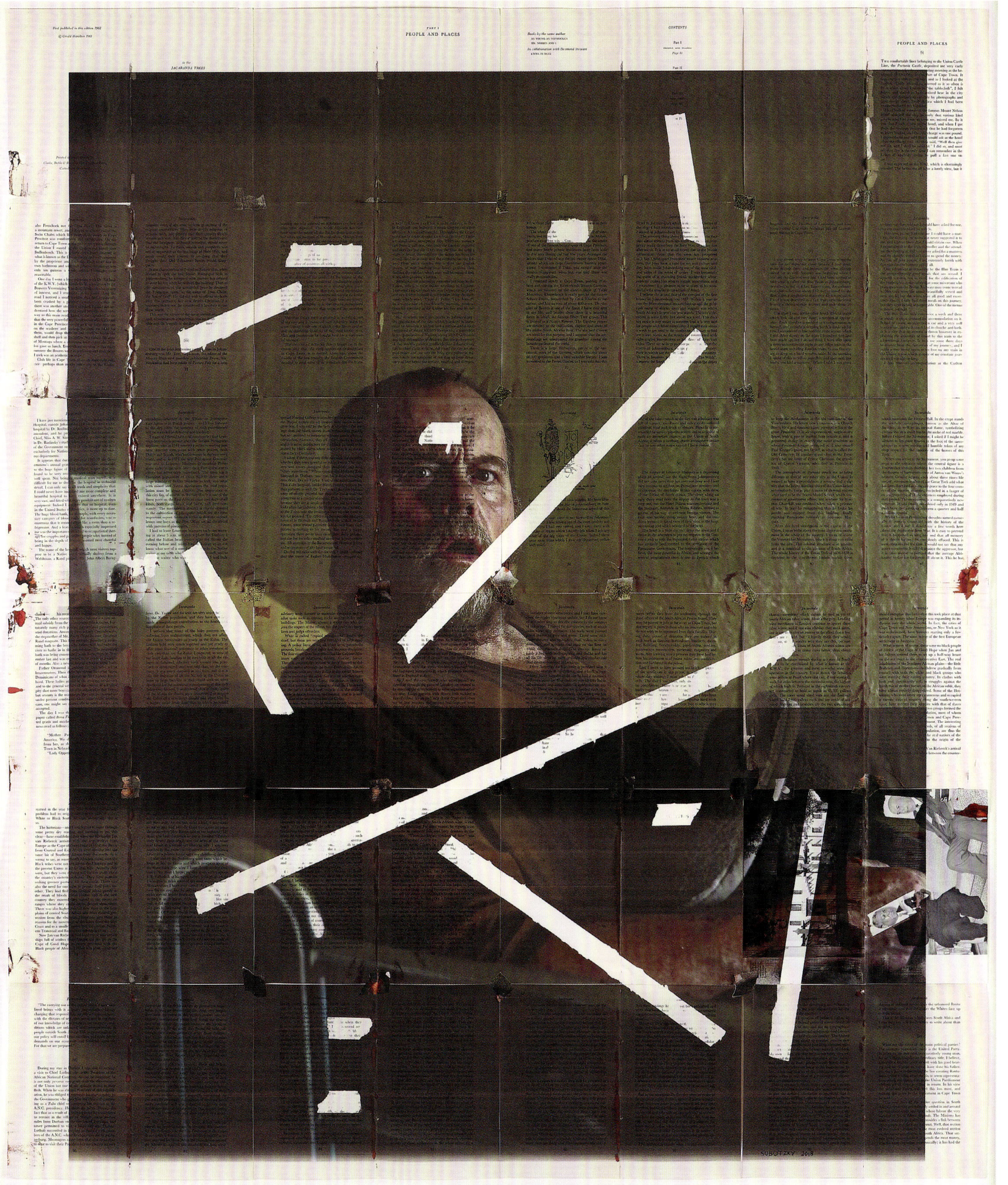

building on the continent. Presented across different media, including towering tableaux of contact sheets mounted on light boxes, the work was first presented at Ponte City and went on to win the Discovery Award after it was exhibited at the Rencontres d'Arles in 2011.

If *Ponte City* invested in the idea of multiplicity, *I Was Looking Back* (2012), an installation of ninety-eight photographs from his archive over the previous decade, allowed Subotzky to confront the construction of the gaze more directly, returning to his documentary photographs and exposing that construction literally by smashing their surfaces. 'I went through every photograph I had ever taken and chose those where the process of looking, or being looked back at, was resonant,' he explains.[4] The act of smashing the glass, Subotzky has said, transforms Barthes's idea of the punctum – a photograph's ability to pierce the conscience – into a physical act. In doing this, he hopes to draw attention 'to the photographic surface itself as an intermediary between the representational world of the subject and the physical world of the viewer, thus reminding the viewer of what they are looking at in objective terms'.[5]

He has continued to interrupt the surfaces of both his own and found imagery using other techniques in subsequent works. In a series of 'sticky-tape transfers' entitled *Show'n Tell* (2017), he used sticky tape to pull at the paper of the pages of South African nationalist propaganda publications, peeling away their fragile surfaces in a gesture that mimics the desire of the work to reveal the relationship between white masculinity and vulnerability, highlighting, in Subotzky's words, 'how the lack of willingness to acknowledge the latter is one of the many reasons why white men have exercised power in such a destructive and violent way over hundreds of years'.[6]

Film and audiovisual works have also become an important part of Subotzky's methodology and concern with white male dominance and privilege. A four-screen film installation, *Moses and Griffiths* (2012), returned once again to the setting of a small rural town, giving his subjects a voice, while *WYE* (2016) was a three-channel, forty-eight-minute film in which the white man is held up as the object of anthropological study. More recent works, such as the series of paintings and sticky-tape transfers in *Massive Nerve Corpus* (2018) and *The Gangsters* (2019), submit the white male to similar scrutiny, to tip the imbalance in looking. 'I'm trying to re-racialize whiteness, because whiteness as we know it disappears and becomes the obscured norm that you compare everything else to,' he explains.[7]

Maplank and Naomi, Pollsmoor Maximum Security Prison **from the series *Die Vier Hoeke*, 2004. Archival pigment print, flush-mounted and face-mounted to toughened glass smashed by the artist, 49.5 x 74.5 cm (19 ½ x 29 ⅜ in)**
Between 2004 and 2005, Subotzky organized photo workshops at Pollsmoor Prison, Cape Town – the maximum security prison where the artist shot the series *Die Vier Hoeke* ('The Four Corners'). The two subjects who appear in this photograph – Maplank and Naomi – were two of ten inmates who participated in the workshops. A few years after he was released from Pollsmoor, Maplank was stabbed to death near his home. Subotzky says, 'At that point I had started smashing some of my photographs. I was retrospectively writing my own feelings of violence, trauma and fear, which came from both my experience of taking the photograph and my ambivalence at the representation I had made, back into the photographic object itself.'[8] The image became part of the series *I Was Looking Back* in which Subotzky revisits his own archive and further complicates his relationship to photography. 'Back in 2005 I still believed that photography could play a positive role in social change, that revealing to the public the unseen violence of incarceration could help to dismantle the system. I also had a big emotional investment in Maplank, not just as a friend but also as a photographer. Of all the prisoners I taught, he was the most talented and we both hoped that he might start getting photographic work as part of building a new life after his release. His death shattered me personally, and also this optimism.'[9]

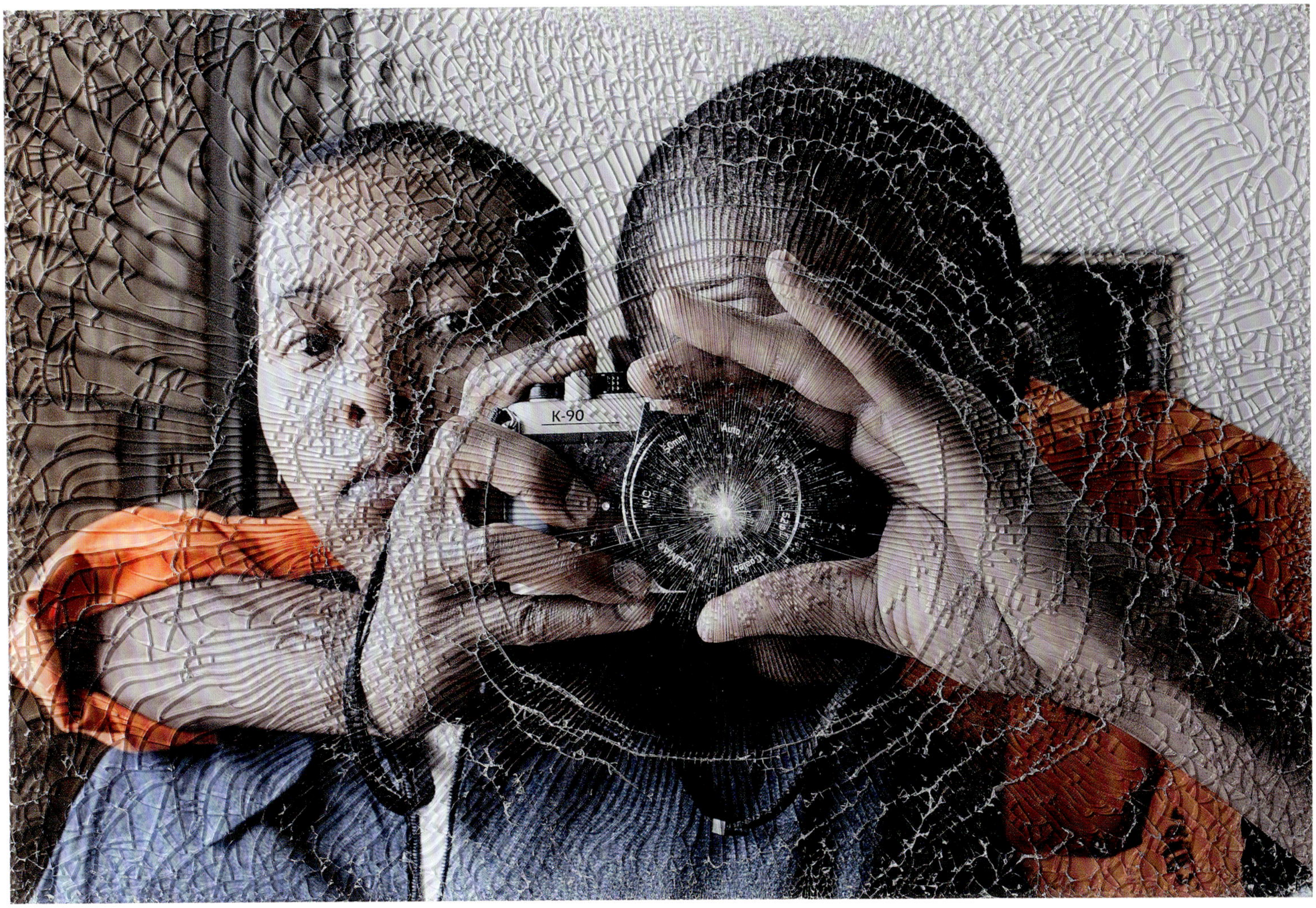
K-90

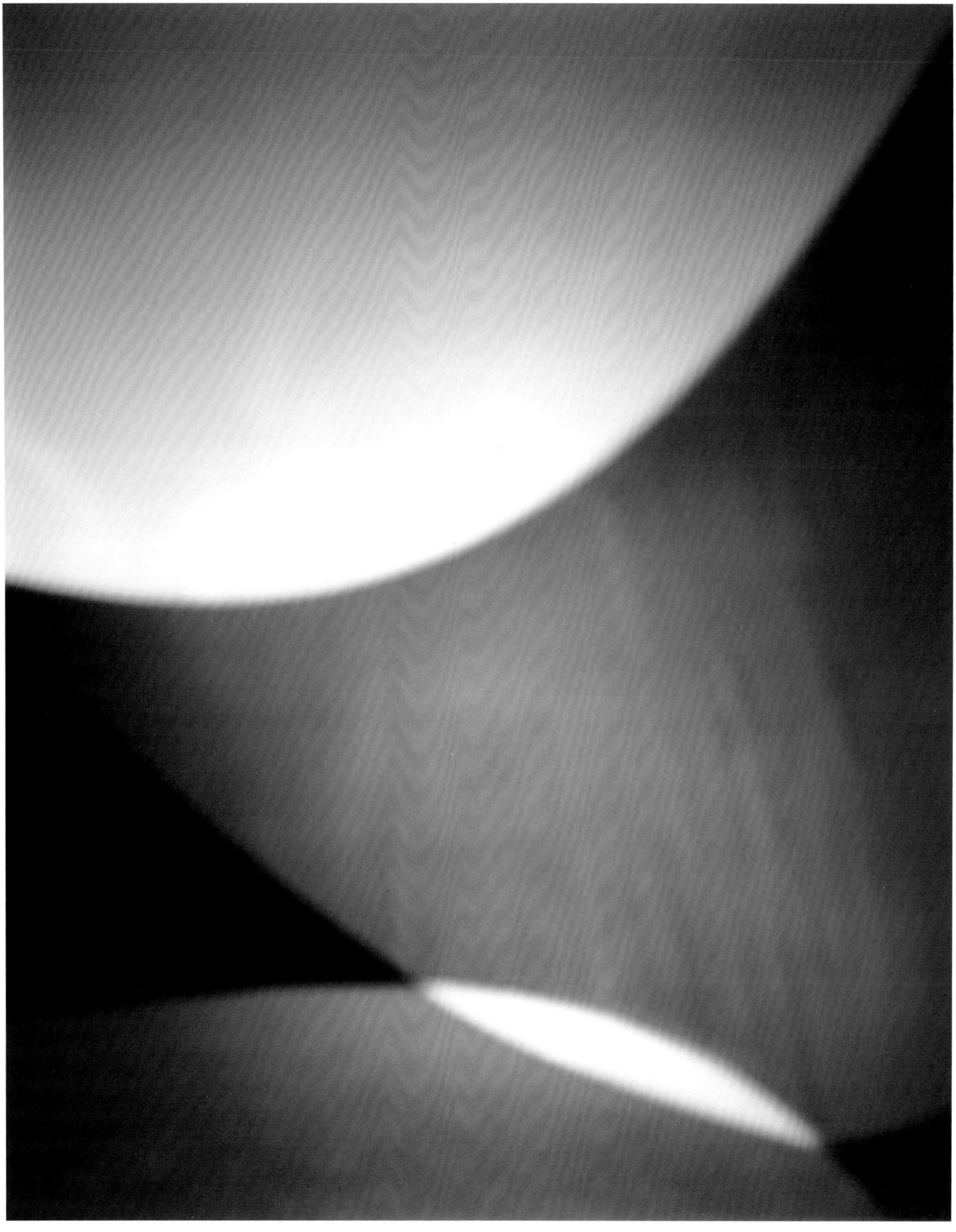

Hiroshi Sugimoto

It takes a certain amount of confidence to photograph nothing, yet that is what Hiroshi Sugimoto does, using the camera like a brush to paint with light. His subjects are barely there, only a blank, luminous cinema screen or the shadows cast by architectural structures, for instance. Sugimoto's work is more about the experience of looking – an enquiry into the quietness of the act of contemplation – than about creating something for the viewer to see. Born in 1948 and active since the 1970s, his work taps into the very core of what photography is, inhabiting an other-worldly dimension between history, space and time.

Sugimoto's rich visual language is rooted in his technique. The artist, who was born in Tokyo in 1948, has made the slow shutter speed his signature, preferring a large-format 8 x 10 camera, which is technically difficult to use because it is both heavy and requires painstaking attention to detail. Sugimoto's chosen tool and methodology contribute to his singular style, which he refers to as 'time exposure'.[1] Each of his bodies of work signifies an attempt to capture the essence of time in an image; eternity, life and death are constant themes, but also relate symbiotically to his way of working.

Rather than confining an object within the four corners of the frame, as most photographs effect to do, there is an astonishing feeling of space within Sugimoto's large-scale prints (often more than a metre by a metre-and-a-half in size). In the 1980s, when he first began to use long exposures of up to three hours, he pointed his lens towards expanses of water around the world, from the English Channel to the Black Sea, the Baltic and the Caribbean. The sea is a perennial subject for all kinds of photographers, but Sugimoto's perspective is unique: using black and white film, he mutes the visual impact of the water, affecting the viewer instead by the mysterious expanse of nothingness. This is the beginning of our 'voyage of seeing', as Sugimoto writes.[2]

The point where beginnings and ends converge is of constant interest to Sugimoto. In one of his most influential works, *Theaters* (1976–2016), he captured an entire film in one frame by fixing his shutter at its widest aperture and clicking it closed only when the film was over. *Theaters* also demonstrates Sugimoto's engagement with the simulation of seeing. *Dioramas* (1974), his first major work, comprises photographs of vitrines of stuffed animals against painted backgrounds on display at the American Museum of Natural History in New York. In the flat, large and intensely detailed photographs, it is impossible to tell that the animals are taxidermied representations, once alive and now 'dead reality'.[3]

***JOE 2053*, 2004. Gelatin silver print, framed, 149.2 x 119.4cm (58 ¾ x 47 ⅛ in)**
Joe is a sculpture by Richard Serra, commissioned by the Pulitzer Foundation for the Arts and installed in the courtyard at the Foundation in St Louis, Missouri. In 2003 Sugimoto visited the Foundation and became fascinated by the way our perception of the torqued spiral sculpture could shift depending on where we stand, the time of day and the season. The artist began to photograph myriad variations of *Joe*, which are both a homage to the magnificence and mystique of art and a paean to the bountiful interactions between memory, space and image.

Revisiting this theme of simulacra in *Portraits* (1999), Sugimoto moves from the natural world to human history in an equally eerie and spectacular way. Here, he ruminates on reality by photographing waxwork sculptures of historical and contemporary figures, many of them borrowed from Madame Tussaud's and in turn based on historical depictions in paintings. Each photograph, then, is a reproduction based on a reproduction based on a reproduction. We identify these people from the past as no longer living and yet what we encounter in the picture is startlingly lifelike. This is the essence of the photograph, and of Sugimoto's theory that 'photography is like a found object. A photographer never makes an actual subject; they just steal the image from the world.'[4]

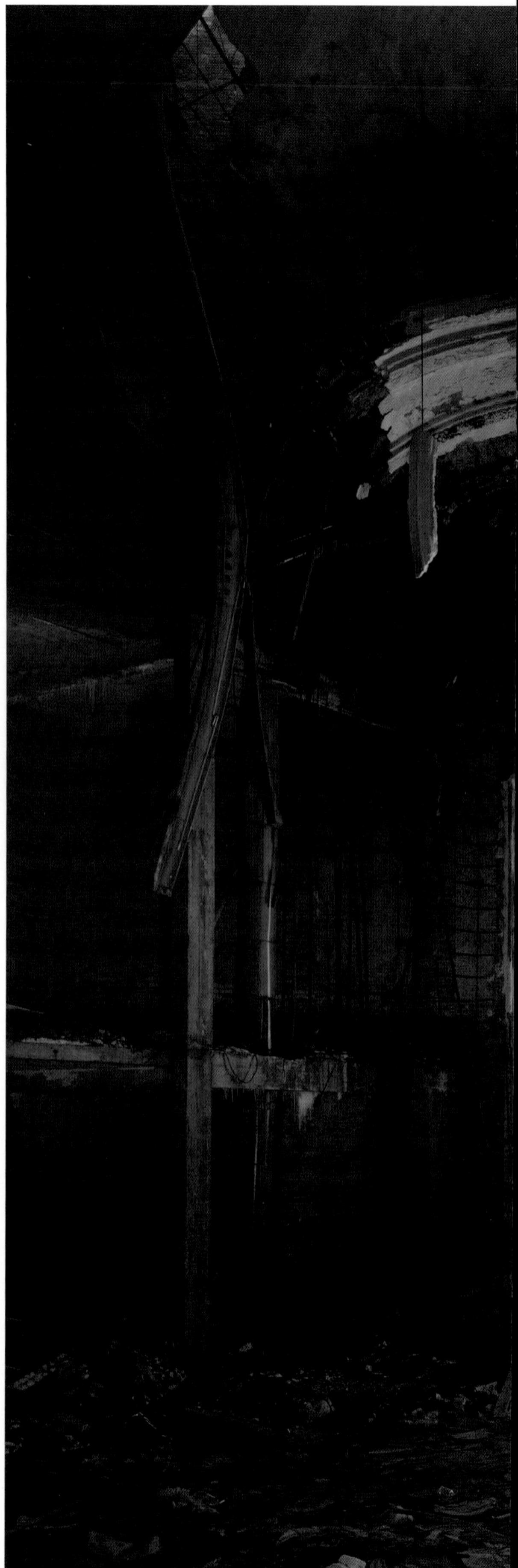

***Palace Theater, Gary* from the series *Theaters*, 2015.**
Gelatin silver print, 119.4 x 149.2cm (47 x 58 ¾ in)
The series *Theaters* was started in 1976, after the artist had relocated to New York from Los Angeles, where he had studied photography at the Art Center College of Design. In New York, Sugimoto has said, he experienced a 'near-hallucinatory vision'[5] that compelled him to set up his camera in the insalubrious St Marks Cinema in the East Village one afternoon. Sugimoto would continue to add to the series, capturing entire films with a single exposure lit only by the projector, for the next forty years. Only in 2016 did he reveal the titles of the films he had captured, in his book of the series.

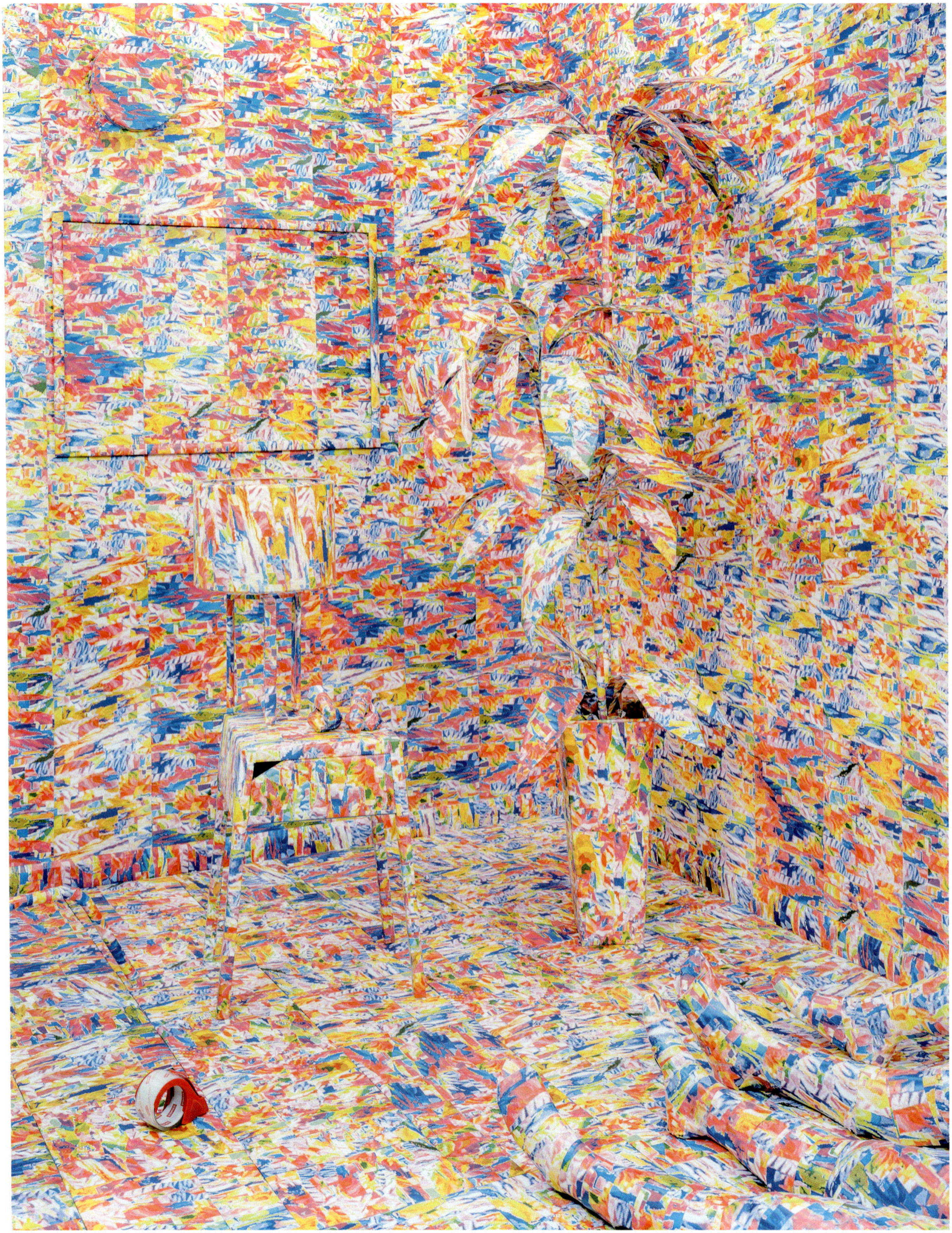

Leonard Suryajaya

***Homeland Security (Souvenir for My Home Country with Bacon)*, 2015**
This hallucinatory image, in which an entire set is wrapped in patterns made by the artist, references the 3D optical illusion prints popular in the 1990s. The fact that everything in the frame is wrapped – the shapes of legs, a nightstand, a potted plant, a clock on the wall are barely visible – is symbolic for the artist. 'When I came out to my mom in 2014, she told me not to tell my dad. I honoured her request because while I enjoy the privilege of being a free queer in America, my family is still vulnerable (to gossip, isolation, complication for having a queer son) in Indonesia. I want to be seen but I can't help feeling unrecognized. I want my experiences to be recognized but I am too fearful to be seen. Yet I long for a place and time where I would finally feel secure in all of my complexities and layers. So with optimism, I made this image.'[4]

'I know in my work I pull from a lot of confusion, conflict and the inability to communicate my potential and suffering,' Leonard Suryajaya reflects.[1] When you first encounter his kaleidoscopic works what strikes you is their irreverent, celebratory atmosphere; but an unexpected sense of pain, chaos and loss is also embedded in each elaborate, intricate display. Making images has provided solace in the wake of trauma for the artist.

Suryajaya was born in Indonesia in 1988 to a Chinese Buddhist family. As members of an ethnic minority, his parents suffered persecution, oppression and violence first-hand, and this was all still in the air as Suryajaya was growing up. Furthermore, being queer in a conservative, traditional family, Suryajaya was unable to freely express his sexuality and he struggled, especially in his relationship with his authoritarian father.

Photography became a form of fantasy for Suryajaya, a vessel for thoughts, ambitions and dreams when verbal communication was impossible. This tension between the isolation and persecution he felt growing up as a queer person and the desire for affection and acceptance has informed the development of his visual language. By the time he emigrated to the USA at the age of eighteen, Suryajaya had sworn never to return to Indonesia. His new home allowed him not only more freedom to express his sexuality but also the distance to begin to process his upbringing through his art. In 2015 he graduated in Fine Art from the School of the Art Institute of Chicago and chose photography as his medium, because, he said, 'the camera is the only thing that leaves me with any sense of independence.'[2]

Suryajaya eventually returned to Indonesia to visit in 2015 and, confronting his past from his present, he asked his family to take part in his art. He started to photograph his parents and other family members, alongside his partner, Peter, by building a set and then letting his subjects improvise within it. The theatrical series *Don't Hold onto Your Bones* (2015) and *False Idols* (2016–20), both shot on a 4 x 5 camera, were the results. 'I made photographs of my family with the fear of rejection from them. If a photograph I make of my family would be the last image I have of them before they shun me, then I want to make sure that includes all of the things – objects, gestures, poses, re-enactment, play-pretend – that I would miss from my time with them at home.'[3]

Suryajaya's works aren't only a personal exploration of his own history and struggle; they explore the complex dynamics of families in a fast-changing world. Suryajaya examines the unique ways family shapes individual identity, and family in turn is defined by tradition, culture and history. Exploding with colour, patterns and cross-cultural references – from Buddhist gods to traditional South East Asian textiles, local food stuffs, selfie sticks and foreign produce – Suryajaya's images embody the contemporary transnational experience, where all the different parts of one's heritage collide and compete. That sometimes looks like chaos and sometimes like bliss, but it is always stimulating: a tableau of the contradictions that face a new generation anywhere.

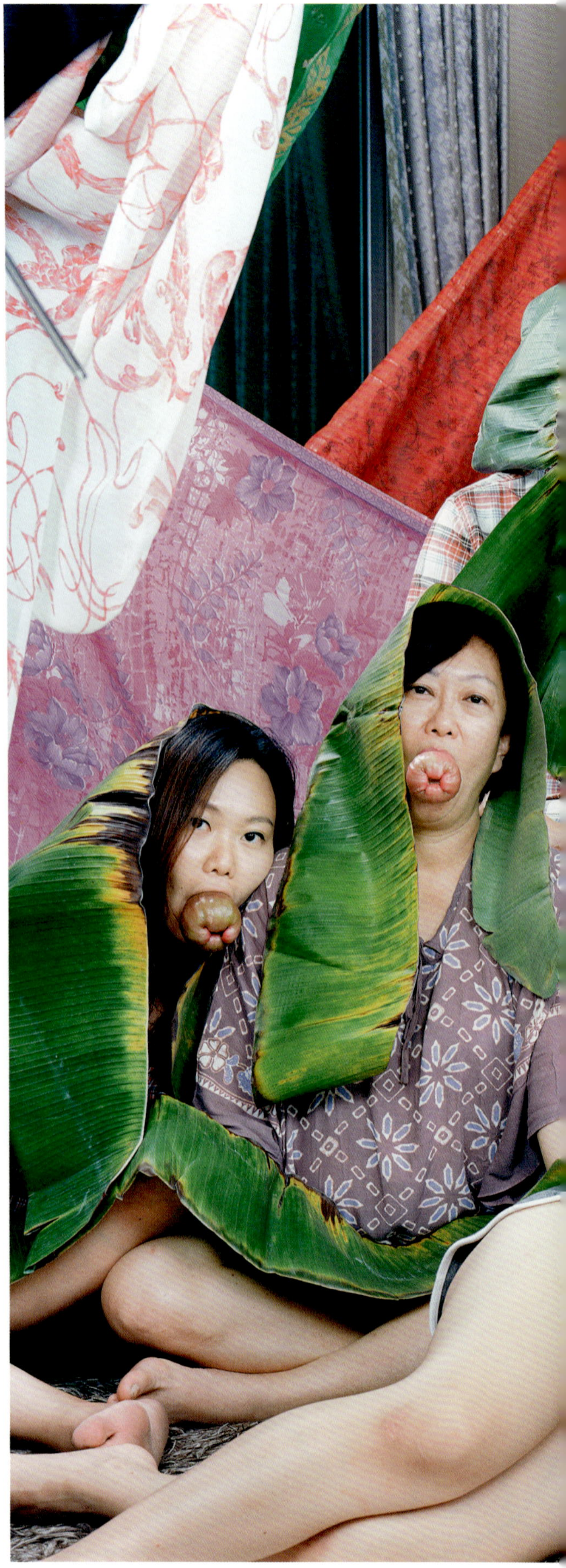

***Kinfolk Lipsync*, 2017**
This image, inspired by the desire 'for closeness and the inability to express love to one another',[5] conveys Suryajaya's experiences growing up queer in a conservative traditional Asian family. The fruit that everyone holds in their mouth is *jambu* (Java apple), a common fruit in Indonesia that the artist grew up eating and one that he is very fond of 'visually for the fact that the base of it looks like a swollen asshole'. Suryajaya visualizes the problems families have communicating with each other by having everyone suck on the fruit, 'making it seem like everyone is talking out of their buttholes'.[6] The family members are wrapped in banana leaves – ubiquitous in Indonesia – and surrounded by fabrics from Chinese, Indonesian and South East Asian cultures.

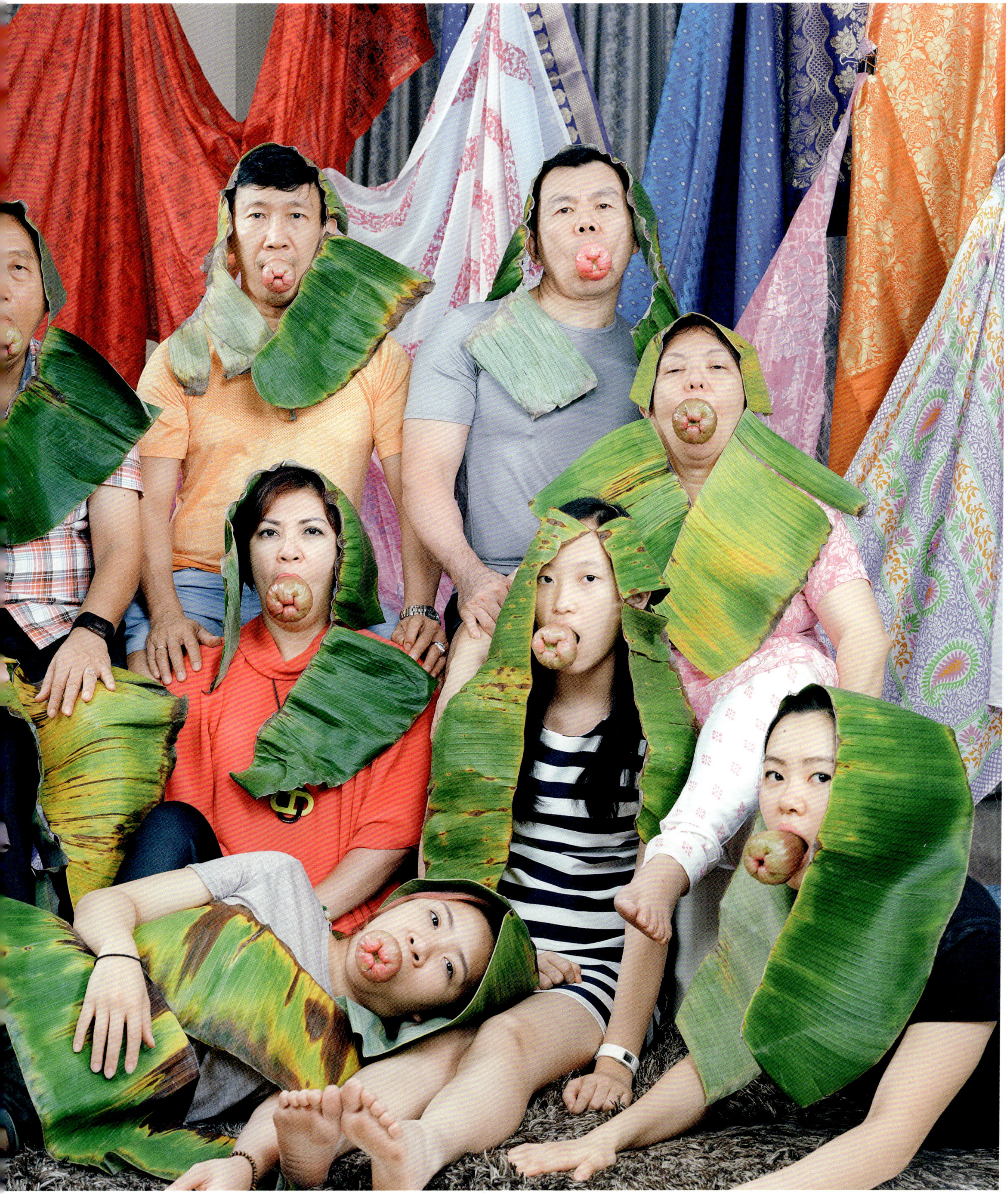

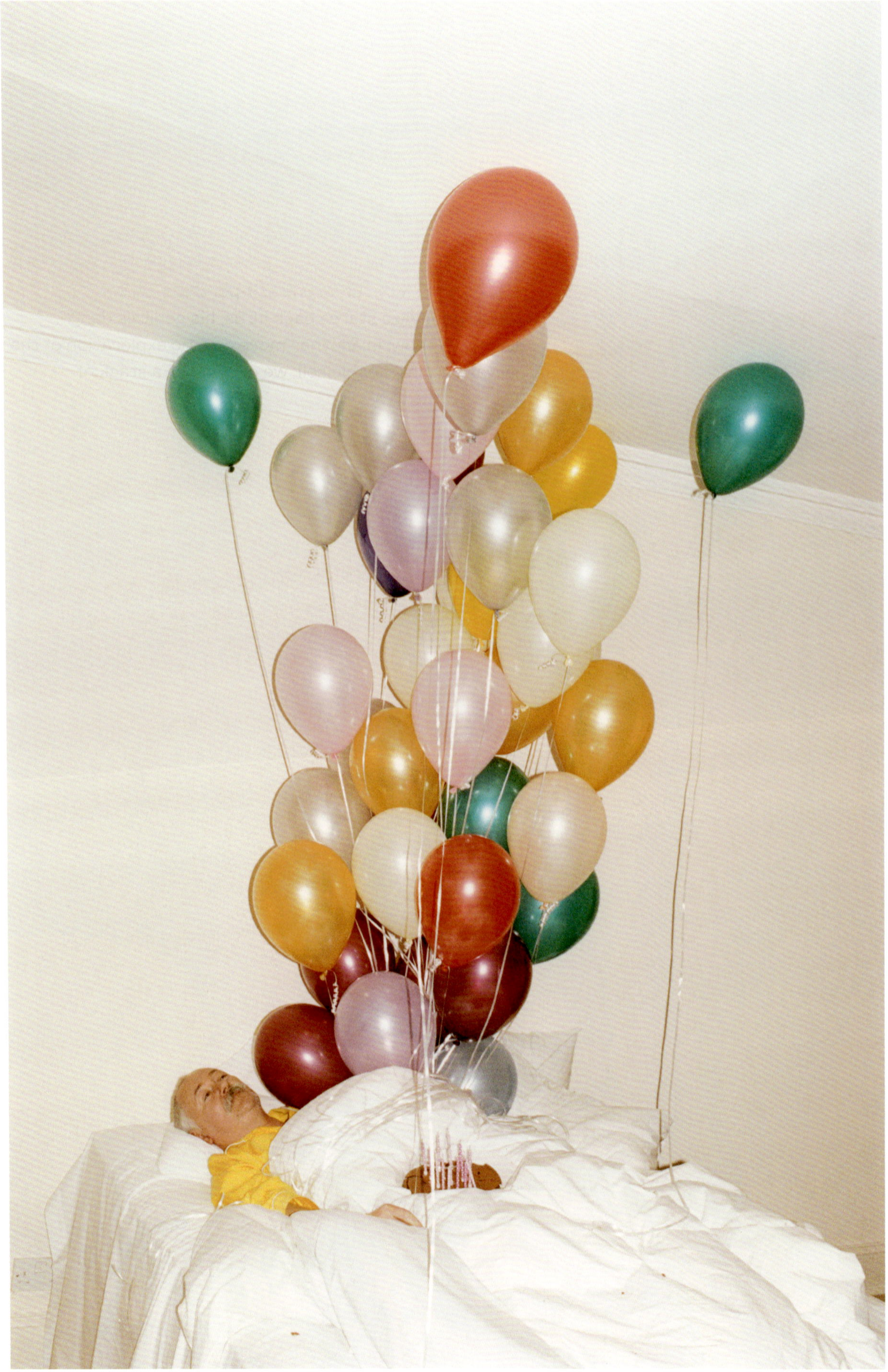

Juergen Teller

Cerith, Suffolk 2011 **from the series,** ***The Keys to the House*****, 2011. Digital C-type, 50.8 x 61cm and 274.3cm x 182.9 (24 x 20in and 108 x 72in)**
Life is a celebration, or a wake, or both at the same time, as this ambivalent image suggests. Underscored with Teller's typical humour, the image teeters between the absurd and the sentimental; the garland of colourful balloons is in stark contrast with the immobile, supine figure who lies beneath them. 'I took this picture at the birthday party of my friend the artist Cerith Wyn Evans. He loves being photographed. When he saw the photo he asked, "Please can we use the picture for my obituary?"' Teller recalls.[4]

Honesty is a quality often ascribed to the artist Juergen Teller, but his photographs make it clear that 'truth' is in the eye of the beholder. Teller's truth is sincere and always subjective, as he himself describes it: 'All of my work is a self-portrait, in one form or another.'[1]

The portraits are characteristically droll, and his subjects – whether it's himself, his son, his mother or the world's most famous faces – are all treated with the same candour and humour. In one self-portrait, Teller's perforating gaze stares back at us, his genitals dangling above the snow; in another more cryptic exploration of the pervasive, inescapable self, we encounter a stack of porcelain plates (in German 'Teller' means 'plate' and this has become a favourite motif for the artist). Teller is the photographer who shot Vivienne Westwood naked, aged sixty-eight, and who got Cindy Sherman to collaborate for the first time (for their Marc Jacobs campaign in 2005).

Born in the Bavarian city of Erlangen in 1964, Teller studied photography in Munich, graduating in 1986. He moved to London soon after to avoid military service. In 1988 his alcoholic father committed suicide and Teller has acknowledged that he could have gone the same way. His photographs often seem to teeter on the brink, to move between life and death, juxtaposing the sweet and the sublime with the bitter and the absurd. 'Life is stupid,' Teller says, 'it's tragic and beautiful, and I want to show all of that.'[2]

Teller cites four photographers as fundamental influences: August Sander, William Eggleston, Nobuyoshi Araki and Borys Andriyovych Mykhailov. What they share is complete confidence in photographing simple subjects in a straightforward manner and it's this that inspires Teller's own frank, no-frills treatment of his subjects, no matter who they are. 'Raw' is an adjective commonly associated with the kind of image Teller creates. In the 1990s he ruptured the glossy, puffy, too-perfect language of advertising and fashion photography. At the same time, he created a new path for photographers who made no distinction between 'personal' and 'commercial' work, shaping his vision through cult youth-oriented magazines such as *i-D* and *The Face*.

Teller's 1999 series, *Go-Sees*, was a professional coming-of-age and remains one of his most provocative works. Amused and annoyed by modelling agencies sending him women they thought he would like, Teller decided to 'turn the whole thing upside down'[3] and asked to photograph all the aspiring models on their books. Over a year, he photographed 462 young women symbolically on the doorstep of his west London studio.

A testament to his own inventiveness, the series is also a prescient interrogation of the 'sense of power you have as a man and the power you have as a photographer', as he explained in a 2008 interview.[5]

Go-Sees also reinvented the way photographers could work with big corporations, setting new standards and using photography as a form of critique from within that could flip the power dynamic between models and photographers, and push back strongly against vanity and the hierarchies that dictate what is beautiful. Teller has always seen his method as collaborative and finds beauty and ugliness equally seductive. His aim is not to flatter but to photograph people in such a way that they recognize themselves in the image – the very reason, he has conceded, that some people don't want to be photographed by him.

***Smiling Ed, London 2005* from the series *Nürnberg*, 2005. C-Type, 30.5 x 40.64cm (12 x 16in)**
Ed is Teller's son and he has featured in many of the artist's photographs over the years. This image of an infant Ed beaming in a bubble bath has become one of Teller's most popular photographs and has been widely exhibited and published. It is the embodiment of optimism, joy and love – one end of the epic scale of human emotions, none of which Teller is afraid to touch on in his work. Like his mother, Irene – another frequent subject in Teller's work – Ed is foundational and intertwined with his explorations of his life through his art. Teller selected this photograph for a curated column in *Die Zeit* (which later became *Pictures and Text*, published by Steidl), after the funeral of his agent and friend, Katy Baggott, who died suddenly in 2010. 'It is good to do normal things with your family. Just that morning I had to change the bedsheets, because Ed weed in it. Normally that would be annoying but that day it was a nice thing to do.'[6]

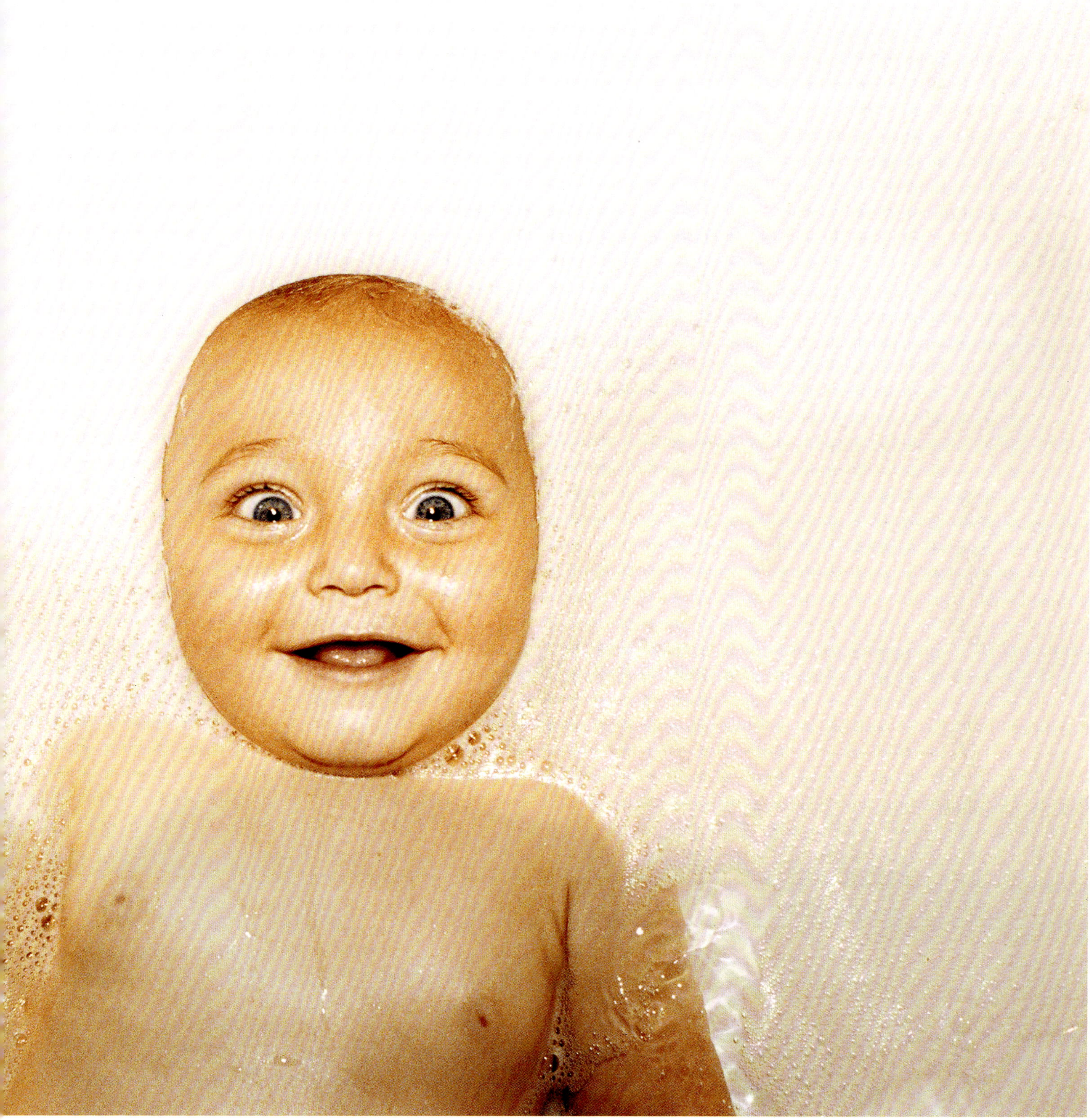

Wolfgang Tillmans

Born in 1968, Wolfgang Tillmans left his native Germany for the UK in 1990. By 1992, Tillmans found himself in London: he went to raves fuelled by ecstasy, sweat and electronic music, fell in love and partied with kindred spirits. His seminal exhibition followed in 1993, held within the three-metre space of Buchholz & Buchholz in Cologne, where he taped his work to the wall with no distinction between the editorial and the artistic.

The personal and the political are never separate in Tillmans's photography. Though his work can be divided into distinct periods and different methods of both taking and presenting his photographs, his aim has remained consistent from the start: 'The multiplicity of myself and my contemporaries – that's what interested me and that's what I wanted to communicate.'[1]

The politics of freedom underscores much of Tillmans's work and everything he captures is the result of a conscious choice. He has chosen to photograph people in the spaces that allow them to be free – nightclubs, raves, underground parties. He has explored the edges and the outer limits of our geography and our understanding of the universe – the sky, the sea, nature, windows, the orifices of the body, these are all motifs to which he returns. What Tillmans omits from his photography, as he himself has suggested, is just as significant as what he includes. Tillmans creates a world that he wants to see – and that he wants us to see with him. Through this visceral visual language, Tillmans conveys that 'if one thing matters, everything matters' – the title he chose for his 2003 exhibition at Tate Britain. Whether it's a portrait of Frank Ocean, a self-portrait in the shower or a still life with an aubergine, there is equal fascination for the photographer's insatiable eye.

Tillmans's photographs can seem desultory and spontaneous, but they are in fact the result of rigorous careful planning. The artist switched the 35mm camera with a 50mm lens (the focal length that best approximates the field of vision of the human eye) he used at the beginning of his career to a digital Canon SLR, but he never retouches his photographs digitally. He is known for producing richly detailed prints and being obsessive about colour. Each of his exhibitions is meticulously laid out in the studio months in advance, using models, so that the display becomes part of the work. Photographs are hung in irregular and unexpected ways, with grids, clusters and isolated prints, each show creating its own intrinsic pace. A Tillmans exhibition is total immersion and, as art critic Tom Morton has written, 'a luminous illustration of how and why we pay attention to the visual world'.[2]

***astro crusto, a* from the publication *Neue Welt*, 2012**
This photograph, one of Tillmans's best-known works, is part of *Neue Welt* ('New World') (2009–12), which focuses on modern life and global production through surfaces and textures. As the title suggests, the works form an expedition of sorts, a voyage of discovery around the world, without ever knowing exactly where we are or what we are looking at – a central theme of Tillmans's work, provoking us to question the reliability of sight. One of the poster images for his survey *2017* at Tate Modern, *astro crusto, a* also appears on the cover of Olivia Laing's 2018 novel *Crudo*. It is in many ways a definitive Tillmans photograph and yet it is a universal image that is hard to locate. It is close up, almost to the point of abstraction. It is classical – the fly resting on the abandoned remains of the lobster reminiscent of a memento mori – yet at the same time contemporary with its sharpness of detail and seductive rich colour. The meatiness of the lobster flesh is both erotic and repulsive, symbolic at once of a lavish lifestyle and the corruption of consumerism.

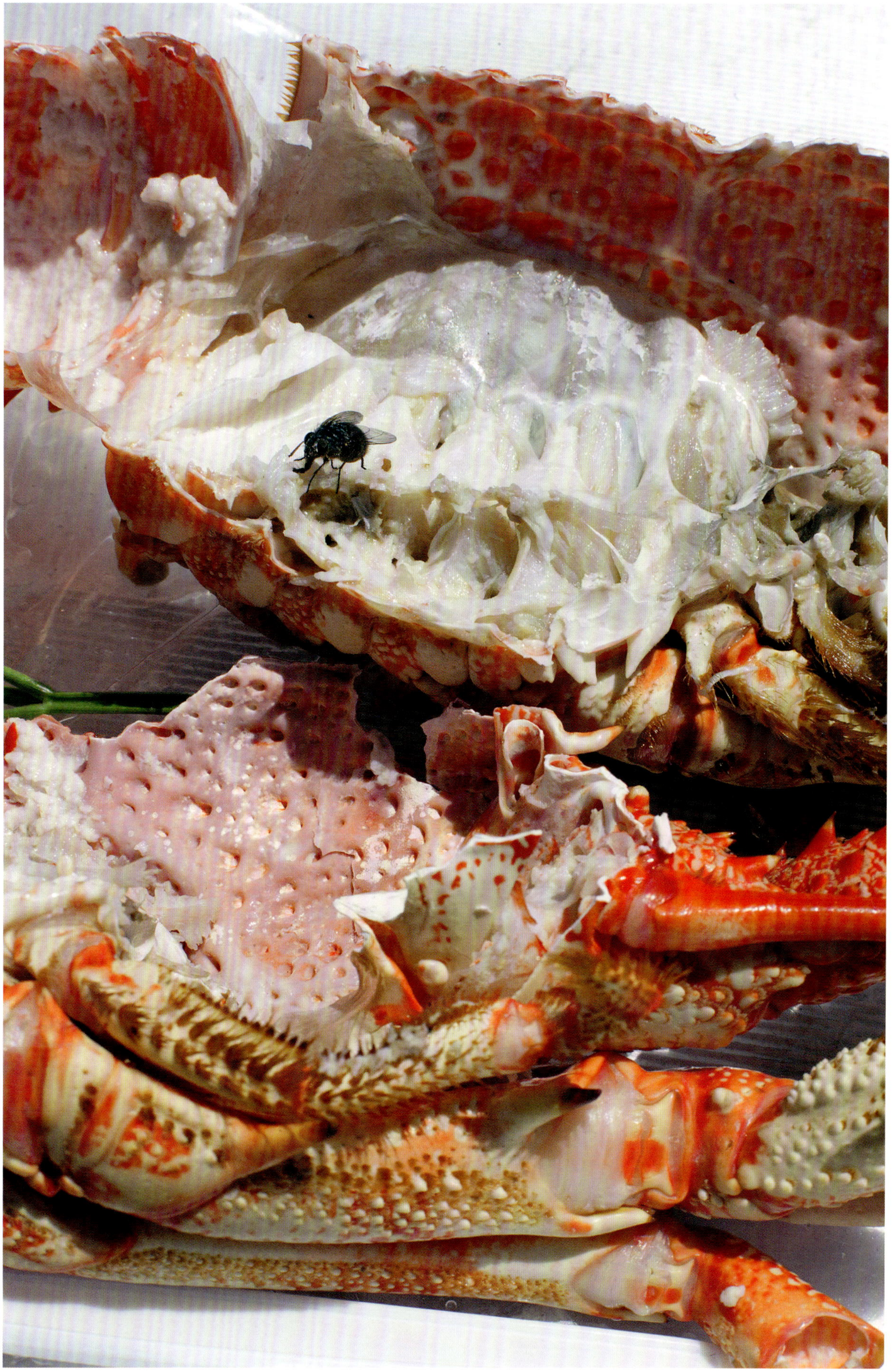

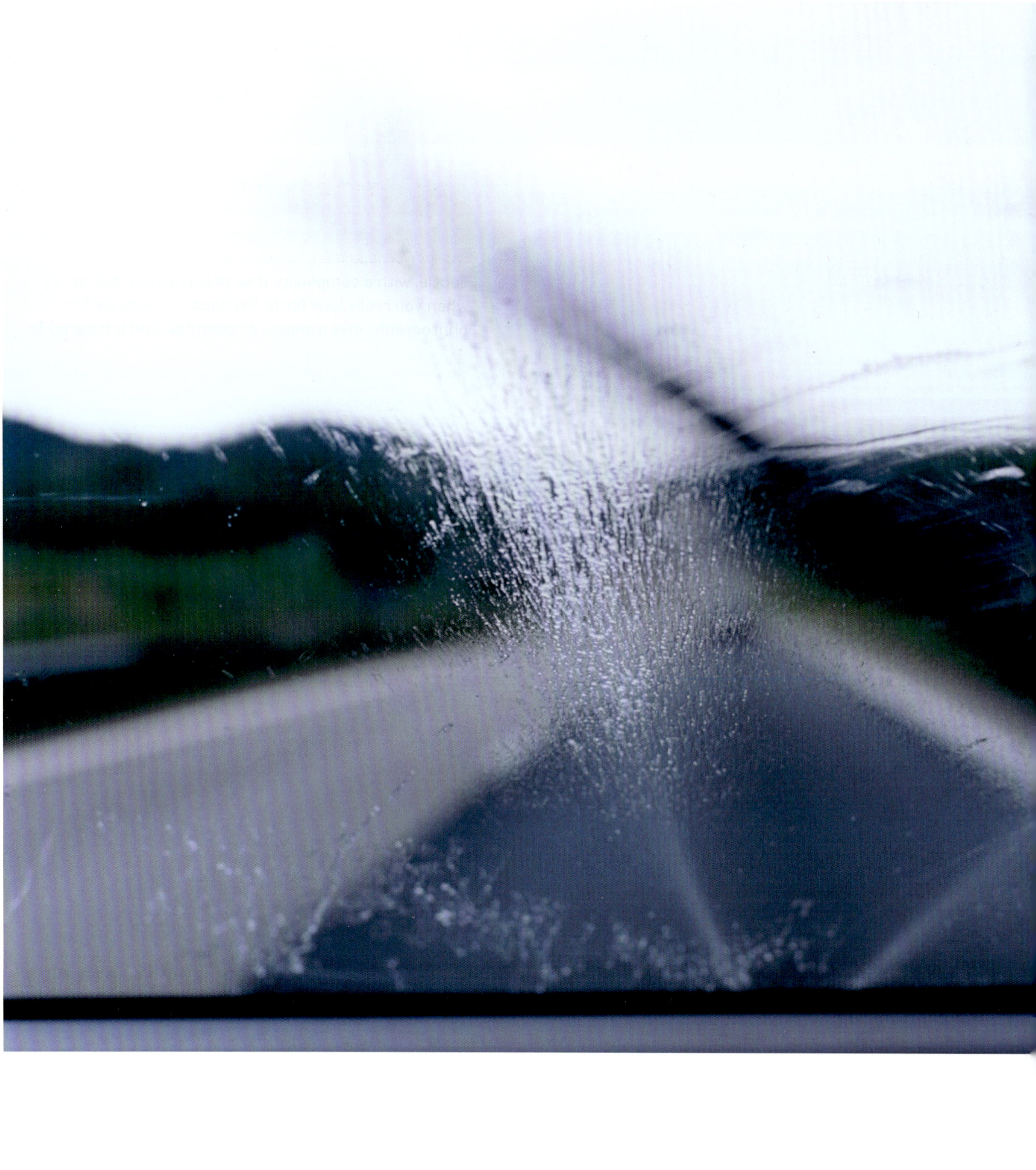

In 2000, Tillmans became the first photographer to be awarded the Turner Prize. The art critic Adrian Searle wrote at the time of Tillmans's 'omnivorous eye, taking pleasure in almost everything he looks at, and eroticising everything his camera sees'.[3] Tillmans was the first foreign-born artist to win the prize for British art. Sixteen years later, before the UK's EU referendum, Tillmans created posters for his pro-EU/anti-Brexit campaign, freely available to download and distribute.

Why is there such a voracious appetite for Tillmans's work? Perhaps it's because it is both immediate and subtle, with a complexity that only reveals itself slowly when you really look for it. Perhaps it's because his photographs give a sense of holding on and letting go at the same time. Or perhaps, as the artist himself says, it is simply because his photographs so acutely represent 'what it feels like to be alive today'.[4]

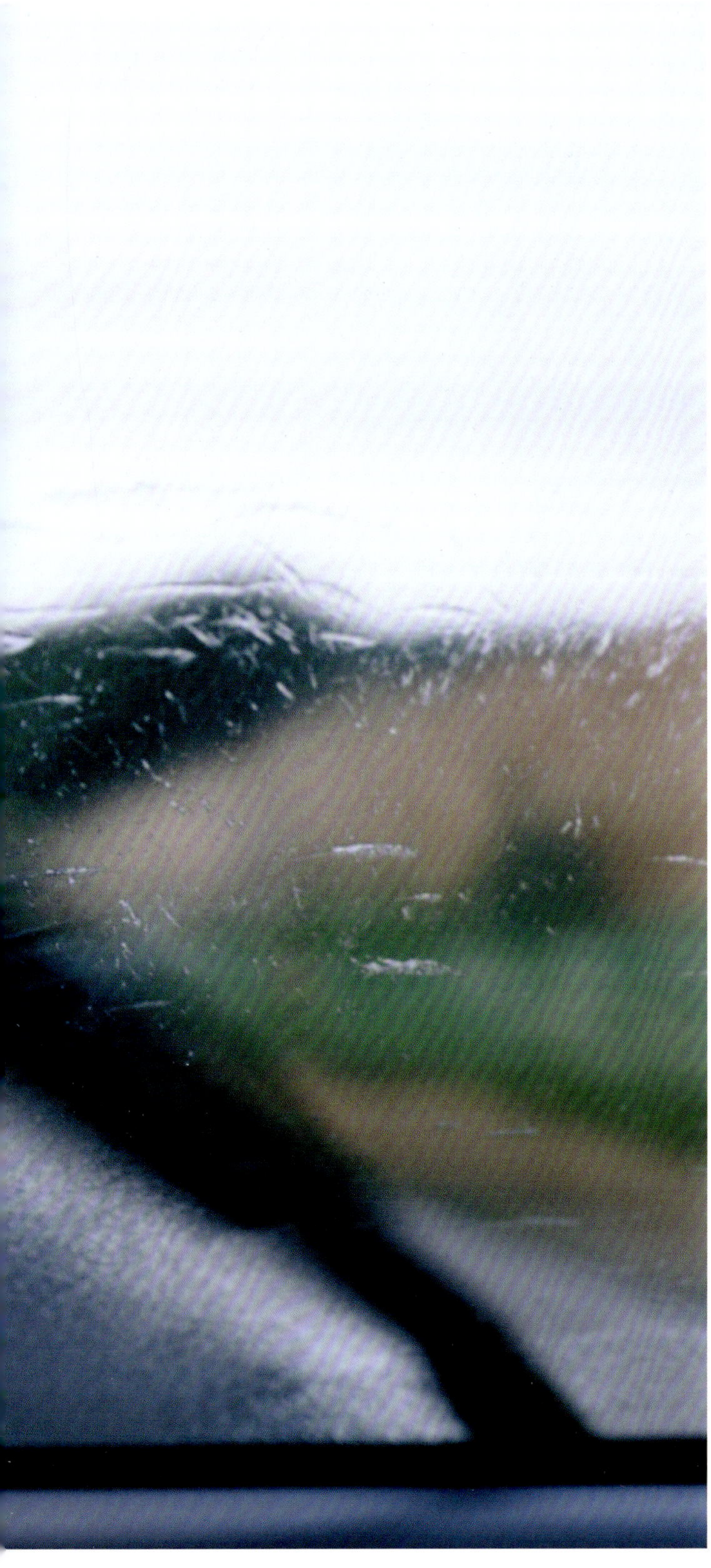

***New Family*, 2001**
Sometimes simple images evoke the strongest emotions, which is the case with this photograph, taken from inside a moving car on the autobahn. Water from a windscreen wiper hits the window as it moves, further obfuscating the view. It is an example, as Tillmans explained at a 2011 lecture at the Royal Academy of Arts in London, of 'the co-existence of abstraction and figuration, and abstract elements in figurative pictures'[5] in his work. *New Family*, made a year after his Turner Prize presentation, represents the semi-abstract language that Tillmans has been exploring since the 1980s.

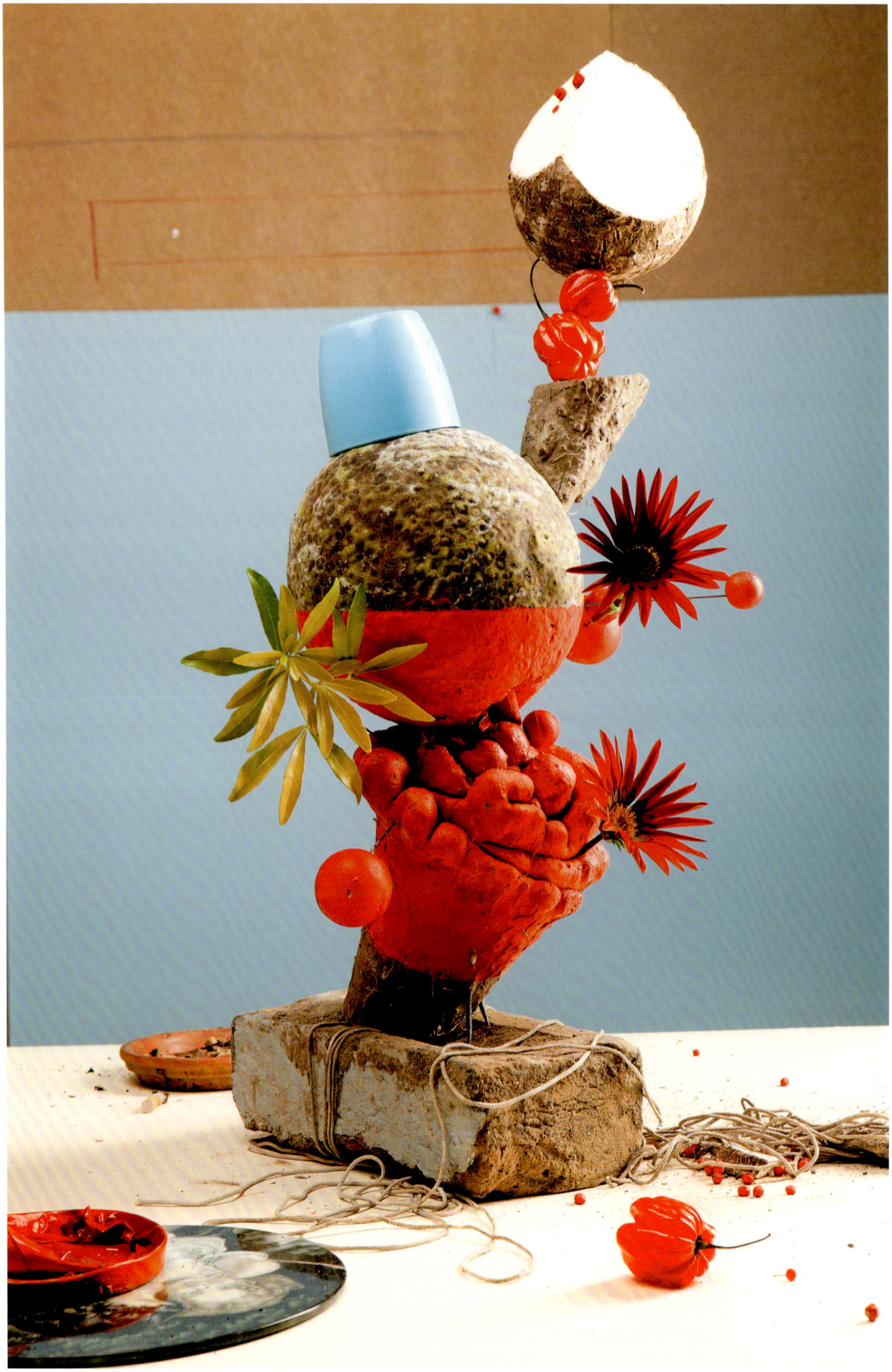

Lorenzo Vitturi

Once you've seen Lorenzo Vitturi's extraordinary photographs, it's hard to forget them. With their unmistakable mastery of colour and form, Vitturi's inventive still lifes, abstract portraits and landscapes bring pure aesthetic delight. But there is more to them than first meets the eye.

It is not a surprise to learn that the London-based artist, born in Italy in 1980, began his career as a cinema set painter. He builds his photographs like a set designer, using photography as part of a process of salvaging and re-presenting. Textures, patterns and shapes collide in what appears to be an impossibly dynamic dance, giving centre stage to the materials – the true protagonists of Vitturi's works.

These endlessly inventive object-oriented photographs are inspired by the rapidly changing urban environment. In 2007 Vitturi moved to east London – an area in the throes of voracious gentrification. His studio was next to Ridley Road Market, one of London's busiest street markets, which would become the subject of his first London series, *Dalston Anatomy* (2013). It was not easy for the photographer to be accepted into the market community, despite his proximity. In September 2012, following an undercover investigation, the national press reported that cane rat meat was being sold illegally to the public and there was an air of deep mistrust, especially of cameras. When Vitturi completed the work, he displayed it first at the market, in the form of a stall.

An urgent question in photography now concerns the position of the photographer in relation to their subject. The negative effects of misrepresentation and cultural voyeurism are present everywhere. As a white Western photographer, the complexities of this dynamic were apparent to Vitturi when he travelled to Lagos for a residency with the African Artists' Foundation and became fascinated by the Balogun market on Lagos Island. 'When I arrived in Lagos I found something very different from the drama that the Western media tends to depict,' he explained. 'The idea behind my collaboration with the African Artists' Foundation is to try and find other ways of representing life in Africa and Lagos.'[1] That included paying all the people who appear in his photographs and collaborating with local artisans. A local writer also produced the text for the series he

***Red #1* from the series *Dalston Anatomy*, 2013. Giclée print on Hahnemühle bamboo paper, 29.5 x 44cm (11 ⅝ x 17 ⅜ in)**
Dalston Anatomy enquires in detail into what makes up Ridley Road Market's unique mix of cultures and communities by looking at the objects sold there and the things thrown away and left to rot. The different organic materials found at the market were reconstructed into delicate new forms at the artist's studio. Imperfect and precariously balanced – as impermanent as the market itself, and enduring only in the photographs – this amalgam of materials is an ambiguous statement about waste and transformation. As the title of the series suggests, everything is the sum of its parts.

published as a book, *Money Must Be Made* (2017). 'It was still difficult to get around the issue of the role of a white Western photographer in Lagos, and it's not that I found any real solutions, but in a way this book sets out to uncover these issues and confront them.'[2]

A market is a microcosm, with its own ecosystem and infrastructure. Working with curator Azu Nwagbogu, Vitturi wanted to capture the vibrant creativity of Balogun and its vendors in a non-exploitative way. In the series, products bought from them were reconstructed as dynamic sculptures in a studio set up inside Financial Trust House – once a base for global conglomerates, corporations and banks, but now empty. The traders were reimagined as abstract forms, juxtaposed with contrasting pictures of the derelict, grey interiors of the disused office block.

The situation at Balogun contrasted with what Vitturi saw at Ridley Road. Both markets were thriving ecosystems full of creative enterprise, but where Ridley Road was under threat from encroaching commercial redevelopment, Balogun was bustling below the now abandoned multi-storey Financial Trust House. This was a rare case when local independent business had thrived while large Western organizations had failed.

The story told through Vitturi's work is primarily material. Using commodity and product – the universal language of a capitalist world – he demonstrates how cultures inherently have the capacity to fuse and transform. People are mostly absent in his pictures, but these are definitely man-made works, composed from the things we manufacture and consume – all of which Vitturi documents in the titles of his works.

In the series *Caminantes* (2019) – Vitturi's most personal work yet – the sculptural forms are larger and anthropomorphic, inhabiting vast open landscapes. Vitturi is retracing the journey his father made in the 1960s, crossing the Atlantic from Venice to Peru to establish a Murano glass factory. There, his father met his Peruvian mother, and Vitturi's upbringing exposed him constantly to the two cultures while also educating him in the strong colours so important in both places. Having travelled to Peru with fragments of glass from Venice, Vitturi fused these with local fabrics, objects and organic matter significant in Peruvian culture. His photographs are a celebration of the richness of material culture and of diversity and coalescence through trade, craft and exchange.

***Painted Calabashes, Aso-Oke and Veneto Leather* from the series *Money Must Be Made*, 2017. Archival pigment print, anti-glare glass, 110 x 73cm (43 ¼ x 28 ¾ in)**
The lively nature of markets and the creativity of market vendors and their use of space – piling their wares vertically, in seemingly impossible physical feats, in order to create the most eye-catching displays – continue to be reference points for Vitturi's series *Money Must Be Made*. This image features a teetering and triumphant sculpture made up of painted *calabashes* (bottle gourds, native to subtropical climates, that can be eaten or made into utensils or instruments), *aso oke* (a handwoven cloth made by the Yoruba people) and Veneto leather from northern Italy.

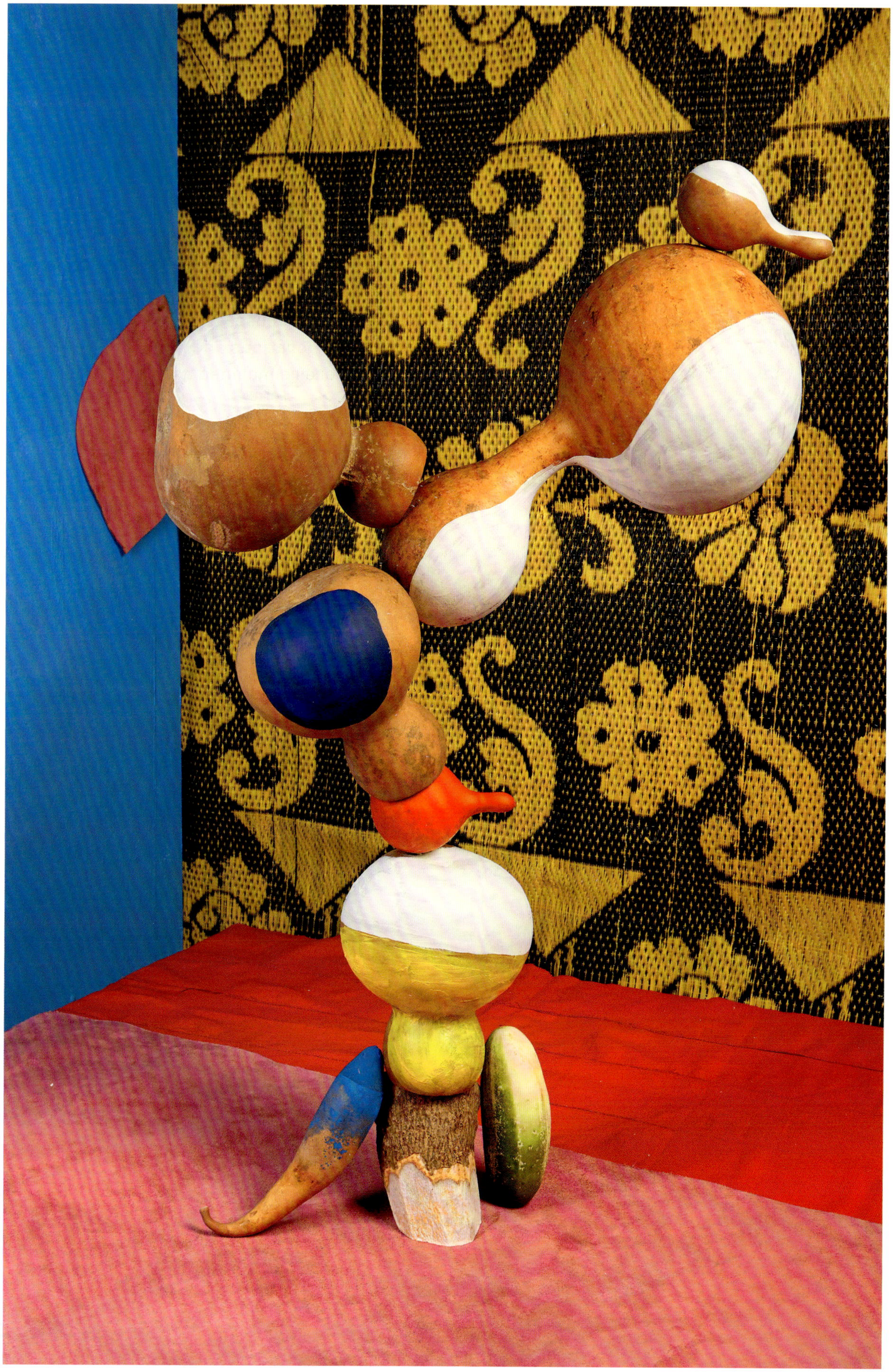

Jeff Wall

Changing Room, **2014. Inkjet print, 199.5 x 109cm (78 ½ x 43in)**
In this apparently ordinary scene, a woman tries on a dress in a changing room. As always with Wall's pictures, though, what you think you see quickly unravels once the details sink in. The figure enveloped in a dress she is pulling on – or is she taking it off? – is in fact already wearing a dress, and an identical dress hangs just in view to the side of the frame. This could of course all be perfectly innocent, but it is enticingly ambiguous. The image is typical of Wall's reconstructed 'near documentary' works, deliberately mimicking the language of documentary photography, based on real-life observations but composed according to his memory.

'I begin by not photographing,' Jeff Wall famously once said.[1] His process starts simply by looking. Later – sometimes after a year or more – he reconstructs his observations with the camera, letting the decisive moment disappear and memory take precedence. 'The reconstruction is a transformation that leads to something faithful,' Wall explains. His work expands on the idea of 'photographic seeing' – an investigation into the way the photographer sees and frames the world through the viewfinder.

Wall was born in 1946 in Vancouver and still lives in the city, which has frequently been the subject of his photographs. It's also the place where he first established his ideas as an artist, being an important contributor to the Vancouver School – a group of photoconceptualist photographers interested in the social mechanism of imagery. After a stint in London where he studied from 1970 to 1973 as an art history postgraduate at the Courtauld Institute, Wall returned to Canada. An 1882 painting by Manet, *Un bar aux Folies-Bergère*, which hangs in the Courtauld Gallery and depicts a barmaid, Suzon, standing in front of a reflected scene at Paris's famous music hall, would inspire one of Wall's most notable works, *Picture for Women* (1979). In Wall's photograph the artist looks at a woman and she looks at the camera, both reflected back in a mirror that frames them. Wall riffs on the different gazes that are exchanged: the male gaze on the woman's body, the viewer's voyeurism and the camera, complicit and right at the centre of the image.

Wall's academic training and close connection with the masterpieces of art history have continued to influence his approach to photography and the way he builds his images; in fact he cites composition as 'one of the most interesting aspects of any form of art'.[2] Restaging his images allows Wall to compose them carefully, choosing the locations and reframing the action to evoke specific emotional responses.

Wall's artistic breakthrough came in 1977, when he produced backlit photo transparencies (photographic film that is processed to produce a transparent image so that it can be projected rather than printed), challenging the boundaries of the photographic form. This led to *The Destroyed Room* (1978), his first light-box work, which measures a commanding 159 x 234cm (5ft 2¼in x 7ft 8in). The room – as the title suggests – is a wreck, but it also reveals itself as a construction, with the joists and joints showing through the battered wall. *The Destroyed Room* was a defining work for Wall, both

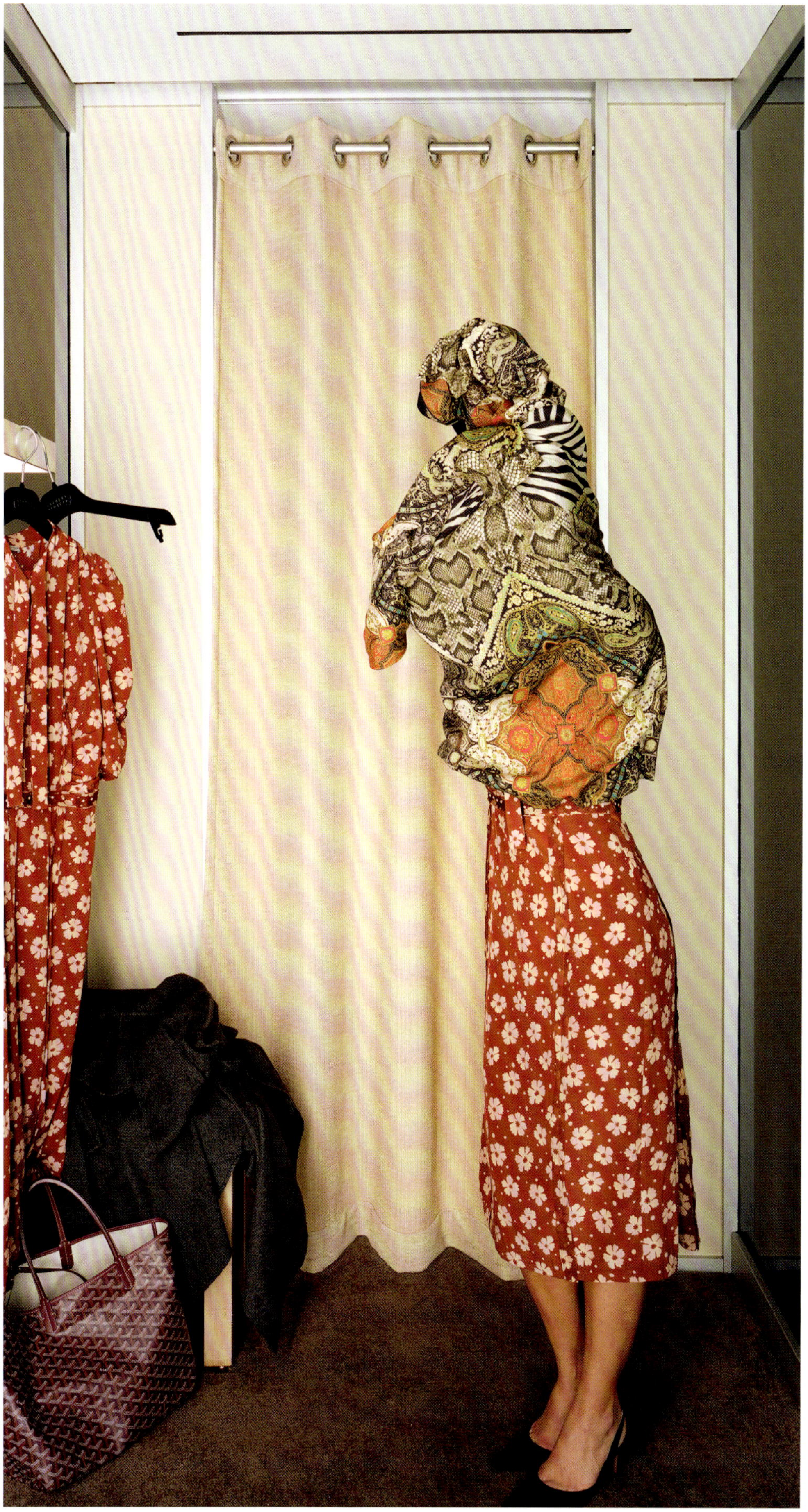

conceptually and in terms of its format, and he has continued to produce imposing, light-box works ever since. With their majestic scale, averaging 180 x 240cm (6 x 8ft), and the glow from the light box, Wall is suggesting that photographs can possess the monumental grandeur of paintings.

Wall also borrows techniques from film-making, such as collaborations with non-professional performers and set building with auteur-like attention to detail to create his pictures. He was also one of the first photographers to makes use of new technologies for digital manipulation in his *Dead Troops Talk* (*A Vision After an Ambush of a Red Army Patrol Near Moqor, Afghanistan, Winter 1986*) (1991–2), which is a deliberately artificial rendition of a scene during the Soviet war in Afghanistan that references canonical war paintings, as well as horror films, with a battlefield of dead soldiers who appear to stagger back to life.

In the 1980s, when Wall began to engage with his cinematographic approach, he created enigmatic scenes and vignettes that comment on the inherently political nature of relationships between people, but without narrating them fully. It is up to us, the viewer, to complete the picture. One of his most famous works from this period is *Mimic* (1982), a reconstruction of a racist incident he observed. At first glance, the picture appears to be an ordinary scene of three people walking down a Vancouver street in summer; on closer inspection, though, the white man walking just behind the Asian man can be seen making a racially offensive gesture.

The title of the work points to the gesture but also introduces Wall's notion of the 'near documentary',[3] a term he coined to refer to pictures of his that appear to be chance snapshots but are in fact choreographed. His close study of reality in the moment allows him the freedom to create what he believes is ultimately a more faithful representation – or at least a more sincere subjective response to what he observes. A photograph, like a painting or a poem, does not have to show something as it happens in order to speak of events that actually occurred.

Rich in references and dense in meanings, Wall's work is nonetheless first and foremost experienced on a visceral level. As he says, 'Artists are sympathetic to being – and I think that's why people like art.'[4] Sharing the enjoyment of looking, the pleasure of appearances, is Wall's main motivation.

***Milk*, 1984. Transparency in light box, 187 x 229cm (73 ⅝ x 90 ¼ in)**

This cryptic image appears to capture an unfortunate explosion as it happens: a man sits on the pavement, turning his head as white liquid erupts from a paper bag in a theatrical arc. However, as we know when looking at Wall's work, this is a carefully arranged restaging: the formal alignment of the brickwork in the background is perfect, the clenched-arm pose of the man is psychologically loaded and ambiguous. The details are peculiar too: the man is missing shoelaces, his hair is wet. The viewer immediately comes up with a series of questions. Who is he? Why is he here? Is that really milk? What has happened? *Milk* shows Wall's interest in creating cinematographic images with intense suggestive power as multiple situations, stories and characters inhabit a single frame.

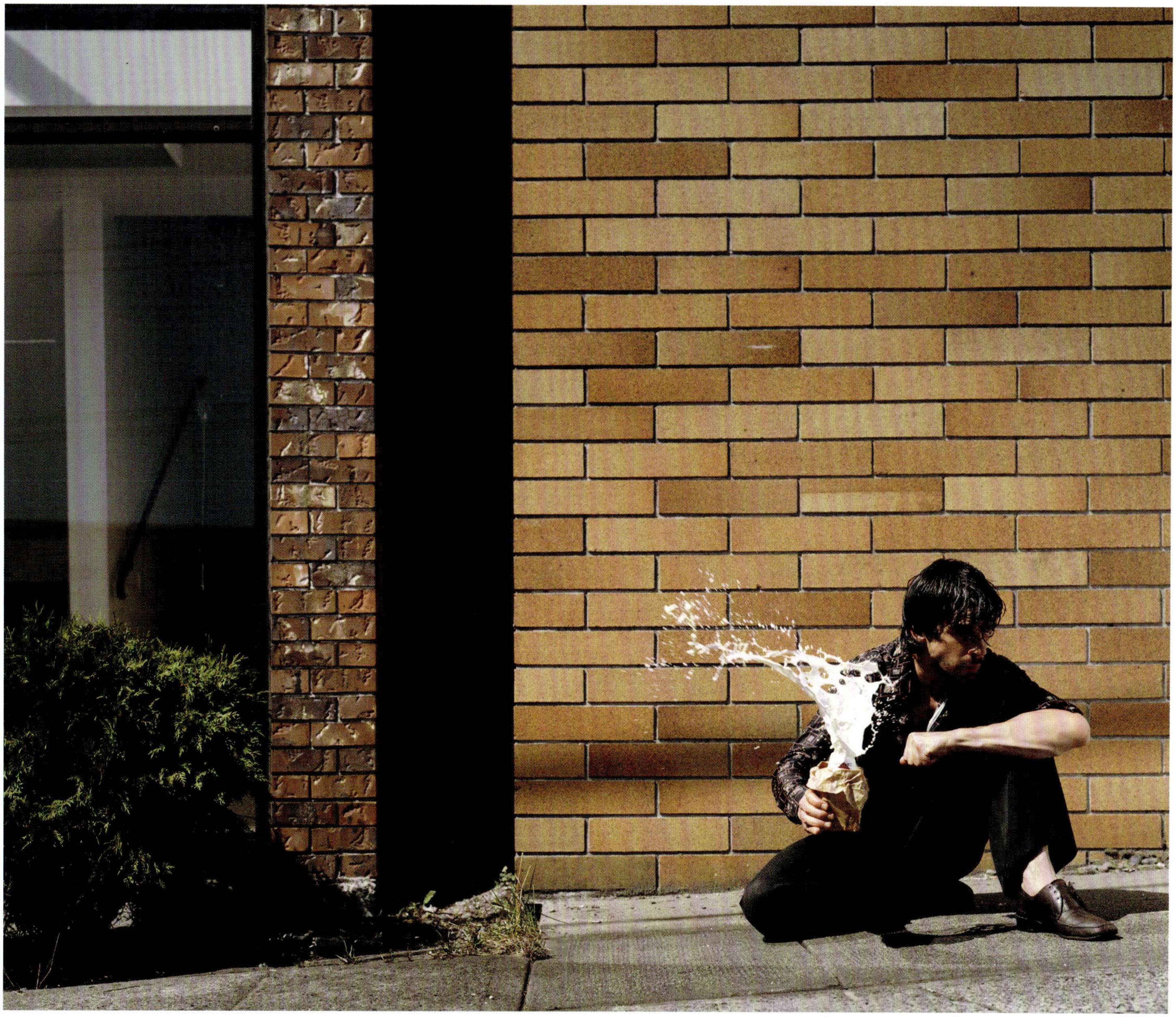

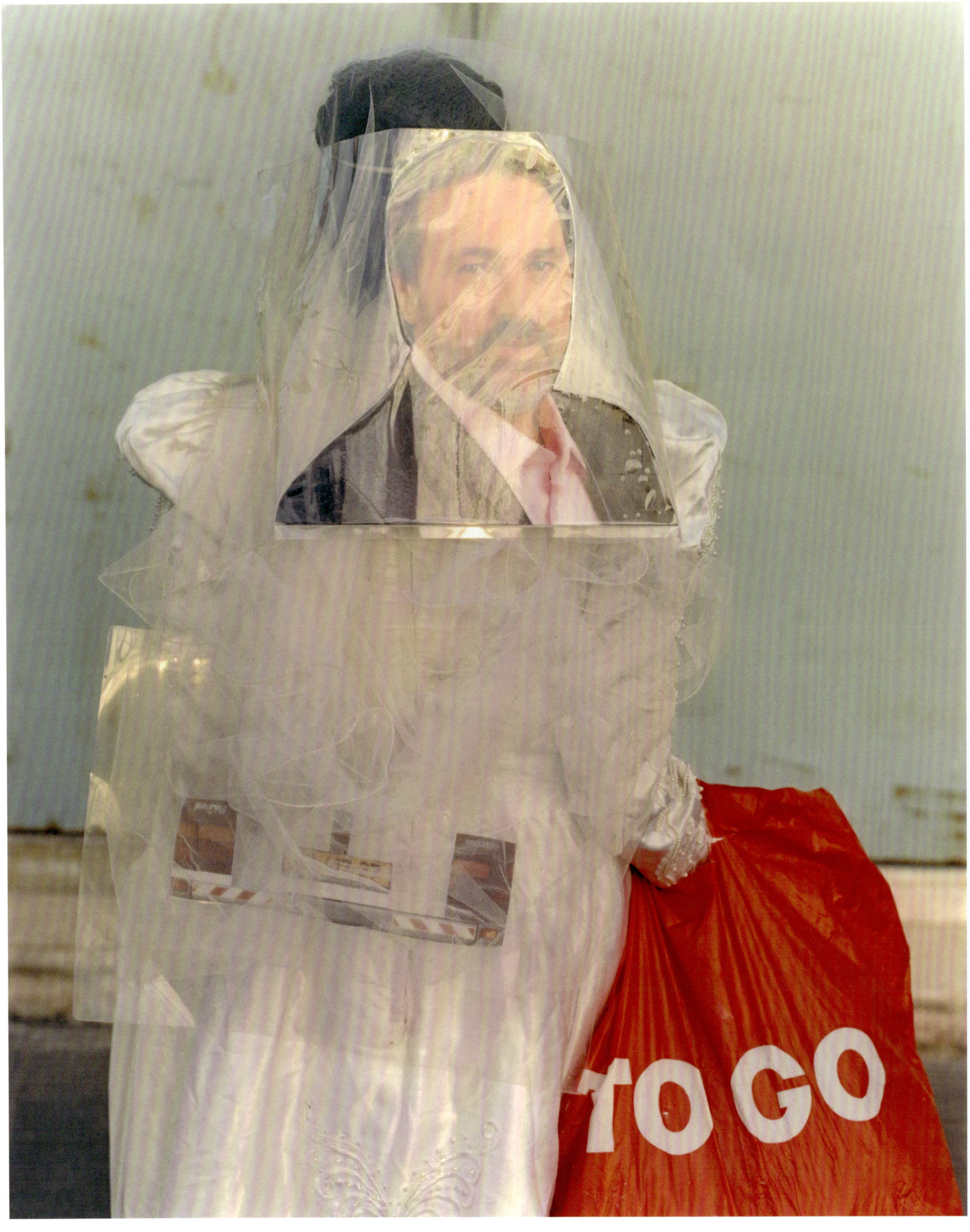
TO GO

Harley Weir

'The relation between what we see and what we know is never settled,' writes John Berger in *Ways of Seeing*. 'Each evening we see the sun set. We know that the earth is turning away from it. Yet the knowledge, the explanation, never quite fits the sight.'[1] The same strange dissonance can be felt when looking at Harley Weir's photographs. We know that what we are looking at is real, but because it is rich in ambiguity and steeped in ambience, we are swept far away from the confines of reality, into a place where the physical meets the metaphysical.

Weir was born in London in 1988 and graduated in Fine Art from Central Saint Martins in 2010. She taught herself analogue techniques, keeping the craftsmanship of working in the darkroom to satisfy a need for making with her hands. Weir has said that her favourite subject is people, but by photographing bodies she often alludes to the experiences that take place outside or beyond them. She wants us to look at things precisely because there is so much we can't understand by looking – the dichotomy in photography that Berger referred to when he wrote of the chasm between seeing and knowing.

Weir's hazy, tender gaze has been lusted after by the fashion world. From the start of her career she has worked with major brands, including Dior, Céline, Balenciaga and Stella McCartney, and influential publications, including the front cover of American *Vogue* in March 2020. Her eye for ephemerality and sensorial beauty gave rise to unexpected results when Weir turned to more politically charged subjects. In a 2014 series entitled *Boundaries*, exhibited in 2017 at Foam, Amsterdam, she captures life on the borders between Israel, Palestine and Jordan with a lightness of touch by focusing on a passing moment in someone's day. In the picture, a young girl in a bikini sunbathes, looking out across the sea towards Jordan, the sky washed with dusky pink and blue hues; a young Hasidic boy wears a fake moustache and Israel Defense Forces (IDF) uniform as fancy-dress to celebrate the Jewish festival of Purim. With her subtle ruminations on the various social, religious, geographic and cultural differences that overlap here, Weir looks at the conflict as it manifests itself in minute details, embodied in ways that are not immediately obvious.

From the series *Boundaries*, 2016
Weir first travelled to Israel for a job in Tel Aviv. She became fascinated by the country and returned several times, visiting Jerusalem, the West Bank and later also Jordan. The imagery of the area we see in the media is intensely politicized, but Weir wanted to create a different way of documenting the conflict. The photographs she shot there, which are almost all close-ups, represent a personal stance – an intimate engagement with the surroundings – that emphasizes her perspective as that of an outsider. 'The situation there is so complicated, the issues are so great – it's beyond my understanding and I didn't want to be disrespectful. Every image is loaded.'[2] In this particular photograph, taken in East Jerusalem, we see a woman in a wedding dress and layers of gauzy veil, with the cut-out photograph of an Israeli soap star attached to the back of her head. The woman was disabled and begging, and Weir deliberately gives us this view, preserving her anonymity. Rather than making a statement about politics or place, she fixes a surreal moment, her focus on the mysterious beauty that results from the meeting between light and materials.

The notorious Jungle refugee camp at Calais, dismantled in 2016 – at which point it was home to more than 8,000 migrants – becomes an almost formal study of materials and design in Weir's series *Homes* (2016). Taken during several visits to the camp, including one after it was destroyed, the pictures are distinct from most of Weir's other work as the focus is not on people; instead she portrays with equal intimacy – by shooting up close – the places where they live. Weir captures colourful makeshift fabrics, tarpaulins and canvases, and finds beauty in the geometric arrangement of toothbrushes strung up inside a tent, or the simple cross that marks one structure as a place of worship.

Whether her subjects are people or their environments, Weir moves in close, silencing the noise of information, focusing on the interaction of colour, light and form. Susan Sontag called photography 'a soft murder, appropriate to a sad, frightened time',[3] which seems to be how Weir approaches her craft, with a gentle regard for a world that is brutal and beautiful, violent and vital. As she herself says, she wants the viewer to feel something, but 'it doesn't really matter what emotion it is'.[4] In today's world, making us feel anything at all is photography's biggest challenge.

From the series *Father*, 2019
The photographs collected in Weir's 2019 publication *Father* are the culmination of ten years' work examining masculinity by looking at different men and their bodies. Weir's gaze on male bodies is empathetic and curious, and is also an intimate look at her own sexuality and desire, and an exploration of how we might explore gender differently, through looking at each other. This photograph depicts Benjamin Kirchhoff in Berlin. His body, cast softly in pink hues, is performative and at the same time vulnerable. A single trickle of blood snakes its way down his back in a perfect curve. Kirchhoff explains that the bloodletting 'is reflective and peaceful, not violent; it's sacrificial, not retributive'[5] and pays homage to the tradition and its resonance in particular with queer performance artists.

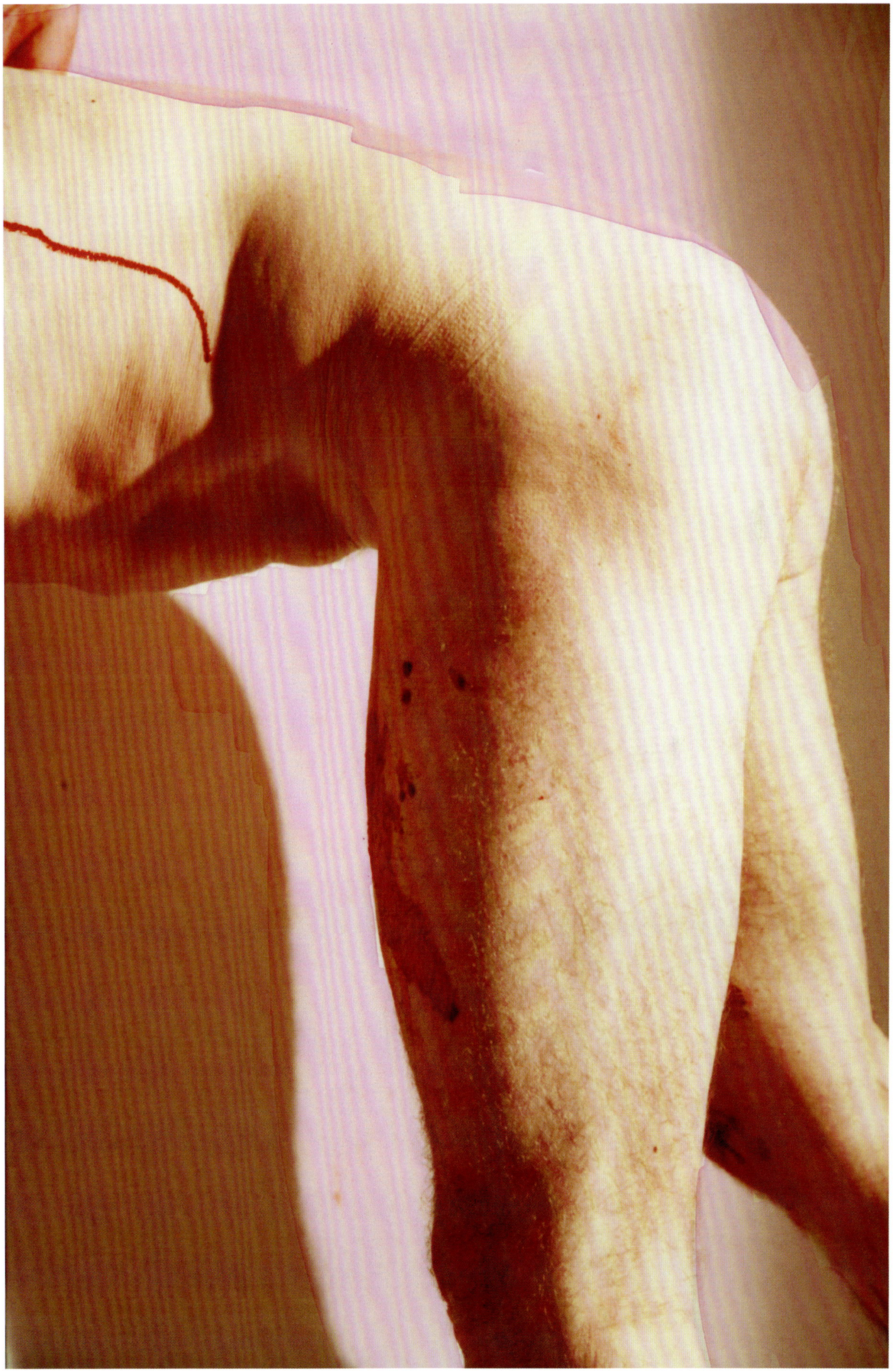

Carmen Winant

Aren't there enough photographs out there already? Photography is young, but its production has accelerated beyond the quantifiable. In our visually saturated world it is easy to be exhausted by photography, but a photograph is also a form of acknowledgement. The artist, writer and teacher Carmen Winant doesn't make new photographs but uses archival pictures to investigate the ways the camera has documented, represented and ratified. 'I collect found pictures because they have their own histories outside of me,' she explains.[1]

Born in 1983 in San Francisco, Winant was a student of Catherine Opie at UCLA and then Larry Sultan at the California College of the Arts, where she attended graduate school. Both artists shaped her practice in a big way, and there is a common thread between the three: a way of turning the lens inwards, on the private, domestic and personal, rather than pointing out and shooting.

Speaking at the Fast Forward: Women in Photography conference in 2019, Winant told her audience, 'My creative practice pivots on photographic objects produced by others which I work to find, compound and recontextualize.'[2] The main area for this photographic research has been the feminist movement of the 1970s, mostly in the USA, and how it has changed the way we see. Winant has looked deeply into matriarchy, alternative communities, different systems of living and ways of reinventing the body outside the patriarchy. Women's bodily experiences are often the starting point for her to navigate these themes, something that also connects in part to her earlier training as a long-distance runner. Female strength, labour, the extreme limits of the body – finding the point beyond which it cannot go – these are the ideas Winant explores in multiple projects, including *Who Says Pain is Erotic?* (2016), *Pictures of Women Working* (2016), *Body/Index* (2018) and *A History of My Pleasure* (2019).

Her work on feminism in the 1970s – a defining period in the history of the emancipation of women in the West – has also highlighted some of the movement's problems and failures. Looking back reveals racial prejudice and a lack of representation of women of colour, non-binary identity and non-heterosexual sexuality. Accounting for absence and questioning who is behind the camera, as well as who is in front of it, what is pictured, how and who it is for, are at the core of Winant's critical and admiring stance towards this formative political era.

***Looking Forward to Being Attacked*, installation view, 2018. Found images, concrete patch, foam**

This photo-based work was presented at a group exhibition at the Sculpture Center, New York, in 2018. The large, boulder-like forms are fashioned from foam, hinged together, coated with concrete and covered in a 360-degree collage of found instructional images of women in self-defence classes. Winant amassed these images from an expansive archive that she had started during the 2016 presidential election campaign. She didn't realize it at the time, but she now sees this as a subconscious response to the national rise of Trump rhetoric. *Looking Forward to Being Attacked* shows how the functional photograph can become a political statement, with the practical engagement of the body a way to combat real threats. It also represents Winant's ongoing interest in the way we encounter photography – on display in New York, this was a work that you had to walk around but that also pushed you physically back against the walls of the small gallery space.

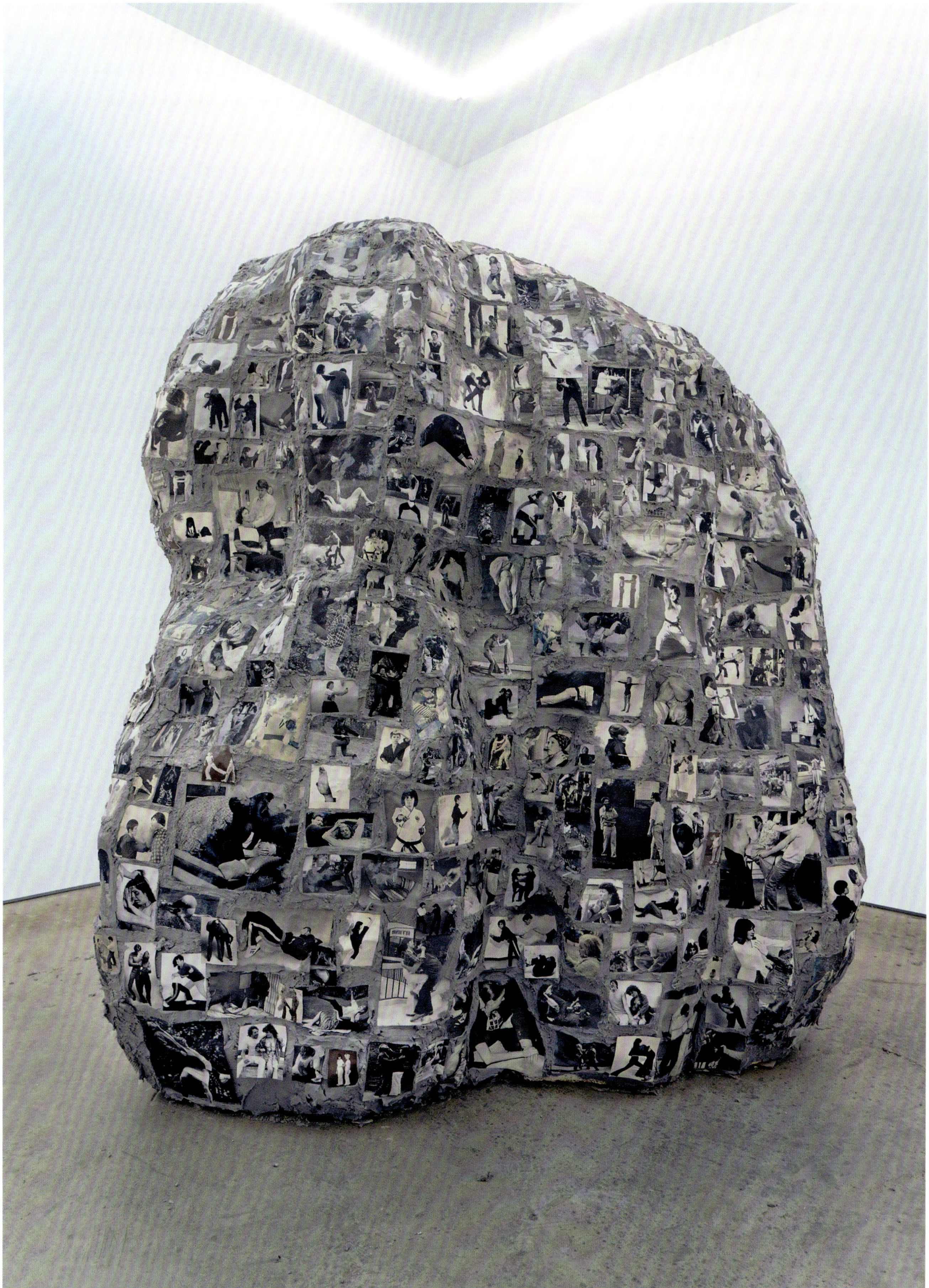

Winant collects and arranges sometimes thousands of images for each new work, presenting them as installations, sculptures or publications. These collages create order out of the chaos of the past, giving a sense of cohesive history, reviving the forgotten and buried histories that have been kept invisible – a welcoming embrace of what we refuse to see. At the same time, the inclusion of such a large number of images makes the idea of any one single 'bigger picture' or coherent story impossible – there are as many narratives as there are women.

This convergence between shared and singular narratives is particularly poignant in Winant's installation *My Birth* (2018), which was shown in *Being: New Photography 2018* at the Museum of Modern Art in New York. *My Birth* comprises written accounts and over two thousand photographs documenting births across the USA, including the artist's birth and that of her eldest son. Winant collected a lot of these images from books and pamphlets produced to provide information for women. The monumental project, also published as a book, was an unprecedented exploration of childbirth, a topic that is rarely discussed or visualized in any public forum. As Winant has said, 'Art history (and its standards) is a reflection of culture; if we live within societies that do not deem birth a worthy subject, we won't see it in art either.'[3]

My Birth is rooted in the body, with thousands of explicit depictions of the birth process, from contractions to crowning and yet, at the same time, these images acknowledge the impossibility of feeling through photographs; the void between seeing and experiencing, between image and body.

***My Birth*, installation view from *Being: New Photography 2018* at the Museum of Modern Art, New York, 2018**
Following the birth of her first son (her second son was born as the installation was presented), Winant realized that she 'wanted to make this experience visible, to examine and study it and take it seriously; it is ubiquitous, but there is nothing normal about birth'.[4] By looking back at birth stories, documented in words and images, from across the USA over fifty years and collating them, Winant expresses both the particularity and the universality of the birth experience.

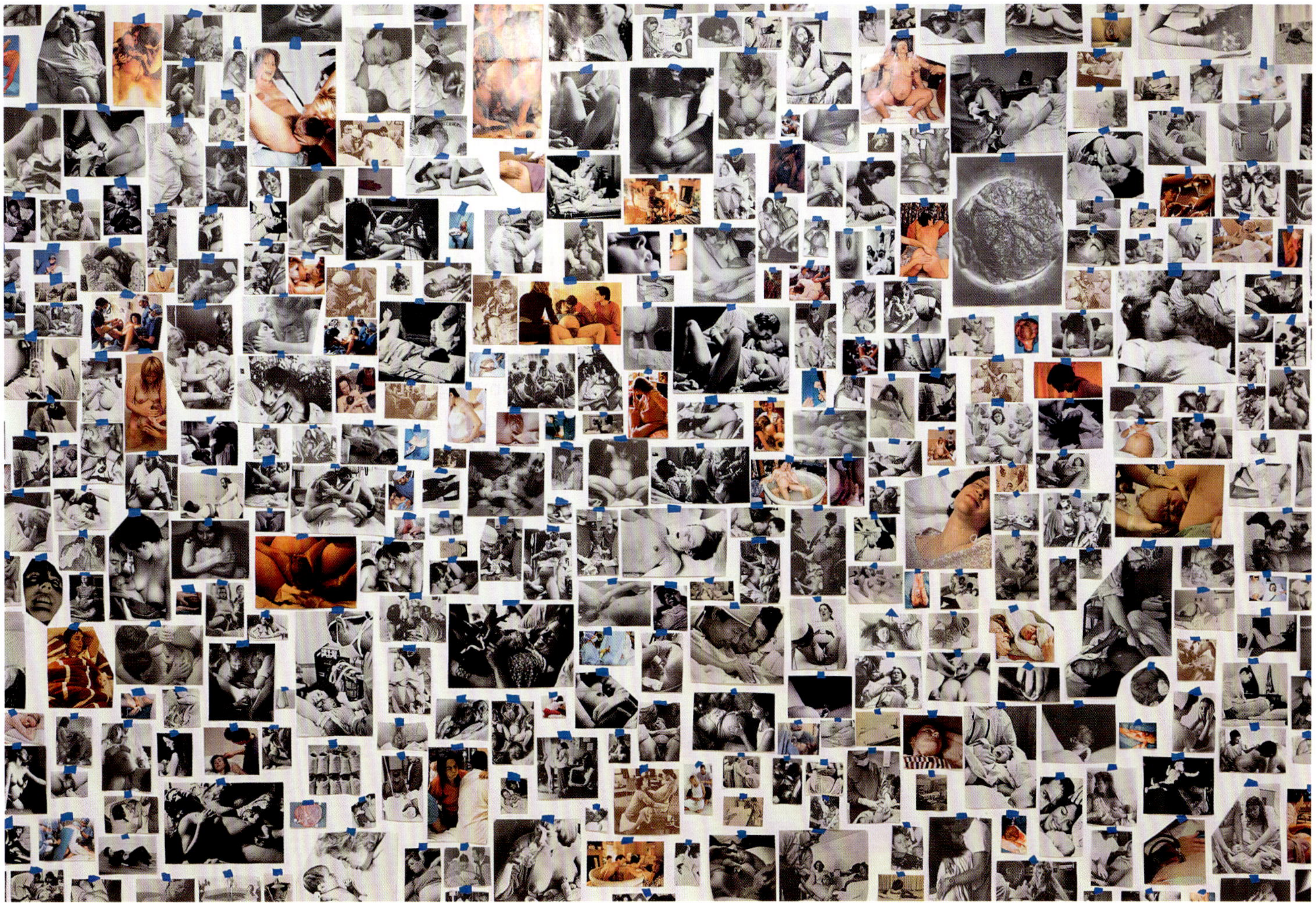

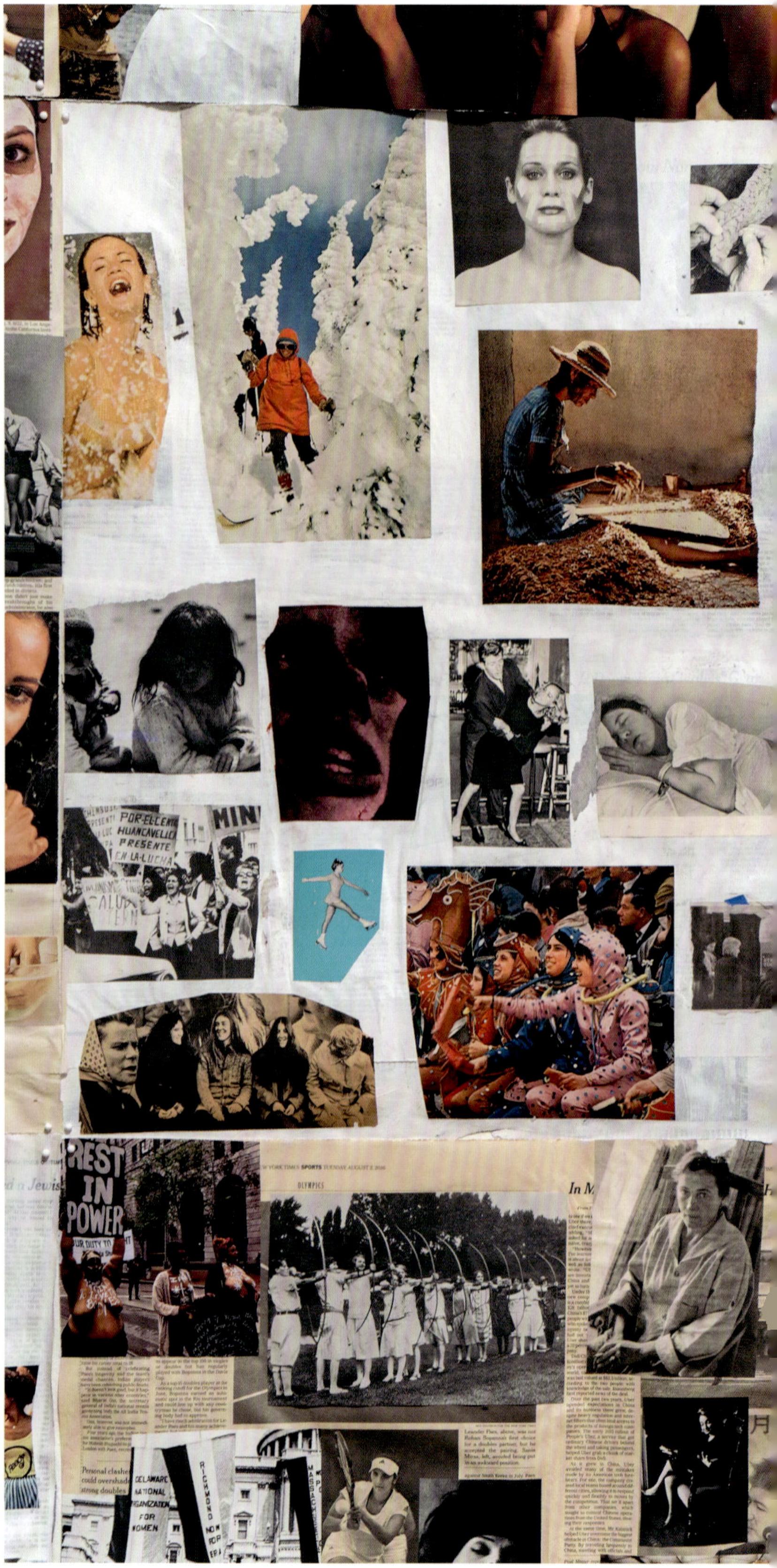

***Pictures of Women Working*, 2016. Found images, newspaper broadsheets, paint, pins**

This work was made while Winant was pregnant with her first son and ruminating on the idea of 'labour'. Inspired by bell hooks's *Feminism is for Everybody* (2000), and the second-wave feminist hope that entering the working world would emancipate women (something the artist notes as problematic in itself), Winant wanted to create something about the breadth of women's work. She began to collate images of sex workers, nuns, builders, athletes and beauticians. The resulting mosaic of images is pasted over broadsheet newspapers that relate similar narratives, barely visible but there. Winant explains, 'They fall into each other as one plane, complicating how we read photographs and collage. Though "fixed" in a certain way, they are intended to shape-shift between each install, such that their sub-narratives are never viewed the same way twice.'[5]

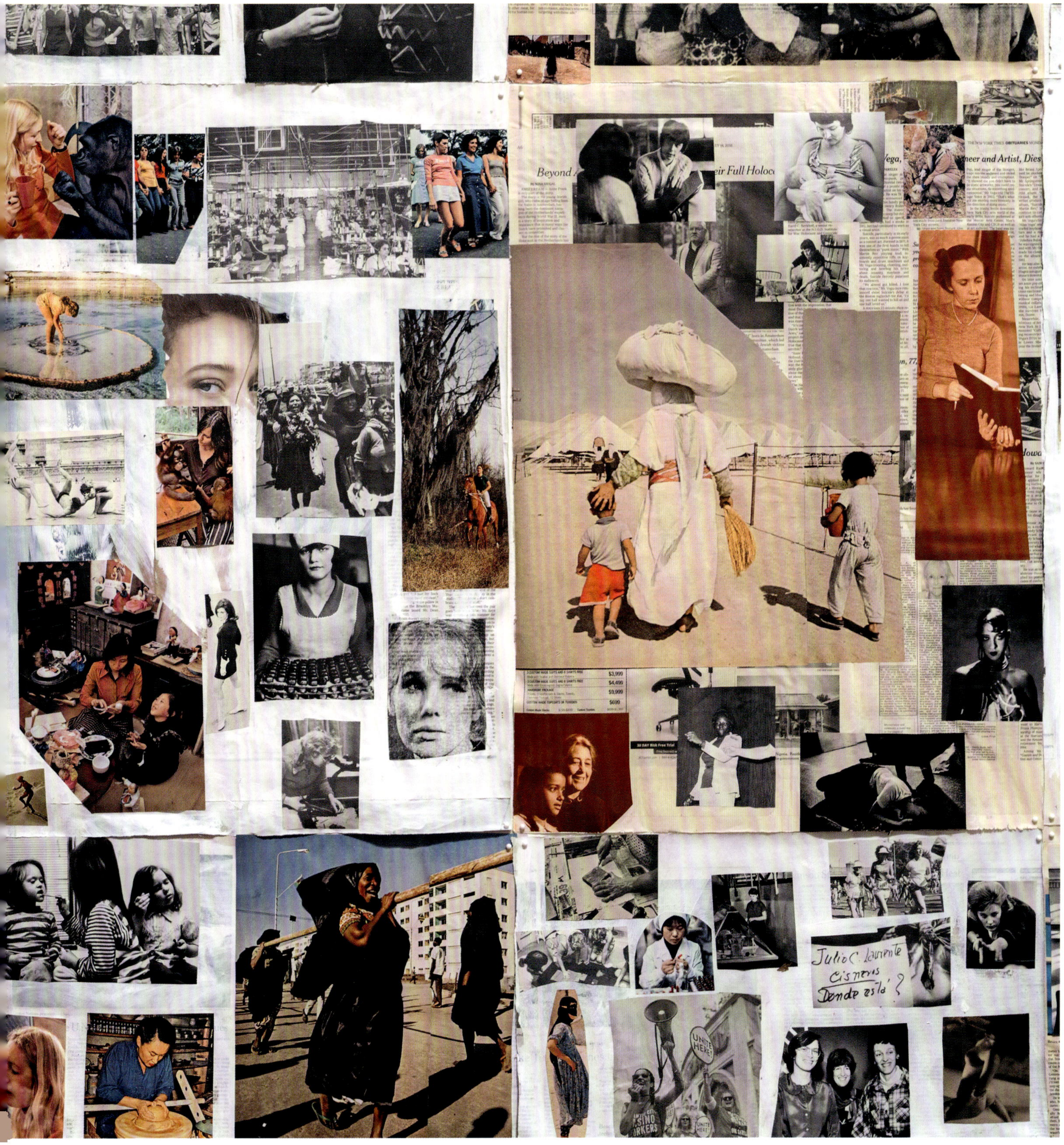

Luo Yang

How do you define a generation? That has been the mission of Luo Yang, who has focused her attention on China's youth for more than ten years, creating an ongoing, evolving record that only gains more meaning and momentum as time moves forward and we look back.

Yang was born in Shenyang, China, in 1984, on the cusp of the new millennial generation. She trained as a graphic designer at the Lu Xun Academy of Fine Arts, but eventually decided to pursue her passion for visual communication through photography. Her first major series consisted of portraits of close female friends, including Zhou Yan, a young woman who was left scarred for life after a brutal attack in which she was doused in petrol and set alight by a boy whose advances she had rejected. She was only sixteen at the time. Yan's story had a profound effect on Yang, who has often since looked at the coexistence of pain and beauty.

Yang's largest body of work to date is *GIRLS* (2007–17), which began as a personal project as an attempt to understand the women she knew and encountered while in the midst of her own adolescent angst. The project also became a way to confront the contradictory demands women face, often caught between personal expression and family expectations. *GIRLS* is not intended as a representative document of a generation, but it is an emotionally rich, candid insight into contemporary femininity, female sexuality and the lives of young women in Shanghai and Beijing today. After centuries of Chinese women being represented by Western men in visual culture, Yang's lens, in tacit complicity with her subjects, redefines women by and for women.

The idea of coming of age is continued in Yang's *New Generation*, which she began to shoot in 2019. While *GIRLS* mostly focused on women born in the 1980s, like Yang, the men and women of *New Generation* are children of the 1990s and 2000s, growing up in a very different context, with increasingly globalized aesthetics of representation. The impact of social media platforms such as Weibo on this younger generation is evident in their interactions with Yang's camera; the next generation appear more conscious and self-aware when it comes to the gaze and their bodies. The subjects of *New Generation* express through their clothes – or lack of them – more fluid attitudes towards gender and sexuality, which represent a much wider cultural shift around the world, not only in China.

Yang insists that her work isn't about indoctrinating the viewer with her ideology and that it has no direct political intention. Instead, she selects her

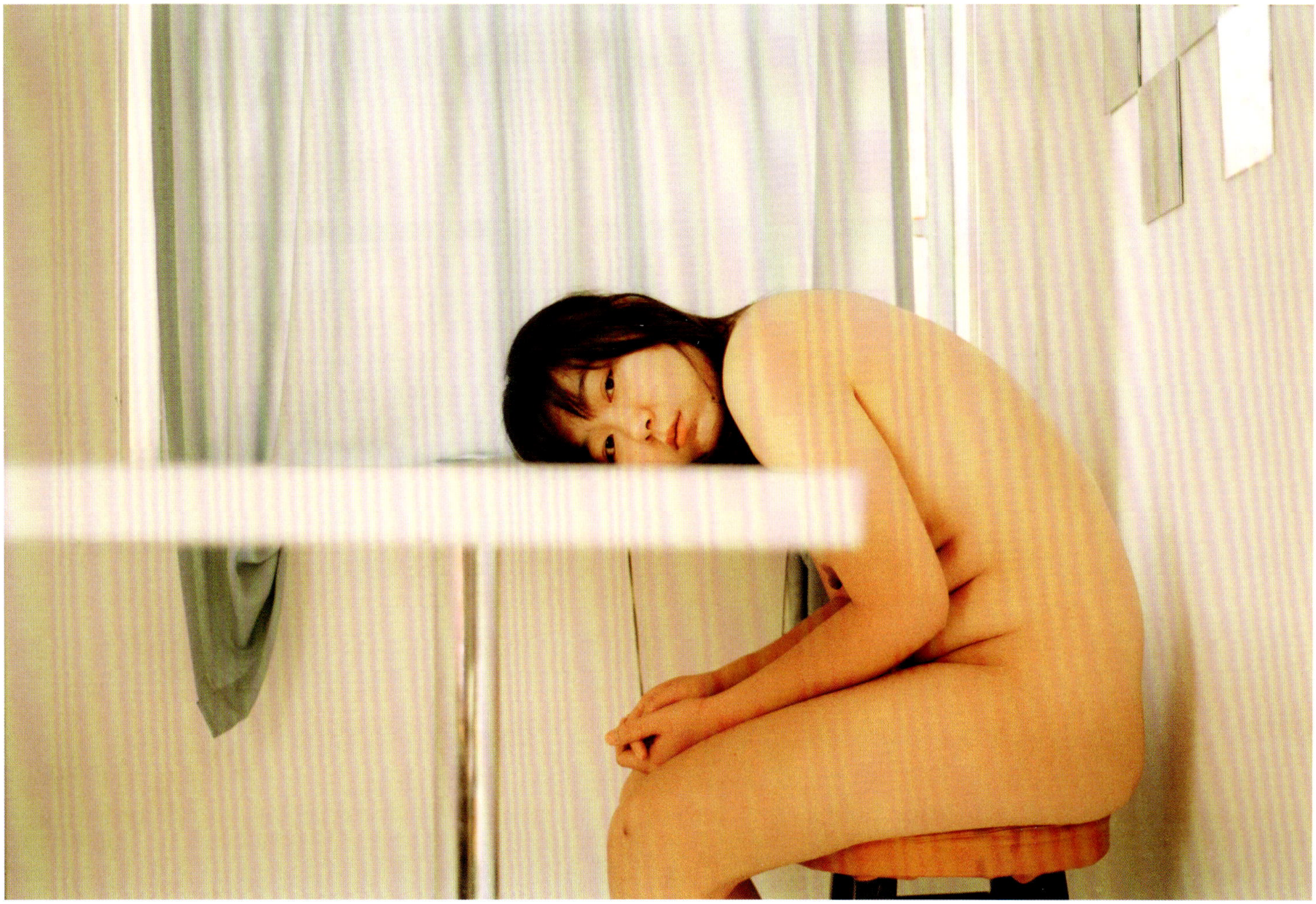

Roro from the series *GIRLS*, 2014
This image typifies Yang's interest in the inner lives of China's younger generations and her desire to depict them in a naturalistic way. Slumped over a kitchen table, in a scene that is both banal and relatable, the young woman in this simple nude portrait gazes back at the photographer-viewer with a frank, straightforward stare. Her pose, meanwhile, suggests self-protection and vulnerability. Finding moments like these, in which her subjects oscillate between control and uncertainty, is Yang's speciality.

subjects according to the emotions they elicit. She is drawn to strong individuals and subculture looks, seeking what she has also called a 'wild vitality'[1] – something with which Yang feels she has an affinity. She sees her subjects as the exceptions that break the rule, making a subtle statement about lifestyle and choice. The urban context is also ever-present in Yang's work and in the background of her images you can often make out highways and soaring tower blocks. She bases herself between Beijing and Shanghai, which are where the majority of her shoots take place, as the architecture of the city seems to unite her subjects and shape the ways they live, dress and interact.

Like her peers Lin Zhipeng and the late Ren Hang, Yang has caught the world's attention with bold portraits that are erotic, playful and provocative. Nudity plays an important role in this – a direct strategy to subvert a Western stereotype of Chinese people as robotic or asexual. Yang, Lin and Hang have become known as the '80s artists', part of a generation that grew up in a more stable and outward-looking China, with greater exposure to Western thought and imagery.

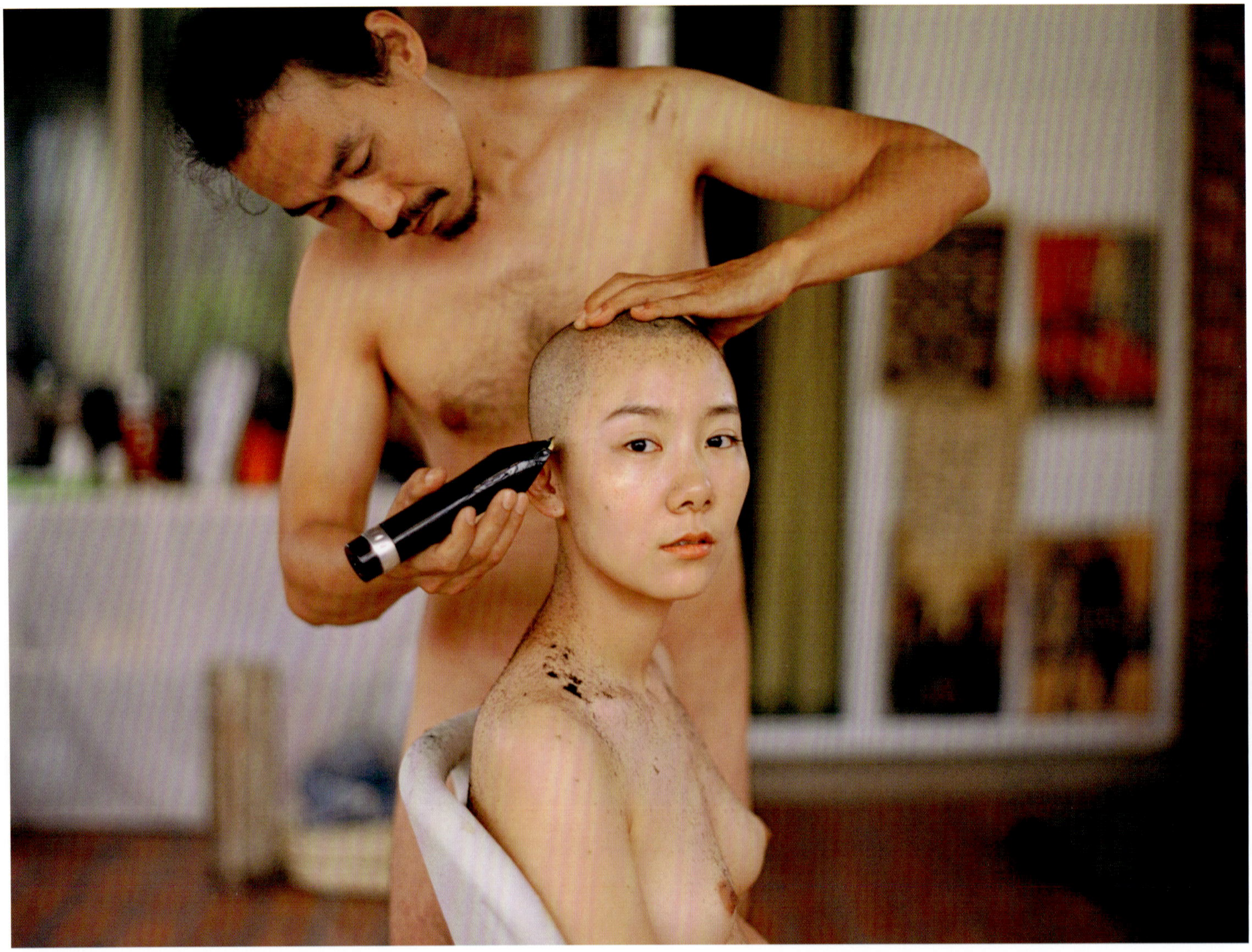

***Wang Yanyun* from the series *GIRLS*, 2016 and 2017**
These two intimate images from the series *GIRLS* depict the same woman, the artist Wang Yanyun, a close friend of the photographer. The earlier image, above, shows Wang having her head shaved by her boyfriend at the time – an act of defiance in the face of conformist femininity, rejecting constructed ideals of beauty. A year later, Yang captured Wang pregnant with her first child, part of an ongoing, personal record of important moments in her friend's life. Wang, Yang explains, is no longer with her boyfriend. This juxtaposition is typical of Yang's work, presenting the multiplicity of the modern female experience. It also establishes another theme that pervades in *GIRLS*, that of women's relationships with themselves, with each other and with their mothers.

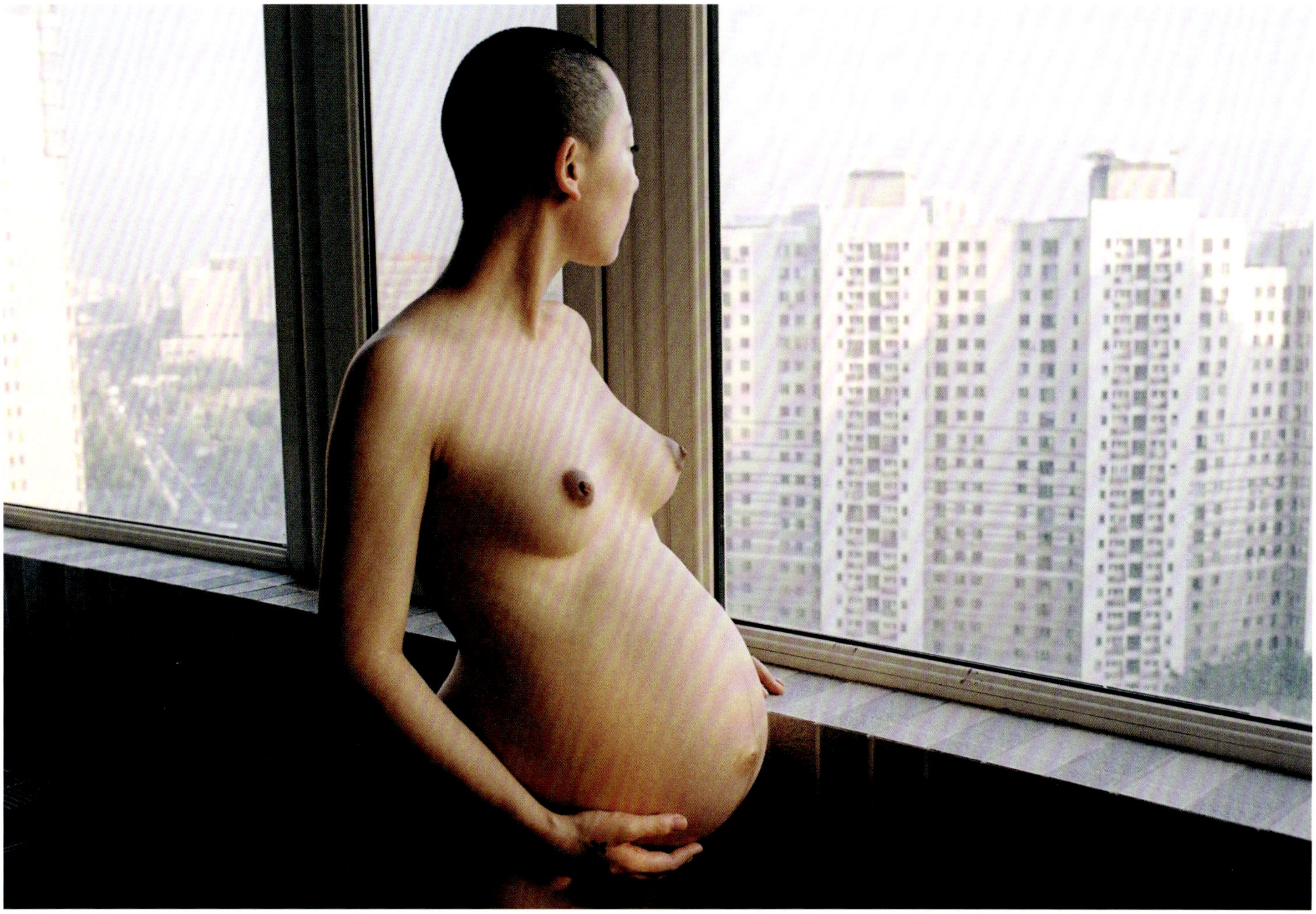

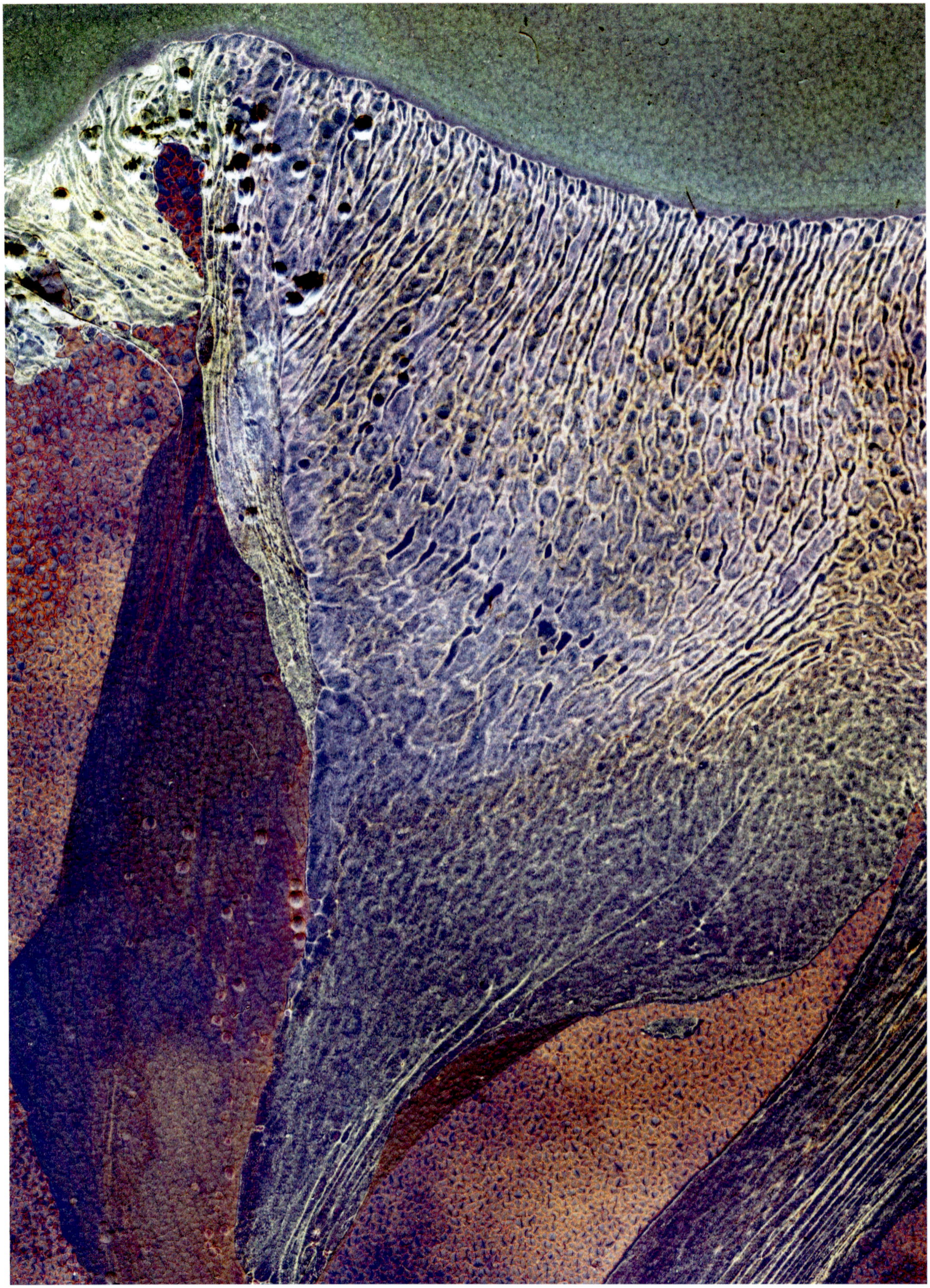

Daisuke Yokota

Is it possible to do anything new with photography in the twenty-first century? That question loomed large for the Japanese artist Daisuke Yokota. Born in Saitama in 1983, he studied at the Nippon Photography Institute, Tokyo, but became frustrated with his chosen medium. He turned instead to music, and it was while playing around with a synthesizer that he struck upon a new way to approach his photography, incorporating methods he had used when making ambient electronic music, such as distortion, reverb and fade, into his photographic process.

The results caused great excitement in the photography world. Yokota was selected for the Outset/Unseen Exhibition Fund in 2013 and Photo London's John Kobal Residency Award in 2015, then in 2016 he won the Foam Paul Huf Award as well as the prominent Discovery Award at the Rencontres d'Arles. Yokota begins with an archive of his own unremarkable digital photographs, printing and re-photographing them with an analogue camera up to fifteen times in order to achieve a level of degradation in the captured image. Then, when developing the negatives at home in his makeshift darkroom, he destroys them with whatever is close at hand: he uses water that is too warm, allows daylight to seep in, applies flame from a lighter, burns them with acid or daubs them with iron powder. Referring to these intrusions as 'visual noise',[1] Yokota creates an entirely new image by destruction. The symbolic nature of this process has not been lost on critics and fans, who have likened it to rebirth. The photographs he produces through this laborious process are dazzling abstract explorations that could be related to the Japanese aesthetic tradition of *wabi-sabi*, where beauty emanates from imperfection and fragility.

The process also transforms our perception of how a photograph might be made and experienced. As the artist has said in an interview, 'There's no element of duration to your experience of a photograph; it's closer to an object. I felt that this was an extremely weak point of photography. So, I'm aware that photography can't function in the same way as films or music, but I wonder whether it isn't possible to create a way for photographs to carry time within them.'[2]

The sense of duration in Yokota's work is essential to its effect, and also motivates other parts of his practice, including live performances in which his

From the series *Matter/Burnout*, 2016
In 2016, at the Aichi Triennial, Japan, Yokota presented an installation entitled *Matter*, which comprised 100,000 photographs printed onto rolls of paper that he had coated in wax. When the exhibition was over, Yokota symbolically burned the entire installation, documenting its destruction. The resulting photographs then evolved, phoenix-like, into a new large-scale project and book, *Matter/Burnout*, of which this photograph is part.

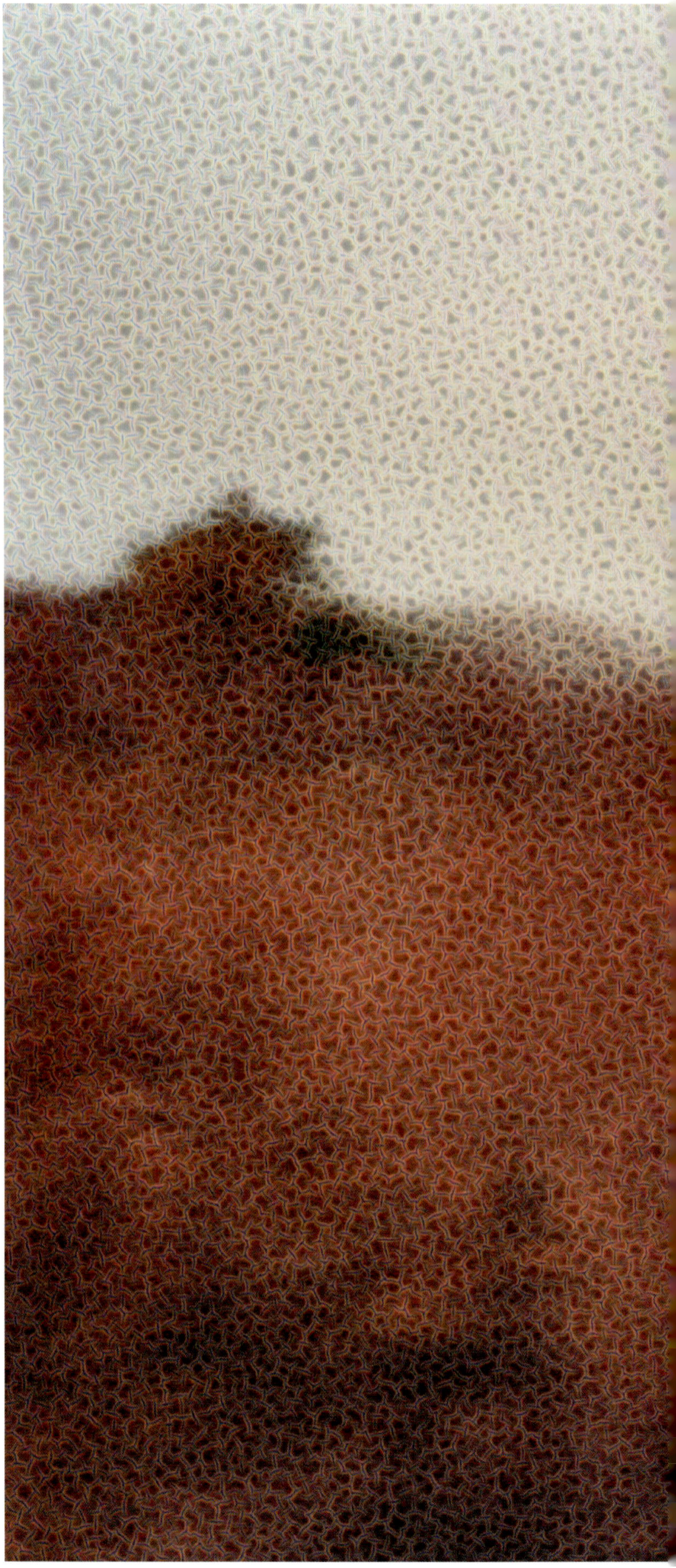

From the series *Taratine*, 2016
Taratine, Yokota's first monograph, brings together two distinct bodies of work that relate to two pivotal female figures in the artist's life: his mother and his girlfriend. It takes the form of an I-novel, a Japanese literary genre that originated in the twentieth century and is characterized by a confessional tone. *Taratine* reveals a more personal, narrative side to Yokota's work, moving between scenes of nature, sensuality and tenderness, fusing his interests in memory, time, tradition and sexuality.

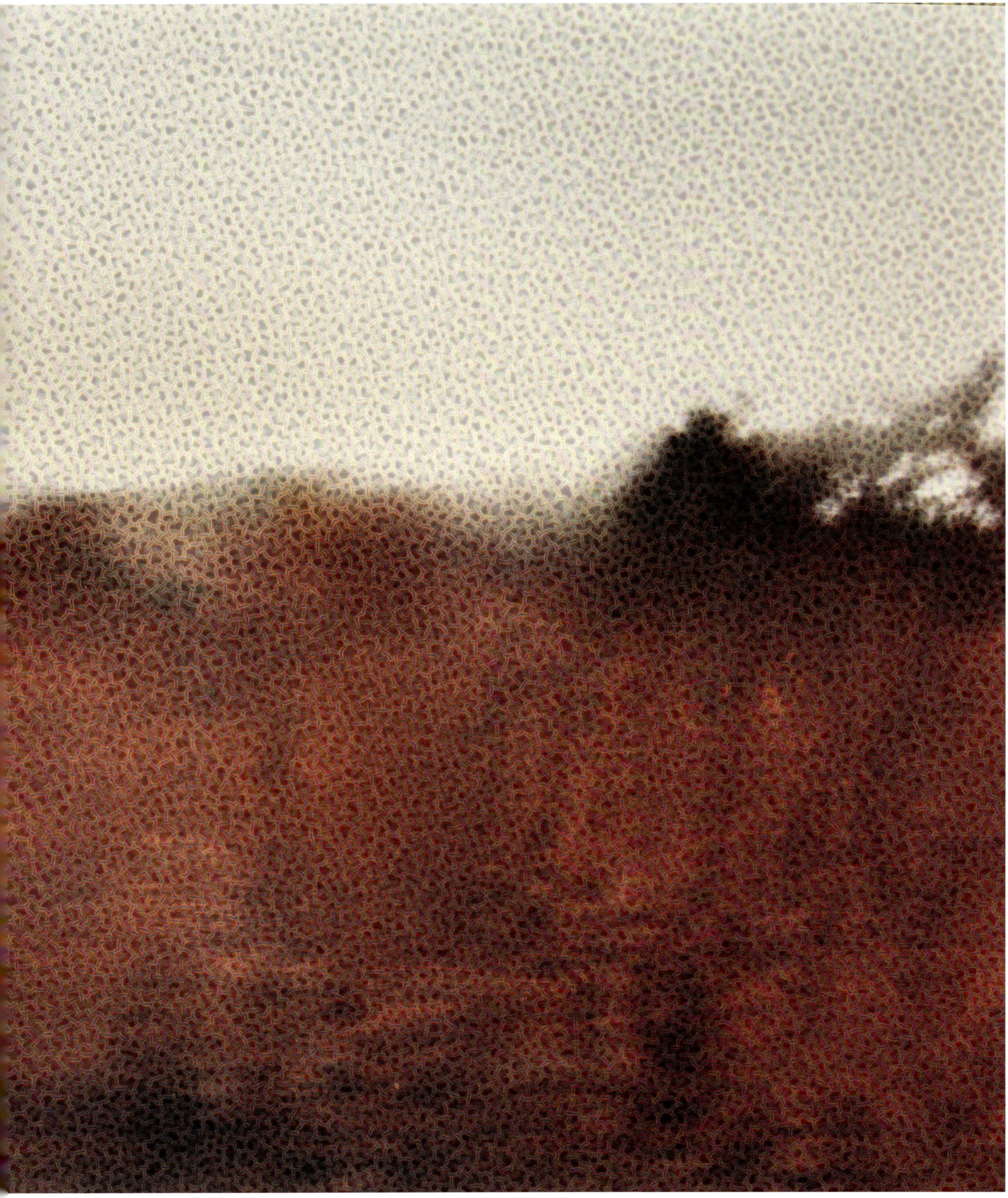

alchemical printing process is on show to the public in real time. Equally important are Yokota's contributions to the avant-garde photobook culture coming out of Japan that has proliferated since the Provoke movement was founded in 1968, pushing photographers to experiment with both subject and medium. In a digitally oriented world, Yokota recalls the physical qualities of the photo-object, in concert with the notions of transience and ephemerality conveyed by his modus operandi.

Yokota leads us far away from photography as we know it, paradoxically by taking us deeper into how it materializes. The beguiling effect of his photographs, whether performed, printed or published, stems from the intense psychic energy the artist channels into them, entering an almost trance-like state. His esoteric approach might have prevented him from receiving more mainstream attention beyond the photography world, but Yokota, like his obvious predecessor Daido Moriyama, is far more instinctive than cerebral, and his photographs are synaesthetic experiences, fluid and feverish. As the artist has said, 'What was I thinking when I took this photograph? I probably did not mean anything special, but I must have been conscious of something.'[3] The precise parameters Yokota sets himself release this consciousness, which surfaces in his photographs.

From the series *Color Photographs*, 2015
In 2015 Yokota's first US exhibition, *Color Photographs*, opened in New York, accompanied by a book of the same name. In sumptuous, liquid pictures like this one, Yokota's aim was to do away with the camera and focus instead on what he calls the 'physical aspect of film'.[4] The photographs were made using large-format colour film, with the artist applying his signature experimental methods in the darkroom and then scanning the results.

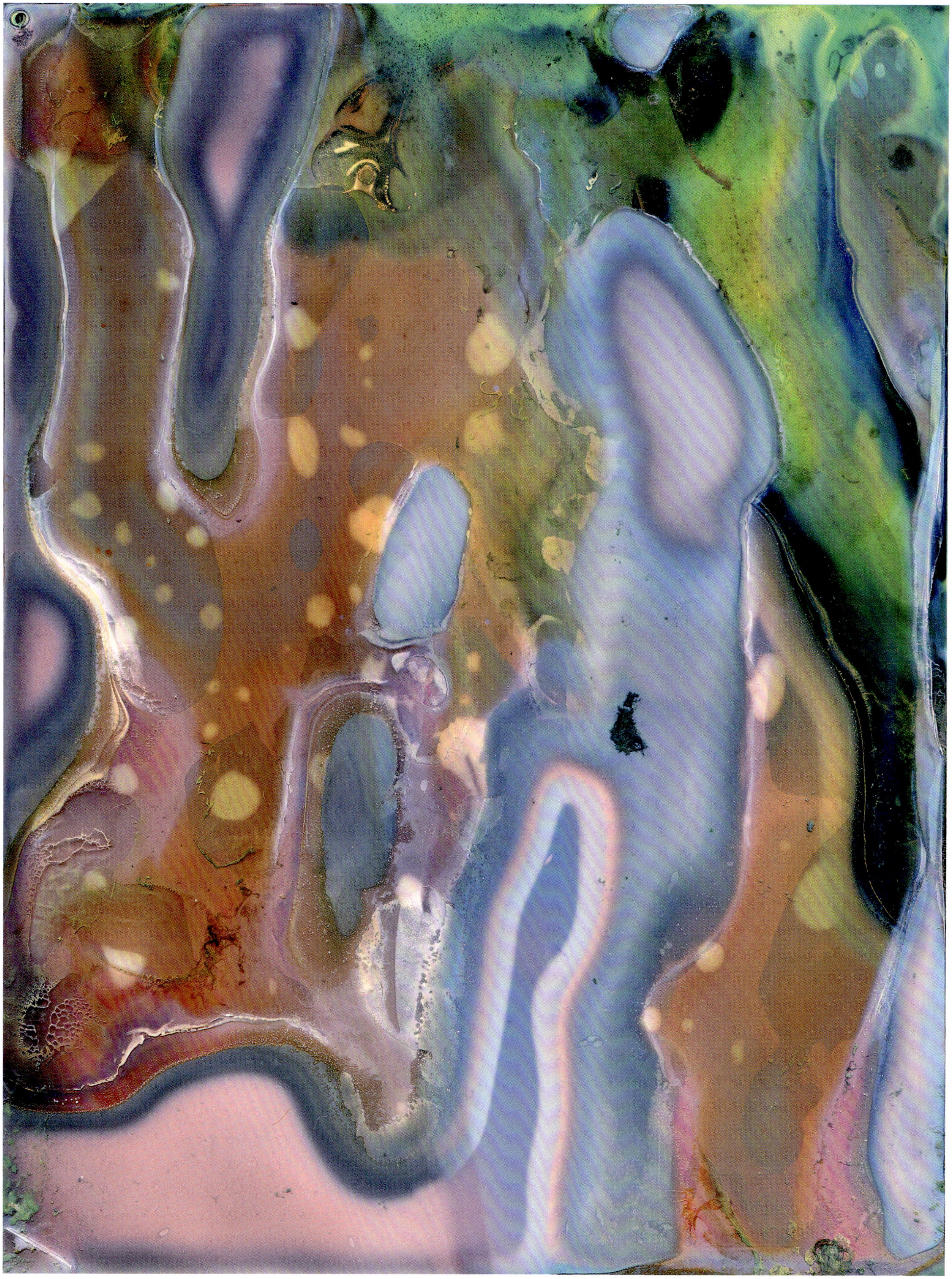

Bibliography

Laia Abril

1 O'Hagan, Sean, 'I've seen horrible things: photographer Laia Abril on her history of misogyny', *The Guardian*, 20 July 2016 https://www.theguardian.com/artanddesign/2016/jul/20/ive-seen-horrible-things-photographer-laia-abril-on-her-history-of-misogyny

2 'Deutsche Börse Photography Foundation Prize 2019 Nominee: Laia Abril', The Photographer's Gallery, 7 March 2019 https://www.youtube.com/watch?v=r8KFnBNS-jQ

Hoda Afshar

1 'The Eyes Have It - Interview Hoda Afshar', *Compass*/ABC, 29 July 2019 https://www.youtube.com/watch?v=VDRngBXEyYU

2 De Maine, Bridget, 'Behind the Lens with Iranian-Born, Melbourne-Based Photographer Hoda Afshar', *Collective Hub,* 10 November 2016 https://collectivehub.com/2016/11/behind-the-lens-with-iranian-born-melbourne-based-photographer-hoda-afshar/

3 'The Eyes Have It', op. cit.

4 Boetker-Smith, Daniel, 'Behold: Hoda Afshar', *British Journal of Photography*, issue 7863, 1 August 2017

5 Email with the artist, February 2020

6 'Interview with award-winning visual artist Hoda Afshar', Migration & Art, 18 June 2019 https://www.youtube.com/watch?v=eijYgDPKgC0

Antoine D'Agata

1 Sturrock, Alex, 'Fear, Desire, Drugs, and Fucking', *Vice*, 1 November 2010 https://www.vice.com/en/article/ppzp78/fear-desire-drugs-fucking-608-v17n11

2 Shamma, Raphael, 'An Interview with Antoine d'Agata: "A Simple Desire to Exist" (2014)', *ASX*, 13 March 2014 https://americansuburbx.com/2014/03/asx-interviews-antoine-dagata-simple-desire-exist-2014.html

3–6 'Antoine D'Agata – Interview', Paris Photo, 2017 https://www.youtube.com/watch?v=cM4mOmP_gyc

7 Cole, Teju, 'What Does It Mean to Look at This?', *New York Times Magazine*, 24 May 2018 https://www.nytimes.com/2018/05/24/magazine/what-does-it-mean-to-look-at-this.html

8 Sturrock, Alex, op. cit.

9, 10 'Antoine D'Agata – Interview', op. cit.

11 Sturrock, Alex, op. cit.

12 'Antoine D'Agata – Interview', op. cit.

13 Sturrock, Alex, op. cit.

Poulomi Basu

1 Cowie, Alix-Rose, 'Poulomi Basu: Through the prism of one culture we may see another more clearly', *WePresent* https://wepresent.wetransfer.com/story/poulomi-basu/

2 Butet-Roche, Laurence, 'Centralia by Poulomi Basu', *British Journal of Photography*, issue 7863, 1 August 2017

3 Cowie, Alix-Rose, op. cit.

4 Email with the artist, August 2020

5, 6 Butet-Roche, Laurence, op. cit.

7 Email with the author, August 2020

8, 9 Vora, Bindi, 'Long Read: Interview with Poulomi Basu', *Autograph*, 30 May 2020 https://autograph.org.uk/blog/long-read-interview-with-poulomi-basu/

Mohamed Bourouissa

1 Berger, John, *Understanding a Photograph*, London: Penguin, 2013

Sheila Pree Bright

1 'In Conversation: Sheila Pree Bright', ICP, 22 February 2017 https://www.icp.org/browse/archive/media/in-conversation-sheila-pree-bright

2 Keith, Naima, 'Vision & Justice Online: Sheila Pree Bright in Conversation with Naima J. Keith', *Aperture*, 22 June 2016 https://aperture.org/editorial/vision-justice-sheila-pree-bright/

3 Bahadur, Nina, '"Plastic Bodies" Series By Sheila Pree Bright Will Make You Think Differently About Beauty', *Huffington Post*, 22 November 2013 https://www.huffingtonpost.co.uk/entry/plastic-bodies-sheila-pree-bright-beauty-identity_n_4324403?ri18n=true&guccounter=1

4 Bentley, Rosalind, 'Sheila Pree Bright's look at "Suburbia" in an unlikely place', *The Atlanta Journal-Constitution*, 10 February 2014 https://www.ajc.com/entertainment/sheila-pree-bright-look-suburbia-unlikely-place/6tuGLSjO8YLOhLr5KW3MYI/

5 Keith, Naima, op. cit.

Jo Ann Callis

1–3 'JoAnn Callis: Other Rooms' Aperture Gallery, 17 June 2014 https://www.youtube.com/watch?v=ZgcULfXD4FY

Juno Calypso

1 Jansen, Charlotte, *Girl on Girl*, London: Laurence King Publishing, 2017

2 Jansen, Charlotte, 'Juno Calypso's The First Night', *Elephant*, 5 November 2017 https://elephant.art/juno-calypsos-the-first-night/

3 Wolf, Naomi, *The Beauty Myth*, London: Chatto & Windus, 1990

Joana Choumali

1–3 Jansen, Charlotte, 'Joana Choumali Reimagines Life in African Cities', *Elephant*, 10 September 2019 https://elephant.art/joana-choumali-reimagines-life-african-cities/

Gregory Crewdson

1 McNamara, Sylvie, 'Submerged and

Interior: An Interview with Gregory Crewdson', *The Paris Review*, 24 October 2016 https://www.theparisreview.org/blog/2016/10/24/submerged-interior-interview-gregory-crewdson/
2, 3 Duguid, Rosalind, 'Gregory Crewdson: Silence in a Small Town', *Elephant*, 29 September 2017 https://elephant.art/silence-in-a-small-town/
4 Crewdson, Gregory (photography) and Moody, Rick (words), *Twilight: Photographs by Gregory Crewdson*, New York: Abrams, 2002
5 Helmore, Edward, 'The Witching Hour', *The Guardian*, 4 October 2006 https://www.theguardian.com/artanddesign/2006/oct/04/photography

Rineke Dijkstra
1 'Rineke Dijkstra Interview', Gallery de Moor, Amsterdam, 1983
2 'Marian Goodman Presents: Rineke Dijkstra | Viewing Room', Marian Goodman Gallery, March 2020 https://www.mariangoodman.com/viewing-room/rineke-dijkstra-2020/
3 Press release, 'Rineke Dijkstra: The French Foreign Legion - Olivier Silva', Marian Goodman Gallery, September 2003 https://www.mariangoodman.com/exhibitions/288-rineke-dijkstra/

Paz Errazuriz
1 Howard, Ellie, 'How one woman used her camera to defy a dictatorship', *Dazed Digital*, 13 July 2017 https://www.dazeddigital.com/art-photography/article/36622/1/how-paz-errazuriz-used-her-camera-to-defy-a-chilean-dictatorship
2 'PAZ ERRÁZURIZ – Interview 2017', Paris Photo, October 2017 https://www.youtube.com/watch?v=a2L9T-IfEyw
3 'Barbican Meets: Paz Errazuri', Barbican, 15 May 2018 https://www.barbican.org.uk/read-watch-listen/barbican-meets-paz-errazuriz
4 Email with the artist, April 2020
5 'PAZ ERRÁZURIZ - Interview 2017', op. cit.
6 Email with the artist, April 2020

Samuel Fosso
1–4 Chatap, Yves, 'The Lives of Samuel Fosso', *Aperture*, 1 June 2017 https://aperture.org/editorial/lives-samuel-fosso
5 Sansom, Anna, 'Me, Myself & I', *British Journal of Photography*, 3 May 2020 https://www.1854.photography/2020/05/samuel-fosso-self-portraits/
6 Quoted in Iduma, Emmanuel, 'The Self-Portraits of Samuel Fosso', *Guernica*, 17 November 2004 https://www.guernicamag.com/the-self-portraits-of-samuel-fosso/

Rahima Gambo
1–8 Email with the artist, April/May 2020

Nan Goldin
1 Quoted in Als, Hilton, 'Nan Goldin's Life in Progress', *The New Yorker*, 27 June 2016 https://www.newyorker.com/magazine/2016/07/04/nan-goldins-the-ballad-of-sexual-dependency
2 Goldin, Nan, *The Other Side*, Göttingen: Steidl, 2019
3 'Nan Goldin: "My work comes from empathy and love", Tate/TateShots, 11 January 2018 https://www.tate.org.uk/art/artists/nan-goldin-2649/nan-goldin-work-comes-empathy-and-love
4 Als, Hilton, op. cit.

Andreas Gursky
1 Jamieson, Tom, 'Andreas Gursky is Taking Photos of Things that Do Not Exist', *The New York Times*, 29 January 2018 https://www.nytimes.com/2018/01/29/arts/andreas-gursky-is-taking-photos-of-things-that-do-not-exist.html
2 Berning Sawa, Dale, 'Andreas Gursky on the photograph that changed everything: "It was pure intuition"', *The Guardian*, 18 January 2018 https://www.theguardian.com/artanddesign/2018/jan/18/andreas-gursky-each-photograph-is-a-world-of-its-own-best-photograph-salerno-harbour
3 Jobey, Liz, 'Andreas Gursky: The perfect image is not something that can be taught', *Financial Times*, January 2018 https://www.ft.com/content/2d52904c-f592-11e7-88f7-5465a6ce1a00
4 'Redefining Photography | Andreas Gursky', Southbank Centre, 7 February 2018 https://www.youtube.com/watch?v=CdOxpTARGx4
5–6 Berning Sawa, Dale, op. cit.

Eric Gyamfi
1 Jansen, Charlotte, 'Making History', *Elephant*, Issue 31, Summer 2017

Hassan Hajjaj
1 Mitter, Siddhartha, 'Hassan Hajjaj Turns Moroccan Clichés Into London Cool', *The New York Times*, 9 October 2019 https://www.nytimes.com/2019/10/09/arts/hassan-hajjaj.html

Felicity Hammond
1 Press release for *Photography into Sculpture*, Museum of Modern Arts, 8 April 1970 https://www.moma.org/calendar/exhibitions/2694
2 Hammond, Felicity, 'Arcades' [commissioned by Contact Photography Festival, Toronto], 2018 http://www.felicityhammond.com/arcades

Graciela Iturbide
1 Jansen, Charlotte, 'Graciela Iturbide's Mexico', *British Journal of Photography*, 7 January 2019 https://www.1854.photography/2019/01/graciela-iturbide-mexico/
2 Nieves, Evelyn, 'Graciela Iturbide's Photos of Mexico Make "Visible What, to Many, Is Invisible"', *The New York Times*, 8 January 2019 https://www.nytimes.com/2019/01/08/lens/graciela-iturbide-mexico-photos.html?smtyp=cur&smid=tw-nytimes

Mari Katayama
1 Black, Holly, 'Mari Katayama Celebrates the Body Beautiful', *Elephant*, 26 January 2019 https://elephant.art/mari-katayama-celebrates-the-body-beautiful/

Keyezua
1, 2 Jansen, Charlotte, '5 Questions with Keyezua', *Elephant*, 20 November 2017 https://elephant.art/5-questions-with-keyezua/
3 Wakiaga, Thomas, 'Panafricanism', TedxYouth@BrookhouseSchool, 9 March 2017 https://www.youtube.com/watch?v=7NNIZG9-RIk
5, 6 Email with the artist, February 2020

Elad Lassry
1 Valentine, Hannah, 'Elad Lassry Questions the Nature of Seeing With an Imaginary Fashion Shoot', *Elephant*, 4 March 2019 https://elephant.art/elad-lassry-questions-the-nature-of-seeing-with-an-imaginary-fashion-shoot/
2–4 'Contemporary Conversations: Elad Lassry and Laura Fried', Contemporary Art Museum St. Louis, 23 February 2011 https://www.youtube.com/watch?v=vzlu_qto8yw
5, 6 Godfrey, Mark, 'On Display', *Frieze*, 1 November 2011 https://www.frieze.com/article/display

Deana Lawson
1–3 Jafa, Arthur & Lawson, Deana, 'A Match Made in Heaven: Deana Lawson and Arthur Jafa on Destiny, Intuition, and Influence', *Garage*, 4 September 2015 https://garage.vice.com/en_us/article/paww9m/deana-lawson-arthur-jafa-interview
4, 5 Smith, Zadie, 'Deana Lawson's Kingdom of Restored Glory', *The New Yorker*, 5 July 2018 https://www.newyorker.com/magazine/2018/05/07/deana-lawsons-kingdom-of-restored-glory
6, 7 Jafa, Arthur & Lawson, Deana, op. cit.
8 'Barbara and Mother', ICA Boston, April 2014 https://www.icaboston.org/art/deana-lawson/barbara-and-mother

Amak Mahmoodian
1, 2 Molloy, Caroline, 'Shenasnameh', *Photomonitor*, Feburary 2018 https://www.photomonitor.co.uk/shenasnameh/
3 Mahmoodian, Amak, 'Mohr', 2008 https://amakmahmoodian.co.uk/Mohr
4 Email with the artist, March 2020

Alix Marie
1, 2 Vacheron, Joël, 'Alix Marie' in *Could You Talk About*, Musée des beaux-artes Le Locle, 2019
3 Marie, Alix, 'MA Work – Orlando', Royal College of Art, 2014 https://www.rca.ac.uk/students/alix-marie/
4 Abel-Hirsch, Hannah, 'Alix Marie's Shredded', *British Journal of Photography*, 9 May 2019 https://www.1854.photography/2019/05/alix-maries-shredded/

Ryan McGinley
1 Quoted in Gregory, Alice, 'Ryan McGinley: Naked and Famous', *GQ*, 11 April 2014 https://www.gq.com/story/ryan-mcginley-photographer
2 Mills, Mike, 'Ryan McGinley', *Interview*, 1 December 2016 https://www.interviewmagazine.com/art/ryan-mcginley-1

Susan Meiselas
1 Quoted in Meiselas, Susan, 'Nicaragua: From Still to Moving', Magnum Photos https://www.magnumphotos.com/newsroom/conflict/susan-meiselas-nicaragua-from-still-to-moving/
2–4 'Susan Meiselas: Creative Activism - A Window Into the World of Artists and Social Entrepreneurs', Skoll.org, 13 May 2015 https://www.youtube.com/watch?v=MVzL8e5C3iM

Zanele Muholi
1 Du Bois, W.E.B., 'The Souls of White Folk' in *Darkwater*, London: Verso, 2016 [original, 1920]
2 Muholi, Zanele, 'Zanele Muholi: "I'm a Visual Activist"', *Financial Times*, 5 January 2018 https://www.ft.com/content/896c582e-f013-11e7-ac08-07c3086a2625
3 Curtis, Elissa, 'Faces and Phases: Portraits from South Africa's Lesbian Community', *The New Yorker*, 21 May 2012 https://www.newyorker.com/culture/photo-booth/faces-and-phases-portraits-from-south-africas-lesbian-community
4 Skidmore, Maisie, 'Yes But Why? Zanele Muholi', *WePresent*/Tate, 2019 https://wepresent.wetransfer.com/story/yes-but-why-zanele-muholi/
5 Muholi, Zanele, 'Brave Beauties: Zanele Muholi on Self-Portraiture', *LensCulture*, March 2017 https://www.lensculture.com/articles/zanele-muholi-brave-beauties-zanele-muholi-on-self-portraiture

Shirin Neshat
1–3 Jansen, Charlotte, 'Why Shirin Neshat Is Turning Her Gaze Away From Iran', *Elephant*, 25 February 2020 https://elephant.art/shirin-neshat-turning-gaze-away-iran-25022020/
4 Sheybani, Shadi, 'Women of Allah: A Conversation with Shirin Neshat', *Michigan Quarterly Review*, Spring 1999 https://quod.lib.umich.edu/cgi/t/text/text-idx?cc=mqr;c=mqr;c=mqrarchive;idno=act2080.0038.207;g=mqrg;rgn=main;view=text;xc=1

Catherine Opie
1 Jansen, Charlotte, 'How to Take a Portrait, According to Photographer Catherine Opie', Artsy, 5 October 2007 https://www.artsy.net/article/artsy-editorial-portrait-photographer-catherine-opie

Martin Parr
1 'Martin Parr – "Photography is a Form of Therapy"', Tate/TateShots, 15 December 2017 https://www.youtube.com/watch?v=wlKrnYWXEK8
2 'Photographers in Focus: Martin Parr', *Nowness*, 9 January 2019 https://www.youtube.com/watch?v=9frLRE49i_A
3 'Martin Parr – "Photography is a Form of Therapy"', op. cit.

Farah Al Qasimi
1 Newell-Hanson, Alice, 'artist farah al qasimi asked emirati photo studios to make her look beautiful, with strange results', *i-D*, 17 November 2017 https://i-d.vice.com/en_us/article/zmz7mj/artist-farah-al-qasimi-asked-emirati-photo-studios-to-make-her-look-beautiful-with-strange-results
2 Press release, 'Arrival: Farah Al Qasimi', The Third Line Gallery, September 2019 https://view.publitas.com/thethirdline/farah-al-qasimi-arrival/page/2-3
3 Vali, Murtaza, 'Farah Al Qasimi: The Third Line', *Artforum*, January 2020 https://www.artforum.com/print/reviews/202001/farah-al-qasimi-81792

Thomas Ruff
1 Jobey, Liz, 'An interview with the artist Thomas Ruff', *Financial Times*, 25 September 2017 https://www.ft.com/content/6fbd0cfa-9746-11e7-a652-cde3f882dd7b
2 Saltz, Jerry, 'Ruff Trade', *Village Voice*, 23 May 2000 https://www.villagevoice.com/2000/05/23/ruff-trade/
3 Ou, Arthur, 'Thomas Ruff', *Artforum*, 12 April 2013 https://www.artforum.com/interviews/thomas-ruff-talks-about-his-ma-r-s-series-40225

Paul Mpagi Sepuya
1–3 'Paul Mpagi Sepuya interview | Modern Art, London | 10 January 2020', Studio International https://vimeo.com/385862627
4 Jansen, Charlotte, 'Paul Mpagi Sepuya Brings a Fresh Gaze to the Male Nude', *Elephant*, 28 August 2019 'https://elephant.art/paul-mpagi-sepuya-mapplethorpe-the-male-gaze/
5 'Paul Mpagi Sepuy interview', op. cit.
6 Email with the artist, October 2020

Cindy Sherman
1 'Under the Gaze: The Art of Cindy Sherman', Heni Talks, 16 May 2018 https://www.youtube.com/watch?v=ED6QhmRchZI
2 Wetzler, Rachel, '"I'm trying to erase myself" – an interview with Cindy Sherman', *Apollo*, 27 June 2019 https://www.apollo-magazine.com/cindy-sherman-interview/
3 Berne, Betsey, 'Studio: Cindy Sherman', Tate, 1 June 2003 https://www.tate.org.uk/art/artists/cindy-sherman-1938/studio-cindy-sherman
4 'How to see Cindy Sherman - with Eva Respini', The Museum of Modern Art, 19 January 2016 https://www.youtube.com/watch?v=bsFsibTO3L4
5 'Under the Gaze', op. cit.
6 Berne, Betsey, op. cit.
7 Respini, Eva, 'WIll the Real Cindy Sherman Please Stand Up' in *Cindy Sherman*, New York: The Museum of Modern Art, 2012

Ming Smith
1–7 Conversation with the artist for 'Ming Smith on Pursuing Her Transcendent Photo Practice despite Decades of Discrimination' Artsy 28 August 2020 https://www.artsy.net/article/artsy-editorial-ming-smith-pursuing-transcendent-photo-practice-despite-decades-discrimination

Mikhael Subotzky
1 Whitley, Zoé, 'How Do You Deconstruct White Male Privilege?', *Elephant*, 11 November 2019 https://elephant.art/how-do-we-deconstruct-white-male-privilege/
2, 3 Email with the artist, June–August 2020
4 Subotzky, Mikhael, 'I was looking back' http://www.subotzkystudio.com/works/i-was-looking-back/
5 *Players: Magnum Photographers Come Out to Play*, Martin Parr & Cristina de Middel ed., Madrid: La Fabrica, June 2018

6 Rankine, Claudia, 'I Wanted to Know What White Men Thought About Their Privilege. So I Asked', *The New York Times*, 17 July 2019 https://www.nytimes.com/2019/07/17/magazine/white-men-privilege.html
7 Whitley, Zoé, op. cit.
8, **9** 'To see as a photographer sees: Mikhael Subotzky at TEDxStellenbosch', Tedx Talks, 17 October 2012 https://www.youtube.com/watch?v=FXMWbWMq4Il

Hiroshi Sugimoto
1 Quoted in Odenthal, Kathleen, 'Hiroshi Sugimoto - The Master of Slow Shutter Speed Photography', *Owlcation*, 5 August 2016 https://owlcation.com/humanities/Hiroshi-Sugimoto-The-Master-of-Slow-Shutter-Speed-Photography
2 Sugimoto, Hiroshi, 'Seascapes' https://www.sugimotohiroshi.com/seascapes-1
3 Sugimoto, Hiroshi, 'How I Photographed an Entire Movie in a Single Frame', *Financial Times*, 3 January 2020 https://www.ft.com/content/baedab88-2792-11ea-9a4f-963f0ec7e134
4 'Hiroshi Sugimoto', Guggenheim, https://www.guggenheim.org/teaching-materials/teaching-modern-and-contemporary-asian-art/hiroshi-sugimoto-%E6%9D%89%E6%9C%AC%E5%8D%9A%E5%8F%B8
5 Sugimoto, Hiroshi, 'Theaters' https://www.sugimotohiroshi.com/new-page-7

Leonard Suryajaya
1–6 Original interview with author conducted in 2020

Juergen Teller
1, 2 'Juergen Teller on How to Be a Radical Photographer | #BoFVOICES 2019', The Business of Fashion, 21 November 2019 https://www.youtube.com/watch?v=_gdFwKiKf_8
3 'Juergen Teller – Studio Visit | TateShots', Tate, 3 September 2008 https://www.youtube.com/watch?v=QY0CCj4ujww
4 Teller, Juergen, *Pictures and Text*, Göttingen: Steidl 2012
5 'Juergen Teller – Studio Visit', op. cit.
6 Email with the artist's studio, April 2020

Wolfgang Tillmans
1 Witt, Emily, 'The Life and Art of Wolfgang Tillmans', *The New Yorker*, 3 September 2018 https://www.newyorker.com/magazine/2018/09/10/the-life-and-art-of-wolfgang-tillmans Emily Witt'
2 Morton, Tom, 'Wolfgang Tillmans', *Frieze*, 10 October 2003 https://www.frieze.com/article/wolfgang-tillmans-0
3 Searle, Adrian, 'An omnivorous eye, taking pleasure', *The Guardian*, 29 November 2000 https://www.theguardian.com/artanddesign/2000/nov/29/20yearsoftheturnerprize.turnerprize
4 Tillmans, Wolfgang, 'Artist Wolfgang Tillmans: "This game can never be mastered"', *Financial Times*, 7 June 2019 https://www.ft.com/content/18398928-86c2-11e9-a028-86cea8523dc2
5 Tillmans, Wolfgang, 'Lecture: Royal Academy of Arts, London', February 2011 https://tillmans.co.uk/images/stories/pdf/2011_Lecture_Tillmans_Royal_Academy_english.pdf

Lorenzo Vitturi
1, 2 Jansen, Charlotte, 'Lorenzo Vitturi: To Market, to Market', *Elephant*, 8 May 2018 https://elephant.art/lorenzo-vitturi-market-market/

Jeff Wall
1, 2 'Jeff Wall: "I begin by not photographing"', San Francisco Museum of Modern Art, 7 July 2010 https://www.youtube.com/watch?v=2yG2k4C4zrU
3 Press release, 'Jeff Wall', Marian Goodman Gallery, November 2002 https://www.mariangoodman.com/exhibitions/244-jeff-wall/
4 'Jeff Wall Interview: Pictures Like Poems', Louisiana Channel, 8 April 2015 https://www.youtube.com/watch?v=HkVSEVIqYUw

Harley Weir
1 Berger, John, *Ways of Seeing*, London: Penguin, 1972
2 Pellerin, Ananda, 'Boundaries by Harley Weir', *AnOther*, 13 April 2014 https://www.anothermag.com/art-photography/3814/boundaries-by-harley-weir
3 Sontag, Susan, *On Photography*, New York: Farrar, Straus and Giroux, 1977
4 Quoted in Morley, Madeleine, 'Fashion photographer Harley Weir's personal work is absolutely breathtaking', *It's Nice That*, 14 July 2014 https://www.itsnicethat.com/articles/harley-weir
5 Email with Benjamin Kirchhoff, May 2020

Carmen Winant
1 Jansen, Charlotte, 'Carmen Winant: Making Childbirth Visible', *Elephant*, 12 May 2018 https://elephant.art/carmen-winant-owns-birth/
2 Winant, Carmen, at *Tate Fast Forward: Women in Photography*, 2019
3, 4 Jansen, Charlotte, op. cit.
5 Email with the artist, February 2020

Luo Yang
1 Benson, Louise, 'Luo Yang's Intimate Portraits of China's Young Generation', *Elephant*, 20 January 2020 https://elephant.art/luo-yang-intimate-portraits-chinas-young-generation-photography-girls-beijing-shanghai-20012020/

Daisuke Yokota
1 Dykstra, Jean, 'In the Studio: Daisuke Yokota', Residency Unlimited, February 2016 http://www.residencyunlimited.org/in-the-studio-daisuke-yokota-by-jean-dykstra/
2 Abbe, Dan, 'Shoot, Print, Repeat: An Interview With Daisuke Yokota', *Popular Photography*, 11 July 2012 https://www.popphoto.com/american-photo/shoot-print-repeat-interview-daisuke-yokota/
3 Daisuke Yokota biography, Christophe Guye Galerie https://christopheguye.com/artists/daisuke-yokota/biography
4 van Veghel, Chris, 'Color Photographs by Daisuke Yokota', *Another Something*, 3 November 2015 https://www.anothersomething.org/2015/11/03/color-photographs

Index

Acknowledgements

It takes a lot to produce a book at the best of times, but staying focused and positive during a pandemic comes with its own unique challenges; I couldn't have done this without the patience, guidance and precision of Ellie, Rachel, Giulia and Lesley at Ilex who have shaped this book and allowed me the opportunity to bury my head in the world of ideas and images.

Thank you to all fifty artists for your permission and for your vitality. Thank you to Gon, Ru and Lev, to Barbara and Martyn, to Alicia and Nat, Millie, Rio, Remi and Ashley; to the many Alons, to Ale and Phil. And thank you to bell hooks, for reminding me that there is always 'power in looking'. If anything, I hope this book is a gesture of hope.

Picture Credits

The publishers would like to acknowledge and thank the following for their kind contribution to this book.

9, 11 Laia Abril/Les Filles du Calvaire; 12, 14–15 Courtesy of the artist and Milani Gallery, Brisbane © the artist; 17, 18–19 Antoine d'Agata/ Magnum Photos; 20, 23 Courtesy of the artist and T J Boulting; 25–7 Courtesy of the artist © ADAGP, Paris and DACS, London 2021; 29, 31 Courtesy of Sheila Pree Bright; 33–5 © Jo Ann Callis. Courtesy of ROSEGALLERY; 37–41 Courtesy of the artist and T J Boulting; 42, 45 Courtesy of and © Joana Choumali; 47, 48 © Gregory Crewdson. Courtesy Gagosian; 50–5 Courtesy of the artist and Marian Goodman Gallery, New York, Paris and London; 56, 59 Courtesy of and © Paz Erràzuriz; 61, 63 © Samuel Fosso, courtesy Jean Marc Patras, Paris; 65, 66–7 Courtesy of and © Rahima Gambo; 69, 70 Courtesy of the artist and Marian Goodman Gallery, New York, Paris and London; 72, 75 © Sunil Gupta. All rights reserved, DACS/Artimage 2021. Courtesy of the artist and Hales Gallery; 76–81 © Andreas Gursky/DACS, 2021. Courtesy Sprüth Magers; 83, 84–5 Courtesy of and © Eric Gyamfi; 87 *Kesh Angels*, framed photography by © Hassan Hajjaj, 2010/1431; 89 *Hamid's Back*, framed photography by © Hassan Hajjaj, 2000/1421; 90 Courtesy of and © Felicity Hammond; 93 Site Specific installation at Cleveland Pools, Bath. Commissioned by The Edge Arts, generously supported by Arts Council England. Courtesy of and © Felicity Hammond; 94, 97 Nadine Ijewere/Trunk Archive; 99–103 Courtesy of and © Graciela Iturbide; 104, 106–7 © Mari Katayama; 109-113 Courtesy of Keyezua; 114, 117 © Elad Lassry, courtesy 303 Gallery, New York; 119-123 Courtesy of the artist, Rhona Hoffman Gallery, Chicago, and Sikkeman Jenkins & Co, New York; 124-129 © Amak Mahmoodian; 131 Courtesy of the artist. Photo © Ben Westoby; 132–3 Courtesy of the artist; 135, 136–7 © Ryan McGinley. Courtesy of Ratio 3; 139, 140–1 Susan Meiselas/Magnum Photos; 143, 145 © Zanele Muholi. Courtesy of Stevenson, Cape Town | Johannesburg and Yancey Richardson, New York; 147 © Shirin Neshat. Courtesy of the artist and Goodman Gallery; 148 © Shirin Neshat. Courtesy Goodman Gallery and Noirmontartproduction, Paris; 150, 152–3 © Catherine Opie. Courtesy Regen Projects, Los Angeles, and Thomas Dane Gallery, London; 155–9 Martin Parr/Magnum Photos; 160–5 Courtesy of the artist and The Third Line, Dubai; 166, 169 Courtesy Mai 36 Galerie © DACS 2021; 170, 173 Image courtesy of the artist, Document Gallery, Chicago, and Vielmetter, Los Angeles; 175–9 Courtesy of the artist and Metro Pictures, New York; 180, 183 Courtesy of the artist and Pippy Houldsworth Gallery, London © Ming Smith; 185, 187 © Mikhael Subotzky. Courtesy of the artist and Goodman Gallery; 188, 190-91 Courtesy of the artist and Marian Goodman Gallery © Hiroshi Sugimoto; 192, 194-5 © Leonard Suryajaya; 196, 198–9 © Juergen Teller, All Rights Reserved. Courtesy Alison Jacques Gallery; 201, 202–3 © Wolfgang Tillmans, courtesy Maureen Paley, London | Hove; 204, 207 Courtesy of the artist; 208, 211 Courtesy of the artist; 212, 215 Harley Weir/Art Partner; 217 Courtesy of the artist. Photo: Luke O'Hallaran; 219 Courtesy of the artist. Photo: Kurt Heumiller © 2018 The Museum of Modern Art; 220-21 Courtesy of the artist. The Columbus Museum of Art, 2016. Photo: Luke Stettner. 223–5 © Luo Yang; 226–31 © Daisuke Yokota.

Wherever possible artwork details have been supplied by the artists or their agents. Caption details vary accordingly.